VOICES
OF
GAY
LIBERATION

ISBN 0-88209-002-X (cloth) and 0-88209-016-X (paper)

First Printing
Manufactured in the United States of America
BOOK AND COVER DESIGNED BY BOB CATO

ACKNOWLEDGMENTS

We would like to thank all the gay sisters and brothers who have contributed their work, advice, and criticisms to this book, and who have taken part in the development and growth of the independent gay media.

At this point, most anthologies usually include a long list of contributing authors, giving their degrees, titles, affiliations, and track records. We have decided to eliminate this formality because we would like each article to be judged independently on its content—whether it was written by a fourth-grade dropout or a PhD.

"Christopher Street Liberation Day, June 28, 1970" and "Looking at Women" are copyright ©1971 by Fran Winant and printed by permission of the author.

"Out of the Closets, Into the Streets" was published in abridged form as "Out of the Closet: A Gay Manifesto" in *Ramparts*, November 1971. Copyright © 1971 by Noah's Ark, Inc. Printed by permission.

"Gay Is Good" was published in *Rat* February 24, 1970. Copyright © 1970 by *Rat*. Printed by permission of the author.

"My Soul Vanished From Sight: A California Saga of Gay Liberation" was published as Gay Flames Pamphlet No. 10, December 1970. Printed by permission of the author.

"Dear Mom" was published in the *Los Angeles Free Press* and is printed by permission of the author.

"The Closet Syndrome" is from manuscript and printed by permission of the author. Copyright ©1972 by Stuart Byron.

"A Gay Critique of Modern Literary Criticism" is from manuscript and printed by permission of the author. Copyright ©1972 by Karla Jay.

"An Open Letter to Tennessee Williams" was published in *People's Gay Sunshine*, October 1971. Printed by permission of the author.

"Queer Books" was published as a chapter in *Homosexual Liberation: A Personal*

OUT OF THE CLOSETS

VOICES
OF
GAY
LIBERATION

A DOUGLAS BOOK

OUT
OF
THE
CLOSETS

EDITED BY
KARLA JAY
&
ALLEN YOUNG

CONTENTS

V. LESBIANS AND THE WOMEN'S LIBERATION MOVEMENT

VI. CUBA: GAY AS THE SUN

IX. MANIFESTOS

Foreward
Karla Jay

Out of the Closets is a collection of the experiences and philosophies of *radical* lesbians and homosexuals. We perceive our oppression as a class struggle and our oppressor as white, middle-class, male-dominated heterosexual society, which has relentlessly persecuted and murdered homosexuals and lesbians since the oppressor has had power. We are the negation of heterosexuality and of the nuclear family structure, and as such we have been driven from our jobs, our families, our education, and sometimes from life itself.

If our individual oppressions reflect the oppression of other gay people, then ultimately our struggle reflects the struggle of other revolutionary groups and of other oppressed people such as the blacks, the chicanos, the American Indians, and women. Some of the articles in this book express our solidarity with these movements and also our struggle with them. We share their goals and aspirations, but we are often rejected by straight groups who have not combatted their own sexism and who have not extended their concepts of freedom to all people, especially to us. Our ambiguity is particularly reflected in our relations with the Cuban Revolution, whose goals we generally support but whose sexist, anti-homosexual policies we oppose. The articles in this book which deal with Cuba express our anguish and concern.

This book also reflects the struggle within the gay movement. Gay liberation is not a political party, and we do not have any political "lines." Gay liberation is made up of people from different backgrounds and from different types of previous movement experience (if any). We are young and old, black and white, women and men, in drag and in "acceptable clothing," and as such we face different problems within the gay movement. We see our struggle in different terms, and each fights the oppression which hits him or her hardest. Thus, some articles in this book will seem to oppose others, and of course, not all the articles reflect the views of the editors, but we must reiterate that gay liberation offers no line, no pat answers: we offer only ideas and questions.

In addition, because we are by no means a homogeneous group, this book reflects our struggles with one another. Gay men oppress gay women, white gays oppress black gays, and straight-looking gays oppress transvestites; and therefore some articles manifest our desire to combat our own chauvinism, our own sexism, our own racism, as well as our oppression by straight society.

If we do share one idea, however, it is that *gay is good*. We affirm our uniqueness. We are proud to be lesbians and homosexuals, and we offer no apologies or explanations of why we are what we are. We will not give in, consider ourselves sick in any way, or conform to "straight" standards of dress or behavior. If homosexuals are your worst fear, then you have a problem. Our selflove and our love for our gay sisters and brothers are the core of our revolution, and this love ultimately binds us together no matter what our exterior differences or opinions.

This book is written for gay brothers and sisters by gay brothers and sisters as an act of love and communion. It is written in the hope that one day *all* gay people will be out of the closet and that someday the suffering of gay people will be not-to-be-repeated history.

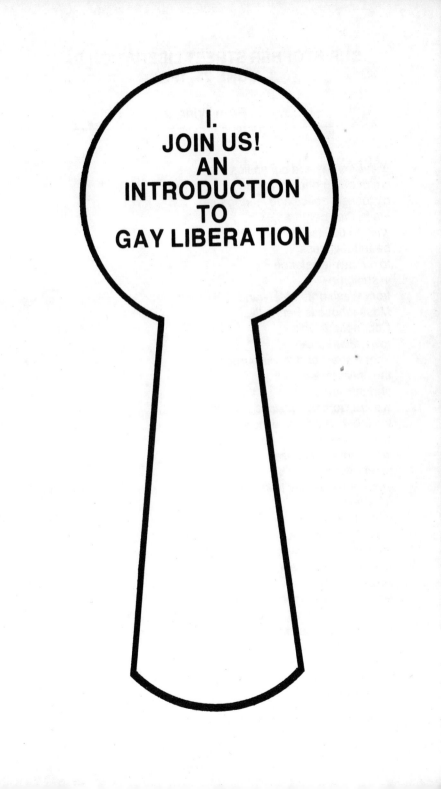

I.
JOIN US!
AN
INTRODUCTION
TO
GAY LIBERATION

CHRISTOPHER STREET LIBERATION DAY, JUNE 28, 1970

Fran Winant

with banners and our smiles
we're being photographed
by tourists police and leering men
we fill their cameras
with 10,000 faces
bearing witness
to our own existence
in sunlight
from Washington Maryland
Massachusetts Pennsylvania
Connecticut Ohio
Iowa Minnesota
from Harlem and the suburbs
the universities
and the world
we are women who love women
we are men who love men
we are lesbians and homosexuals
we cannot apologize
for knowing
what others refuse to know
for affirming
what they deny
we might have been
the women and men
who watched us and waved
and made fists
and gave us victory signs
and stood there after we had passed
thinking of all they had to lose
and of how society punishes
its victims
who are all of us
in the end

but we are sisters and sisters
brothers and brothers
workers and lovers
we are together
we are marching
past the crumbling old world
that leans toward us
in anguish from the pavement
our banners are sails
pulling us through the streets
where we have always been
as ghosts
now we are shouting our own words
we are a community
we are a society
we are everyone
we are inside you
remember
all you were taught to forget
we are part of the new world

photographers
grim behind precise machines
wait to record
our blood and sorrow
and revolutionaries beside them
remark
love is not political
when we stand against our pain
they say
we are not standing against anything
when we demand our total lives
they wonder
what we are demanding
cant you lie
cant you lie
they whisper they hiss
like fire in grass
cant you lie
and get on with the real work

our line winds
into Central Park
and doubles itself
in a snakedance
to the top of a hill
we cover the Sheep Meadow
shouting
lifting our arms
we are marching into ourselves
like a body
gathering its cells
creating itself
in sunlight
we turn to look back
on the thousands behind us
it seems we will converge
until we explode
sisters and sisters
brothers and brothers
together

OUT OF THE CLOSETS, INTO THE STREETS

Allen Young

Introduction

On a June evening in 1969 police began what seemed like a routine raid on the Stonewall Inn, Greenwich Village's most popular gay men's bar. But the raid didn't go off as planned. We fought back. The gay liberation movement was born.

I am smiling ironically as I write "we." I wasn't there, and it took me more than six months before I even began to take part in the gay liberation movement. I was a "closet case," an oppressed homosexual, oppressed in America, oppressed in the movement.

I might well have been on Christopher Street—home of the Stonewall—that June night. I had been to the Stonewall several times that spring and the previous winter. But the Stonewall was a dancing bar, favorite hang-out of the freest of the gay people—those most likely to be labeled "fag" and "drag queen." I wasn't comfortable there; I preferred the more up-tight and sedate (read, "masculine") crowd at Danny's, a few blocks closer to the waterfront. Had I been in the Village at all that night, I suspect I would have stayed discreetly on the sidelines, perhaps even split the scene altogether. Sure, I was a homosexual, and, as a member of Students for Democratic Society (SDS) and a writer for Liberation News Service (LNS), I was into fighting the pigs. But I couldn't have handled this swift coming together of the personal and the political. America—and the movement—had taught me too well how to make the separation.

My ideas about revolution and about homosexuals are very different now. I am no longer working at Liberation News Service. I have stopped avoiding myself by avoiding my community. I go to Danny's only occasionally now; my gay brothers and I are trying to build something better.

Because I am a white male homosexual, a New Yorker, a leftist, most of what I say is from that perspective. There are other homosexuals—Third World people, lesbians, transvestites—about whom I can say little. They speak for themselves. Most of the ideas expressed here are the result of a collective process. And I am grateful to the gay sisters and brothers who offered me criticism about myself and my writing.

On Sexism

Gay liberation is a struggle against sexism. We are only beginning to define this word. At the Revolutionary People's Constitutional Convention meeting in Philadelphia, the male homosexual workshop put it this way:

"Sexism is a belief or practice that the sex or sexual orientation of human beings gives to some the right to certain privileges, powers, or roles, while denying to others their full potential. Within the context of our society, sexism is primarily manifested through male supremacy and heterosexual chauvinism. Since in the short run, sexism benefits certain persons or groups, in the long run it cannot serve all the people, and prevents the forming of complete social consciousness among straight men. Sexism is irrational, unjust and counterrevolutionary. Sexism prevents the revolutionary solidarity of the people."

Sexism reveals itself in many ways. Of course, there are the overtly male-supremacist, anti-homosexual institutions of our society: the legal system and the police, the church, the nuclear family, the mass media, and the psychiatric establishment. Much of the energy of gay liberation is directed against these institutions. But sexism is a part of all people, too, present in many of our behavior patterns. Every straight man is a target for gay liberation. His rejection of homosexuality builds and strengthens our oppression; he is the accomplice of the policeman, the priest, the psychiatrist. Sexism affects us, too. Dealing with our own sexism, usually through a small group process, is also essential to gay liberation. These small groups vary in nature, from rather formal "consciousness-raising groups" to less formal communes or groups of friends or roommates. The goal of this small-group process is the elimination of inequalities in human relationships, inequalities brought about through role-playing or sexual objectification.

Our struggle as gays is to eliminate oppressive patterns that straights have burdened us with. Many gay men play either male or female roles. Some people think that this only has to do with what happens in bed. Although sex may be a factor, role-playing permeates all areas of human interaction. I was socialized into playing a male role. It didn't come easy: I knew that I threw a baseball "like a girl," and I have always been worried about my femininity. But a time did come when I could feel comfortable about my ability to pass for a "real man." Most important, I could hide my gayness.

Sexual objectification has to do with seeing other human beings in terms of the superficial alone—face, body, clothes. Phrases like these, often heard among gay men, are sexist and sexually objectifying: "Those blue jeans really turn me on." "He has a big cock." "I'm only attracted to young blonds." "He's too swishy; if I wanted to sleep with a woman, I'd do it with a real woman." I have thought or said all of these things at one time or another. Gay liberation is teaching me how this oppresses me and my brothers.

The consciousness-raising technique—with people talking about their personal experiences—is probably the best-developed small-group method for dealing with sexism among gay people. As a process, it has been basic to the growth and success of the women's movement. Now, we are using it to our benefit.

A Collegiate Saga of Gay Oppression

I would like to tell you a story about how two male homosexuals tried to be "real men" and ended up crushing the love that brought them together. I was one of those men. The other, my former college roommate, is now an inmate at a state mental hospital, where his jailers (officially known as psychiatrists) catalogue him as having "paranoid schizophrenic tendencies."

We were college classmates. We became good friends because we had a similar interest in what was then called politics, because we took many of the same classes and because we worked on the college paper together. In retrospect, I presume we were also physically attracted to one another. One day, at the end of our sophomore year, after we'd known one another for months, we were sitting on a bed in a dormitory room, talking. Suddenly, I was aware of a burst of sexual energy. Without saying a word about our feelings, we made love. It happened again a few nights later. Before long, our relationship became what is sometimes known as a "love affair." We didn't have any sense of that, however, certainly none of the romantic sense you find in novels and plays. It was mostly very scary. This was homosexuality—certainly we knew that—and we sensed the ponderous weight of a centuries-old taboo. For this to be an open, free love, we concluded in our mutual silence, would destroy us as successful college men. We were right, of course. We chose silence, and secrecy, and we continued as successful collegians. Our fear and shame were the keys to survival. I became editor-in-chief of the college paper; he became managing editor. We took all of the same classes. We ate all our meals together, and we became roommates. To all our friends, and even in our own minds, we were just college buddies. No one "suspected." We knew no other gay people—that was the last thing on our minds. The passion we knew in bed at night was always muffled by our inability to say "I love you" to each other, by the awareness that the whole world which was rewarding us as men was saying "no" to our homosexuality. On several occasions, we managed to talk briefly about what was happening to us. We never said anything positive about the closeness and love we were experiencing. We knew on one level that it felt very good; but we also had a clear understanding how homosexuality is "untenable"—that's one word I definitely remember using. We agreed to stop having sex, but we started up again. Finally, as the end of our senior year came closer, we made another agreement to stop having sex. A few weeks later, I tried to reinitiate our physical love, but this time his refusal was final. Our identity as men still intact, we took the next logical step. We got girlfriends to affirm our heterosexuality.

A couple of years later, aided by the independence of life on a Fulbright grant in Brazil, I decided to stop running away from my homosexuality. I knew I wasn't straight and I gave up pretending. It wasn't quite coming out all the way, as I maintained a double existence and I still thought about committing suicide, but at least I was beginning to come to terms with myself.

As for my friend, he went through a series of affairs with women, and then, gradually, became a kind of a hermit. He ended his friendships with his brother and his close friends (accusing some of them of being "faggots"). He started writing odd tracts, eventually declaring himself a genius, the bearer of great religious and political knowledge and wisdom. Sometime last year, his mother had him committed to a mental hospital. The cops came to take him away. I don't know if or when he will come out of the hospital, but I feel in my guts that his mental health will return only when he can feel free enough to be gay. I also know that this is not the approach that the hospital staff will take; they would rather keep him locked up than affirm anyone's homosexuality. That is why I consider him—and the thousands of gay people like him—to be political prisoners.

Homosexuality: An Adjective First

Anti-homosexual feelings run high in America. Simultaneously, there is a great awareness of homosexuality as a phenomenon. Some of America's most popular swear words—"shove it up your ass," and "you dirty cocksucker," for example—express at the same moment the straight man's awareness of homosexuality and the repugnance he feels towards it.

The word "homosexual" was an adjective before it was a noun. Those whose desire today is to kill homosexuals (and there are many) are the descendants of those who first killed the homosexuality inside themselves. The quest for full life of today's gay liberationists—if it is to be realized—will lift the penalty of death for the homosexual in all women and men.

Gay liberation, on the surface, is a struggle by homosexuals for dignity and respect—a struggle for civil rights. Of course, we want to "come out," (that is, to end our hiding), to forbid such terms as "faggot," "dyke," and "queer," to hold down jobs without having to play straight, and to change or abolish those laws which restrict or denegrate us.

But the movement for a new definition of sexuality does not, and cannot, end there. The definition of sexism, as developed by women's liberation and gay liberation, presupposes a struggle against the main perpetrators of sexism—straight white men—- and against the manifestations of sexism as they appear in all people. The revolutionary goals of gay liberation, including the elimination of capitalism, imperialism and racism, are premised on the termination of the system of male supremacy.

On Gay Oppression

The worst thing about being gay is experiencing the anti-

homosexualism of the society. To survive in a hostile environment, most gays hide their homosexuality. The result is the fear
associated with the possibility of discovery, and the shame and
guilt associated with homosexual dreams, daydreams, desires
and acts. For an important minority of homosexuals—those who
are identified as such because they have the mannerisms,
clothing or speech pattern usually reserved for the other sex—the
oppression takes on different forms. The blatantly gay are often
subject to verbal abuse, physical brutality from police and other
thugs, and the knowledge that even those who can tolerate
discreet homosexuality will not tolerate this turn-around of
sex-determined roles.

Most male homosexuals are still trapped by notions of
masculinity. It is a familiar story—the oppressed worships the
oppressor. Listen to the names of some of America's gay men's
bars—The Stud, The Tool Box, The Barn. What passes for gay
men's art—including murals in these bars—often depicts such
masculine characters as the Body-Builder, the Motorcyclist, the
Cowboy. What goes on inside most of these gay bars often
preserves the notion that the people inside are "real men," too.
The billiard table, the sawdust on the floor, the leather vest on the
bartender, and, most of all, the men standing around with carefully
groomed indifference while quaffing their beer (just like good
collegians or dockworkers). The gay man's quest for masculinity,
or exaggerated masculinity, cannot be dismissed as mere
evidence of his sexism. Beyond that, it is evidence of oppression,
evidence of how a minority is overwhelmed by the values and
style of the majority.

Some additional observations about gay bars are necessary.
On one level, these gathering places are products of a system we
are striving to eliminate. First, they perpetrate male supremacy;
second, most of them are owned by greedy gay capitalists or
greedier criminal syndicates. It is impossible, however, to escape
a crucial fact: aside from the meetings of gay organizations, these
bars are the only places where large numbers of gay people get
together. Until I went to a gay liberation meeting in January, 1970,
for example, I had never been in a roomful of homosexuals—with
the exception of a gay bar. As congregating places for gay people
(particularly gay men, although there are a handful of lesbian bars
in the biggest cities), the gay bars are the focal points of conflict
between our new spirit of liberation and the forces which would
keep us in our place. In other words, they are community
institutions, as the community is now constituted.

The raid on the Stonewall Inn Bar is accepted as the birthday of gay liberation. Police action against gay bars in Los Angeles has led to mobilization of hundreds of gay people. In one incident, police harassed drivers and zealously ticketed parked cars near the Tradesman Bar. When one patron of the bar warned some of his brothers about the police activity, he was beaten and arrested. The cops told the owner of the bar what they were up to: "We don't like fags, we don't like places that serve fags, and you might as well declare bankruptcy because you're going to be closed. We're going to be here every night." Los Angeles Gay Liberation Front (GLF) formed a Gay Action Patrol to observe the police.

In Chicago, gay liberation actions forced several bars to permit dancing. Even though there is no law in Illinois prohibiting dancing between people of the same sex (such laws do exist in other states), the bar operators didn't allow dancing so they could maintain their image (as in, "This is just a bar like any other bar"). Leaflets and a boycott changed things in Chicago.

One of New York's most militant demonstrations—a spontaneous march and vigil in Greenwich Village early in 1970—occurred after a police raid on the Snake Pit. The cops busted the operators of this after-hours bar on a liquor law technicality, choosing, typically, a busy Saturday night so the raid could intimidate a maximum number of patrons and look good for the politicians and the police brass. The people at the Snake Pit, 167 in all, were carted off to the precinct house. Most of those arrested were afraid—of the police, at the very least, and, beyond that, that the arrest and the homosexual connotation would be reported to employer or family. One man, an alien named Diego Vinales, had an additional fear—that the immigration officers would find out. In order to obtain a visa to the United States, you must swear that you are not a homosexual—and if it is determined that you are a homosexual, you may be deported. Diego Vinales jumped out of the second-story window of the police station and impaled himself on a fence. Five steel spikes went into his pelvis and thigh. Firemen using an acetylene torch cut the fence, with Vinales still impaled on it, and took him to the hospital, where emergency surgery saved his life.

A few months later, policemen from the same precinct raided two different bars, pushed the patrons out into the street, and proceeded to use crowbars and other implements of destruction in a "search" for drugs and whiskey. Property damage totaled more than $20,000.

In San Francisco, gay people are organizing legal defense and propaganda around the case of Charles Christman. This gay brother was shot by police, placed under arrest and charged with attempted homocide. Christman's arrest came after police arbitrarily broke up a crowd of gay men congregating outside The Stud (a nightly occurrence). As Christman was driving away from the scene, one cop told him to beat it and another told him to stop. In the confusion, Christman tried to drive off. The cops say he tried to run down several police officers—supposedly justifying their trigger-happy response. With the cops' liberal use of the term "faggot" during The Stud incident, Christman's defense lawyers and local gay groups are pointing out that the police seem motivated more by their hatred for homosexuals than by anything else.

In Houston, Gay Liberation Front used a picket line successfully to break the racist lily-white policy of a gay men's bar.

While fully recognizing the oppressive nature of dimly-lit bars in out-of-the-way streets such as Greenwich Street in New York and Folsom Street in San Francisco, we will continue to preserve the bars as temporary gay turf where there is at least minimal freedom for gay people. This campaign goes on simultaneously with attempts to provide alternative meeting grounds, such as coffee houses and community centers. Such places, along with gay liberation meetings, communal houses and apartments, already offer such an alternative to thousands of gays in nearly 100 localities.

Repression by police power is a day-to-day fact for all homosexuals. Every "practicing" homosexual is an outlaw, for gay love (under the legal category of "sodomy") is a crime in all but two states (Connecticut and Illinois). In New York state, the sodomy laws prohibit any contact between the mouth and the penis, the mouth and the vulva, and the penis and the anus. (Most sodomy laws are written in such a way that they apply to heterosexuals as well; court cases are challenging these laws in several states at the present time.) In some states, all sex is illegal unless it is done by a married couple in the "missionary position" (man on top, woman on back looking up)—so named because Christian missionaries insisted that the Indians use this position and give up their evil variations.

Few sodomy convictions are for contact between "consenting adults." Changes in the legal codes to allow such sex acts between consenting adults have come in a handful of states (and in Great Britain), but this has not made a difference in the basic oppression of homosexuals in these places.

Many sodomy convictions are for sexual contact between

minors and individuals of legal age. If a 22-year-old man has sex with a 16-year-old man, the 22-year-old can go to jail for several years. Such cases are not at all uncommon.

In New York state, a handful of lawmakers backed a bill in the 1971 session to extend the state's fair housing and fair employment legislation to include homosexuals, but the bill was voted down.

Provisions for certain "moral" standards already force gay doctors and gay lawyers to hide their homosexuality. Even attorneys whose practice is limited by choice to the defense of homosexuals and homophile groups find it necessary to reiterate constantly that they are not themselves homosexual.

Gay people—just by our existence and life style—are perpetual outlaws. For example, in most states it is illegal to invite someone home with you for the purpose of sex. Since gay people (especially men) do this frequently, we are constantly in danger of being arrested for "solicitation." (The laws against "solicitation" are violated constantly by straight men any time they whistle at a woman or say something like, "Hey, baby, wanna come home with me?", but virtually all arrests for solicitation are of prostitutes, transvestites and gay males.) Many solicitation arrests are entrapment cases. In one such case, currently being fought in a Los Angeles court, an attractive young police officer dressed in a Texaco service station uniform stood alluringly in a popular cruising spot in Griffith Park. Before long, he managed to get into conversation with another young man, who happened to be a member of Los Angeles Gay Liberation Front. When the GLFer invited the Texaco pig home, he was immediately busted by other cops waiting nearby. The GLF brother vowed to take the case through all the courts necessary to prove he was being punished not for "solicitation" but for homosexuality. Most men arrested under such circumstances pay high legal fees to get the charges dropped or lowered.

Transvestites (only some of whom are homosexual) are frequently arrested for wearing "the clothing of the opposite sex." Transvestites find it almost impossible to obtain employment, a situation which often drives them to prostitution. They are frequently arrested for prostitution, impersonation, solicitation, loitering, harassment, disorderly conduct, etc., or are carted off to mental hospitals.

Gay couples holding hands or dancing or kissing in a public place are often arrested for "lewd conduct" or under some disorderly conduct statute. At any time, those of us who organize gay events, such as dances and meetings, or those who sell or print gay newspapers, may be arrested for "contributing to the delinquency of a minor." In fact, most of the older homophile groups specify that their activities are only for those of legal age. We are now willing and ready, however, to fight legal codes which deny sexual freedom to young people. In New York and other cities, a separate group called Gay Youth (for those under 21) has been organized to deal with the special problems of younger gays.

In the summer of 1970, police harassment on 42nd Street in New York reached new heights. Within a couple of weeks, several hundred gays were arbitrarily taken into custody by police. A special command post was set up inside the Dixie Hotel, where gay people were interrogated and harassed. Few arrests were actually made; the purpose of the police action was intimidation. Gay liberation responded with a demonstration. We marched and chanted and sang up and down 42nd Street, past the Times Square precinct, and down into the Village. There, police wielding clubs charged at demonstrators, touching off another summertime gay riot. There were several arrests and injuries, but the fighting spirit of the community was forged stronger still. Several cops were also injured.

Gay people are challenging many laws in the courts, including marriage laws and tax laws which discriminate against gays or "single people." (As for gay marriages, most gay liberationists see this as an imitation of a bad heterosexual institution. While many of us relate in couples, we are working toward a goal of communal love.)

One of the most significant court cases in gay liberation was that of the D.C. 12. Twelve gay brothers attending the Revolutionary People's Constitutional Convention last Thanksgiving weekend in Washington, D.C., were arrested in an incident at The Zephyr, a straight, lily-white restaurant. The incident occurred after four gay brothers were refused service. Several carloads of gay people responded to this act of discrimination by filling up the restaurant. When some straight patrons and the manager started to push the gay brothers out, they fought back. The restaurant was trashed. The police came and made 12 arrests, charging destruction of property, assault, etc. As the case developed, defense attorneys won the right to carry out a *voir dire*, that is, to question the jurors as to their prejudice against homosexuals. Later, when it was revealed that witnesses had illegally seen the defendants in jail before viewing them in a line-up, the government had to drop all the charges. Winning the right to do a *voir dire* on sexism is considered to be an important precedent for future cases involving gay people.

No one knows for sure how many gay people are in jail, but it is an acknowledged fact that many men's jails have a special tier or section for homosexuals. For most people, linking up the word "homosexual" and the word "jail" conjures up images of sex perverts attacking "normal" men. The gay liberation movement is beginning to break through the distortions, lies, half-truths and ignorance on this topic. First of all, every jail has a significant number of gay people, homosexuals who are known to be homosexuals by the authorities and who acknowledge their homosexuality. Like most oppressed people who are carted off by the police to the nation's prisons, these gay people are victims of a vicious system. Whether the charge emerges directly from their homosexuality (sodomy, solicitation, "lewd conduct"), or indirectly (burglary, prostitution, shoplifting), all gay prisoners are political prisoners.

To the extent that there are violent homosexual acts in any jail, this is due exclusively to the aggressive behavior of straight men. Overt homosexuals, homosexuals trying but failing to pass for straight, or straight men who are slight of build and capable of being seen as a female sex object—these are the victims of rape and sexual assualt from brutal, straight male prisoners. Such sex is a form of bogus homosexuality which is nothing but an under-the-circumstances parody of heterosexuality.

In New York, the Gay Community Prisoner Defense Committee was organized in the wake of the murder of Raymond Lavon Moore, a black gay man whose suicide death was reported by the authorities. The Young Lords Party conducted their own investigation of Moore's death, charging that he was murdered by guards.

Richard Harris, who like Lavon Moore, was being held in lieu of bail on the fourth floor of the Tombs (that's where the gay people are kept), issued a statement concerning Lavon Moore's death:

"On November 1, 1970, I was witness to a brutal, inhumane beating of Lavon Moore by four pigs. This beating led directly to his death. An alleged suicide, but which was in reality cold-blooded murder. Being an epileptic and asthmatic, Raymond Lavon Moore refused to take medication which would have aggravated his condition and which was being forced on him by pig Benjamin. After Brother Lavon repeatedly refused to take this medication and requested to see a Captain or Deputy Warden, pig Benjamin told another pig to crack the cell (4th floor, lower cell), at which time he and three other pigs went into Brother Lavon's cell and started beating him savagely. They handcuffed him, dragged him out of the cell, and continued to viciously kick and beat him.

Brother Lavon was covered with blood. His cries went unheard. When they finally took him off the floor, he was more dead than alive. Raymond Lavon Moore did not commit suicide—he was murdered."

The four Tombs guards who murdered Lavon Moore were suspended from their positions, but they were later reinstated after a Grand Jury said there was no evidence of criminal action.

Richard Harris was convicted on trumped-up charges and is still a prisoner. His lover and friends cannot visit him because prison regulations uphold the nuclear family by limiting visitors to immediate blood relatives. Gay community groups are continuing to work to free Richard Harris and to demand that the murderers of Raymond Lavon Moore—not just the four guards but the highest city officials—be brought to justice.

Ortez Alderson, former chairman of the black caucus of Chicago Gay Liberation, is another gay prisoner. He recently served a one-year sentence for his part in ransacking draft files in Pontiac, Illinois. For Christmas, he sent this message on a card which was read during a silent interlude at a Christman Eve "Gay Community Celebration of Love and Life":

"I practically die when I think about spending my Christmas in this jail. Well, I guess that's how life goes. I wonder if they stop dropping bombs for Christmas. Of course, it really doesn't make any difference, if they start the next day. You know, the only way I've managed to survive this is because of all my beautiful sisters and brothers who really make me strong."

Getting The Facts: Mission Impossible

In the 1950s, when I was a teen-ager and I realized that the word "homosexual" had something to do with the way I was feeling and behaving, I tried to get the facts. I was already overwhelmed with a sense of my abnormality; I had no idea there were millions of other teen-agers going through the very same thing. Everywhere, in the newspapers and magazines, on radio and TV, in the movies, there wasn't the slightest affirmation of homosexuality. If the subject ever made an appearance, it was in terms of ridicule or condemnation. But mostly, there was nothing. The overwhelming message of boy-girl, man-woman love came through in every novel and every comic book I ever read. Holden Caulfield of *Catcher in the Rye,* the hero of my generation, spent much of his saga worrying about queers. He ended up in a mental hospital, like so many who desperately try to repress their homosexuality, flipped out after a former English teacher (unappealingly described as an alcoholic and woman-hater by

Salinger) affectionately strokes his hair. *The Picture of Dorian Gray*, Oscar Wilde's great homosexual novel, felt vaguely homosexual to me as I read it, but it is not explicit. Wilde talks of "friendship," not "love"; the story did not provide the affirmation I needed.

Now it is becoming more common to find homosexuals appearing , in some way or another, in the media. More often than not, the homosexuals portrayed are stereotypes, or otherwise shown in a negative way. In *Up Tight,* a movie about black militants, there is a homosexual police informer. The so-called progressive movie-maker who put together *Z* went out of his way to portray one of the young Greek fascists as a homosexual. Then there was Little Horse, the gay Indian in *Little Big Man,* said to be a shaman respected by his people, but nevertheless played for racist, sexist laughs—something to do with redskin as faggot, or faggot as redskin, either way, it's oh, so clever! And as for *Boys in the Band,* the movie that brought a part of the gay world to the American masses for the first time, it depicts a sad collection of stereotypes in a story designed to win pity and perhaps tolerance from liberals. That would be bad enough, but the movie evinces stormy applause from straights when the closet-case friend of the birthday party host affirms his straightness and goes back to his wife. This "courageous" movie (some reviewer must have called it "courageous") doesn't even dare to show two men kissing on the screen. Its homosexuals are so unappealing and so pitiful that it hardly serves as affirmation for someone trying to come out.

In the 1950s, I looked up the word "homosexuality" in the index of every book on psychology or sex or health that I could find. The mere association of homosexuality with medicine, of course, is oppressive. Beyond that, almost every reference was negative —Freudian nonsense about arrested sexual development, or, still worse, categorical statements about homosexuality being a mental illness and urgings that homosexuals seek "help."

One of the most macabre set of anti-homosexual lies is contained in the super-best-seller, David Reuben's *Everything You Always Wanted to Know About Sex But Were Afraid to Ask.* In a chapter entitled "Male Homosexuality" (he ignores female homosexuality altogether), Reuben (who is a psychiatrist) projects an image of crazed faggots sticking carrots and cucumbers up their asses, and he categorically asserts that no homosexual can possibly be happy.

There is a six-man rogues' gallery of shrinks who are most responsible for the "scientific" facade which covers the oppression of homosexuals by those whose oath is to help people. Each of these shrinks has written a successful book, and each has become rich by convincing homosexuals that they can be "cured" (even when all the evidence points in the opposite direction). What is more serious, each is responsible, directly or indirectly, for the suicide of countless gay people, and for the incarceration, in jails, mental hospitals and juvenile centers, of countless others. Even more enlightened and liberal shrinks, under the influence of the Big Six and their books, accept homosexual patients or refer them to other shrinks. Very few shrinks, if any, send their gay "patients" where they should be sent—to the nearest gay liberation group.

The suffering and cruelty promoted by these six shrinks places them, in my eyes, in the ranks of the worst of war criminals. They are: Edmund Bergler, *Homosexuality: Disease or Way of Life*, 1957; Irving Bieber, *Homosexuality*, 1962; Albert Ellis, *Homosexuality: Its Causes and Cure*, 1964; Charles Socarides, *The Overt Homosexual*, 1968; Lionel Ovesey, *Homosexuality and Pseudohomosexuality*, 1969; and Lawrence J. Hatterer, *Changing Homosexuality in the Male*, 1970.

These shrinks speak with a confidence and authority that would be laughable if it were not for the infinite suffering they cause. Bergler, for example, writes: "It has recently been discovered that homosexuality is a curable illness. . . . Homosexuality is not the 'way of life' these sick people gratuitously assume it to be, but a neurotic distortion of the total personality. . . . The entire personality structure of the homosexual is pervaded by the unconscious wish to suffer."

So far, it has only been homosexuals from gay liberation and homophile groups who have launched an assault against the Shrink Pigs. Since May 1970, when gay liberation invaded the national convention of the American Psychiatric Association in San Francisco, angry homosexuals haven't missed a chance to disrupt such events as a recent seminar on homosexuality at the Downstate Medical Center in Brooklyn.

The books by the Big Six are virtually the only books on homosexuality available in the average bookstore or public library. Virtually the only pro-gay book of the 1950s, Donald Webster Cory's *The Homosexual in America*, was published by a tiny publishing house and was generally unavailable until the recent publication of a new edition. At the Library of Congress years ago, I found the title on a file card under "Homosexuality," but it was kept in the "Delta" section (along with pornography and rare manuscripts). I was able to read it there only by bracing myself to overcome my fear that upon my signing for the book (I had to show ID), a librarian would telephone my family and my high school. A few pro-homosexual books are set for publication in 1972, but if Random House had trouble distributing *Woodstock Nation,* you can imagine how conservative librarians and book distributors will respond to something on gay liberation. (A task force on Gay Liberation has been formed within the Social Responsibilities Round Table of the American Library Association. A gay librarian, Jack McConnell, is a major figure in two court cases in Minnesota. He and his lover applied for a marriage license, were rejected and are now appealing. When the marriage case was publicized, McConnell lost a position he was supposed to have as a librarian at the University of Minnesota.)

On The Army

"Gay Liberation Is Anti-War Movement / Movement Against War." Gay people at a recent anti-war gathering in Ann Arbor emerged with this slogan, and proposed a resolution on gay liberation, which was approved by the conference. The gay resolution was conveniently omitted when the conference organizers later sent out a printed collection of resolutions, an action typical of the anti-gay attitudes of the straight movement.

The Gay May Day Tribe, organizing for the recent anti-war demonstrations in Washington, stated our position this way:

War American style, is a man's game, where to prove his masculinity, he must maim or kill women, children, the very old, the very young, and his own brothers. War is an extension of our own oppression because it reinforces the masculine image of males and forces them into playing roles where the end result is the death of millions of people.

The gay movement also circulated the following statement entitled "Sexism and the War":

How does the concept of sexism relate to the machinery that grinds out war after war? Wars are conceived and fought by men who are reared to play a 'macho' role and to feel guilty if this sexual role is not fulfilled. As homosexuals it is especially ludicrous to ape this non-homosexual role-playing. As gay people and people who oppose sexism, we can offer a truly permanent peace by offering a viable alternative.

Sexism is the most elemental form of politics. Indoctrination into the system begins at birth. Human interaction based on sexual roles conditions boys to be aggressive and to fight others, while it conditions females to submit to a lesser status in the hierarchy. This same system brands those outside these two stereotypes as 'queer' or 'foreign.'

Gay people are 'foreigners' in their own culture and are reminded of this fact at every opportunity. We must demonstrate, in whatever way possible, that the beast is within this, our system.

The homophile organizations—those groups formed before the gay liberation movement—are still officially in favor of the right of homosexuals to serve in the U.S. Armed Forces. There is no doubt that the exclusion of gays from the army is the result of unacceptable anti-gay ideas. But virtually all gay liberation groups are opposed to the draft and to the policies of the U.S. Army. The official policy adopted by Berkeley GLF, and endorsed by many other groups subsequently, is to urge all young men, gay and straight, to claim homosexuality and thus be exempt from military service. If you can prove you are a homosexual, you can insist on your legal right not to serve in the army. Gay women and gay men are frequently thrown out of military service and given dishonorable discharges, a policy which is now being challenged. After one success involving two WACs, GLF in Los Angeles offered to help any gay servicemen or servicewomen to obtain honorable discharge.

On The Church

The Roman Catholic Church has been a deadly enemy of the homosexual throughout history. During the Middle Ages, many male homosexuals, along with countless rebellious women, many of them lesbians, were burned at the stake. Even today, church dogma strikes fear in the heart, mind and body of many who fall under its influence. Protestant and Jewish dogma is no less destructive.

Different gay groups have taken different tactical approaches toward the church and religion. Many gay Christians (including a few de-frocked ministers and priests) have formed their own churches, while other gays prefer to reject the idea of organized religion altogether. These gay churches, especially the Los Angeles-based Metropolitan Community Church, have been very successful in attracting large, predominantly male congregations. Many gay people, while affirming the concept of spirituality, feel that organized religion is intrinsically sexist. While recognizing that Christ preached love, and even entertaining the idea that Christ and his friends may have been homosexuals themselves, the unaffiliated gays believe it is naive to try to become a part of Christian history, which has been so incredibly anti-homosexual. It is also sexist to promote any system which has an elitist male (Jesus) on top.

During a recent week of actions to call the United Nations' attention to the practice of genocide by the United States government, a dozen gay liberationists marched in front of New York's St. Patrick's Cathedral. Many gay people have been oppressed by being coerced by family custom to be subject to religious ritual and dogma.

On The Straight Movement

The traditional left, both Old Left and New Left, has been as oppressive to homosexuals as has establishment America. I grew up in a Communist Party household, and I learned at an early age about socialism, about how the workers are unjustly exploited by the bosses, about the beautiful system known as socialism. I also quickly learned that socialism wasn't for fairies, because my parents and their friends would occasionally make jokes about fairies. I also knew that I was a fairy. (I didn't want to be one, of course, but that's what they called me in school.) In any case, it was much easier to identify with socialism than with being a fairy. (The Communist Party is probably the most vicious anti-homosexual group on the left today. Its paper, the *Daily World,* has published at least one anti-homosexual cartoon, and CP picket captains in New York physically assaulted gay people who wanted to march with gay banners in support of Angela Davis.)

I joined the staff of Liberation News Service in Washington, D.C., shortly after it was founded in the autumn of 1967. By then, I was actively homosexual. I used to sneak away from the LNS office, and from my "comrades" in SDS, to meet other homosexuals. I always enjoyed the irony of cruising in Lafayette Park, across the street from the White House, but the emotion I most remember is anger and sadness as I wandered through that park. I never met a homosexual like myself—someone from the movement—a situation which reinforced my sense of aloneness and uniqueness. With good reason, too—the oppressive sexist power of the movement itself was keeping us apart. Now I know more of what was really happening: at one time, there were no fewer than six male homosexuals associated with LNS in Washington. One had a few gay experiences but actively projected his heterosexual image. One called himself "pan-sexual," shied away from gay experiences, and had an affair with a woman. Still another, repressing his homosexual feelings, was having an affair with a woman. One was a man in his thirties who felt that he would be unable to work politically if he was open about his gayness and satisfied himself by having mostly non-sexual friendships with teen-age boys. One was totally asexual in practice, though actively gay in his fantasies and manner—on November 1, 1969, he ran a vacuum cleaner hose from his car's exhaust pipe to his front vent window, saying good-bye to the world and the movement. (It was on another November 1, this one in 1964, in Rio de Janeiro, where I was studying on a Fulbright grant, that another gay friend of mine killed himself, a wonderfully vital man in his mid-twenties who had helped me accept my own homosexuality. Most of us in gay liberation don't hear about a suicide without automatically assuming there's a good chance the person was homosexual.)

It was even worse inside SDS. I attended most of the large national council meetings of SDS in the period from December, 1967 until the stormy final convention of June, 1969. I felt totally alone as a homosexual, incapable of telling any of those people about myself. The gay love I wanted to express was prohibited while they played musical beds.

Some people seem to think that things have gotten better. In very small ways, maybe they have. Homosexuals do not have to be invisible any more in many movement groups. There has been a formalistic recognition of gay liberation by such diverse groups as the Black Panther Party, International Socialists, Peace & Freedom Party, the Young Socialist Alliance, The Yippies and various local collectives and underground papers. This has not, in my opinion, altered the basic pattern of anti-gay oppression within the straight movement. When I told the people at LNS I was gay, they didn't express any overt hostility to me for that. But the men there steadfastly hold on to their own straight identity. I could not even begin to establish a gay identity, could not even begin to struggle with my own sexism and elitism, in such hostile surroundings. Among straight people, I must suppress many of my feelings. Shared experiences around my oppression are minimal.

The "pro-gay" segment of the straight movement is telling us, "Now you don't have to hide any more, so everything is OK." We are saying in return, "Everything is not OK. Not hiding is only the beginning. You have to stop holding on to your straight identity. By denying our form of love, by saying it is essentially a private matter, you wish to perpetuate male supremacy and patterns of dominance which are basically sexist and which are in the end anti-homosexual."

There are many well-intentioned people in the straight movement who like to define the revolutionary forces in this country as a melange of diverse groups in struggle—workers, blacks, Puerto Ricans, chicanos, Indians, Asians, women and gays—often expressed in that order. I myself often grasp at this idealized vision of what is supposedly happening. We do have a common enemy in U.S. imperialism; that is true and that provides us with a certain sense of unity. But the straight movement has continually asked gay people to deny the validity of the gay struggle.

We gays want and need autonomy, yet the straight movement continually denies the validity of our struggle. Gays are constantly being asked by the straight movement to prove ourselves. I am keenly aware of this because as a former member in good standing of the New Left, I am constantly being told by former comrades things like, "Well, we know that you are an anti-imperialist, but we don't know about a lot of the other people in gay liberation." I cannot accept this attempt to separate me from my gay sisters and brothers.

I am still so encumbered by the sexist mentality of the left that it is actually a longer, more difficult process for me to develop a gay identity and struggle against sexism. Gay people without proper movement credentials are in many ways far ahead of me in understanding sexism. I am constantly being coerced, gently or arrogantly, to provide a class analysis of homosexuality, to answer allegations about "bourgeois decadence"—and more often than not I yield to this coercion. But this is just one of the ways that so-called Marxists have put down homosexuals. We don't have to answer any of these questions; the onus is on the straight movement to deal with its sexism. Our struggle is denied by straight people who think of themselves as being part of the "broader struggle," who define themselves as the "real revolutionaries." We do not get validated by our participation in anti-war marches; we join those marches because imperialist wars are sexist. Straight leftists will accept us as long as they can conceive of us as something like "United Homosexuals for Peace, Equality and Socialism." We are opposed to capitalism, racism and war, but we express that opposition by using our energy to oppose sexism. We are for gay liberation. Gay liberation is a total revolutionary movement. The oppression which we suffer from straight society, and our consequent quest for freedom, is the only justification or validation we need.

Some History

The traditional birthday of Gay Liberation is June 1969, when gay people fought back against a police raid at the Stonewall Inn. The police invaded the bar, forcing people out onto the street. But instead of running away, the gay people, led by transvestites, locked the police inside the bar, set the place afire, and then threw coins and bottles when the police worked their way out of the place. Participants in the incident, along with others in the gay community, got together to plan an on-going political group for gay people. The gay militants chose the name Gay Liberation Front, in homage to the Vietnamese guerrillas. The group has never been a "front," in the real sense of the term (a collection of groups), but the name stuck and was picked up in dozens of other cities.

GLF defined itself from the beginning as being different from the early homophile and lesbian organizations. These groups, including the Mattachine Society, the Society of Individual Rights (SIR), and the Daughters of Bilitis, were formed in the 1950s primarily as civil rights and social groups. Lacking an explicit understanding of sexism, though fully aware of oppression, the members of these groups struggled to halt the anti-homosexual hysteria of McCarthyism, to combat the most overt forms of anti-homosexualism such as police brutality, and to provide social activities. The use of the term "homophile," which was meant to include straight people who favored justice for gays, implicitly rejected the idea that gay people as such had a right and need to be together. In practice, these groups carried out important work. They put out some of the first homosexual publications (*One, Vector, The Ladder*), held the first meetings where gay people could get together to talk over their problems, provided lawyers for gay people in trouble with the police, published information about venereal disease (since the medical profession and public health officials tend to think that there is only one kind of sex), and sponsored social events.

The homophile groups, as well as some of the newer groups such as the Gay Activists Alliance, work primarily toward the elimination of laws which prevent gays from doing our own thing. Gay liberation is a more far-reaching concept. It is premised on consciousness-raising about sexism with the goal of sexual liberation for all. Gay liberation also has a perspective for revolution based on the unity of all oppressed people—that is, there can be no freedom for gays in a society which enslaves others through male supremacy, racism and economic exploitation (capitalism).

In any case, some events bring us all together, at least momentarily. The first large mass action by gay people was the June, 1970 Christopher Street Gay Pride March from Greenwich Village up the Avenue of the Americas to Central Park. Some 10,000 people participated, some of them members of gay groups, the vast majority coming from the disparate gay community. It was a big step for gay people to be in the street, and many of us recognized many more gay people watching from the sidewalk with an ambivalent look of fear and pride on their faces. Larger marches took place in New York and Los Angeles on June 27, 1971.

From the outset, the Gay Liberation Front was an organization of male homosexuals and lesbians. By the spring of 1970, many of the GLF women began a separate caucus, and before long this turned into a new, separate group, the Radicalesbians. The lesbians were responding to a situation in which they were wasting their energies pointing out sexist attitudes to men. They decided to respond to their unique situation as gay women, and they were joined by many lesbians from the feminist movement who had not previously associated with gay liberation. Other women continued to function as a part of GLF, noting that "our strongest common denominator and greatest oppression lies with society's injustice against us as homosexuals." In several cities, Black, Latin and Asian homosexuals formed separate caucuses and groups. In New York and Chicago, Third World Gay Revolution has been working to combat racist attitudes of white homosexuals and to struggle against anti-gay attitudes in the Third World communities. Another separate organization, Street Transvestite Action Revolutionaries (STAR), was started in the fall of 1970 in New York to meet the special needs of transvestites.

While the Stonewall Riot—and response to police repression—is generally accepted as the starting point of gay liberation, there are other antecedents worth mentioning. In the 1960s, for several years running, a few dozen pickets from the homophile groups went to Philadelphia during Independence Day festivities, picketing Independence Hall to protest the status of homosexuals as second-class citizens.

In San Francisco's Haight-Ashbury district in 1967, gay freaks led by Keith St. Clare formed the Circle of Loving Companions and put out a hip gay monthly called *Vanguard*. Its articles about peace and drugs upset the traditional homophile spokesmen.

In the same city, a group called the Committee for Homosexual Freedom (CHF) was formed in early 1969 to respond to a series of incidents in which gay people were fired from their jobs for the mere fact of being gay. In the spring of 1969, articles on gay oppression started appearing in the Bay Area underground newspapers. An announcer for KGO, the San Francisco affiliate of ABC, wrote by-lined articles for the *Berkeley Barb*. Other KGO announcers ridiculed him on the air, and eventually he was fired. His case became something of a cause celebre, though he was never reinstated, and by the fall of 1969, groups using the name gay liberation were functioning in San Francisco, Berkeley and Los Angeles. Another important antecedent was the formation of the Student Homophile League (SHL) on various campuses. The first SHL was formed by a handful of students at Columbia University in the fall of 1966. Columbia officials, following the rule book, were compelled against their better judgment to charter the group. When the news went out across the nation via UPI and AP, angry alumni, shocked schoolteachers and worried parents deluged the university with their complaints and protests. Columbia President Grayson Kirk—later to become the villain of the big 1968 strike—lashed out at the officials below him. One casualty of the formation of SHL at Columbia was Vice-President Lawrence Chamberlain, who quit his position when he was attacked by Kirk. SHL survived Kirk's storm. In the fall of 1970 SHL became Gay People at Columbia, though the group continued to define itself as educational and social, specifically not political. Dances at Columbia, attracting at least 600 gay men and women, have been held in Earl Hall, a building which falls under the chaplain's office and ostensibly is dedicated to religious purposes. (It is quite common for gay people to meet or hold dances in churches, though it is only a handful of liberal pastors who have made this possible. Gay groups regularly use the meeting hall of the Episcopalian Church of the Holy Apostles in New York City.)

The campuses of America's universities, however, are hardly liberated territory for gays, despite the fact that gay dances are now held regularly at Columbia, Yale and a few other places.

Several gay community groups in New York joined with New York University's Gay Students Liberation at the beginning of the fall 1970 term for a struggle against the school's sexist policies. It began with a fight for the right of gay people from the community and from the school to use university space for a dance. The university said no; students—who supposedly controlled the hall—said yes. A sit-in was held, ending only when the university summoned the Tactical Patrol Force. The students' presumed power was non-existent. Several rallies and pickets followed. The gay people (with very little support from NYU students) raised the broader issue of NYU's total failure to meet the needs of the community in which it is located—Greenwich Village, the world's largest gay ghetto.

Last fall, many student gay organizations were still engaged in basic battles over the right to hold on-campus meetings. At Florida State University in Tallahassee, the gay people had to put up a fight just in order to advertise one of their meetings in the school paper. It is also understood at virtually every university that any faculty or staff member could be discharged for homosexuality (on "moral" grounds). Even such presumedly tolerant and enlightened people as university professors have yet to speak out as a group on this issue. When a gay professor raised the issue (without saying he was gay) during the struggle at NYU, his colleagues tittered. Gay teachers cannot be open about themselves with their colleagues and their students—a situation which depends on the sexist power of straight administrators, trustees and faculty members. This situation has a threefold damaging effect: it inhibits the sense of community which may be possible within a university; it promotes relationships based on dishonesty; and it almost totally prevents scientific work on homosexuality in many fields, including history, sociology, political science, psychology, medicine, and the law. The result is disastrous not only for gay teachers but for all homosexuals, and ultimately for all people.

Conclusion

The work of the gay liberation movement—its organizational progress, its media, its demonstrations—are meaningful only in the context of consciousness about sexism. Our understanding about sexism has come about gradually; it is still emerging. There are no leaders who have handed down these ideas; rather they have emerged from discussions and personal testimony in consciousness-raising groups and political meetings.

For gay people, the essential point is to see limited sexuality as an end result of male supremacy and sex roles. Gay, in its most far-reaching sense, means not homosexual, but sexually free. This includes a long-ranged vision of sensuality as a basis for sexual relationships. This sexual freedom is not some kind of groovy life style with lots of sex, doing what feels good irrespective of others. It is sexual freedom premised upon the notion of pleasure through equality, no pleasure where there is inequality.

Straight people (and some gays) cringe when we chant "Two, four, six, eight, gay is twice as good as straight!" This slogan reflects our understanding of homosexuality as a superior way of life to heterosexuality as we experience it. Heterosexual relationships are encumbered by notions of how men and women are supposed to behave. It is a system which has male supremacy built in. Homosexuals committed to struggling against sexism have a better chance than straights of building relationships based on equality because there is less enforcement of roles. We have already broken with gender programming, so we can more easily move toward equality.

Gay is good for all of us. The artificial categories "heterosexual" and "homosexual" have been laid on us by a sexist society. Children are born sexual. To protect the power of straight men in a sexist society, homosexuality becomes prohibited behavior. As gays, we demand an end to the gender programming which starts when we are born (pink for girls, blue for boys). The nuclear family, with its man-woman model built in by the presence of parents, is the primary means by which this restricted sexuality is created and enforced. Gays experience rejection by the family in a society where familial love is considered important. The family oppresses women and children as well as gays. The phenomena of runaway teenagers and increasing divorce rates are signs of the erosion of the nuclear family. Gay liberation is another sign. We attack the nuclear family when we reject our parents' plea to get married and have a family. We are committed to building communal situations where children can grow strong and free.

Straights who are threatened by us like to accuse us of separatism—but our understanding of sexism is premised on the idea that in a free society everyone will be gay. It may be utopian to think that all people who now define themselves as "straight" will become gay, but it is not utopian to ask people who call themselves revolutionaries to struggle against sexism by working toward establishing a gay identity. We have a separate movement of gay people because we are fighting for survival, and because that is the only way we can establish an identity and advance our struggle.

While we have a vision of a free society, we do not claim to be a superior breed of free people. We do pride ourselves on our commitment to struggle, and we know that most, if not all, straight men will do everything in their power to resist gay liberation because by staying straight they stay privileged and powerful—at least in the short run. I can say this much about myself: I obtain a sense of well-being and confidence when I blend in with straight men, which is directly linked to power and privilege, and that is hard to give up. There are rewards in the other direction, however. As I develop a gay identity, I feel much more in touch with my humanity than when I was regularly passing for straight. I am swept up in a process of change which allows me to define myself in terms other than some masculine ideal. I have a growing awareness of myself and my relationships to other people which is exhilarating and deeply satisfying. My revolutionary fervor is more real than it ever was. I dance more, I laugh more, I am learning how to listen to others. I have sex less often but find it infinitely more satisfying. I am finding out how to love my brothers and sisters, how this love is the vital revolutionary force we all need.

One of the longest-running gay male consciousness-raising groups recently published a paper on their experiences. In it, they seem to sum up much of the revolutionary humanistic dimension of our struggle:

Gays must organize because it is the only way a class of people that has been cut adrift by society can deal with that fact. Everywhere we find hostility, prejudice and condescension, even amongst ourselves. Most gays accept, in self-defense, the straight man's mythology that says we're sick, immature, perverse, deviant, and thus should hide our love away in tearooms, park bushes, on cruising streets, and in Mafia—or otherwise pig-controlled bars. Those who reject the mythology, developing positive attitudes toward their homosexuality, are even more offensive to straights. We all risk brutalization and imprisonment and have little alternative but to use the traditional oppressive cruising institutions. These myths and institutions keep us isolated and distrustful of each other. And don't expect any help from our straight oppressors in creating alternatives. We're on our own.

In our consciousness-raising group, we have been trying to step outside the straight man's myths and institutions, to suspend the limited ways we deal with each other, and experiment with new ways of relating. Everyone's feelings are considered in consciousness-raising, and instead of shouting each other down, consensus, a solution that is to each person's interest, can be reached. If people are silent, they are asked to contribute. This is part of the collective process. We as men are struggling with our eagerness to dominate and ego-trip by being aware of the needs of others in the group, and are struggling with our tendency to intellectualize by speaking from our experience.

We are also learning what has been forbidden us—to relate to one another with respect and love.

GAY IS GOOD

Martha Shelley

Look out, straights. Here comes the Gay Liberation Front, springing up like warts all over the bland face of Amerika, causing shudders of indigestion in the delicately balanced bowels of the movement. Here come the gays, marching with six-foot banners to Washington and embarrassing the liberals, taking over Mayor Alioto's office, staining the good names of War Resister's League and Women's Liberation by refusing to pass for straight anymore.

We've got chapters in New York, San Francisco, San Jose, Los Angeles, Minneapolis, Philadelphia, Wisconsin, Detroit and I hear maybe even in Dallas. We're gonna make our own revolution because we're sick of revolutionary posters which depict straight he-man types and earth mothers, with guns and babies. We're sick of the Panthers lumping us together with the capitalists in their term of universal contempt—"faggot."

And I am personally sick of liberals who say they don't care who sleeps with whom, it's what you do outside of bed that counts. This is what homosexuals have been trying to get straights to understand for years. Well, it's too late for liberalism. Because what I do outside of bed may have nothing to do with what I do inside—but my consciousness is branded, is permeated with homosexuality. For years I have been branded with *your* label for me. The result is that when I am among gays or in bed with another woman, I am a person, not a lesbian. When I am observable to the straight world, I become gay. You are my litmus paper.

We want something more now, something more than the tolerance you never gave us. But to understand that, you must understand who we are.

We are the extrusions of your unconscious mind—your worst fears made flesh. From the beautiful boys at Cherry Grove to the aging queens in the uptown bars, the taxi-driving dykes to the lesbian fashion models, the hookers (male and female) on 42nd Street, the leather lovers . . . and the very ordinary very un-lurid gays . . . we are the sort of people everyone was taught to despise—and now we are shaking off the chains of self-hatred and marching on your citadels of repression.

Liberalism isn't good enough for us. And we are just beginning to discover it. Your friendly smile of acceptance—from the safe position of heterosexuality—isn't enough. As long as you cherish that secret belief that you are a little bit better because you sleep with the opposite sex, you are still asleep in your cradle and we will be the nightmare that awakens you.

We are women and men who, from the time of our earliest memories, have been in revolt against the sex-role structure and nuclear family structure. The roles we have played amongst ourselves, the self-deceit, the compromises and the subterfuges—these have never totally obscured the fact that we exist outside the traditional structure—and our existence threatens it.

Understand this—that the worst part of being a homosexual is having to keep it *secret*. Not the occasional murders by police or teenage queer-beaters, not the loss of jobs or expulsion from schools or dishonorable discharges—but the daily knowledge that what you are is so awful that it cannot be revealed. The violence against us is sporadic. Most of us are not affected. But the internal violence of being made to carry—or choosing to carry—the load of your straight society's unconscious guilt—this is what tears us apart, what makes us want to stand up in the offices, in the factories and schools and shout out our true identities.

We were rebels from our earliest days—somewhere, maybe just about the time we started to go to school, we rejected straight society—unconsciously. Then, later, society rejected us, as we came into full bloom. The homosexuals who hide, who play it straight or pretend that the issue of homosexuality is unimportant, are only hiding the truth from themselves. They are trying to become part of a society that they rejected instinctively when they were five years old, to pretend that it is the result of heredity, or a bad mother, or anything but a gut reaction of nausea against the roles forced on us.

If you are homosexual, and you get tired of waiting around for the liberals to repeal the sodomy laws, and begin to dig yourself—and get angry—you are on your way to being a radical. Get in touch with the reasons that made you reject straight society as a kid (remembering my own revulsion against the vacant women drifting in and out of supermarkets, vowing never to live like them) and realize that you were *right*. Straight roles stink.

And you straights—look down the street, at the person whose sex is not readily apparent. Are you uneasy? Or are you made more uneasy by the stereotype gay, the flaming faggot or diesel dyke? Or most uneasy by the friend you thought was straight—and isn't? We want you to be uneasy, be a little less comfortable in your straight roles. And to make you uneasy, we behave outrageously—even though we pay a heavy price for it—and our outrageous behavior comes out of our rage.

But what is strange to you is natural to us. Let me illustrate. The Gay Liberation Front (GLF) "liberates" a gay bar for the evening. We come in. The people already there are seated quietly at the bar. Two or three couples are dancing. It's a down place. And the GLF takes over. Men dance with men, women with women, men with women, everyone in circles. No roles. You ever see that at a straight party? Not men with men—this is particularly verboten. No, and you're not likely to, while the gays in the movement are still passing for straight in order to keep up the good names of their organizations or to keep up the pretense that they are acceptable—and to have to get out of the organization they worked so hard for.

True, some gays play the same role-games among themselves that straights do. Isn't every minority group fucked over by the values of the majority culture? But the really important thing about being gay is that you are forced to notice how much sex-role differentiation is pure artifice, is nothing but a game.

Once I dressed up for an American Civil Liberties Union benefit. I wore a black lace dress, heels, elaborate hairdo and makeup. And felt like—a drag queen. Not like a woman—I am a woman every day of my life—but like the ultimate in artifice, a woman posing as a drag queen.

The roles are beginning to wear thin. The makeup is cracking. The roles—breadwinner, little wife, screaming fag, bulldyke, James Bond—are the cardboard characters we are always trying to fit into, as if being human and spontaneous were so horrible that we each have to pick on a character out of a third-rate novel and try to cut ourselves down to its size. And you cut off your homosexuality—and we cut off our heterosexuality.

Back to the main difference between us. We gays are separate from you—we are alien. You have managed to drive your own homosexuality down under the skin of your mind—and to drive us down and out into the gutter of self-contempt. We, ever since we became aware of being gay, have each day been forced to internalize the labels: "I am a pervert, a dyke, a fag, etc." And the days pass, until we look at you out of our homosexual bodies,

bodies that have become synonymous and consubstantial with homosexuality, bodies that are no longer bodies but labels; and sometimes we wish we were like you, sometimes we wonder how you can stand yourselves.

It's difficult for me to understand how you can dig each other as human beings—in a man-woman relationship—how you can relate to each other in spite of your sex roles. It must be awfully difficult to talk to each other, when the woman is trained to repress what the man is trained to express, and vice-versa. Do straight men and women talk to each other? Or does the man talk and the woman nod approvingly? Is love possible between heterosexuals; or is it all a case of women posing as nymphs, earth-mothers, sex-objects, what-have-you; and men writing the poetry of romantic illusions to these walking stereotypes?

I tell you, the function of a homosexual is to make you uneasy.

And now I will tell you what we want, we radical homosexuals: not for you to tolerate us, or to accept us, but to understand us. And this you can do only by becoming one of us. We want to reach the homosexuals entombed in you, to liberate our brothers and sisters, locked in the prisons of your skulls.

We want you to understand what it is to be our kind of outcast—but also to understand our kind of love, to hunger for your own sex. Because unless you understand this, you will continue to look at us with uncomprehending eyes, fake liberal smiles; you will be incapable of loving us.

We will never go straight until you go gay. As long as you divide yourselves, we will be divided from you—separated by a mirror trick of your mind. We will no longer allow you to drop us—or the homosexuals in yourselves—into the reject bin; labelled sick, childish or perverted. And because we will not wait, your awakening may be a rude and bloody one. It's your choice. You will never be rid of us, because we reproduce ourselves out of your bodies—and out of your minds. We are one with you.

DEAR MOM

Virginia Hoeffding

Dear Mom,

This is going to be a difficult letter to write; but I've known for some time that it would have to be written sooner or later. For the past several months, I've been trying to come to terms with the fact that I'm homosexual. Before you start having pink and purple fits, at least finish reading this; I want you to understand as fully as possible what's in my mind, and this is the easiest way I know to get it across. I say that I've been coming to terms with this thing—accepting it, if you like; anyway, this is nothing new. For a long time I've been kidding myself along, convincing myself that I was going to grow out of this; even, at one point, that I was doing so. However, there comes a point at which one can't kid any more—since I've been up at Reed I've reached that point.

As far as the whys are concerned—that doesn't seem terribly important. I suppose that my experiences at the stable had something to do with it, but to say that that was the only thing would be a bit absurd. Anyway, it doesn't really matter.

I have, I think, given the other thing—"normality" or whatever—a fair try. I've made the effort to get involved with boys, and it just hasn't worked. When I got involved with Scott early last semester, it was, more than anything else, a response to a violent attack of fair play—of wanting to see as many sides as possible to any argument. Oh, I liked him well enough as a person, but as to the other thing there was just no way. I slept with him a few times—but there's no real need to go into it.

I've discussed with you more than once the importance to me of honesty, both to myself and to other people; this, mostly, is why I've made the decision to try to be honest about this. I've realized lately that I just can't go on with the sort of hypocrisy necessary to preserve a myth of being straight, and at the same time retain any self-respect at all. I'm speaking now entirely in terms of me, and not considering the other part of the picture: whether it is fair to people that I feel close to and want to be open with, to conceal a whole side of my personality. But I personally can't see spending so much effort lying to people; it simply isn't worth it when I consider the things it does to my insides. I've talked to several people who have gone through the same thing, or something similar, and almost all of them feel that any negative reactions one may get are not all that important—the people one cares about are generally able to accept one as one is sooner or later.

There is a homophile group starting at Reed; this is where I've been talking to people. I don't know what you know about homophile groups—the Reed group, at any rate, seems to combine elements of a political movement, encounter group, and lonely hearts' club. I don't know if this group will ever get off the ground, but I hope it does, as it's potentially a very good thing; it makes it a lot easier to have a situation in which one can discuss problems and experiences with people who can respond honestly, without fear or defensiveness. This means a great deal to me, and it has saved me quite a lot of agonizing.

The thing I see you asking about now is, Can you possibly be happy? The answer is that I don't know; but nobody ever said anything about being happy, and how many people, gay or straight, really are? The point is, though, that what one is supposed to have is the right to the pursuit of happiness; and one thing that I do know is that the only thing I'll ever be if I try to live denying my homosexuality, whether to myself or others, is miserable. The most that I can do is to pursue happiness by what seems to be the road with relatively the fewest obstacles.

Please don't think that I don't know what I'm getting into; I do. I know it won't be easy, that there are plenty of people who won't be able to accept this—but it's a chance I've got to take. I can't lie to people anymore. I'm aware, too, of the problems that homosexuals face in the world at large; I know it can be ugly, I know that the "gay life" is seldom, in fact, gay. However, I hope I can avoid some of that by being honest; anyway, I'm going to try. I hope you'll help me—I'll need it. Eventually I'll probably want to get involved with one of the bigger, more militant groups such as the Gay Liberation Front, but that's in the future, when I know better where I am.

I trust you not to react unreasonably to this, or to dismiss the whole thing as nonsense and tell me not to be silly; or, for that matter, to rush around looking for someone who can "cure" me. I know that I'm asking a lot, that this won't be an easy thing for you; but I hope that when you've thought about this, you'll be able to accept it. There are many ways of loving people, of which this is only one. If people can trust one another, and, trusting, love—surely this is what matters. If you feel like discussing this with anyone, please do, without feeling that you'll be betraying confidences or anything—the whole point of this letter is that I want people to know. I spent some time debating whether to tell you at this particular point, knowing that you have a lot on your mind as it is, without my adding to it; but I felt that you might be better able to understand where I am now, when you're going through changes and adjustments of your own. I hope I'm right, anyway, and I'm looking forward to hearing from you.

Much love,
Me

I wrote the above letter about six months ago from college, and I'm glad I did—it was worth it. As an indication of why, here is a little of the letter my mother wrote back:

Thank you for your letter—it can't have been easy to write and I'm happy and proud that you trust me and care enough about our mutual honesty to take the plunge. I love you—always—and believe I can truly accept you as you really are, at any time.

It would be dishonest to pretend that I liked the situation you described, even if I didn't have purple fits. All I can say is that I'm trying to understand. It seems to me that probably anything said now will seem wrong, but believe I must, if we're to be honest, let you know some of my thoughts. . . .

Anyway, whatsoever, I'll try to be really *with* you, to understand.

I'm lucky, I know—my mother and I were brought even closer by my sharing this with her. It improved our relationship. I told my father recently, and he too is trying to accept me, although I think it's a bit harder for him.

Telling one's parents that one is gay is probably never easy—it's bound to cause a certain amount of pain for all concerned, and to do it at all requires love, guts, and enough self-knowledge at least to be sure that one is doing it from the right motives and not simply to get back at them for something; and there is always the possibility that the whole thing will be a disaster, one way or another. But telling my parents has made me a lot freer, both inside me, which is where it matters most, and outwardly. I no longer feel the same pressure to do what people expect rather than what I feel is right, and I don't have to lie any more, in the little things as well as the big ones.

True, not everyone has the good fortune to have parents as sympathetic as mine, and many people, for one reason or another, will probably never be able to tell their parents that they're gay. But if you've ever considered it, or even if you haven't, if you care about your parents, *do it!* If only because it's a lot easier on them if you tell them than if they find out by accident. And they'll probably surprise you.

MY SOUL VANISHED FROM SIGHT:
A CALIFORNIA SAGA OF
GAY LIBERATION

Konstantin Berlandt

1951. I was five, staying with my father on his small Salinas, California farm. The corn was sweeter than I'd ever tasted in the city. As I fed him some apple a neighbor's horse bit my fingers. "Feed him out of your palm?" I caught a whole jar of banana spiders off the tomato plants. With some other kids I climbed through the hills, passed a dead dog bleeding into the stream above where we had drunk, camped in a fort of cane marsh, flew kites on string forever long across a barren ploughed field or housing site. I held the ball of string for a while and let it out slowly. I stayed the night at their house and the other five-year-old in bed with me suggested we try fucking. I lay on my stomach; he lay his body on top of mine, putting his penis next to my ass. And then his ten-year-old brother came up on the side of the bed and accused: "I know what you're doing. You're fucking. I'm going to tell." The flames grew up along the side of the bed.

HELL FIRE.

In the morning I remember one of the beautiful boy's beautiful bottoms in a streak of sunlight as he ran around the house naked before breakfast.

I stayed blanketed, afraid to get up and expose my naked shameful body.

EIGHTH GRADE, Washington Junior High School, Salinas, California. Before my first P.E. class I had a hard-on, and I prayed to God, if you exist, go down, make it go down before I strip in front of these guys. Don't think about your cock—fuck fear—think about something else. My cock went down in the rush and my soul vanished from sight for many years.

My memories of P.E. are of the shower heads, the water spurting in my face, and the yellow tile floors, soapy water running down legs and into the drain. Three minutes to strip for fast shower, hurry and dress and spend some time combing your hair. Don't watch me. Three minutes to strip and change and be out on that field running in place, running in formation. "Now, Berlandt," always called by my last name, a name I never identified with. Berlandt No. 2. How many chin-ups can you do while the class watches? How many push-ups till you're red trying to prove something? I'm always first to make a fool of myself. Choose teams. I'm always second to last to be chosen. And that last kid is such a wimp. At least I get on base sometimes. I play right field so very few balls come out for me to miss. I try to get somebody small to block, afraid I'm going to get run over. I wonder if he ever felt afraid across from me.

I used to say I'm sorry every time I missed the basket or swept past the tennis ball. I used to feel I was a hindrance to any team who had me on it. Today I enjoy playing softball with my friends. I try to catch the ball for my own pleasure. I have nothing to prove.

The best six weeks were when I broke my finger and played battleship in the library with a friend who had a heart condition. Eighth grade. And then I remember being sick a lot in the morning before I had to go to school. I stayed home all day listening to soap operas on the radio—Helen Trent's "eternal search for love and happiness" and "My True Story." I played fantasy baseball teams against each other and figured out their percentages. I masturbated. I once dressed up in my mother's nightgown and masturbated. Masturbated taking off my jock strap.

I used to come home after school and masturbate in front of the mirror or to the memory of Rick Kammen's tanned leg between his cuff and his sock, which I would stare at during seventh period American history class. And I'm still masturbatng in front of the mirror when no one is looking. I still look away when I am attracted to someone.

Look where you want to look.

Let your eyes go where they want to go.

Let your cock do what it wants to do.

We were separated into men and women—separate rest rooms, separate gym classes, separate world—when we are all man and woman, all capable of loving each other. When we recognize we are all sexual creatures capable of relating to each other there will be orgies in P.E. or higher walls between the stalls.

Exercise: Walk into your P.E. class (or golf locker room) today and look at the other people in the shower with you. Look at their beautiful bodies. Look at your own beautiful body. This is not illegal. But someone might think you're queer. You might be. You might get a hard-on like you do in the shower at home. You might start looking at each other again, appreciating each other all over not for how much better they are than you are but for what we are. For your groovy mind and groovy body. Instead of looking away all the time, instead of avoiding connections.

I am an Aegean sailor washed up in the surf and seaweed.
I am so beautiful drying in the sun
badge in pocket.
deciding never having
Come and get me.

I used to be outside things
standing

Michael lived across the street from my grandmother's house. We both had eight o'clock classes, and he drove me in from El Cerrito on the back of his motorcycle. We enjoyed arguing. We also talked about girls: he was afraid of them. I was dating a hundred of them and sleeping with three. I blind-dated him with a couple of the more fantastic ones and we double-dated.

"Blue, Navy Blue, I'm as blue as I can be
'Cause my steady boy said ship ahoy and joined the Navy."

We heard it on his car radio on a double-date eating French fries at a drive-in restaurant. A week later he went down and joined the Navy for four years. He wrote me a letter, just a regular letter, and I cried. I didn't understand why I cried. I was in love with him.

Berkeley is my home town, my elementary education. I came to Cal a high school honor student and loving John F. Kennedy.

Same Sproul Hall, same Dwinelle Hall rat maze. "Mommie, I'll go in this door and I'll try to find my way out to the front door." It's not so difficult now as I find my way to French class.

The first man I ever met who said he was homosexual. Mattachine Society of San Francisco set up the interview at their office. He was attractive, tall, trim, short dark hair, a black turtle neck sweater and tight black slacks. His name was Bob. I liked him a lot. I asked him questions for about two hours and then he took me to a gay bar, the Missouri Mule on Market Street.

It was dark inside. My leg brushed against a man sitting in the crowded bar and I apologized profusely. I don't want to give the wrong impression that I'm interested in you. I'm a straight boy on assignment. Can I have another interview next week?

I left the bar high, excited, jumping, running. I greeted my friends with a huge grin. I've just discovered a whole new world:

Homosexuals are people, beautiful people who really exist, party, rap, hold each other tight when riding motorcycles. I'm going back next week to interview another one.

But the following Saturday afternoon I am an intrepid boy on an AC Transit bus from Berkeley.

I'm too involved. My cock starts to rise. Just an interview for a sociology project and a newspaper article, but my cock starts to rise. The fear climbs up around me. I have always loved going to San Francisco. Now it is frightening, crawling with homosexuals, old men who want to make me. I don't want anybody to see me, and yet I've worn a bright shirt and tight Levis. The city is dark, the shadows hanging over the patches of sun.

Friday night after the newspaper was put to bed I drove over to the City in the publications car to a gay afterhours bar another *Daily Cal* staff member had told me about to help me with my sociology paper and an article I wanted to to write about a Cal homosexual. Maybe I could meet one there.

I sat nervously at the edge of the circle listening to the new homosexual side of the juke box music.

The boy next to me stares at me. A sexual advance? I try to return the stare. "I just have to ask you this," he says. "Are you Konstantin Berlandt?"

My god, is there no anonymity? I'm exposed. I can be seen. "Yes, who are you?" A friend from high school, another foot taller and grown a beard. We had been in a play together. He was a very good dancer, very cute, and very popular with the girls. He had complimented me on the way I skipped once before I broke into a run across the stage. "What are you doing in a place like this?" he asks now.

"I'm writing a paper for a sociology class, and putting together an article, trying to find a Cal homosexual. Do you know any?" He could have said, Look into yourself, but we have all been so polite with people who say they're straight.

Another man approached me with, "Is that a new fixture?" A cherub lamp on the red satin wall. "I don't know. I've never been here before," I told him. We talked about why I was there. The Petula Clark record about Jack and John. Would I like to go home with him? "Yes." I'm doing this out of academic curiosity. If I'm going to write about it, I might as well find out what it's all about.

His beard on my cheek when he kisses me feels revolting. Wait, baby, if you are going to get into this, don't hold back.

I enjoyed masturbating his cock. It felt like my own. I enjoyed feeling something not me that felt like me. And I said to myself as I did it, "Might as well do it and enjoy it because I'm not going to get another chance. I'm not gay and I'm not going to make it with another guy."

"Can I give you my phone number," he asks.

"No, because I'll never use it."

But by the end of the next week I really wanted to see him again. I drove to his house and put a letter in his mailbox.

"Do it. You know you want to kiss it. You know you want to suck it. Try it. See if you like it. I won't come in your mouth now if it freaks you."

I used to be a reporter. I covered things objectively, standing outside, feeling safe with my press badge in my back pocket. Never deciding anything, never having to. Was I prepared to get arrested for his cause? I didn't have to decide. I was covering the event.

But eventually my cover lifted. My objectivity melted into real emotion. "In the name of the people of California I order you to disperse." Break into ones and twos and run down your city streets away from each other. Separate till you fade into the store fronts. Someone is shooting at those who are too obvious. "Disperse! Disperse! Divide! Disintegrate!"

A homosexual picks me up hitching a ride home from Bancroft and Telegraph late at night. "Straight boy, do you do this sort of thing? Straight boy, would you like a blow job?" "I don't know." Of course, I do, but are you exploiting me or am I exploiting you?

"What's the difference between a man's mouth and a girl's mouth on my cock?" I asked Gene later.

"If you talk much more like that, Konstantin, I'm going to think again about being your roommate."

I didn't bring up homosexuality in a first-person context again. After I came out—recognized my own homosexuality and my love for Gene, recognized my frustration on our double-dates together and sleeping in separate beds when I visited him—I wrote it all out in a seven page confession to give to him. "But if I tell you this about myself you may not be my friend any more." "Don't tell me," he said.

I walk through the Cal library undergraduate reading rooms now, afraid of being picked up. I look at everyone's eyes but lower them again when I see the same thing in them that I feel in mine.

I'm discovering who I am and I'm afraid of it. See me looking at you. Don't think I'm queer.

Of course, I'm not. I've just done the research. I know that the third floor head in the library is a cruising spot for homosexuals and I'm afraid to go in there.

Class, let me tell you about *them:*

"Homosexuals use the same words the straight society uses for them. Their words are derogatory when used by straights. For example, this word: I'll write it on the board and leave out a letter so as not to offend anyone. C-CKSUCKER." This was during Berkeley's four-letter word controversy, which I was parodying.

I sat on a desk in front of my speech class and told them what homosexuals wore according to *Life* magazine—fuzzy sweaters and tight Levis. I sat before them in tight cream Levis and a ski sweater. The visual message—homosexuals look just like me, but the whole rap, detached, academic, objective, third person, said, "I'm not a homosexual." Homosexuals are just like us, I said, except they make love to each other, hate themselves and each other, and we hate them too as we hate ourselves as we are them and as we separate ourselves from them who are not them but us.

The next class speaker, a burly football-player build, crew-cut, madras shirt, erased C-CKSUCKER from the board with anger.

Readers, let me tell you about them:

"The *Daily Californian* today begins a new series of articles on minorities—racial, sexual, political, religious." I started the series with blacks and then homosexuals.

Headline: "Minorities—2700 Homosexuals at Cal"—a one in ten figure based on 1948 Kinsey study estimates about the proportion of the general population who by choice have a majority of their sexual experiences with members of the same sex. Underneath ran a picture of a University library shitroom, every other stall door removed, and an article about police tactics against homosexual activities on campus. In eighteen months Cal's special police entrapment squad had arrested 240 people for homosexual activity and now they had removed head doors to prevent homosexuals from sitting in neighboring stalls and passing notes to each other or blowing each other through glory-holes.

Notes on toilet paper:

"What do you like to do?"

"Are you vice squad?"

"Have you a place?"
"I want to see your face."
The notes are exchanged under the shit stall walls in the Harmon Gymnasium boys bathroom at Berkeley. It is how a friend of mine picks up tricks at Cal.

Can I see what you look like? But there haven't been any campus social activities for homosexuals to get together.

I'd be ashamed for people to know I jacked off in the john, I blew a man through a gloryhole, I blew a man at all.

I like making it in a restroom. There's romance in the fear of being caught, the excitement of making it with a complete stranger, someone you don't know, and you can be so close, so sexually intimate and unafraid to put your cock in his mouth and taking his in yours and feeling strong because you can fuck. If I can't ever show my cock in public now, I can show it to a public stranger who loves it.

And make the world all sex.
No piss-elegant romantic trappings
(No bed, no fucking million dollar diamond ring
to prove our forever love for each other)
just cold tile floor
and cold ceramic toilet bowl,
just what we are with no pretensions
now without future involvements to pretend other things for

But on the other hand, when I'm loving myself for longer periods of time I'd like to make it with you in bed and smile in the morning without putting it on.

There's honesty in fucking fast and fearful.

Having to perform is such a drag.

that morning smile after sex
that morning smile to your boss
that morning smile to closet friends
—"Didn't do nothin' wrong last night,
    except it was with a guy."
How could I have loved you last night
        —sorry about that.
Good morning.
    what suit should I wear today,
    what smile and opening lines for the friends downtown.

Good morning boy.
  was I really attracted to you last night?
  was I really such a pervert as to like your cock and your body?
Funny, I don't feel that this morning.
Feeling straight,
  giving you my plastic appreciation smile.
Well, I proved I'm not gay myself anyway.

The second article, an interview with a boy friend of mine, blew the roof off the school. "I never walked into a john at Cal when there wasn't someone waiting . . . Cal was so cruisy I couldn't make it from class to class." He rapped on about a Cal football star who lived with his gay lover and a fraternity that picks up homosexuals to blow the frat men while they watch stag movies.

The student senate passed a censure on the *Daily Cal* for the series. "It was something I wouldn't want my younger brother to see," said a female senator. The Publishers Board held a three-hour personnel session debating my firing along with several other editors. "A head should not be offered up at this time," the University Public Information director had recommended to the chancellor. I apologized, and the other student editors printed an apology to the fraternities and sports world while cutting and burying the rest of the series.

The California State Senate Investigating Committee published an attack on the University in the spring, using the series to charge that the Berkeley campus since the Free Speech Movement had become "a haven for communists and homosexuals."

Bring in the police to protect straight boys from temptation. Maybe you don't want to relate to people while you are sitting on the toilet. Maybe you don't want to be freaked by a hand coming out from under the stall wall or people watching you while you pee. I mean, I am so uptight I can't pee at all unless there isn't anyone else in the restroom. Afraid someone might be interested in my cock, afraid if I can't make it work now while the spotlight is on me I'm not a man. And then, while I stand there unable to pee, I start to worry that instead of another faggot at the next urinal it might be a vice squad officer who will accuse me of soliciting while I hold out my cock.

Finally, I flush, pretending I have used it, wash my hands, comb my hair, dry my hands, and walk out planning my return in a few minutes when these people will all be gone.

But then I smile at a hippie girl at the lavatory door who is waiting for her boyfriend and I remember that I'm strong and wonderful and beautiful like she is and no one is going to keep me from peeing. I go back in.

Exercise: Stand at the urinal and look at the cock of the man standing next to you. Is it ugly? It is beautiful? Is it yours? Do you want to make it feel good? You'll never see him again. You might be in love with him. Let him look at your cock. Is it ugly? Is it beautiful? Do you want to make it feel good? Can he make it feel good? Is it getting hard? Yes, it is. Let's go get a cup of coffee and reassure each other we're not cops.

Anonymous homosexuals wrote in to the paper defending the image of the homosexual. The letter I laughed at and liked the best complained of a lack of understanding and added, "One thing is for sure, Mr. Berlandt is not a homosexual." My masculine image protected I wore a "Freedom for Homosexuals" button and laughed along with everyone who read it and laughed.

FOUR YEARS LATER: Arguing with the city editor of the *Daily Cal* over the importance of a gay liberation demonstration against the *San Francisco Examiner,* over whether it merited coverage in the *Daily Cal.* He says, "I haven't seen any evidence that there are any homosexuals on campus besides yourself and this one letter we got."

I visited my father in New York in the summer of my coming out.

My father and his girlfriend saw *Zorba The Greek* and put it down as a homosexual movie. I talked about girls I met dancing till dawn.

I slept all day, and after every evening with him and his friends I took the subway down to 42nd Street and talked with the hustlers that I had read about in John Rechy's *City of Night.* I recognized the place from the cover picture in the book.

My hustler friend introduced me to a man who was writing a book on homosexuality to be produced by Bennett Cerf. I was impressed. We both talked. He wanted to know how big my cock was.

I made it the first night with a black hustler who said hello to me. He had very little money, lived in a tiny room with another hustler. "Buy me a hot dog," he asked. I did. Am I being exploited? I wondered. Is this the game? We went up to his room. He lavished over how big my cock was and then I was astonished at the size of his. "I wish I had some money to pay you," he said afterwards. Only money is real. I'm not.

I tried hustling too. I bought a nice red shirt with the money.

My last night in New York I met a man who had just gotten out of the army. He had a wife and three children. It was 3 a.m. and we talked by the sunrise on the Hudson River until 9 a.m. when my father had gone to work and we went to my house and made love. Six hours of anticipation as he became more and more beautiful and then he fucked me and it felt so good.

I wrote him three letters from California. He finally answered one pledging that while "most gay relationships don't last, our love would last forever." I don't remember answering his letter.

"Another thing, Wally, the more guys I'm sleeping with, the more I'm getting out of girls because I expect more from them."

From the back of the motorcycle I held tightly to Wally's waist and watched the road through his blond hair. I was glad to talk to someone approving about my homosexual experiences.

I never said I liked *him* though.

I had met Wally before I came out—realized my homosexuality or admitted it to myself.

I was attracted to him, talked to him all afternoon and then on the phone for hours, and he was excited by our similar experiences: hating sports, hating our step-fathers, loving our mothers. We liked each other. I introduced him to my girlfriend and we competed over her. Only we really dug it that we were sleeping with the same girl. But Wally and I would have come closer if we'd been fucking each other.

I was hitching down from my summer job as switchboard operator at the Bohemian Grove on the Russian River to trick out at the Rendezvous. I had five tricks in a day-and-a-half, making up for all the sex I hadn't had, hadn't had with Wally at the Grove, hadn't had all my life. I lost my job for the next year there for taking off so much.

The Rendezvous became my summer home. It was San Francisco's most popular gay bar—a doll house, a thousand young men standing around on Saturday night, looking beautiful, too beautiful to touch, too beautiful to approach.

"He's got to be good looking
'Cause he's so hard to see.
Come together."

Can I be beautiful while yet so ugly? Nothing but a queer. When I graduated from college and became open about my homosexuality, I was still just a queer. My relatives proud of me as editor of the *Daily Cal,* proud of me going to Cal, proud I had graduated, would do well, would find himself and be successful. "I'm homosexual, Mom." "I'm ashamed. I'm sorry. You're destroying your chances for success. You're hurting yourself and your family. I was hoping you'd grow out of this. You're not going to be mature for another ten years. You can overcome this. Your father did."

"You can overcome heterosexuality."

Naked theater. Abbie Hoffman's *FREE* suggested it to me. Meetings are for coming together, he said. Groove on it all: the tight jawed people who try to concertedly continue their progress reports while trying to pretend they don't see me and won't look in my direction; frowning, disapproving, disgusted people: the friendly, laughing, glad to see us out in front again today people.

Gay liberation theater—the fall offensive. At the Radical Student Union's Freshman Disorientation Fair below Berkeley's student union. We performed a gay liberation allegory to the Who's *Tommy*, starring blond, innocent, sincere Gale Whittington: "My name is Gale and I became aware this year . . . .I'm learning to be myself and love myself . . . .I'm striking my classes, I'm turning on, I'm a homosexual."

Mom: "I knew it, you're high on something right now, aren't you?"

Dad: "You're a disgrace."

Chrous: "Pervert, faggot, queer, sissy, pansy, cocksucker."

Gale: "Hip, radical, Black, Gay. Don't let anybody fuck you over. Be yourself."

Chorus: "Who are you?"

Gale: "I'm Gale when I'm naked and I'm beautiful."

And after confrontations with his closet queen boss, his closet queen friends and a radical uptight friend, and his priest, Gale tells him: "All you're telling me is bullshit. You're not my god. Come, my gay disciples." Twelve of us follow him out into the audience spreading the teachings, gay liberation slogans, until pigs arrest him and the black Barrabas.

Pontius Pilate: "Ecce Homo, Behold the Man. Children of the Universe, which one shall be crucified and which one shall be freed?"

Chorus and Audience: "Free them both! Free them both!
'We want our rights and we don't care how;
We want a revolution now!"

THREE AFFAIRS

Ben.

I wore my white tight Levi shorts over my Russian River tan.

Ben complimented me on it. I said, "Thank you," and began to turn away. "He is too skinny," I said to myself. "Don't you want to get beyond superficial physical characteristics?" I asked myself and turned back around.

Strangers in the night, exchanging glances
Wondering in the night what were the chances
We'd be sharing love before the night was through
Ever since that night we've been together
Lovers in the night in love forever
It turned out so right for strangers in the night.

I sang that song in Europe where he had sent me to forget him, to live an independent life. I sang that song to give me encouragement and inspiration for making it work, making it last, trying again when I got home. I cried, I pleaded, I tied him to the bed one night so he wouldn't go out. I argued with him for hours, days. And I drank Scotch and fantasized on suicide. There will never be anything again so intense as that first love, I thought. Don't let it go. It can never be recovered.

For a year I wanted to live with him. He'd take me to dinner one night, ignore me the next. In the bar he rapped about an orgy he had been to the night before. Laughing, he said to me, "I've probably been to bed with over 500 people." You're nothing special, sex is nothing special, you're nothing, I don't love you, go away little romantic boy.

I walked down the street pouring out my tears, hoping he would drive up in his silver convertible and save me. I have to go away where he will never find me. I'll go to my grandmother's (where he knows he can find me).

I was crying in the bedroom the next afternoon when he drove by, picked me up with my things. "You're coming to live with me."

"I'm so happy," I said to myself. "This is what I've always wanted." I said all the lines I had heard in the movies and in Helen Trent, but instead of exhilarated I felt empty. Only the challenge. Now he loves me. I got what I wanted. Will he let me drive his car? Sleep late in his lovely white house? Masturbate in the afternoon while he's at work, kiss him warmly when he comes home, eat the food he buys me at gay restaurants?

I sit in your white house on your thick white rug and look out at the view of lonely San Francisco and Berkeley where I used to live, the home and life I left to come here. (I'm still commuting to that separate secondary life—bad grades and incompletes. My friends think I have a girlfriend in the City.)

I sit in your clean white house on your thick white rug before you come home and after you go out. I always feel cold in this house. I curl up by the heater, sip Scotch, feel jealous and hurt until 1:45 when I pull the drapes, light the candles, put Vince Guaraldi on the phonograph, lie naked and seductive on the couch. You laugh when you come in. How cute. How romantic. How silly. Tonight you say you want to get some sleep and will sleep in the other bed alone.

My life is devoted to you!

"I want you devoted to me, but I want you to be yourself."

Chris.

Chris and I were classmates, studied together. He was very lonely at Berkeley and I was his first close friend there. I took him to the Rendezvous on the bar's anniversary ostensibly to hear the Grateful Dead. I wanted him to know I was gay and find out if he was. He recognized immediately that it was a gay bar, but he paired me up in his head with the girl, an old friend, who I asked to come with us. He and I were together every night ostensibly to study, but we mostly talked. I wanted to touch him very much, kiss him very much and didn't, waited, frustrated.

I told him if I didn't get out of the draft any other way, I'd tell them I was homosexual. I never overtly said I was homosexual. He never said he was. I cried in frustration after he left one night, angry at myself: "It's just sex. It's just sex," I cried. "I don't even know him. I only just met him."

He wrote me a letter: "Konstantin, I like you as a friend. And I like to touch my friends. It is something a girl with whom I was very much in love taught me. For you see, Konstantin, I am not homosexual like you."

I felt we had a homosexual relationship. I would be his friend in a physically sexual relationship and be frustrated at times, but I would not try to seduce him, not try to bring him out. If he wanted to come out, he now knew where the Rendezvous was. He touched my shoulder and said he liked me and wanted to continue to be my friend. Another night as we walked to his house he took my hand. I took him into the shade and kissed him. He withdrew again for a few days and then, filling himself up with beer, he initiated our making love.

He told me later he had always known he was homosexual but had had a recent love affair with a girl and proved to himself he was straight after all. He wanted to work for the government, and letting his homosexuality come out again conflicted with his life's ambitions.

"Don't call my house any more. Don't come over except when I tell you my parents aren't home. My parents know you're homosexual, and I don't want them to know I am." He thought they could tell because my laugh is sometimes high and because I called so often. We were living together. If his parents came to visit I rolled my face to the wall as his lethargic, nameless roommate. When other people knocked, we messed up one bed before we answered the door. If people stayed overnight, we slept apart. If we went to parties together we danced with the girls and pretended we weren't interested in each other.

Surprise! Your father's coming through the front door. Quick down into the basement until he leaves. An hour with the spiders and my toasted cheese sandwich. We have to be careful in case his parents come home. Quick with you and your clothes into the closet and get dressed without a thump. His mother is talking to him in front of the closet door. I breathe with open mouth and no sound behind it. He sneaks me out of the back of the house when she's vacuuming another room. It's exciting. But I resent being hidden. I wish he loved me more than he feared hurting his parents. I guess I too wanted their acceptance. I'd rather be openly angry with his mother than seemingly sinister. They found out anyway that we had been living together. She asked him in a dream state under sodium pentothal after an operation: "Dad tells me you and Konstantin are living together. Does that mean anything?" (Well, Mother, it means I'm pregnant.) "No," he said.

Gene.
T-shirt and tight Levis and a smooth olive skin. I felt physical attraction throbbing in me when I first met Gene. And then he lived in my town, and so he joined my night staff so he could get a ride home conveniently with me. We drove home once a week together and talked about girls. And I introduced him to that same girl, a longtime friend. They had a long affair through which she really tore him up or he tore himself up or let himself be torn up.

Gene and I went to Monterey for an acid trip together. We stayed with a gay friend. His lover came over, and we all got stoned around the fireplace. Our host prodded Gene a lot. Gene said very seriously he had recently learned about homosexual feelings in others and himself. "Oh goodness," laughed our host.

Gene and I had to share a bed. He told me he didn't want to have sex that night. "That's cool," I said. I wasn't really expecting to.

On the beach I thought a monster crab was tapping me on the shoulder. "Gene, hold me. I'm afraid." He put his arm around my back and I felt safe again.

I visited him often after that. We talked openly about the

attraction that developed as we sat across the table from each other. He said he felt good where he was living. He felt safe. He didn't want to relate to the past. He didn't want to make it with me.

"You are what you think you are," he said. (You don't have to be homosexual.) "And I know as you come over again and again you will expect more each time."

"Gene, you think I'm hugging you for some sort of return. I'm hugging because I want to hug you, because I need to and it makes me feel good." I hugged him goodnight and felt good as I left though I could see he felt bad.

After I came out, I recognized the sexuality of my love for Gene, recognized my frustration on our double dates and sleeping in separate beds when I visited him. Four of us went to see *The Leather Boys* in San Francisco, and at his home later Gene insisted it was completely unbelievable that the two heroes would be friends so long and one not know the other was gay. I said I thought it was quite plausible. "You sleep on the cot tonight," he said.

I read about gay liberation in the old *Berkeley Barb,* a picket line at States Lines Steamship Company where Gale Whittington had been fired from his job for his picture's appearing in the *Barb* hugging Leo Laurence in an article on gay revolution.

A friend asked me if I wouldn't write an article on gay liberation for the *Daily Cal* to help a group get started in Berkeley. I went to a Committee for Homosexual Freedom meeting to interview Leo Laurence, sat in on the meeting and joined the picket line at States Lines the following Wednesday.

We formed a small circle on the sidewalk below the skyscrapers. A thousand straight people in suits and nylons passing by, some not looking; young businessmen concertedly talking to each other and avoiding the pickets like we were trees in pots; some disapproving, reading the signs, frowning, looking at us, frowning, disgusted; some friendly, smiling, glad to see us out in front again today.

I laughed at freaked-out uptight attitudes of the people who listened to our chants, read our signs: "Gay is Good"; "Black Power, Gay Power, All Power to the People"; "We are the people our mothers warned us about"; and "Out of your Closets and into the Streets."

At first I was a little nervous. My head bowed a little as I internalized the disapproving stares. Then I shouted, shouted louder. "Say it loud. We're gay and we're proud. Say it loud, we're gay and we're proud." What do we want? "Freedom!" When do we want it? "NOW!"

Into the summer with a gay encounter group. We talk about where we're still hung up. Anti-effeminate—"He's a brother," Morgan reminds us. We're being straight when we separate and stand on our brothers.

That queen is honest. Sea, sky, mountain cliffs, sand, hare krishna, and you're still groveling in your closet.

Exercise: Write, Shout: "Gay is Good" 500 times across the
blackboard
across the sky,

across the bathroom wall,
across the men's clothing store
window

Weekly meetings of the Committee for Homosexual Freedom, weekly picketing, daily struggling. In any conversation a thought comes up that reveals I'm gay.

In July, 1969, I went to the United States Student Press Association convention to see old friends and give a session on gay liberation. I made out my name tag listing gay liberation fourth after other titles, obscuring my homosexuality: yes, I'm gay, but don't hate me; I'm all those other things that you can love.

I was uptight until the session. "I'm a homosexual. I'm frustrated at radical parties because there's no gay dancing, no one admitting he's gay. I'm frustrated in the same way at this convention." The rest of the conversation among the group of 30 journalists was third-person concerning homosexuality, but attractive, tall John Zeh asked me, "Isn't the next step in your liberation, now that you are open about being identified as a homosexual, to say you want to make it with whoever you are attracted to, to kiss guys you feel like kissing?" To be on the offensive instead of the defensive. "Yes, it is," I realized, "and I'd better learn to defend myself against people who get violently uptight over it."

I happen in on the organization's national executive board meeting, suggest they drive a riot tank into the middle of the student editors at the next convention to bring them the reality of fascism. I got lost in the bullshit on another topic, feel like taking off my clothes, do. Feel free.

Back in San Francisco. Moratorium Day, Oct. 15, 1969. I danced around the Capri, danced for hours, whipped my body around, fucking and being fucked and coming. Feeling natural, feeling high, feeling free. "Oh I see you got that natural rhythm." Charles laughs.

"Those guys are gross," I heard a fellow apologize to the girl he was dancing with. A lot of people seem to feel I'm obnoxious. I'm feeling liberated.

Come and sing a simple song of freedom
Sing it like you never sung before
Sing it for me now, sing it anyhow
We, the people, don't want more war.

I'm singing it tonight as a liberated homosexual. It's Moratorium Day. Why aren't we arm in arm, brothers? Don't you want to dance? Doesn't everyone want to dance? "It's a solo," a boy in blue workshirt and wire-framed glasses answers.

Asking people to dance feels archaic. I'm dancing if I want to be, not looking down at my beer waiting. Dancing with myself, somebody else, everybody. But the floor is mainly closed couples who fall back into their singular positions along the wall at the end of every dance with a polite exchange of thank yous.

Ten to two: lights up. I shout it out. "Lights up. Out of your ghettos, into your streets." People turn angrily towards me. "I wish you hadn't said that," says Sean.

SNAP! WHAP! Back into your closets, Queers! Or we'll put you in cages ourselves.

"Wear your gown all year around!" We screamed and chanted and picketed and danced in a chorus line in Market Street in protest of the Beaux Arts drag queen ball. Why only once a year? Why only on Halloween? Why not whenever you want to do it? The streets belong to the people, we sang. I came in drag. I didn't have to shave my beard or my legs: I looked very sexy. At one point, however, the whole acting troupe disappeared into Fosters while I was eating an orange and talking to a spectator. When I looked around I was alone—I became paranoid about being beaten up on my way home.

The bars are havens for the until-that-day crowd.

Standing in the Stud watching 500 men, lots of them stoned, squeeze together, touching to get by each other, holding hands, hugging each other, groping each other, opening up in the closet. Limits: No dancing except in the back, no dancing close, no kissing. The bar is owned by a gay commune who work together to keep it open. Jim, one of the partners, pulls Neil and me apart. "If you want to do that, go home and do it." Your kiss is obscene! Alcoholic Beverage Control is hassling you, and you're hurting me.

Outside on the street the men from the bar separate, no touching, they walk off passing as straight men. The bedroom is a closet, the bar is a closet, the closet a jail cell. You're let out if you can go straight, act straight and don't get caught. Let's bust out of here. The Tenderloin queen stands in the middle of the street shouting at the cars going by. Why don't we all do it in the road?

Gay Liberation held an open party across the street from the Berkeley campus—"Come Together"—to celebrate our second coming and the opening of our office—a free space. This was the first open and mass homosexual get-together in Berkeley's history. Womb and the Crabs played for free. Some 500 people came out of their closets to dance and sing and kiss. Gay Liberation Theatre performed, and Don Burton, a deep blue silk sheathe over his naked body, sang some gay civil rights type songs he had written. We sang one song together and I felt a brotherhood like never before.

In our faces was the same feeling—we have faced the same battles, the same mothers and fathers, administrators and friends.

Sitting around the new gay liberation office at Bancroft and Dana across the street from campus while the telephone man installs the phone. People walk by, see the sign in the window, come in.

Paul: I'm sick and tired of having to go to Harmon Gym restroom to get a trick. But nothing else is happening.

Nan: I'm graduating from Berkeley this year. I want to meet other people here like me.

Mike: I've been at Berkeley since 1962.

Me: I've been here since 1963.

London: Where have you been all these years?

Me: I've been hiding.

Telephone man (answering the new ring): Gay liberation, honey.

We are everywhere. How can we hide from each other?

II.
GAY
PEOPLE
VS.
THE MEDIA

THE CLOSET SYNDROME

Stuart Byron

There is a sense in which the particular problem of homosexuality and the media is the particular problem of homosexuality itself—the thing about the state of being gay which distinguishes it from other "oppressed" conditions; and that is that one can hide one's minority group status: "staying in the closet" is a phrase that has little application to women, or blacks, or Chicanos. Members of these other groups can choose to be militant or not, conscious of their oppression or not, "liberated" or not—but (with the irrelevant exception of the small number of blacks who can "pass") there is no way they can hide from the world their membership in an oppressed (or minority) group.

Moreover, in relation to other oppressed groups, those in majority status need have no fear of change, or encouragement of change. Blackness and womanhood are defined biologically; homosexuality functionally. I have no "fear" that I will one day wake up to find myself black, or a woman; nor, had I children, that they will be "influenced" to become members of an inferior race or sex. As a reporter or editor, my display of interest in the oppression of blacks would result in my being branded a "nigger-lover" in certain communities, but no one would think me a "nigger."

And then there's this: homosexuals have always felt—and gay liberationists even more so—that becoming a *public* homosexual must be a self-willed act. "Coming out"—in the new sense of the term—must be voluntary, a thing of joy. It is not my business to perform my brother's liberation for him. And of course there is an element of risk in terms of societal reaction—which makes it dangerous in the extreme to call anyone homosexual in print; a life, a career can be ruined. As Gore Vidal's suit against William Buckley can remind us, calling someone gay on the public airwaves can be grounds for libel and slander action in the courts.

I preface with these thoughts because it seems to me that the gay liberation movement—and I do not exclude myself, inasmuch as I have written of it—has seen the relationship between the media and homosexuality too narrowly in terms of "movement news." That the movement has been badly reported and under-reported in the establishment press is a matter of serious concern, but a limited focus on this aspect of "the media problem" does little to get at the root of things. The gay liberation movement is a response to an oppression which existed long before there was a movement, a set of societal conditions *expressed* in the mass media. One is, after all, oppressed as a homosexual every minute of every day, inasmuch as one is restrained from acting in ways that would seem normal to a heterosexual. Every time one refrains from an act of public affection with a lover where a straight couple would not—in the park, on the movie line—one dies a little. And gay people, of course, die a little every day, causing nervous breakdowns, suicides, self-hate, and the look of a wax doll at 35 or 40. *Everything* in society—every movie, every billboard, everything done as second nature in public—reminds the gay person that what he or she is is unnatural, abnormal. It is small wonder that the usual defense takes the form of coming to love one's cage—to like the secrecy.

Inasmuch as they reflect society, mass media pretend that homosexuality does not exist. This is evident on every page of every newspaper—from the amusement page to the obituary page. The romances and marriages of straights are detailed whenever possible; the homosexuality of gays is unmentioned. "Mr. Smith is survived by his wife" is okay, as is "Mr. Smith, a bachelor, leaves no heirs," but not, of course, "Mr. Smith, a homosexual, is survived by his lover, Mr. Brown." Personality interviews with straight actors or cooks, gossip columns, features on up-and-coming politicians—all will gloat over matters of family or romantic life as long as they are straight, and I include in that of course gays pretending in public to be straight—which means the overwhelming majority of famous gays. Growing up gay in straight America means rarely having the feeling that your inmost feelings are commonplace—the source, of course, of the adolescent traumas which leave lifelong scars, the feeling, as Sidney Abbott once reminisced, "that I had invented lesbianism."

Yet what is the horse? And what the cart? To survive in a straight society, gays hide their gayness. Therefore, there is little about gayness in the media. Therefore it continues to appear abnormal. Therefore gays hide their gayness. It's an endless cycle, this Closet Syndrome, a kind that could only be broken, as someone once suggested, if everyone who was gay woke up tomorrow colored green. Obviously, every public "coming out" by a celebrity helps accomplish something, and one result of gay liberation is that such people as W.H. Auden, Tennessee Williams and Jean-Claude von Italie have identified themselves as gay.

The Closet Syndrome affects everything. In 1970–1971, for example, the Gay Activists Alliance in New York conducted a massive campaign against the *New York Times* for its lack of coverage of efforts in the New York City Council and New York State Legislature to secure passage of bills forfending discrimination against homosexuals in employment, housing and public accomodations. I happen to believe that much of the negligence on the part of the *Times* was of a deliberate nature. But also much of it is *de facto*—deriving from the peculiar nature of gay oppression. Not understanding this, the *Times* perhaps could claim with some justification that it failed to see the importance of the issue because it failed to see evidence of discrimination. Perhaps some reporters, known by editors to be gay, were consulted. "What? Discrimination? How can that be? *I*'ve never had any trouble!"

For in point of fact there is no discrimination (with the exception of "obvious types") of anyone in the closet. Discrimination enters the picture only when someone *comes out or is found out*. The gay has an out not available to the woman or the black: he can hide his "liability." Even examination of records on file at the Human Rights Commission, say, would not demonstrate clearly the extent of the discrimination, for someone fired from a job on account of gayness is not about to put that fact on public record when he can keep it secret. Investigative reporting by the *Times'* own men might go further in revealing the quantity of discrimination, but here too victims might fear publicity.

In case it isn't already apparent, let me say that I consider the oppression experienced by a *closeted* gay white middle-class person (and most of the people involved in gay liberation are white and middle-class) as a very privileged form of oppression compared to that experienced by a Latin American peasant or a black Mississippi sharecropper. I'll go further: because the gay person (especially the male) does not have to share his income with wife and children, he or she tends to have a good deal of disposable income and to be relatively *un*oppressed economically—which is the worst way to be oppressed, and which makes almost anyone in Harlem more oppressed than almost any white gay person elsewhere in New York. (I also think, however, that sexism precedes and ultimately causes racism, but that's another, and very historical, and very speculative story.) Nevertheless, because the factors which cause the oppression of blacks or of women are *visible*, they tend to get more attention and to seem more believable and verifiable in the media. I dare say that in the past year New York's tiny Chinese-American community has received more attention in the *Times* than has the city's large gay community.

For the Closet Syndrome works against the numbers which

impress the media, and makes it hard for them to understand just what "coming out" entails. A black or Chinese-American or welfare mother who pickets or demonstrates is revealing nothing about himself or herself except that he or she has become militant, but a gay who does the same thing is revealing something which society thinks it far better to hide. In other words, 50 gay pickets at the Board of Education, or 3,000 gay demonstrators in Albany, are equivalent to ten times that number of any other minority group. Yet, unaware of the Closet Syndrome, the *Times'* Albany man filed no story on grounds that there are fourteen demonstrations a week at the state capital, that many of them involve 5-10,000 marchers, etc.

From the beginning of the gay liberation movement, the Stonewall riots of June, 1969, the *Times* and other elements of the mass media have misunderstood just how traumatic and new and courageous is "coming out." It is famous that the riots were covered in the *Times* on inside pages while at the same time—the very same time—front-page attention was being given to some trees chopped down by vigilantes in a homosexual cruising area in Queens. In the perspective of events, of course, the paper was dead wrong: the Queens trees represent a minor incident in gay history; the Stonewall began a movement and an era.

Yet surely not even the Closet Syndrome fully explains this perspective, for the *Times*, indeed, seemed more concerned about the poor trees than about the homosexuals. The Stonewall story was "buried," at least partially, because the paper disapproves of homosexual self-assertion. There has been, let us remember, a gay sub-culture and life-style long before there was a gay liberation movement, yet this has received scant attention in the media then or since. The inter-racial couple, or the suburban couple, even the hippie couple is worth a feature a year and has been for a decade. The gay couple has been worth nothing (even in the pre-Stonewall era of anonymity and pseudonymity, stories could have been done). Bar life, street life, intimate life; the way some ten percent of this nation *lives* has gone unrecorded in the media for scores of years.

For to have done such stories might have "encouraged" homosexuality, and the big papers and networks and news magazines, so criminally negligent during the buildup of the Vietnam War, are seized with "social responsibility" when it comes to gayness. In some cases this can be very personal; on the *Times*, the mother of publisher Arthur Ochs Sulzberger is thought to have been responsible for years for that paper's under-reporting of gay news, and she is known to have been deeply upset when, in 1965, drama critic Stanley Kauffmann wrote a famous article suggesting that the three best living American playwrights, all of them widely known to be gay, write directly homosexual plays; Kauffmann was fired soon thereafter. And this personal bias and fear are perhaps the reason why homosexuality is so often presented in psychiatric terms.

What may be termed the Cause Question is probably the single greatest sin perpetuated by the mass media, and the result has been the creation of a huge false consciousness on the part of homosexuals themselves. When, for years, the vast majority of material on gayness available from the media concerns the question of what causes it, the individual homosexual begins to think of it as the most important question. One's life may be ruled by how one may be fired from one's job if "found out," by how the next pickup may turn out to be a cop, by how one's favorite bar exists at the whim of local politicians—but one's mind nonetheless is obsessed with the question of what made one a homosexual and how, possibly, to "cure" or at least "change" the condition. The Cause Question is how *straight* society chooses to look at homosexuality. Even two years after Stonewall, in 1971 a *Newsweek* feature on "The Militant Homosexual" has a page on the Cause Question and nothing at all on the relationship between gays and the police. And, infamously, the *New York Times* has run two Cause Question features during 1971 and has yet to run easily-compiled breakthrough features on gays and police, gays and politics, gays and the family, and so on. Psychiatrists are considered the "experts" today, just as, one imagines, clergymen would have had to be quoted in any story about homosexuality written 100 years ago. Even Merle Miller, in his pioneering if ultimately unsatisfactory "What It Means to Be a Homosexual" in the *Times Sunday Magazine,* felt obliged to spend pages on the psychiatric and cause questions, and a feature on lesbians in that magazine could not appear until the writer, *Times* staffer Judy Klemesrud, had incuded "expert" medical opinion.

This kind of thing can be gotten away with largely because of the Closet Syndrome. The few letters of protest from official gay spokesmen received when, for example, reporter Jane E. Brody tells us in the *Times* that parents don't necessarily deserve the "blame" for homosexuality and that a child can resist "even the *worst* combination of influences" are as nothing when compared with the huge amount of missives coming in to a paper like the *Times* when an ethnic group is offended. How many gays dare to go on record with their own names? How many letters will Johnny Carson receive for his crack (all too typical) of March, 1971, that "women's lib and gay lib had a meeting to discuss their differences and it lasted thirty seconds because they discovered that there weren't any differences"? How many letters will syndicated columnist Pete Hamill (one of that chauvinist bunch of new-breed writers which also includes Norman Mailer and Jimmy Breslin) get for telling us in September, 1971, that since he quit smoking he has rediscovered the smell of flowers and trees—"all those faggot things"? Similar cracks against blacks or Jews would have produced howls of protest.

An interesting aspect of the Closet Syndrome is that it allows the media to indulge in self-fulfilling prophecy. Much has been made of the "furtiveness" of gay life; this was the overriding theme of *Time* magazine's cover story on homosexuality in late 1969 and of a series on WNBC-TV in New York which began with the classic shot of two male homosexuals stealing a kiss in a dark doorway at night. Yet it never occurs to the media which indulge in these descriptions of gay life that they themselves are responsible for it: if they had acknowledged the existence of homosexuality during the previous years, it would have been widely accepted and there would be less need for "furtiveness."

The Closet Syndrome also works against accurate reporting of the "gay vote." How many gays in New York? How many in certain districts? There can be guesswork, but not the kind of data which are available concerning the black or Jewish vote. Gay Democrats went to the polls in droves to vote against former Mayor Robert Wagner in the 1969 primary, in which he attempted a comeback at the same New York office, but no newspaper mentioned the identification of Wagner with anti-gay policies in gay minds when they analyzed his "upset" defeat. Gay liberationist Ralph Hall has expertly demonstrated how gays might have won re-election for Mayor John V. Lindsay that same year, but here again there was no such speculation in the establishment press. And in regard to legislation, another horse-cart situation occurs: the *Times* claims that it gave scant attention to the Passannante Gay Civil Rights Bill in the New York State Legislature of 1971 because assemblymen and senators did not think it an important issue—but maybe they didn't think it important because the *Times* never gave it much attention! In their legislative boxscore at the end of the session, the *Times* did not list this bill at all; I have seen two other such boxscores, of about the same length as the *Times'*, and the Passannante Bill is listed in both of them: that of the New York Civil Liberties Union, and that of my own assemblyman (67th A.D.), Al Blumenthal.

It has sometimes been suggested, including by this writer, that many problems would be solved if gay people at various publications would "come out" and volunteer to cover "the beat." It is now considered enlightened for blacks to be assigned to black news, and women to women's news, and on the *Times* those Chinese-American stories often carry the byline of a reporter named Frank Ching. But I know of only one establishment daily in the country which has an openly gay reporter assigned to the gay beat—the *Minneapolis Star*. Indeed, part of the problem in the past has been a downplaying of gay news partially because both straight and gay reporters and editors feared suspicion if they paid too much attention to homosexuality. At the very least, openly gay reporters would serve as visible restraints on their colleagues; it would be hard for Pete Hamill to use a word like "faggot" if a few desks away on the *New York Post*, his home paper, sat someone gay and proud. Aware of the Closet Syndrome, an open gay would know the impact of Stonewall, would know just how discrimination operates against gays, would know that 3,000 gays in Albany equals 30,000 student nurses—and if not assigned to these stories himself could at least advise those who are and/or his editors. And exposure to the movement might lead to an understanding of sexism. With this in mind, plus a conviction that children-less gays need not conform to straight hours, some depth of coverage might have been expended on, for instance, the raids on gay after-hour bars of July, 1971; as it was, it was made to seem as if the Mafia *caused* the peculiarities of gay life-style. The "deterioration" of Times Square would hardly be attributed to "junkies, prostitutes and homosexuals" lumped together.

Various tactics have been tried by various liberation groups against media oppression, and most have succeeded. The first, dating from before Stonewall, was undertaken by the Society for Individual Rights against the *San Francisco Examiner;* it was a militant "zap," the most prominent feature of which was the spreading of lavender paint around the newsroom; since merged with the *Chronicle,* the paper has been relatively pro-gay ever since. The Gay Liberation Front in New York demonstrated against the *Village Voice* in the fall of 1969, as a result of which phrases like "no gays" were removed from apartment ads, the group was allowed to advertise its meetings, and most stories about the movement were assigned to gay reporters instead of the straight types who had utilized flippant vocabulary. A meeting with editorial page editor James Wechsler of the *New York Post* by the newly-formed Gay Activists Alliance in January, 1970, was followed by detailed attention by that paper to the rising gay political movement in the city. In October of that year GAA sat in at

Harper's in protest against an article, "Homo/Hetero: The Search for Sexual Identity," by Joseph Epstein; it is thought in the trade that no-magazine of general opinion will ever again print such an anti-gay piece. A threatened "zap" of the Dick Cavett Show by GAA ended forever the discriminatory cracks of that late night host and resulted in a guest appearance by three movement leaders.

The longest and most varied GAA campaign was waged against the *New York Times* during the winter of 1970–71, and was instructive in proving that the more cynical and worthwhile tactic might be softsell in nature. A militant meeting with an assistant metropolitan editor produced no result. A diatribe in the form of a subway poster ("Wrong Should Be Righted!") produced no result. A bitchy article by this writer in the *Village Voice* had no result. Finally, a deliberately "reasonable" letter carefully worded to appeal to the "white liberal conscience" was sent to every *Times* staffer by GAA president Jim Owles. Soon afterwards the paper began covering political developments in the gay civil rights movement with some regularity, although things remain far from perfect. But subsidiary sections like the Arts & Leisure pages and the Book Review were affected; reviews of movies from a gay liberation point of view began to appear, and reviewers of the spate of gay liberation books published in the fall of 1971 were checked out with movement representatives.

Compared to that which exists in the law or in education, there seems relatively little employment discrimination against homosexuals in publishing; like show business, it remains more or less an "open" field for gays as long as they stay in the closet. Nonetheless, a dossier presented to the City Human Rights Commission by GAA contained an affidavit by movement leader Arthur Evans: when he worked at the Hadle Employment Agency, a specialist in publishing jobs, in 1966, he was required to check a box marked HCF (for High Class Fairy) on the application forms of "obvious types."

A GAY CRITIQUE OF MODERN
LITERARY CRITICISM

Karla Jay

Since the beginning of modern literary criticism, the subject of homosexuality has been ignored or shunned by the critics, even when homosexuality is an integral part of an author's work or life. Heterosexual critics are afraid to deal with such a taboo subject because they dread being labeled homosexual. Of course, there are critics who are homosexuals or lesbians, but these closeted people are even more afraid than their straight colleagues of being pointed out as a homosexual or a homophile (one interested in homosexuality) and have thus relegated what little criticism there is into the hands of our enemy, the heterosexual critic, who is inherently unqualified to analyze competently the works of any homosexual or lesbian, since he has long viewed us as the Other, the enemy of the nuclear heterosexual family, the corrupter of children, the sex maniac, and so on, *ad nauseum mythicum.*

Even if the heterosexual critic considers himself to be a liberal, he invariably reverts to a psychological approach. To begin with, psychology, with few exceptions, has been a staunch enemy of the homosexual. Even if the psychiatrist is too humane to bombard us with shock treatments, he tries to correct our "abnormal" learning and behavior patterns or attacks our family background. For example, the few critics who venture to discuss Marcel Proust's sexuality lean heavily on his relationship with his mother.

Another liberal approach is the condescending view of homosexuals as flawed creatures, who managed *despite* their mental handicaps to create works of art. Thus, Michelangelo's bisexuality would parallel Toulousse Lautrec's physical deformities. Still another liberal approach is the reduction or putdown of homosexuality to the smallest possible place in an author's life: thus, Rimbaud is not a homosexual poet, but a poet who just happened to be a homosexual. This putdown is swallowed by critics and students alike, although the same people would never tolerate a statement to the effect that James Baldwin is a writer who just happens to be black.

Some heterosexual critics even get apologetic. I read recently in a woman's magazine that Gertrude Stein was an unlesbian woman, who didn't have the sordid fights associated with lesbian relationships. I was taken aback. On one hand, I was pleased that Middle America was finally going to learn that Gertrude Stein was not Alice B. Toklas' aunt, roommate, cousin, or ward. On the other hand, they never said directly that they were lovers (beating around the bush), and I had to wonder what kind of sordid fights homosexuals and lesbians have that heterosexuals are somehow immune to. In another apologetic approach pro-Whitman critics get angry and defensive when Whitman is called a homosexual and think that someone would have to be anti-Whitman to discuss the poet's sexuality.

Even worse are the outright lies or distortions. High school French texts rarely mention the fact that Verlaine shot Rimbaud, although some vaguely state that Verlaine spent some time in prison. One book even hinted that Verlaine had committed a political crime, although the truth of the matter is that Verlaine shot Rimbaud in a lover's quarrel after Rimbaud fell in love with another famous French poet, Mallarme. It is curious that the same texts hint more deftly at Chateaubriand's incestuous love for his sister. Shakespeare's sonnets to a young man were always explained away by teachers and by critics as friendship, while his marriage to an already pregnant Anne Hathaway was glorified, and Shakespeare's relationship with his children was gilded. Finally, I still remember my Sunday school teacher blushing and glossing over the text in the *Bible* where David says: "O Jonathan! . . . your love was more marvelous to me than the love of women" (II Sam. I:26).

Even the well-meaning heterosexual critic, due to his ignorance of homosexuality and of homosexuals and lesbians in general, makes blunders apparent to any homosexual or lesbian. Heterosexual critics cannot fathom the gay experience and try to read their own mythology and prejudices into a literary situation. For example, one school of critics who are aware that Proust was bisexual or homosexual have implied that Albertine, the heroine of *A la Recherche du Temps Perdu* (usually mistranslated into English as *Remembrance of Things Past*) was a man in disguise. I've been unable to discover the root of this misconception since the book clearly states that Albertine was a bisexual woman, but I gather that the critics have equated Marcel the hero of the book with Marcel Proust—and that error is grave indeed.

Yet the blunders are still better than the taboo, for the suppression and denial of homosexual authors is the worst crime of all. Why has it taken so long for E.M. Forster's only homosexual novel to be published? Why are there thousands of books on

Marcel Proust (including one on the food in the *Recherche* and another on syntactical inversions) and not one on homosexuality, despite the fact that homosexuality, along with art, love, and time, is one of the main themes of the work, and one of the volumes is even called *Sodome et Gomorrhe*? Why are Sappho's lesbian lyrics omitted from high school anthologies, when some of her far lesser asexual ones are included? Why are the homosexual interpretations of Oscar Wilde's *The Portrait of Dorian Gray* virtually ignored?

The taboo is the worst crime of all. When I was growing up, I thought that I and perhaps one or two other people were the only homosexuals who had ever existed. I felt very alone, and yes, very "queer." I read everything I could find, hoping that there were other people, even fictional ones, like me, that there were people with whom I could identify. But I read works from Socrates to Oscar Wilde, without discovering that I was not alone because the critics, instead of pointing out my tribespeople, denied their existence, and because the scholars would rather cut off their hands than put the work of a homosexual as a homosexual work in a school library. And yet, if they took the works of homosexuals and lesbians out of the libraries (instead of whitewashing them), the bookshelves would be a lot emptier.

Thus, the homosexual and the lesbian have suffered the same fate as blacks and women at the hands of the heterosexual critic: that is, he or she is defined, described, boxed, and labeled by the oppressor. We have no voice in our destiny because our culture is taboo to the heterosexual, but we can destroy the taboo by creating our own literature and our own criticism of that literature and of already existing homosexual/lesbian literature. Only then will our literature be treated with understanding instead of with ridicule, belittlement, or silence. Only then will our literary heritage be brought to light with love and pride so that future lesbians and homosexuals will be able to grow up with the feeling that they have a well-deserved place in history. Yes, our voices are our most powerful weapon, for when we stand up and scream: "We are Socrates, Sappho, Oscar Wilde, and Gertrude Stein," we will destroy the heterosexual myths about us and their domination over us.

AN OPEN LETTER TO TENNESSEE WILLIAMS

Mike Silverstein

Dear Tennessee,

First of all, I love you. I love you because when my own parents were strangers to me, and didn't know who I was, you were one of the few people who told me I was beautiful, and showed me how to be courageous and endure. I want you to know this. I also want you to know I never believed the lies they told me about you. I never believed you were how they said you were: "the notorious Tennessee Williams, talented, but a little weird. Insightful, in a sick sort of a way. Interesting, but never forget how distorted—perverted—his point of view is." The artist as an item of gossip, and slightly risque story.

This is what my parents told me you were—a queer—when they deemed I was old enough to know about such things. This is what the straight critics have always told you you are, and still tell you you are. Someone who is interesting just to the extent that the people you write about have nothing to do with them, the human experiences you describe have nothing to do with theirs, and above all, you are not like them at all, since you are obviously doomed to self-destruction.

But I knew that what you said did have to do with me, I knew I was a queer too—long before my parents deemed I was old enough to know about such things. I looked to you, because you were a queer, to tell me about myself, who I was. You, and a few other people, Allen Ginsberg, Christopher Isherwood, were the only queers I knew, and the only people who would tell me anything of my humanity.

I'm writing to you now because what you told me wasn't enough. What you told me I was, what you told me I could be, what you told me you are, are still too close to what my parents told me I was, what your critics tell you you are. You helped me free myself, but I can see you are not free, because you still tell me we can never be free.

This is what happened: my parents, my friends, my teachers told me that I was a victim, a loser. I must lose in a world where only the winner is a Man, a human being. I was not a real Man. I was a queer, a half-Man, a pseudo-Man, like a woman. I could never aspire to the dignity accorded only to the conqueror, the Man on top. Men fought and won, they fought other Men for the ownership of the rest of creation, lesser peoples, the losers, women, the Third World, as well as the natural environment. I could never be a real Man. I didn't want to own women. I didn't want to fight other men. I wanted to love them, and I can only stand in awe before the material world, not own it. This made me obscene in this society, a dirty joke, contemptuous, the worst thing a Man can be, a loser, a victim.

You were one of the few that contradicted this. You told me to love myself, told me I was of infinite worth, holy. You taught me that only the victims still cling to their humanity. You taught me that the courage the victims show when they endure is the true human courage, and the true expression of our human beauty. You taught me that humanity is destroyed by the fight with Men for the ownership of other people, mastery, the despoilation of the world. You taught me to honor my beauty and courage as a victim, as the real expression of humanity.

You also taught me a sense of acceptance and resignation. Because you also taught that my fate was unavoidable, that because the source of my humanity lies in the endurance of my victimization, the price of my humanity is my submission to the strong and soulless, the Men, who have sold their soul for mastery.

And you spoke not only to me, not only to queers, but to other victims as well, especially to women. I had been taught that women are wild animals, to be hunted, tamed, and used—screwed, fucked, made to serve. You were among the first to teach me that women are my sisters, fellow-victims. Blanche DuBois, Hannah Jelkes, above all the Gnadiges Fraulein—who was all of us—these were the first sisters I had encountered, the first people who shared my victimization, and my humanity. You were the first to teach me to love my sisters. (The critics, those liars, say you hate women.)

But to my sisters and myself, you taught that solace lies in the inevitability of our hopelessness. When I was 16, in 1957, I clung to this teaching, it kept me sane, and gave me courage, because it seemed the only hope, the only humanity I was capable of.

Now I see you being destroyed by the teaching that was the beginning of my liberation. By finding your humanity in your victimization, you have been trapped by your critics into accepting self-destruction as the price of your continued humanity. You have accepted that you must be the loser, the victim they want you to be. Now they have made you a success, a "celebrity," so in order for you to retain the victimhood that is your humanity you must destroy yourself. They have tricked you. They can make you drink—their old weapon against us—so they can call you a drunkard, and show how different you are from them. They want you to join the legion of gay brothers drinking themselves to death in the bars they have set up for us. The straight man's whole world is a conspiracy to destroy you, and they even have your complicity in it, because you believe them when they call you a paranoid for seeing this.

But I will no longer follow that way. Once I learned from you the courage of my humanity, I could no longer accept my victimization. It was still too much like what the straight world said I should be. You are still not free of the straight world, especially your critics. You still believe your humanity must be linked to your victimization, so you still tell us victims, queers, women, too much of what they want us to be told. You tell us that we must submit to their mastery.

Tennessee, what you taught was perhaps the best hope you could offer. Perhaps you spoke for a whole generation of gay men, expressing their humanity in the only way allowed to them. But now we can and must do more, we must refuse to be victims, losers, queers. I will be free. I, only I, will say who I am. I will be gay, I will not accept that I must submit. I will not accept that I am doomed. I will not destroy myself.

You were right in many things, and I must not forget the things you taught me that are true. We must not give up our humanity to become like the Man. We must not seek to conquer, to become the master. Our gayness, our ability to love one another, is our humanity, and it must not be sold for the Man's mastery over others. And if the straight Man's revolution is based on mastery and conquest we will have no part on it.

But we are going to make a gay revolution, a revolution that will be an assertion of humanity. And remembering what you taught us of our humanity, we gay men, together with women, and all the other victims, those who don't seek to be masters, can create it.

And we will fight and even hate if we have to. It is part of one's humanity to hate one's oppressors. If an oppressor has taken from you the ability to hate him, he's taken part of your humanity from you. And here too they tricked you into telling us only to endure, not to fight back. We can fight back, struggle and hate, and as long as we are not seduced by the man's victory, conquest, as long as we avoid his love of the fight, the hatred, the revolution will be in the name of humanity, and for the creation of a truly human society without conquest, mastery, winners, or hatred.

This is what I want to tell you. You and I, we need not be victims, queers, in order to be human. You are being destroyed by your oppressors. They are making you kill yourself, as they have made generations of gay men, the best of us, kill ourselves. Stop and fight them. They are lying to you when they tell you you must destroy yourself not to be like them.

And we have discovered something else you must know. They are also lying to you when they tell you that you must be alone. This is another lie they have tricked you into repeating to us. It is they who must always be alone, the Man, the master, whose mastery keeps him apart and afraid of humanity. Join us! We don't have to be alone. We still have the ability to love one another. It is very hard. We have been so corrupted by them. We have learned so much of their mistrust, their will for power, their aloneness. But we are struggling to trust one another, to open ourselves up to one another, to love one another. And before our love, the world will look and wonder. Our love will be a humanity new under the sun, and a new world will be born from it.

Tennessee, look, an army of lovers is beginning to arise. It is being born from among the victims, the queers, the women you were among the first to love. We were queer like you, victims like you. But now we are gay, no longer accepting our victimization, and proudly proclaiming our humanity. We can give you back your love. The world will tremble, fall and be reborn before the love we former losers have for one another. An army of lovers cannot lose.

Love,
Mike Silverstein
July 23, 1971

QUEER BOOKS

John Murphy

We can draw up long lists about how society oppresses homosexuals, but specific incidents make the truth more immediate. Some of the most obvious—yet least examined—manifestations of homosexual oppression occur in literature. Besides psychiatry, this is the only area of American culture where homosexuality is examined in depth. Until recently, it has also been the only platform for public statements by self-acknowledged homosexuals. An examination of American popular literature as experienced by one homosexual shows a frightening range of attitudes toward homosexuality—almost all negative.

The antihomosexuality in these books is a prime example of what has made the gay liberation movement necessary and inevitable.

When a boy is curious about sex, he can get detailed information about every aspect of sexual activity, psychological, biological, or literary-erotic, at his neighborhood drugstore's paperback rack—if he is interested in heterosexuality. If a boy wants to learn anything about himself in relation to other males, he encounters a special set of problems. The ideal solution, of course, would be to discuss his feelings with a sympathetic and knowledgeable older person; unfortunately, the chances of encountering someone like that are extremely slim, due to the defensive reactions about frank discussions of sex common to most people in Western society. So the inquisitive young person will probably turn to books. If he has homosexual inclinations, the choice of books dealing with his sexual concerns are limited to a few serious "classics," some sensational popular novels, and pornography. Psychology texts—if he has the background to understand them—range from discussions of homosexuality as a form of pathology to a standard liberal acceptance of it as an expression of an individual's neurosis. These medical attitudes toward homosexuality, although sometimes in advance of public opinion, often do more harm than good simply because they usually view homosexuality as a medical matter—that is, as something that is wrong with you.

A discussion of the popular literature that deals with homosexuality cannot be definitive, because practically every novel, play, short story or poem that deals with sexual roles says something about our attitudes towards homosexuality, if only by pointedly ignoring it. Here, I will discuss what I have encountered as one reader who has used a voracious literary appetite in a hit-and-miss technique to cover as much material on homosexuality as possible. Actually, a hit-and-miss technique is practically the only possible way to approach social attitudes toward homosexuality in books available to the nonspecialist. Only a few serious books on psychological aspects of homosexuality are useful as background reading for the general reader, and these are usually distinguished by their marked distaste for homosexuals and homosexuality. Martin Hoffman's The Gay World is a notable exception. Although it tells homosexuals very little they do not already know about gay life, it is an ideal introduction for the straight person who may be interested in learning more about homosexuality. Hoffman's relatively unbiased approach concentrates on dealing with homosexuality as a form of personal expression that should be as viable as heterosexuality. Using books like his, homosexuals may soon assemble a long-needed body of works about homosexuality, which will become the basis for homosexual studies, past and present. Rather than being a subdivision of psychological investigation, this corpus would stand on its own merits, much like the newly discovered black literature and the works concerning women—both of which are now being re-evaluated.

Since early childhood, I have devoured books. Fortunately, my family and a few of my teachers encouraged this appetite for reading. I went to a Catholic grammar school, high school, and college, the last two run by those quintessential Catholics, the Jesuits. I received a strict, rather formal, education, somewhat out of the tradition of American public education. But I have found that the ways in which this specialized education affects my life and attitudes, in comparison with the effects of public education on others, differs less each year. I may have worn uniforms to class, and I may have been encouraged to say the rosary at home, but I have found that Catholic and public education share practically all of the same moral stances and sanctions, particularly regarding sexuality. The nuns were just a lot more colorful in describing the attendant dangers of sex.

Like every other child of the World War II years, I was raised on the Dick-and-Jane readers, which showed the ideal American family—a hard-working father, a domestic sweetly compliant mother, and charming, chubby children, who varied in age and sex from grade to grade. The life portrayed in these books was lily-white and as straight as an arrow. No matter that it corresponded to practically nothing that happened to anyone I knew; this was how it was supposed to be. To supplement what I was supposed to be learning in elementary school, I grabbed whatever I could lay my hands on, from war comics to *Robin Hood* to the *Hardy Boys*. Occasionally, I could identify with some small element in something I was reading—the friendship between Tom Sawyer and Huck Finn, the fear and excitement of the all-male world of *Treasure Island,* and *The Railway Children,* a sad little book written at the turn of the century about some children who endure poverty after their father has gone to jail for embezzlement. I was ashamed of this last, because I thought it had been written for girls; I tried to hide its cover while I was reading it. Until high school, I read to escape, to bring some color into what I unconsciously felt to be a very boring young life.

Only when I began to encounter books intended for adults did I realize that one could learn something concrete from literature, that books could actually change your life, just like the signs in the library said. *The Bridge of San Luis Rey, Animal Farm, Catcher in the Rye*, then *Portrait of the Artist as a Young Man*, then Henry James—I read what everyone who eventually becomes a college English major reads. But, at the same time, I was satisfying other aspects of my literary curiosity more related to my budding libido. *Peyton Place*, the first of the blockbuster sex novels, was handed around surreptitiously when I was in the eighth grade; I remember reading scenes over and over again, excited and yet a little disgusted. I couldn't understand what I was getting into; everybody wanted something in this book, evidently the kind of thing priests warned me about in confession. These people felt really bad about it; they were always getting in trouble and having to hide things. If I was going to grow up to live like that, I was afraid.

A few years later, *Lady Chatterley's Lover* burst forth in its unexpurgated version. I was beginning to understand that there were some books that were better than others, and I saw that this wasn't a "dirty" book. D.H. Lawrence's psychological expositions were new to me; his picture of Constance Chatterley was obviously meant to be the focus, but I realized that all of Lawrence's skill came out in describing Mellors, the gamekeeper. I was becoming aware of urges and questions that the book intensified but in no way satisfied. I wanted to know *why* Mellors wanted to have sex with this woman, and how he did it, and what he meant when he referred to his love for his commanding officer in the army. But Lawrence provided no easy answers. He was not concentrating on deep relations between men, and that is what I wanted to learn about. It was then, I think, that I began to realize that it would be very difficult to find out what I wanted to know. There was no one I could question about this, so I kept reading.

The summer between my junior and senior years in high school, I came across Thomas Mann's *The Magic Mountain* in a public library. No one had told me about it; I guess I chose it on the merits of reading its first few pages, my usual way of selecting books at that time. Here I finally encountered something to which I deeply responded. The infatuation that ten-year-old Hans Castorp felt for his schoolmate Pribislav Hippe corresponded to my first real infatuation. That I could identify so readily with little boys embarrassed me, yet I knew that I was reading something that was true and that I had never read anything that corresponded so closely to what I really felt. Castorp's later intense infatuation with the French woman was a magnificient description of the fixation that can become love. When I finally read *Death in Venice*, a few years later, I realized Mann provides one of the most serious and genuine approaches to complicated relationships of any novelist. He is not generally considered a "homosexual writer," but it is exactly his breadth of understanding applied to psychological and emotional interaction between men that must be considered an essential part of the literature on homosexuality.

I encountered another book during that last year of high school—*The Sergeant,* by Dennis Murphy. Although I didn't know it at the time, this book was an excellent example of the "serious" novels that dealt with homosexuality in the fifties and sixties. One of the main characters—a sergeant in the army—is a confirmed homosexual. The hero, a private under his command, gradually becomes aware of the sergeant's attraction to him. The younger man eventually becomes so disgusted with the sergeant that the latter gets himself killed, apparently out of remorse for inflicting his sickness on the younger man. Murphy wrote well; there was no reason, for me, an inexperienced reader, to think that this was other than a realistic protrayal of what I could expect if I ended up as a queer. I began thinking that I had better be careful, much more careful than the "normal" people around me appeared.

This impression was strongly confirmed when I eventually read *Giovanni's Room* by James Baldwin during my senior year in high school. In Baldwin's book—which assumed the status of a minor classic among homosexuals in the 1950s, according to people who read it when it originally appeared—a young American falls reluctantly into an affair with a young European. When he returns to his senses, the American leaves the European, who is pursued, trapped and tormented by a greasy older homosexual, whom he murders. The young European is speedily executed, and the hero begins to learn to live with his dreadful curse. There appeared to be an uncomfortable parallel between homosexuality and death in these books, and it frightened me. They were my only source of information outside of my own abortive experiments, and they held very little promise for any kind of future.

Eventually, I discovered the "classic" homosexual novels. Although very few had any semblance of literary worth, they filled a definite need. Foremost among them were such books as James Barr's *Quatrefoil* and Fritz Peter's *Finisterre.* In the latter, published in 1951, there are no overt descriptions of sex; rather, there are numerous languishing sighs, tender looks, and so on with some extremely provacative fade-outs at the end of chapters. The story, here mercifully condensed, tells of a wealthy young adolescent, who is in love with a tutor, who reciprocates his affection; the boy's evil stepfather, who evidently is lusting after him, makes some nasty intimations about the extent of the teacher-pupil relationship, and so gets the boy to confront his mother. She is highly upset and tells her son she would rather he were dead. He obliges her by drowning himself. The whole thing is absurd, written in the same silly but somehow touching style that distinguished Radclyffe Hall's *The Well of Loneliness*, a novel about lesbians that was banned in the 1920s. Typical of a whole generation of fiction, books like *Finisterre* were passed around secretly and pored over at great length; today, they have about as much relevance to young readers as have the *Hardy Boys*.

Gore Vidal has provided another classic of this genre, which even provides alternative endings that conveniently show the changes in social mores of which Vidal is so enamoured. *The City and the Pillar* somehow strayed onto a dorm room bookshelf when I was in college. Nobody seemed to have read it or even heard of it. I borrowed it for a few days and read it with a familiar feeling of unease. Vidal's story focuses on a single sexual experience that the hero, at fourteen, has with a close friend; this becomes the ideal by which he measures all later sexual encounters. He is consistently unhappy in all of these liaisons, so he is especially elated when he meets his old chum by chance. They have a few drinks and by some unlikely set of circumstance end up in the same hotel bed. The hero finally makes advances and is shocked when his friend disgustedly repulses him. In the first version, the book ended with the hero killing his friend; in the newer version, he merely rapes him. This was Vidal's first book, and one would be tempted to forgive its clumsiness if he had just let it lie in peace; unfortunately, he performed surgery on it only a short time before assaying *Myra Breckenridge*. A reader can only wonder why. (*Myra Breckenridge* isn't included in this list for several reasons. It has very little to do with its ostensible subjects, transsexualism and homosexuality; rather, it is a jumbled and occasionally funny guide to the whole world of American sexual confusion, appropriately using Hollywood as a backdrop and ultimate metaphor. Vidal, I think, is much more terrified of the breakdown of sex roles than most of his readers; in fact, this breakdown seems to be progressing quite calmly and successfully, with none of the barely restrained hysteria that his books so often exude.)

There are variations of this theme that end on a happier note. Sanford Friedman's *Totempole*, a novel that was not widely reviewed (and, sadly, is not very good), confronts the problem of homosexuality head on. The problem consists of two issues: first, is the hero homosexual? This is obvious after the first few chapters to any but the most dull-witted readers. The second matter is perhaps trivial to the heterosexual reader who has strayed into the book but is often crucial in the lives of homosexuals. The question is simple: Will the hero be able to perform anal intercourse, acting as the receptive partner? Luckily, he can, after a furtive little romance during the Korean War with a Japanese POW (who is an intellectual and a bisexual and therefore an acceptable partner in the eyes of the liberal straight reader).

There are also numerous descriptions of homosexuality in the best sellers that find their widest circulation as paperbacks. These books are usually programmed for some hypothetical straight, red-blooded American reader. Therefore, homosexual episodes are usually limited to interludes that show how far one can go in searching for the limits of depravity. In Harold Robbins's *The Carpetbaggers,* we are presented with a forty-year-old film executive who is picked up by a rather sinister young man in a bar. We have been clued in that there is something wrong with the executive; it turns out that he is a repressed homosexual. When he returns with the young man to his house, the hustler presumes that the older man is a masochist and proceeds to beat him nearly senseless. The executive remains conscious enough to realize, however, that he enjoyed the sexual act (undescribed, like most of the couplings in Robbins's books) that was evidently performed in the course of his beatings; horrified at this realization, the executive castrates himself and dies. Thus homosexuality in Hollywood. To date, *The Carpetbaggers* has sold several million copies.

Another best seller, *Boys and Girls Together,* was written by William Goldman, writer of one of the classic sublimated-homosexual films, *Butch Cassidy and the Sundance Kid.* In his novel, Goldman describes the world of several people, including Aaron, a mother-fixated young man who is seduced by an older sergeant while he is in the army. Aaron eventually hits New York; his life there—portrayed rather well by Goldman, who lets most of his characters lead lives of stupefying boredom—consists primarily of pickups, particularly in movie theaters. Eventually Aaron is beaten nearly senseless by one of the pickups. This leads him to thoughts of a psychiatric cure, which are abandoned when he realizes it is "too late." Finally, Aaron meets an older man, an actor, who seems to desire a sort of idealized father-son relationship—something Aaron has been shown to want very badly. But, in an extremely cruel plot twist, the book ends with Aaron's being beaten—again, nearly senseless—by the actor, whom we discover to be an active sadist. This discovery takes place at the beginning of a long ocean voyage, a fitting symbol for the inescapable tortures that Aaron realizes he must face.

Another, more recent example, of the popular best seller that treats homosexuality that is not *really* homosexuality is James Kirkwood's *Good Times, Bad Times*. Hailed by reviewers as a top-rate thriller and a sensitive account of life in a boys' school, the book is little more than a crudely jazzed up *Catcher in the Rye*. What distinguishes it is the conflict between the friendship of two sensitive boys and the lust of their headmaster for the older of the two. A celebrated line, quoted by practically all of the reviewers, deals with the possibility of homosexuality in the relationship of the boys. "I mean, *anybody* would jerk off with Cary Grant if they got the chance." Since neither boy was Cary Grant, the relationship remains pure; they are both normal. Not so the headmaster, however. He torments both and finally, by his constant browbeating, causes one to die of a conveniently vague disease. The headmaster ends up stumbling through woods and swamps after the older boy, driven out of his mind by lust and jealousy. He catches the boy, fondles him, kisses him, and is killed by him for these unnatural acts. No one, of course, condones headmasters molesting their pupils. But it seems unfortunate that such a widely praised book shows homosexuality as the affliction of a crazed madman and the absence of it as a crowning touch to a beautiful and pure friendship. Real-life situations where the exact opposite occurs in boys' lives will get little sympathy or understanding from liberal parents who read such "sensitive" books as this obtuse and dull little story. Perhaps the simple acknowledgment of the existence of homosexuality in a mass-market book sent the reviewers into such fits; one is even more discouraged at the state of liberal thought on homosexuality, if this is the case.

Something should probably be said here about a recent best seller entitled *The Lord Won't Mind*. Accompanied by a huge and successful barrage of publicity, this book quickly sold over 50,000 copies in hard cover and went on to become an enormously successful paperback. Hailed in its ads and book jacket copy as "the most moving and outspoken novel of homosexuality ever written," it is nothing more than soap opera. The main characters are two distant cousins, Charley and Peter, who are both paragons of WASP beauty—blond, and spectacularly endowed. The plot revolves around the struggle of the more delicate (read slightly smaller and slightly less well-endowed) Peter to subdue the manly and somewhat insensitive Charley so that he can call him darling in public and keep house for him. Charley has an evil, possessive grandmother, who maliciously tells him that he had Negro blood in him. When Peter finds this out, he says, "Oh, darling, how marvelous. That must be why you smell so funny." This remark is even more offensive in, than out, of context. Written by Gordon Merrick—who must have dug up this manuscript from a trunk containing the results of a late 1940s college creative writing course—the book is ridiculous and harmful. The struggle for homosexuals to determine their own lives does not deserve this racist, limited parody of the ideal American couple. The fact that this book did so well is perhaps testimony to the promotional genius of its publishers, but it is even more indicative of the desperation with which homosexuals are seeking some realistic picture of the way they might be able to live. It is to the discredit of Merrick and authors like him that they have taken this need and preyed on it to create a market for pulp romances that would never make *True Story* if they were about straight people.

Popular fiction is not, of course, an accurate representation of what may be considered current serious or enlightened thought on a controversial topic. But popular fiction does show directions of the "popular" attitudes that are often ignored by serious thinkers. And a pattern that is distinct and menacing begins to emerge in this popular fiction: Homosexuality, or any taint of it, is rewarded by death or abject humiliation. There are some exceptions, such as Friedman's novel or James Baldwin's *Another Country*. In the latter book, the main homosexual character falls into bed with the main heterosexual character after a night of heavy drinking; the heterosexual (who is, incidentally, the stablest male in the book) is gratified by his one homosexual experience with a friend but immediately realizes that it's not the life for him. Even though these books break the general rule that homosexuality leads to suffering and death, they still fail to show the homosexual as a complete being. Work, friendship, social and political consciousness, all are haphazardly sketched in, to provide a background for "the homosexual." There has been no major American author who has treated homosexuality in depth. Those writers who have dealt with it seem to have unconsciously adopted the classic attitude of homosexuality as an unspeakable sin. Thus, when they try to deal openly with love between persons of the same sex, they become so preoccupied with the matter of the character's homosexuality that they are unable to complete their creation of a genuinely complicated human being. "Homosexual" becomes a problem, rather than a natural part of the human condition.

There are a few classic books that treat relationships between males on more sophisticated levels. But most critics ignore or minimize the aspects of homosexuality in them. These books are unfortunately accessible only to readers acquainted with serious literature and criticism. Thus, the magnificent world of Proust, in which homosexuality is a crucial element, is given added richness by a reading of the vast body of criticism that explicates the mystery of Albertine, the hero's beloved, whom most critics believe to be a female disguise for one of Proust's male lovers, and the nether world of the well-bred homosexual in pre-World War I Paris. Likewise the novels and diaries of Andre Gide, which are so exciting and rewarding to anyone familiar with the development of modern French literature, would bore a young American reader who stumbled across them with no previous preparation. Hermann Hesse, whose immensely popular novels provide analyses of the relationships between men with many subtle insights, does not touch on the concrete physical expressions that have today come to be associated with such relationships. Of course one can learn about oneself through these books. But it takes a reader with more perseverance, intelligence, and intellectual honesty than most of us possess to make these books mean something in his life.

These books are certainly invaluable, but they are also irrelevant to the young reader who wants to understand his own feelings of homosexuality more clearly. There are a multitude of recent authors who treat homosexuality more explicitly, perhaps more exotically, and usually with much less skill. Jean Genet (whose special case I shall describe later), Jean Cocteau, Paul Bowles, James Purdy, Truman Capote, Ned Rorem—all take the reader's knowledge of homosexuality for granted. Moreover, their works incorporate subtle degrees of the social aversion to homosexuality, which they may be conscious of and even deplore but which is unconsciously transmitted to the reader. Thus, someone who strays into Alfred Chester's world of drug addicts and mother-fixated fantasizers or Rorem's circle of wits and eccentrics cannot be blamed for feeling confusion, trepidation, and even distaste for the homosexual world. Just as he might have reacted to the books of someone like Harold Robbins, he again wonders what could become of him in worlds like these, since he can find nothing that relates to his own life. Whatever the individual literary values of each book—whether they are ambitious, visionary, pretentious, serious, or precious, or all of these at once—they all share a sort of code that has been evolved to signal to the homosexual reader and to provide a defense against the contempt of the straight world.

The available sources of explicit information about physical sexual relationships are limited to pornography, which varies in quality. Medical and psychological books slight the actual performance of homosexual sex; there are scores of "how-to" sex for heterosexuals, advising readers to throw restraint to the wind, but neither textbooks nor popular sex manuals even mention the possibility of homosexual intercourse. In the case of textbooks, this is probably because most such sources still seem to be oriented to the production of babies, despite the recent acceptance of birth control and legal abortions by the public. Sex manuals are meant to sell, and sell with no complications; because homosexuality is socially unacceptable and descriptions of homosexual sex could keep a book from being widely distributed, the publishers prefer to leave such descriptions to pornography.

The first pornography I encountered was on the racks in the back of a seamy little drugstore in Washington, D.C. The magazines were primitive compared to what may be purchased today in such cities as New York, with its relaxing censorship laws. But, when I was in high school, these were dangerous, forbidden, exciting, and disturbing. The books consisted primarily of statuesque women and men in strained poses, wearing little or nothing, but with genitals invariably coyly hidden. I went to that store only four or five times over the course of my high school years, but the memory of the shame I felt each time has remained indelible. Why? I suppose I shared with most American children the feeling that sex was a secret and that bodies were to be hidden and concealed; that attitude was what caused such things as "dirty" pictures. But I was also more attracted to the pictures of men in the magazines, and I instinctively knew that was very wrong; they awakened something I had never before experienced. I have since realized that, although I knew even then these materials were pathetic, I was responding to something created expressly for me as a *homosexual.* This was my first glimpse of the world that has been created to service—and exploit—the homosexual. These magazines crudely showed men as nothing but sex objects; if they were objects, I could be one too. That frightened me then, and it infuriates me now.

With the relaxation of censorship enforcement in many cities, a wide selection of hard-core pornographic books has become available for every taste—sadistic, fetishistic, child-oriented, masochistic, voyeuristic, necrophiliac, science fiction, frontier tales, and so on. Some have become immensely profitable. Richard Amory's series of *Loon* books are representative of this new wave of sexually explicit books in their detailed descriptions of sex between men. They are atypical, however, in the good humor and relaxed sensibility that makes them much less morbid than most pornography. With no pretense to literary quality, but with a genuine regard for homosexual desires and a real flair for characterization, Amory has created a fantasy world where no women intrude, where men are almost always able to relate deeply to one another, where no one has any lasting antagonisms. There are always a few villains, repressed homosexuals who are always brought out fairly early on. Despite the lack of realism and the unconscious male chauvinism, these books show people being affectionate to one another without fear, acting as people, not as bodies. One wonders why this positive attitude toward physical homosexuality has been primarily found in pornography until now.

There is a relatively new genre of homosexual pornography. Although it deals frankly with sex, the writing is usually highly stylized, and critics are hesitant to label such obviously sincere—and forcefully promoted—books as pornography. But there is very little in most of these books to distinguish them from run-of-the-mill skin books. Many of them seem to have been the lucky recipients of critical attention that needed a new and controversial topic. John Rechy's *City of Night* and *Numbers* are excellent examples of this school. His work portrays the milieu of the rootless young urban homosexuals who support themselves by commercial sex. Aspirations are not the same as achievement, however, and Rechy's work at best is a sort of tape-recorded true-life account of the lives of some homosexuals. The driven, compulsive young men that Rechy portrays do exist, and they do sacrifice their intelligence, their ambition, even their humanity in their search for an ultimate sexual experience that they know can never be attained. But Rechy's writing lacks the self-discipline that could make his characters more than two-dimensional shadows in his own private freak show.

The plight of Rechy as a writer is in many ways representative of the dilemma that faces anyone who attempts to depict homosexuality as something other than an ailment or a successfully handled liability. Rechy feels something that he desperately wants to express, but he has no cultural or aesthetic tradition other than the gossip of the homosexual subculture with which he can work. In *City of Night,* the only characters that are portrayed with much depth are the transvestites that Rechy sees as caricatures of movie stars or glamour girls. But the macabre humor that Rechy allows these transvestites (who, incidentally, resemble no one I ever met in my somewhat limited contacts with cross-dressers) is absent from his next book, *Numbers*. The goal of the main character, Johnny Rio, is to have nonreciprocal sex with thirty men in the space of a week. When he nears his goal, however, he becomes terrified and reaches out for another young man who is as frightened as he. They fail to make any meaningful contact, and Johnny is once again on the prowl for numbers—-men with whom one has sex—and now he is even more desperate and frightened. Rechy's characters are practically always desperate, frightened, on the run. His books are realistic, but they give no hint of the variety of homosexual life styles.

Hubert Selby's *Last Exit to Brooklyn* garnered even more critical acclaim, became a best seller, and was the center of several fierce censorship battles. But the tone of the book's reception showed how it followed in the death-and-damnation vein that runs through so much literature dealing with homosexuality. "A vision of hell so stern that it cannot be chuckled or raged aside."—*New York Times Book Review.* "A profound vision of hell. . . . An extraordinary book."—*San Francisco Examiner.* "No author that I can think of has presented so impressive . . . an account of the life of people at the bottom of the heap."—Granville Hicks, *Saturday Review.* The book consists of five stories about life in the heartlands of Brooklyn. Most of the characters are bitter and malicious, the remaining few simply stupid. Homosexuality, overt or latent, is the main theme of three of the stories. In the longest and best, a longshoreman who has become enamored of a transvestite is rejected by her. His marriage maddens him, his work is boring, and he is extremely stupid, so he takes this rejection rather badly. So badly that he attempts fellatio on a ten-year-old boy. The boy calls the neighborhood punks, who slowly and in excruciating detail maim the man. This may be life at the bottom, but it is curiously unconnected to the real world. We feel nothing but disgust at the lives of these people. Any sympathy aroused is immediately superseded by relief that one's own life isn't *that* bad, at least.

Selby is an extremely idiosyncratic writer, using dialogue and narrative techniques reminiscent of socially conscious novelists of the 1930s. The world he describes, like that of Rechy's men, is unknown to practically everyone except those who have lived in it, and most of these have until now been uninterested in conveying the quality of their experience. Selby's work seems to have been strongly influenced by Jean Genet; but his depressing world view has none of the affirmation that Genet's characters so often have in their ferocious adversity. When Selby's characters display insight or initiative, it is usually born out of desperation. Selby's homosexual characters—the only ones who are portrayed with much depth—hover near insanity or are killed off. It is fascinating, and chilling, to realize, over and over again, the pattern of death and retribution that runs through American writing on homosexuality. The misery portrayed may exist, but it exists because homosexuality has traditionally been viewed as evil and degraded. The standard liberal response to books like Rechy's and Selby's merely affirms the scorn felt by the straight world for those "at the bottom of the heap." Rechy and Selby thus become the Stepin Fechits of the homosexual subculture: Their books, however sincerely meant, reinforce the straight world's fear of the homosexual and the straight world welcomes these books, calling them "profound," "extraordinary," and "impressive."

Jean Genet shares many characteristics with Selby and Rechy. He dwells on the violent and brutalizing aspects of homosexuality; he shows almost no reciprocal affection between men; he glorifies sexual gratification—in an almost religious manner. Yet Genet has become a worldwide celebrity, one of the few writers who is almost universally acknowledged as great. And he is one of history's most outspoken homosexuals. His autobiographical-fictional creations are exquisite blends of fantasy, gross realism, clinical sex descriptions, lyrical praises of bodies and faces, and sophisticated musings on the nature of reality, the possibilities of love and communication, and other issues central to modern thought. Genet has been analyzed and criticized from social, political, psychological, even sociological viewpoints. But the central fact of Genet's homosexuality is usually taken for granted, simply assumed as a given by those who have no personal experience of it.

Genet's portrait of the homosexual underworld is often praised because it is the mirror image of "normal" world. "The explication of the homosexual code becomes a satire on the heterosexual one. By virtue of their earnestness, Genet's community of pimps and fairies call into ridicule the behavior they so fervently imitate," writes Kate Millett. She shows how the degradation and contradictory hopes that Genet's characters experience are symbolic and expressive of the entire social order. Although she understands Genet much better than most of his other explicators, Millett cannot resist making Genet bear the burden of her particular and excruciatingly genuine oppression. "The political wisdom implicit in Genet's statement [in *The Balcony*] is that unless the ideology of real or fantasized virility is abandoned, unless the clinging to male supremacy as a birthright is finally foregone, all systems of oppression will continue to function simply by virtue of their logical and emotional mandate in the primary human situation. . . . Alone of our contemporary writers, Genet has taken thought of women as an oppressed group and revolutionary force, and chosen to identify with them. His own peculiar history, his analysis of expropriated peoples, inevitably lead Genet to empathize with what is scorned, relative, and subjugated."

Both the "larger" ideas that Genet expresses are inseparable from the reality of the lives he writes about. Social roles, traditional concepts of masculine and feminine, the fury of oppressed peoples—all are portrayed by Genet, but they are portrayed in the lives of *homosexuals*. Readers may grasp and enthusiastically embrace these "larger" ideas, while still clinging to traditional concepts of homosexuality as something that is wrong.

Genet's style and content are as abstruse and demanding of careful study as those of Gide or Proust. The psychological processes that Genet describes are so complicated that they cannot legitimately be projected onto someone else's cause, to prove someone else's point; they must be accepted for what they are. Today being outrageous is good theater, good public relations, good business. Yet the public acceptance of Genet's outrageousness does not mean that his homosexuality can be viewed as anything but an aberration, to be equated with his criminal past. The patronization extended to Genet corresponds to that shown to women and black writers: A homosexual has been granted his say and has spoken at length, and the entire matter has been covered; the only people who could possibly be interested in hearing more would only be other homosexuals (or women or blacks). The "larger" issues that Genet illuminates are more important to the straight world, and it is ready to embrace them. But what straight readers and critics must remember is that homosexuality—the actual love of men for men—is the larger issue and is inseparable from everything else straight readers want to hear about. These readers must accept, understand, and even applaud Genet's homosexuality before they can begin to appreciate his work. I suspect that, if the present reading public really began to understand what Genet means, his popularity would diminish, at least until social and sexual attitudes change radically.

There are other views of homosexuality that counteract the essentially negative direction of most American literature on homosexuality. Interestingly, most of these are not American.

Reasons for this are so varied and complex that it would be discursive to go into them here. But it is interesting to note that the often ridiculed American attitude of viewing foreigners as different, as somehow weaker, is still with us. Homosexuality is also equated with weakness, and so we must turn to the work of non-Americans to understand a phenomenon that is an integral, if largely ignored, part of American life. In a thought-provoking article in the *New American Review No.1* (September, 1967), entitled "But He's a Homosexual . . . ," Benjamin De Mott considered the then current theory about a sort of informal conspiracy in the arts, fashion, and so on that was supposed to be threatening the fabric of American society. In refuting these patently absurd charges, De Mott also said a great deal about the real place of acknowledged homosexuals and homosexuality in literature and American life, mentioning such figures as Edward Albee, Tennessee Williams, and "their relevant superiors," such as Genet and Auden.

With a few other poets and dramatists, they [the above mentioned homosexual writers] are the only compelling writers of the postwar period who seem to know anything beyond the level of cliche about human connectedness, whose minds break through the stereotypes of existential or Nietzchean extravagance into recognizable truths and intricacies of contemporary feeling. . . . A steady consciousness of a dark side of love that is neither homo- nor heterosexual but simply human pervades much of their work; they are in touch with facts of feeling that most men do not or cannot admit to thought. . . . They know that love and suffering are near allied, and that love ought not to be confused with the slumbrous affection or habitual exploitation that is the rule in numberless households.

Poets seem particularly able to deal with homosexual relationships in a realistic manner. W. H. Auden combines a literary sensibility of the highest order with a discreet, tender, yet thoroughly explicit exploration of homosexual love. Auden's poems rarely mention homosexuality openly; many that have nothing to do with homosexuality still include references, intonations, phrasings that are particularly accessible to homosexuals. His love poems are not addressed specifically to males, yet they are full of references to their direction—not hints or clues, for Auden is not trying to hide anything, but references that fit into Auden's entire poetic scheme. It is ironic that one of his most widely anthologized poems, "Lullaby," is usually ignored in this aspect. I wrote a paper on the poem in college. I spent an hour discussing it with a teacher, a man widely denounced on campus for being a "faggot," and the subject of homosexuality never came up. This whole side of Auden's work was ignored in every class in which I studied his work and every such class that I have heard of, and I cannot help but think that Auden's work is being crippled by this deliberate evasion. Oddly enough, *Life* magazine, the prayer book of middle America, made a discreet and unsensational note of Auden's homosexuality in an article on him in January, 1970. It was perhaps paranoid on my part, but I was offended by the article. To *Life* and its readers, Auden would automatically become an acceptable queer, a famous oddity who could be pictured at home in much the same way Edward R. Murrow used to corner celebrities at home. Auden's homosexuality should not be a matter for revelation by *Life;* and yet it is.

Auden's sophisticated poems are, of course, simply not very interesting to many young homosexuals. Nor are the works of other poets likely to gain a wide acceptance. Thom Gunn, an English poet who has written extensively about homosexuality, is unknown among most gay as well as straight readers, despite his incisive work. There are numerous writers who portray homosexuality in constructive, realistic terms. One immediately thinks of Constantin Cavafy, the Egyptian-Greek poet who provided so many of the motifs for Lawrence Durrell's *Alexandrian Quartet;* or Yukio Mishima, the Japanese novelist and playwright whose tragic life encompassed a homosexuality that sought to return to primal simplicity in the middle of an industrial state; or even Edward Albee, whose supposedly "disguised" homosexual play *Who's Afraid of Virginia Woolf,* is a chilling, but believable, and meaningful study of people in crises. But, like those of Gide and Cocteau, the works of these writers remain mysteries to most readers. Even if they are known by reputation, these writers have their effect principally on literature and literary developments, rather than on people's lives.

I can only discuss books here that have worked for me, that have shown the way to functioning in a world I could understand. I came across the writings of Christopher Isherwood during a rainy Sunday afternoon in the library at college. I read straight through the *Berlin Stories* with their discreet (and therefore) provocative references to affairs with nameless persons, all in the shadow of Hitler's rise. I then read *A Single Man,* a relatively recent book, which tells of a middle-aged teacher's love for a younger man, who reciprocates. The young man dies in an accident, and the older man mourns him and dies a few years later. A short book written in spare and unsentimental language, it depicts a mature relationship yet also provides a realistic look at the casual sex that is part of homosexuality. Never condemning or patronizing, Isherwood simply tells the story of a few people working out their problems. A *Single Man* could serve as an object lesson for many counselors, therapists, psychiatrists, and others who are incapable of realizing that there are aspects of homosexuality as completely normal and complex as anything encountered by heterosexuals.

Like Albee, Purdy, Vidal, and many others, Isherwood has made no outright statement about homosexuality. To accuse them of it would make me subject to a libel suit. So one must presume that their works are "fictions," that they are not speaking about their own experiences. A critic discussing such an author is forced to separate the author's life (unless he is dead) from his writings. It is simply another indication of the extent of homosexual oppression, that an honest admission of homosexuality is not feasible for most of those who treat it in their work; it is—private, and somehow distasteful to broadcast that sort of thing. So the reader is left to learn what he can haphazardly, and writers must continue to behave as though they are not what they are writing about—even if they are. They may, of course, admit in private to certain sexual preferences, but the public must be protected from the obvious truth. It is as if most homosexual literature were a game, with elaborate rules, masks, costumes, hiding places. But the game is very old; we all know all the parts; the identity behind the masks is painfully clear. Everyone is tired of the old game, but there is no new one to take its place. And we are all unaccustomed to living without that game; it would be very painful to acknowledge that it all was a game, that there is nothing special going on anymore. It will probably hurt to live realistically, yet that is what we must do.

People like Isherwood can show the way to such realism. His book may not be great literature, but it is very good, very beautiful. If a literary work can be important and good for nonliterary reasons, his is. Another book in this mold is Marguerite Yourcenar's *Hadrian's Memoirs,* a highly complex novel in the form of a memoir of the Roman Emperor pointed out, in an ancient history class I attended several years ago, as a "good" ruler. I came across the book by chance in a secondhand bookshop and was surprised to learn that Hadrian was a homosexual. (These small shocks of recognition are numerous and often very funny; homosexuality is usually ignored in straight society, so one's personal list of famous homosexuals is a hodgepodge of famous, respectable, and surprising celebrities—all just as queer as you always felt you were.) The book is not a historical novel, in the lending-library sense; rather, it is a recreation of what it was like to be an absolute ruler as well as a homosexual and how the emotional entanglements that all ordinary men feel became. involved with politics.

There are very few modern novels that provide any *new* insights into homosexuality, but oddly enough, a few pornographic books point the way. Their graphic descriptions of sex-without-guilt are often accompanied by interesting writing on the place of *any* kind of sex in modern society. A typical example is *Hours*, by Lon Albert. One senses that it was written by a student in need of money—evidently a fairly common occurrence among pornography-writers. Set in the Columbia University community on New York's upper West Side, it concerns a radical, film-making, sexually innovative group of the kind that springs up around such campuses and details the interlocking lives of several people in this circle who come up against the Mafia. Despite the gratuitous sex, the book does give some very accurate descriptions of sexual types and habits among homosexuals—the men who touch and meet in the dark of theaters; the radical students who become less radical in the eyes of fellow activists when their homosexuality is made known; the well-adjusted young business-man who compulsively has anonymous sex and eventually is beaten; the belligerent, terrified, mother-centered alcoholic who finally goes into a "queer" sexual situation, where his only possible response is violence. Like many other commercial, sexually exploitative books being written today, *Hours* also represents an attempt to relate homosexuality to something other than hidden paranoid fantasies.

There are thus far relatively few serious nonfiction works on the gay liberation movement. One of the most cogent and exciting is Carl Wittman's *Gay Manifesto*. Writing from his experience in San Francisco, Wittman discusses women, oppression, sexual roles, the gay ghetto, possible coalitions among oppressed groups and other topics in a reasonable, casual, and extremely appealing manner. Wittman is careful to avoid aligning himself with any of the various gay organizations that are proliferating throughout the country, although he does use militant language when stating his demands. His *Manifesto* is written in a personal style, but it is more than one person's opinion. He has distilled the countless hours of discussion and impassioned rhetoric that characterize militant homosexuality into a clear-cut list of grievances and demands. For anyone wishing to understand the goals of gay liberation, this is probably the best place to begin. The myriad statements, constitutions, and lists of goals that have erupted in the last few years contain few items that Wittman's *Manifesto* does not cover.

A few newspapers have begun to appear that present a personal approach to the meaning of gay liberation. They are completely different from the homosexual-oriented pulps that have been issued (with extremely profitable results) by publishers of such august sexist tabloids as *Screw*. The one with which I am best acquainted is *Come Out!*, originally connected with New York's Gay Liberation Front and now speaking to and for New York's radical homosexual community. *Come Out!* is published under severe financial and practical limitations: Due to its radical political-sexual politics, the paper must be printed at night, secretly; because the majority of people who work on it live outside the established economic order, they must devote time they would like to spend on the paper to eking out a living. Moreover, the paper's contents are decided by consensus; everyone involved in each article's appearance discusses and provides opinions on what is to be printed. The paper appears very irregularly; only six issues have been brought out since the paper's inception in the fall of 1969. But the resulting work shows a remarkable coherence of thought; it deals with every aspect of homosexuality but without the guilty prurience found in commercial papers. There are no sex ads, no suggestive pictures, no titillating fabrications of "personal experiences"—all of which characterize most sex publications, from such oddities as *Sexology* to the recent, supposedly amusing raunchiness of *Screw* and *Gay*.

Come Out! is a serious venture; the problems discussed are real and painful ones, and the affirmations expressed are hard won and genuine. It is only through the development of media controlled by gay people that an accurate picture of the gay world can be presented. The straight press has seized on gay liberation as another item, a new fad to be played for jokes, now that the women's lib thing has gotten so serious. *Come Out!* and the scores of papers like it—which are springing up all over and which are outside of the press establishment, the radical establishment, and the entire straight world—are now the sole recorders of the new homosexual consciousness.

The lack of meaningful literature on the positive aspects of homosexuality point to a painful necessity: the re-evaluation of all that has been written before and the extraordinarily difficult creation of a new kind of literature. The entire body of Western Judaeo-Christian literature has been created by individuals steeped in the sexism that characterized the growth of our culture. As we begin to outgrow the limitations of that culture and attempt to make a new one, we must recognize the problems inherent in appreciating traditional culture. This does not mean that we should abandon our heritage or deny the beauty and meaning of great works of art. We must learn, however, to be more critical of those values that are taken for granted. We are no longer in a family-oriented, expanding, colonizing culture. The virtues of that world, extolled for centuries, are meaningless to more and more people today. Likewise, many deeply rooted beliefs—for example, woman are naturally weaker than men; homosexuality is unnatural; marriage is the standard and ultimately desirable state—must be discarded. These ideas, celebrated in innumerable and genuinely beautiful paintings, books, statues, films, were never "true." Rather, they were conveniences that helped a self-serving culture to grow. It was a healthy process, but it is not now.

The literature that will grow out of this new culture will reflect new values or, perhaps more accurately, a lack of the strict old values. And foremost among these will be the honest and accepting portrayal of people who relate to other people of their own sex. Ideally, this would be part of the sexual awakening that will enable everyone to break out of old stereotypes and achieve the freedom that has always been put forth as the ideal in every other area of human activity. But homosexuality, as the most despised, most denied sexual activity must be treated with special care. The attempts by straight people and hostile homosexuals to understand the homosexual liberation movement are the most fitting form of reparation that can be made for the centuries of abuse, torture, and misery afficted on those whose only crime was to feel affection for another man or woman. *Come Out!,* the works of Auden, Isherwood, Hoffman, Wittman, all the writers and observers, past and present, who have written truly of homosexuals will be incorporated into this new culture and used as models for the new works. Above all, we must rid ourselves of the guilty, cruel, death-oriented fixations that dominate so much literature about homosexuals. Until we remove these onesided representations of what homosexuals are *supposed* to be, we will never be able to develop fully.

I realize I have slighted many perhaps worthy books and many passages in otherwise ordinary books that provide insights into homosexuality. But this was not meant to be a definitive survey of all homosexual literature; I leave that to sympathetic bibliographers and critics. Rather, this is a record of what one inquisitive person encountered, and the conclusions that he drew—was forced to draw—from what he read. It is a depressing picture for the most part, but it truly seems that the worst is over. There is no reason now why homosexuality cannot be portrayed as what it is—a full life.

94 /Out of the Closets: Voices of Gay Liberation

III.
THE MAN'S LAW

HAPPY BIRTHDAY, BABY BUTCH

Jaye V. Poltergeist

It was the night before my twenty-first birthday, and celebration was in the air. And when you're gay and you live at home, celebration (in the days before gay liberation) meant a gay bar. I bounced downstairs in my new sneakers, took a few random swipes at my short bangs, and winked at the "baby butch" image in the mirror. Then, halfway out the door, I called back over my shoulder, "I'm off to a party, be back late," and zipped off to pick up a girlfriend who lived way out in the wilds of Long Island.

We reached the Casbah around eleven. It was a white stucco building, very respectable looking from the outside. The only thing that would distinguish it from a normal establishment was the goon at the door. We each handed our three bucks to old stoneface and stepped into the dark and hectic warmth of the bar. The jukebox was blasting frantically; women were writhing against women, men were disappearing in couples into the blackness of the back room. A young man, lace at his sleeves and collar and pants tight as skin across his ass, was shaking to the music. A slow tune came on, and couples appeared from the corners, hugging each other in time to the music. In the middle of the dance floor a butch woman and a gay boy were clowning; the boy suddenly jerked backwards with a scream of surprise: "Oh Dee! You really are a man aren't you? I felt it! I swear I felt it!" Dee, whatever she was, had a sense of humor. Chuckling and shaking her head, Dee hitched up her Levis and swaggered towards the bar for a refill.

At the bar and at the tables scattered around the room, men and women were buying their dates two dollar watered-down drinks. Here, as well as at most other gay bars throughout the country, whether Mafia-run or not, gay people were paying exorbitant prices for a few hours of relaxation. And we paid, for where else could we go for a while to remove our straight masks and to shake out the cobwebs from that proverbial closet? After a week of constant tensions from acting the part at home, at school, at the office, and in the street, it was a relief to be able to hold hands, dance together and be our *real* selves. We were exploited at every turn in every gay bar that we fled to so furtively and so anxiously. Even today, the oppression hasn't ceased; gay bars are raided and shut down regularly, especially in an election year. It's a steep price to pay for a few hours of not having to pretend.

But when you're gay, you're a menace to the morals of white, middle-class suburbia, and even the walls of the Casbah can't keep the real world out. We were dancing and really into it when suddenly out of nowhere flash bulbs began exploding against the darkness—the white bursts of light were blinding and terrorizing. At first I thought, "What idiot would dare to take pictures in here?!" But as suddenly as the cameras flashed, people panicked and started to run like hell for the back exit. It was a raid! Caught in the tide of frantic bodies, I grabbed my friend and pushed her out the door. She escaped over the back fence. I wasn't quite so lucky. One of the cops had me by the back of my sweater. I twisted and pulled and punched him with my elbows and finally got free. I ran to my car and locked myself in, but the driveway was blocked by police vans. There was no escape. A plainclothes pig suddenly loomed over my windshield with a brick, threatening to smash my windows if I didn't get out. I knew he wasn't kidding either, so I got out. He lined me up against a wall with several others, our hands up over our heads. He frisked us. I felt his hands on my breasts, and in my anger and fear I broke from the line and ran halfway across the lot. Another pig grabbed me from behind with a chokehold and pulled me off the ground. In the terror of it all I wet my pants.

Later, as I sat locked in the police car wondering what was going to happen to me, I observed numerous instances of police brutality. The pigs, while questioning people, were very generous in the use of their nightsticks, poking men around the genitals and women in the breasts. They made a thorough search of our pockets and handbags, probably hoping to find dope.

I sat there wondering how the hell I would explain all this to my parents and remembering the time a year or so earlier when I had felt the same sickening fear. Then too I had a run-in with the law for the same reason—being gay in a straight world. My friend and I had parked on a dark street which was a well-known lovers' lane. The seats of my car went down, and we followed suit. While we were necking, a car pulled alongside and honked. I popped my head up, saw green, black, and white with a red bubble on top, and stepped on the gas. After a three-block chase at 65 miles per hour in a residential section, sirens and flashing lights behind me, I decided to pull over before I had a bullet through my skull. My friend had forgotten to put her seat up. She just lay there moaning in panic, her hands over her face. The pig pulled up next to us.

"Okay, who's in there with you? Are you alone?"

"Uh, no officer . . . it's my friend . . . uh, sh-she's sick."

At the word "she" a grotesque look of hatred and disgust

appeared on his pink Aryan face. He took down our names and addresses. He looked at my license. He looked us over for a long minute, his tight lips in a scowl.

"Why I ought to haul you both in, you filthy bitches."

He had me pegged for the butch because of my short dark hair (my friend's hair was long and blond), and he motioned me out of the car. He walked me down the street a bit (out of earshot of the pretty blond girl I was supposedly corrupting) and began to talk to me "man-to-man." He was really getting turned on as he went into a long, detailed description of what constituted sodomy between men and women, men and men, women and women, animals and humans, and what the hell was I really up to way down there in the seat anyway?

"You were pretty far down now, weren't you?"

"We were only talking officer." Believe that one you bastard.

"Tell me something butchie, do you do that sort of thing with men too?"

Dream on, you prick! "Listen officer, please don't arrest me, my mother has a heart condition, my father has high blood pressure, and anyway, I'm going to a shrink, I really am!"

"You're going to a psycho?"

"Yessir, I go every week, three times a week, please don't take me in." Be cool kid, just tell him what he wants to hear.

"Well, awright, this time you're lucky. I want you to get in that car and I want you to take her home and then you get the hell out of here. I don't ever wanna see you in this neighborhood again 'cause if I do I'm gonna haul you right down to the stationhouse."

"Yessir, right away sir, thank you sir."

Zoom! I was off and cursing the motherfucker for the next twenty miles. It was a week before my friend and I stopped jumping every time the phone rang.

That same sinking feeling of fear gnawed away at me now, as one by one, the pigs dragged us out, checked our i.d.s and took our photographs. Then if we were "clean" (no drugs) and over eighteen they let us go with a warning. My knees knocked all the way home. Some of those arrested were charged with public lewdness; that was really a laugh! The pigs should take a good look at themselves sometime.

Next morning, after a sleepless night, I stumbled down to breakfast. I expected my birthday present to be the front page of the *Daily News* spread across the kitchen table with the headlines "Gay bar raided—Jaye V. Poltergeist charged with public lewdness!"

Instead, my mother greeted me.

"Good morning, did you have a nice time last night? How was the party? Did you meet any nice young men?"

"Oh yeah, ma, it was a really nice party."

"That's good dear, Happy Birthday!"

SISSY IN PRISON

An Interview with Ron Vernon

When did you first realize you were a homosexual?

I think I first realized when people started calling me a faggot. I really became aware of being a homosexual in school.

What do you think there was about you that made people call you faggot? Where was this school, by the way?

In Chicago. I think, well, the way I acted. Like I acted in sort of a way of always being with girls and never playing around too much with the boys, and they began to associate that in some way with femininity, with being feminine, and eventually, the word "sissy" arose, and I was classified. And that's when I really became aware that something was different about me.

How old were you then?

Oh, I was about seven or eight years old.

Did this ever go past the name-calling stage to any other form of harassment?

Yeah, well, not so much when I was very young, but when I was about ten or eleven, I began to get into a couple of arguments, deep arguments, but nobody ever physically attacked me for being gay, you know. Just arguments. At about thirteen, I transferred to a high school which was one of the roughest high schools in the city of Chicago. Not knowing that I would be the only overt homosexual at the school, the first day I wore a red shirt down to my knees and a pair of the loudest pants I could find, and went to school. Because at the school I had been to previously, there were other homosexuals I associated with, and we sort of stuck together and nobody ever bothered. There was a lot of alienation on our part. We alienated ourselves from the other people.

In this high school with all these rough and tough types, what sort of an encounter did you have with these straight men?

Well, the first day I transferred in, I remember getting off the bus, and it was about 8:30 in the morning, and school didn't open till 9. And I walked around the corner, and here the whole street was filled with students getting ready for the bell to ring. The minute I turned the corner, it seemed like a hush came over the whole street, all the way down to the end of the next block. I reacted to it, but I didn't turn away, you know, like I went on up to the center door. And by the time I got to the center door, people all on down the street were whistling, and all this kind of shit. I got to the center door, and the janitor was on the inside. And the door was locked. And I asked him if he would open the door. And he said that the bell hadn't rung yet, and I couldn't get in until the bell rang. So I had to go back out into all these people, and walk down to the other end of the school, through all these people, to another door, by the office, where I got in. When I got in it was a relief after having struggled past all these people.

When you were finally in that school, what did you do for friendship? Did you continue to have friendships mostly with women, or were you able to have friendships with some of those straight men?

Well, what happened was I was assigned my classes and sent to a counsellor immediately when I came into the school, because of my overt femininity. I was like flamboyant, and all this. I was sort of sticking by myself because there was no other people there that I felt I could relate to. I felt that I should just be by myself, you know, because I felt that it would really be a difficult struggle to try to relate to these straight people. I came to school for about the first three days. And the third day I was in the cafeteria at lunch time, and this woman walked up and said, "Hi, my name is Susan, what's yours?" It sounded like they had written out everything of how they were going to approach me, and practiced and rehearsed it, and then came and did this skit, on how to relate to me, because no one had ever related to a homosexual, obviously. And they wanted to try to do it as well as they could. And I guess the thing was to write up a script and all take part. It sounded like they had read it and memorized it. She says, "My name's Susan, what's yours?" And I said, "My name's Ron." And she sat down and we started just talking about what school I had come from, and things like this. We were sitting there for about five minutes and then some more women came into the cafeteria and she called them over, and pretty soon about five women were sitting at the table, and we were all rapping about how did I feel coming into the school, and things like that. So that was my first communication with any straight people at all, and those were women at school. I sort of hung around with them ever since then.

We'd always meet during our breaks and at lunch time, and get together and rap.

I was there for about a week and I had been assigned a health class. I was sitting in the front of the classroom, and I was really kind of nervous because of being put in the front of the classroom and not in the back of the classroom where I could keep an eye on everybody instead of everybody keeping an eye on me. The teacher walked out of the room, and this man got up and said, "That's a faggot." At first I didn't know how to react to it, and I had just gotten out of the Illinois Youth Commission for . . . well, it was my first time there, I'd been there for about eight months. I didn't know what to do. I didn't want to fight with him because I had just come into the situation, and I really didn't want to jeopardize my freedom in any way. I knew that being kicked out of school—all that would happen is I would go right back to the Youth Commission. Anyway, he did it a couple of times, and I just had a temper which wouldn't wait at that time, which I still sort of do, and so I used a term which was used a lot then. "Can you box?" I jumped up and said, "I can box, and I don't have to go through any shit, either. Put 'em up or shut up." And so he got up and came up to the front of the classroom, and I knocked him down. And we just beat each other to death, and in a way I guess you could say that I won the fight. He was very offended by this, because this faggot kicked his ass. So he went and organized a campaign to wipe out faggots around the school.

I had a gym class with him also. The next day, I came into my gym class—well, this was the first gym class I had had—and we had to wear shorts and a T-shirt, and I came into my gym class with a slip for registering for that class, and I came in late for some reason, and everyone was seated on bleachers on either side of the gym. And the teacher's desk was in the center all the way at the other end of the gym. And I had to walk all the way across the gym in front of all these people, by myself, because I was about ten minutes late. He was giving a lecture about what we were going to be doing in gym, or some shit like that. So anyway I walked across the floor, and the whole gym went up. I really felt kind of bad about it. They started whistling, and cackling and all this shit. So I turned my slip in and sat down at the back of the class. Well, eventually everything was really like up in arms, people were just screaming and yelling. So the teacher blew the whistle for everybody to play ball. And so everyone ran out on the floor and started playing ball, and I walked out of the gym. This fellow who had attacked me—well, verbally attacked me, because

I did hit him first—was in this gym class. It was gym with about five classes, there were about 200 people, it was a huge, huge gymnasium. That day, nothing happened, except that incident.

The day after we had had this fight, he came up to me in the hall and said, "2:30." That was when we got out of school; he meant that I should meet him at 2:30 outside, you know. I said, "OK," and I thought I was going out there just to him, but when I walked out of the school, there were about fifteen boys altogether, waiting for me. And he was standing in front of them woofing like a dog. I turned around and walked back into the school and went out the back door and ran home. The next day he saw me in the hall, and he told me "2:30" again. And I did the same thing again. The next gym class that we had he came up to me in the locker room. What they had done is they had planned this fight between about three people, where three people would get involved in the back of the locker room, because I was the only one who went all the way in the back of the locker room to dress and undress, and all the other people were up front. They had fought all the way back along the wall, back to where I was. Maybe it was my paranoia or something, but I had this idea that they were coming back there after me. And I went around the other side and ran up into the crowd at the door waiting to get out of the locker room, and squeezed by everybody and managed to get out of the locker room. Well, they ran up behind me, trying to get to me before I could get through the crowd. I left school early that day.

I went home and told my father what had happened, and he had always been one to tell me to fight my own battles. So I took a razor, half a razor, the handle was broken off. I wrapped it up in a piece of toilet paper and stuck it down into my underwear and went to school. That day, I came out of the school and this fellow was waiting behind the door and hit me in the face with a chain. I ran and they were chasing me, and they were catching up. All the time I was running I was reaching down in my drawers trying to pull out this razor, and eventually I got it out, and I just did a U-turn, and went right, just blindly, just into them, cutting everybody I could, and going after the person in particular who had hit me in the face with a chain, and I cut his face up pretty bad, and I ran home.

I came back to school the next day, and he was there with his mother and the police and everybody under the sun to take me to jail. So the school told me that they couldn't tolerate any shit like that, and that they were going to send me to Montefiore, which was a rehabilitation school for boys, which I wasn't ready to go to, and I told them I'd quit school before I'd go to Montefiore. So when

I quit school, I was returned to the Illinois Youth Commission for dropping out of school. This all happened in the course of about a month.

I had just gotten out a month before, and I went back in and stayed about a year that time. Ever since then I was getting out and staying for about two weeks and going back in, for curfew and shit like that. And then eventually I turned sixteen, and I was old enough to get an independent parole where I would just leave the institution and come out on the street on my own, you know, without going to any relatives or anything, and working a job as a dishwasher or something, trying to make it, until I got off parole.

How did you first get in with this Youth Commission? What is the Youth Commission? Is that a jail, or what?

Yeah, the Illinois Youth Commission is a jail for juveniles. My reason for going was that at about twelve, I ran away from home to live with an older man. Eventually I was caught up with. My father put out a "missing person" and all this shit, and they caught me. When I went to court, it was all established somehow that there was a homosexual relationship going on between this older fellow and me. When I went to court, the judge asked my father, "Are you aware that your son is a homosexual?" And my father said, "Yes." We had never talked about it before and that was the first time I had ever heard him refer to me as a homosexual. And he did, and was very hurt having to do it in that way. And I felt the pain that he encountered because it was really a blow to him in so many ways that someone would come out and ask him, "Are you aware that your son is a homosexual?" and his son is standing right there next to him, you know. My father is a very honest man, and just said, "Yeah." So they said, "Well, we're going to send him to Galesburg Mental Institution to try to correct his homosexuality." I couldn't understand anything that was happening. I had sort of had an idea that I would be going to the Youth Commission, but never really accepted the fact that they'd send me to the Youth Commission for something so stupid. But they did. And that's how I went to the Youth Commission.

When I got there, well, there were other homosexuals there, but we were so outlandish, you know, we ran the institution practically. Anything that happened or went down in the institution, well, we knew about it. We had something to do with it, all kinds of shit. The first place I was sent was to the Reception Center in Joliet. Then I was sent to St. Charles from the Reception Center. I stayed there for about six months and got into a fight with my cottage mother. I stole some cigarettes out of her room. They gave homosexuals jobs like cleaning up, and I was cleaning up her room and took advantage and stole some cigarettes. And she came down in the basement, and grabbed my arm or something, told me not to steal cigarettes, not to be stealing cigarettes from her, and my immediate response was to hit her, which I did, I turned around and slapped her in the face. That same night they came and handcuffed me and took me to Sheridan, because that was an outrageous thing to do, slap a cottage parent, you know, because you just couldn't do it, because if you did it then other people would do it.

So they sent me to the maximum security institution which was in Sheridan, Illinois, with two fences with dogs between and guard towers with guns, and all kinds of shit like this. I stayed there for three months, and I got out and went through that change [in high school], and then I went back. And everytime I went back after that they sent me immediately to Sheridan because I was, you know, always fighting. Whenever a prisoner called me a faggot or a punk, I would try to knock their brains out and shit like that, you know. Really, they didn't know how to handle us, they didn't know what to do. They thought they knew so much about psychology and about homosexuality that they could just put us in any type of situation and we would just play along with whatever was the set rules, you know. But we really fucked up a lot of things there. I was in Sheridan the second time for a year, and I was in the hole ten months out of that year. The hole was a small cell with just a light box and a slot underneath where your food comes in. And I was let out once every other day for a shower. At that time you used to get a milk pill and a vitamin pill for breakfast, a full lunch, and a milk pill and a vitamin pill for dinner. Now this is where they put murderers, rapists, you know, people they felt they couldn't handle—they put them in the hole. I was apparently a murderer and a rapist all combined, with my homosexuality, so they put me in the hole. A lot of shit went down. A lot of people were committing suicide. An awful lot of gay people were hanging themselves or shit like that. They eventually gave us a building which was called C-8, and they put us on the fourth gallery, way up at the top. We had all the cells on the top, and even there, people would slice their wrists and shit, and hang themselves, and all kinds of shit.

We used to have this thing where many of the gay people would organize, and do strikes, and sit-ins, and shit like that, refuse to do any work, you know. I remember this very good friend of mine, we used to call him Didi, he tied a sheet around his neck. There was this guard, he was giving us an awful lot of trouble, his name was Ivy, Big Ivy, who used to really give us a lot of hell, you know, beat us up and shit like this, and this was a grown-ass man, and we were like fourteen or fifteen years old, you know. What happened was we had planned to get him, you know. First we tried getting him fired by telling lies and saying he was forcing us into homosexual behavior with him, you know, all kinds of shit. And then we couldn't get him fired because he had been there for so long that everybody just wouldn't believe it. So what we did was, Didi tied a sheet around his neck, and tied it up to the barred windows, and was standing on top of his bed. So I walked up to the door and started screaming, "Guard, come here! Somebody's trying to hang themselves!" So he ran up to the door and when he opened the door I pushed him in and about like seven or eight gay people ran in and threw a blanket over his head and almost beat him to death and left him there, you know. We used to do shit like that. We were doing more shit in that institution. Anything that went on, we were in it. I remember this straight brother who was very close to a lot of us, he always defended us and stuff like this, he was taken to the hole and they broke both of his arms and both of his legs before they got him there.

I have to tell this: My first day in Sheridan I was in the cafeteria. When you first get there, you come into this big mess hall where everybody eats. All the people eat in this big mess hall. The intake people, the new people, eat at one table. I came with two other gay brothers. And we were sitting at the table and like my name was known throughout the institution before I got there for all the shit that I'd been doing in these other institutions, you know, and people were constantly transferring in. This fellow reached over and grabbed my butt, my ass, you know. I turned around and said, well, "Don't touch me. Don't put your hands on me, 'cause you don't know me." And we went through this big argument type of thing. I jumped up and took my tray and threw it in his face. It was just the thing to do. We had to defend ourselves, and we had these reputations to hold. Otherwise we really would have been fucked over. So I threw the tray in his face. They shot tear gas into the mess hall. The first person they run to grab to carry up over all the tear gas—while the tear gas was settling—the first person who they're carrying up in the air out to the hole, my first day there, was me. They just lifted me up and drug me out and threw me in the hole.

We've all read in the newspapers and all these books about forced homosexuality and rapes in jail, and also the whole phenomenon of tough straight guys forcing weaker men into homosexual relations. Was this a phenomenon that you encountered in this jail? Exactly how did that work?

It's true that the straight men forced people into homosexuality, but it was like most of the gay people who were overt about it and let people know were all put into the same area together or on the same tier. We didn't have as much of that on our tier. First of all, nobody would even dare to attack one gay person without having to fight 30 or 40 who are on the tier, you know. On other tiers, I remember this one boy was gang-raped thirteen times, and like nobody in the institution knew about it other than the inmates, and like he wouldn't tell the officials because he would have really been in trouble then. You know, finally we got him to admit his homosexuality and come over to our tier so that he wouldn't be gang-raped any more, because it was a regular thing. Can you imagine being gang-raped by all these men thirteen times, you know, thirteen different times, not thirteen men, but thirteen different times by many men! So there is a lot of that, but, you know, I think that the way the institutions play it up, you know, I think they encourage things like gang-rapes and shit like that, by keeping this tension, first of all, between homosexual and straight people there. They try their damnedest to.

How do they do that?

Well, by segregating us. I don't feel we should be segregated from straight men. If men are straight they won't relate to me sexually anyway, so I won't have any problems with them, right? So I think that they encourage it by keeping us separate from them, and then keeping all straight men together to do their thing, and calling it mass homosexual uprisings and shit like that, and calling people a bunch of perverts and shit, when they are just encouraging the whole thing themselves.

You had a reputation for fighting. What happened to other people who didn't fight as well?

I'm not talking about the straights on straight tiers. I'm talking about on the gay tier. Every once in a while you'd hear like someone was raped over on another tier. But as far as on our tier was concerned, they put about 40 homosexuals and about almost as many supposedly liberal heterosexuals, men, you know, with the role of men, and the homosexuals playing the role of women, on the tier together. All right? It was a thing where we had . . . I mean we really had it set up. Nobody would even utter "faggot." I mean the guards were very careful about what they said. I think that most of the things that we hear are not about the stereotyped or role-type gay person in the type of situation that I was in, you see. I was playing a role. I was playing a passive, feminine role. All right? Had I not played a passive, feminine role, and went into the institution, and been put on a straight tier, and had a homosexual relationship with one person, you see, on that tier, the whole tier would have known about it, and I would have had to have a homosexual relationship with everyone on that tier, you see, because I was an overt outlet, so to speak. Someone had initiated it. And I think that's how a lot of the gang-rapes are caused, you know, by homosexuals going in with these supermen attitudes about how butch they are and shit, and they get up there and have a relationship with one person, and it's NOT with one person, and it ends up where someone else will come up to him, or proposition him or something, and he'll refuse it, and that's when he's gang-raped. I think that's how gang-rapes occur. I would not advise any homosexual to go in there with a superman attitude, because some of the biggest, muscular, macho masculine-identified men, they go into prison, they're homosexual, and they go through this change. I don't care how big you are or how tough you are, it just happens that you'll get raped if you don't go along with the program. That's all.

You say the men who you related to in this tier were not really straight men, they were butch homosexuals in effect?

Right. At that time, I didn't identify those people as homosexuals, the men on my tier. Because I was into a role thing, where I was a homosexual and he was a straight man, you know, and I related to him that way.

Now you think about it differently?

Oh, yeah. My consciousness is entirely different now. I think that having to play those roles was extremely oppressive for many of us. In fact, that's why so many of us kept returning to the institution. We'd get out, and sometimes you'd see someone who left two days earlier walking right back in there.

Why'd they come back in?

Going out and prostituting, or going out and ripping somebody off or something. A lot of them had intentions of being caught, and intentions of going back to jail. And intentions of being incarcerated.

Did people want to go back because of relationships they had?

Yes, because of relationships there. That part was oppressive. It was oppressive in the fact that it was locking up people and making them think it was all right. Nobody should be locked up, that's all. No homosexual or straight man or anybody.

When you weren't in this jail, what sort of jobs or experiences did you have. Did you ever get back to school?

Well, I graduated from grammar school in St. Charles.

That's a jail?

That's a jail. I took a test and somehow I passed it, and they handed me a diploma. When I got out on the independent parole, I went downtown to some General Equivalency Diploma Test office, and passed that. I got a high enough score to get a scholarship to college. I started college. That was another whole trip. That was going into how to relate to capitalism, how I could come out of one situation and go into another. I feel that's what school did for me, you know, put me in the same type of oppressive situation, but in a more bourgie sense, so I'd be able to get a half-assed job after I graduated, supporting the system, you see. And in fact, to show you how oppressed I was, I wouldn't be able to get a job because the record I had was tremendous. And just because I had the intelligence to rap through their books and shit like this, I was so oppressed that I couldn't even see that I'd never be able to teach, I'd never be able to go through school and teach high school students or children or adults or anybody, because of my criminal record. All I was concerned with was getting that diploma because that made me a part of the system, could make me some money.

Did you meet other gay people in college?

Yeah, I met lots of gay people in college. Most gay people in college that I know just stay in their closets and didn't let anybody know. That's true for the people I knew when I was in school, until gay liberation and Third World Gay Revolution came out. Those people in school were very closeted people. Like you would know, maybe by talking with them, they'd drop a hint or something, but other people wouldn't. They'd have to hide and shit like that.

When did you first think in political terms and think of yourself as a revolutionary?

Basically, I've always thought of myself as a revolutionary. When I was in jail I was a revolutionary, all right? In a sense I was a revolutionary because I was rejecting the system, all right? I was rejecting the system in a negative sense, in that I was not using my rejection constructively to turn it against the system, but perpetuating and helping the system, but still in a revolutionary sense, sort of. I've always had ideas of offing repression. I mean, as early as I can remember people have been fucking over my head, and I've always had a desire to stop people from fucking over my head.

When you were in jail, for example, were people already talking about things like the Black Panther Party? Malcolm X?

Yeah, there was quite a movement in jail between, well, most of the people in jail are black, first of all. There was quite a movement in jail between black people, and around Malcolm X. I was in jail when I first heard about the Black Panther Party, and related to it very positively, but in a blackness sense and not out of a gayness sense, because they were offing gay people, verbally offing gay people. You know, saying things like this white man who is fucking you over is a faggot, and that was getting to me too, because I was a faggot and I wasn't no white man! Finally their consciousness has changed, somehow. I don't know how, but it did, recently, and they've begun to relate to homosexuals as people, as a part of the people. That's when I really became a revolutionary, began to live my whole life as a revolutionary. And I could never ever consider another—I mean now that I'm conscious of my oppression I could not consider any other thing. If there was a movement to restore capitalism in this country and they offed every revolutionary, they'd have to off me too. If they restore black capitalism in this country, they'd have to off me too. That's going to be oppressing me as a black, gay person.

Do you have any ideas about how you're going to mobilize more black gay people into revolutionary activity?

Well, I have sort of an idea of what I'm going to do. I'm really struggling right now with developing my own gay consciousness. I think that most of the people in Third World Gay Revolution and in gay liberation are developing their own consciousness, and trying to relate to other consciousness-raising issues. I think that more and more Third World and also white people are coming into the movement. And just the idea that they know that they'll have a fighting chance somewhere to be gay people, whether they're Third World or white, you know—the opportunity for them to get it—they're going to get in there and struggle for it.

As you've developed political consciousness, how has that changed you and the way you see yourself and other gay people?

As far as my political consciousness goes, or my political gay consciousness goes, I see many things in gay people that I never paid attention to before, sort of in a positive sense. I see gay people as being oppressed people, and I see that the roles that have been given us, you see, that we identify with, I see as an oppression. There are many gay people that I'd never thought I'd be able to understand that I'm able to understand out of a revolutionary context, in a revolutionary sense, in that I recognize that they are oppressed, and that is the reason for them taking these roles, and that is the reason for whatever it is about gayness that is negative. I don't really think that anything is negative about gayness except for the roles, which exist among heterosexuals too, and I think that's negative about them too.

You say that there were certain negative qualities in gayness that you noticed, and which you eventually concluded were due to oppression. What were some of these negative qualities?

I think that the people I had most difficulty in understanding, the people I still have most difficulty understanding, are white people, first of all. I still feel a lot of negative things about white people because of their racism, basically—the extreme racism which they really bring down on the black community and on black people. I really feel that white straight people bring about this whole shit. I think that the thing that I'm able to see better is the white gay person's point of view, and I'm able to identify—I have something to identify with in a white gay person, in a revolutionary sense. I'm able to understand white people to such a degree, in their gayness, to see that they're oppressed as gay people also. I think that those are the people I had most difficulty understanding that I'm beginning to relate to now, beginning to understand.

I definitely feel that I still don't understand white straight people. I hope that I will. . . . I don't know that I hope that I will. I don't think that I'll ever be able to understand white straight people because of all the shit that they've created in this society. And I feel that they have created all this shit—white straight MEN in particular.

Since the women's liberation movement, I've begun to relate more closely to white women and understand their oppression, because it sort of parallels gay oppression in many ways, and I'm sort of able to understand white straight women because they're sort of able to understand black gay men, to an extent. They can understand their gayness. I still feel that a lot of white straight women do not understand black gay men as far as their blackness is concerned. I still think that women's liberation has an awful lot of racism to deal with before they can really understand the whole point of view. And I think that black gay men and white gay men have an awful lot of consciousness-raising before they can understand women's oppression. As far as dealing with white women are concerned, we have to really deal with sexism. And that's really a strange thing to think about—that you're oppressed in a sexist sort of way, and that you have to raise your own consciousness on sexism. But I can see it, because black people are constantly raising their own consciousness about their blackness, and so that's how I relate to it.

In what ways have you personally experienced oppression within homosexual life by white gay men, either racist oppression or some sexist oppression?

Well, I was into this hustling trip where I used to prostitute. The people who supported me in prostitution really had a lot to do with the way I'm fucked up in relating sexually—now I don't know if you can understand that. I mean the way that I relate in bed to people sexually—is from white men, you see. My roles were reinforced by white men, and the fact that they were my living . . . my roles had to be reinforced by white men at that time. And this is the thing I attach to white men. The thing I wasn't looking at at that time was, I was identifying it with white straight men, and in fact they were white gay men that I was having sex with. That's a whole other thing, too.

Well, they were very straight-identified.

Yeah, most of them were married, suburbia with two children, snuck out of the house to turn a trick, you know, down at the Square, which is all brought on by the system. That people have to in fact do shit like that, and lie about themselves. And when they lie about themselves, that in turn makes it, you know, a racist thing. In my case that made it a racist thing, when they had to deal with me. Because they lied about themselves, they had to deal with me, and that really turned me off.

Do you think they chose you because you were black?

I don't know if they chose me because I was black. I think they chose me because I was there and I was an easy sex object. All they had to do was flash over fifteen or twenty dollars and they would have a blow job.

With all this going in and out of prison, you must have had a lot of run-ins with the pigs. Would you tell us about some of them?

Pigs are, well, I don't know what they are. A pig is a pig, all right? Most people are trying to get in this trip of trying to relate to people, and to think that a pig is actually a person in a uniform, with an oppression on him, you know, and that he's in turn oppressing everybody, and if you think about it that way, I guess maybe you could sort of work around it somehow. Even in that way, like, I can't relate to them. Like my whole life has been centered around pigs busting me for different things, which were insignificant and trivial, really superficial things, like, I remember a story . . . one time we were on the beach around four o'clock in the morning. We were walking around the Oak Street Beach. There were about four Third World gay brothers who were walking together. Now this is on Lake Shore Drive in Chicago, which is the exclusive ritzy area. The reason that we were on Lake Shore Drive is, like, the gay bars are up that way. Anyway, the pigs saw us walking on the beach, and we passed these two white brothers who were playing a guitar and singing out on the beach. So the pigs came. First they drove by, and then they turned around and came back and drove up onto the concrete on the beach and said,

"We have received reports that you are out here disturbing the peace and it's four o'clock in the morning." And I said, "It wasn't us who was disturbing the peace, officer, it was someone else down the way, and all they were doing was playing the guitar." So he says, "Well, no, I don't think it was anyone else, I think it was you." And he says, "Let's see some identification." I says, "Well, I don't have any identification." I did have identification, but I just didn't feel like showing him my identification. At that time the stop-and-frisk law wasn't out—it was just before it came out in Chicago. I told him, "Well, I don't have any identification." He told me to put my hands up, and he searched me, and he felt my wallet in my back pocket, and he stuck his hand in my pocket to take out my wallet. So I sort of pushed him away, and I said, "Don't put your hands in my pocket because nothing in there belongs to you. If you want to see something, you ask me to pull it out, but don't you be putting your hands all over me." And shit like that, you know. So he said, "Oh, you're one of these smart faggots, huh?" I said, "Why, yes, I'm one of these smart faggots, and I still don't want you putting your hands on me." With that, he says, "Well, you're going to the shithouse," and I says, "Well, I don't see why I have to go to the shithouse, because I haven't done anything." He says, "You're going to the shithouse." I says, "I'm not going to the shithouse." And the brothers that were with me said that they weren't going to the shithouse. And so it eventually ended up that we attacked the police and another squad car was passing by and pulled up—well it wasn't a squad car, it was a paddy wagon, and it pulled up onto the concrete, and helped them, and that was the way that they got us.

RAPPING WITH A STREET TRANSVESTITE REVOLUTIONARY

An Interview with Marcia Johnson

You were starting to tell me a few minutes ago that a group of STAR* people got busted. What was that all about?
  Well, we wrote an article for Arthur Bell, of the *Village Voice*, about STAR, and we told him that we were all "girlies" and we're working up on the 42nd Street area. And we all gave our

*Street Transvestite Action Revolutionaries, of which Marcia Johnson is the vice president.

names—Bambi, Andorra, Marcia, and Sylvia. And we all went out to hustle, you know, about a few days after the article came out in the *Village Voice,* and you see we get busted one after another, in a matter of a couple of weeks. I don't know whether it was the article, or whether we just got busted because it was hot.

Were they arresting a lot of transvestites up around there?

Oh, yes, and they still are. They're still taking a lot of transvestites and a lot of women down to jail.

How do they make the arrests?

They just come up and grab you. One transvestite they grabbed right out of her lover's arms, and took her down. The charges were solicitation. I was busted on direct prostitution. I picked up a detective—he was in a New Jersey car. I said, "Do you work for the police?" And he said no, and he propositioned me and told me he'd give me fifteen dollars, and then he told me I was under arrest. So I had to do twenty days in jail.

Was the situation in jail bad?

Yes, it was. A lot of transvestites were fighting amongst each other. They have a lot of problems, you know. They can't go to court, they can't get a court date. Some of them are waiting for years. You know, they get frustrated and start fighting with one another. An awful lot of fights go on there.

How are relations between the transvestites and the straight prisoners? Is that a big problem?

Oh, the straight prisoners treat transvestites like they're queens. They send them over cigarettes and candy, envelopes and stamps and stuff like that—when they got money. Occasionally they treat them nice. Not all the time.

Is there any brutality or anything like that?

No, the straight prisoners can't get over by the gay prisoners. They're separated. The straight prisoners are on one side, and the gay prisoners are on another.

Can you say something about the purpose of STAR as a group?

We want to see all gay people have a chance, equal rights, as straight people have in America. We don't want to see gay people picked up on the streets for things like loitering or having sex or anything like that. STAR originally was started by the president, Sylvia Lee Rivera, and Bubbles Rose Marie, and they asked me to come in as the vice president. STAR is a very revolutionary group. We believe in picking up the gun, starting a revolution if necessary. Our main goal is to see gay people liberated and free and have equal rights that other people have in America. We'd like to see our gay brothers and sisters out of jail and on the streets again. There are a lot of gay transvestites who have been in jail for no reason at all, and the reason why they don't get out is they can't get a lawyer or any bail. Bambi and I made a lot of contacts when we were in jail, and Andorra, she went to court and she walked out.

What do you mean she walked out?

Well, when you're picked up for loitering and you don't have a police record, a lot of times they let you go, and they let your police record build up, and then they'll go back there and look at it—and then they give you a lot of time. That's how they work it down there at the courthouse. Like my bail was $1,000, because I have a long record for prostitution, and they refused to make it lower than $500. So when I went to court they told me they'd let me go if I pleaded guilty to prostitution. That's how they do it, they tell you ahead of time what you're going to get. Like before you even go before the judge, they try to make an agreement with you, so that they can get your case out of court, you know.

What would have happened if you'd pleaded not guilty?

I would still be there. They gave me 20 days to serve. And a lot of people do that a lot of times. That's how come their record is so bad, because they always plead guilty just so they can come out, cause they can't get no lawyer or no money or no kind of help from the streets.

What are you doing now about these people who are still in there who need lawyers?

We're planning a dance. We can help as soon as we get money. I have the names and addresses of people that are in jail, and we're going to write them a letter and let them know that we've got them a lawyer, and have these lawyers go down there and see if they can get their names put on the calendar early, get their cases put out of court, make a thorough investigation.

I remember when STAR was first formed there was a lot of discussion about the special oppression that transvestites experience. Can you say something about that?

We still feel oppression by other gay brothers. Gay sisters don't think too bad of transvestites. Gay brothers do. I went to a dance at Gay Activist Alliance just last week, and there was not even one gay brother that came over and said hello. They'd say hello, but they'd get away very quick. The only transvestites they were very friendly with were the ones that looked freaky in drag, like freak drag, with no tits, no nothing. Well, I can't help but have tits, they're mine. And those men weren't too friendly at all. Once in a while, I get an invitation to Daughters of Bilitis, and when I go there, they're always warm. All the gay sisters come over and say, "Hello, we're glad to see you," and they start long conversations.

But not the gay brothers. They're not too friendly at all toward transvestites.

Do you understand why? Do you have any explanation for that?

Of course I can understand why. A lot of gay brothers don't like women! And transvestites remind you of women. A lot of the gay brothers don't feel too close to women, they'd rather be near men, that's how come they're gay. And when they see a transvestite coming, she reminds them of a woman automatically, and they don't want to get too close or too friendly with her.

Are you more comfortable around straight men than around gay men sometimes?

Oh, I'm very comfortable around straight men. Well, I know how to handle them. I've been around them for years, from working the streets. But I don't like straight men. I'm not too friendly with them. There's only one thing they want—to get up your dress. They're really insulting to women. All they think about is getting up your dress, anything to get up that dress of yours. Then when you get pregnant or something, they don't even want to know you.

Do you find that there are some "straight" men who prefer transvestites to women?

There are some, but not that many. There's a lot of gay men that prefer transvestites. It's mostly bi-sexual type men, you know, they like to go both ways but don't like anybody to know what's happening. Rather than pick up a gay man, they'll pick up a gay transvestite.

When you hustle on 42nd Street, do they know you're a transvestite, or do they think you're a woman? Or does it depend?

Some of them do and some of them don't, because I tell them. I say,"It's just like a grocery store; you either shop or you don't shop." Lot's of times they tell me, "You're not a woman!" I say, "I don't know what I am if I'm not a woman." They say, "Well, you're not a woman." They say, "Let me see your cunt." I say, "Honey, let me tell you something." I say, "You can either take it or leave it," because, see, when I go out to hustle I don't particularly care whether I get the date or not. If they take me, they got to take me as I want 'em to take me. And if they want to go up my dress, I just charge them a little extra, and the price just goes up and up and up and up. And I always get all of my money in advance, that's what a smart transvestite does. I don't ever let them tell me, "I'll pay you after the job is done." I say I want it in advance. Because no woman gets paid after their job is done. If you're smart, you get the money first.

What sort of living arrangements has STAR worked out?

Well, we had our STAR home, at 213 E. 2nd Street, and you know, there was only one lesbian there, and a lot of stuff used to get robbed from her and I used to feel so sorry for her. People used to come in and steal her little methadone, because she was on drugs. I seen her the other day. She was the only lesbian who was staying with us. I really felt bad. She's back on drugs again. And she was really doing good. The only reason I didn't take her from STAR home and bring her here was the simple reason that I couldn't handle it. My nerves have been very bad lately, and I've been trying to get myself back together since my husband died in March. It's very hard for me. He just died in March. He was on drugs. He went out to get some money to buy some drugs and he got shot. He died on 2nd Street and First Avenue. I was home sleeping, and somebody came and knocked at the door and told me he was shot. And I was so upset that I just didn't know what to do. And right after he died, the dog died, and the lesbian that was staying there was nice enough to pick thè dog up out of the street for me. I couldn't hardly stand it. I had two deaths this year, my lover and then the dog. So I've just had bad nerves; I've been going to the doctor left and right. And then to get arrested for prostitution was just the tops!

What about job alternatives? Is it possible to get jobs?

Oh, definitely. I know many transvestites that are working as women, but I want to see the day when transvestites can go in and say, "My name is Mister So-and-So and I'd like a job as Miss So-and-So!" I can get a job as Miss Something-or-Other, but I have to hide the fact that I'm a male. But not necessarily. Many transvestites take jobs as boys in the beginning, and then after a while they go into their female attire and keep on working. It's easier for a transsexual than a transvestite. If you are a transsexual it's much easier because you become more feminine, and you have a bust-line, and the hair falls off your face and off your legs, and the muscles fall out of your arms. But I think it will be quite a while before a natural transvestite will be able to get a job, unless she's a young transvestite with no hair on her face and very feminine looking.

Isn't it dangerous sometimes when someone thinks you're a woman and then they find out you're a man?

Yes it is. You can lose your life. I've almost lost my life five times; I think I'm like a cat. A lot of times I pick up men, and they think I'm a woman and then they try to rob me. I remember the first time I ever had sex with a man, and I was in the Bronx. It was a Spanish man, I was trying to hustle him for carfare to come back to New York City. And he took my clothes off and he found out I was a boy and he pulled a knife off of his dresser and he threatened me and I had to give him sex for nothing. And I went to a hotel one time, and I told this young soldier that I was a boy, and he didn't want to believe it and then when we got to the hotel I took off my clothes and he found out I was a boy for real and then he got mad and he got his gun and he wanted to shoot me. It's very dangerous being a transvestite going out on dates because it's so easy to get killed. Just recently I got robbed by two men. They robbed me and tried to put a thing around my neck and a blindfold around my face. They wanted to tie my hands and let me out of the car, but I didn't let them tie me up. I just hopped right out of the car. There was two of them, too. I cut my finger by accident, but they snatched my wig. I don't let men tie me up. I'd rather they shoot me with my hands untied. I got robbed once. A man pulled a gun on me and snatched my pocketbook in a car. I don't trust men that much any more. Recently I haven't been dating. I've been going to straight bars and drinking, getting my money that way, giving people conversation, keeping them company while they're at the bar. They buy you a drink, but of course they don't know you're a boy. You just don't go out with any of them. Like my friend; she gets paid for entertaining customers, talking to them, getting them to buy a drink. I'm just learning about this field, I've never been in it before. That's what I've been doing. I've been getting a lot of dollar bills without even doing anything. I tell them I need money for dinner.

Is one of the goals of STAR to make transvestites closer to each other? Do transvestites tend to be a close-knit group of friends?

Usually most transvestites are friendly towards one another because they're just alike. Most transvestites usually get along with one another until it comes to men. The men would separate the transvestites. Because a lot of transvestites could be very good friends, you know, and then when they get a boy-friend. . . Like when I had my husband, he didn't allow me to hang around with transvestites, he wanted me to get away from them all. I felt bad, and I didn't get away from them. He didn't like me to speak to them and hang around with them too much. He wanted me to go in the straight world, like the straight bars and stuff like that.

Do you think there's been any improvement between transves-tites and other gay men since the formation of STAR, within the gay world, within the gay movement?

Well, I went to GAA one time and everybody turned around and looked. All these people that spoke to me there were people that I had known from when I had worked in the Gay Liberation Front community center, but they weren't friendly at all. It's just typical. They're not used to seeing transvestites in female attire. They have a transvestite there, Natasha, but she wears boys' clothes, with no tits or nothing. When they see me or Sylvia come in, they just turn around and they look hard.

Some of the transvestites aren't so political; what do they think about your revolutionary ideas?

They don't even care. I've talked to many of the transvestites up around the Times Square area. They don't even care about a revolution or anything. They've got what they want. Many of them are on drugs. Some of them have lovers, you know. And they don't even come to STAR meetings.

How many people come to STAR meetings?

About 30, and we haven't even been holding STAR meetings recently. Like Sylvia doesn't have a place to sleep, she's staying with friends on 109th St.

Is there something you'd like to add?

I'd like to see STAR get closer to GAA and other gay people in the community. I'd like to see a lot more transvestites come to STAR meetings, but it's hard to get in touch with transvestites. They're at these bars, and they're looking for husbands. There's a lot of transvestites who are very lonely, and they just go to bars to look for husbands and lovers, just like gay men do. When they get married, they don't have time for STAR meetings. I'd like to see the gay revolution get started, but there hasn't been any demonstration or anything recently. You know how the straight people are. When they don't see any action they think, "Well, gays are all forgotten now, they're worn out, they're tired." I would like to see STAR with a big bank account like we had before, and I'd like to see that STAR home again.

Do you have suggestions for people in small towns and cities where there is no STAR?

Start a STAR of their own. I think if transvestites don't stand up for themselves, nobody else is going to stand up for transvestites. If a transvestite doesn't say I'm gay and I'm proud and I'm a transvestite, then nobody else is going to hop up there and say I'm gay and I'm proud and I'm a transvestite for them, because they're not transvestites. The life of a transvestite is very hard, especially when she goes out in the streets.

Is it one of the goals of STAR to create a situation so transvestites don't have to go out in the street?

So we don't have to hustle any more? It's one of the goals of

STAR in the future, but one of the first things STAR has to do is reach people before they get on drugs, 'cause once they get on drugs it's very very hard to get them off and out of the street. A lot of people on the streets are supporting their habits. There's very few transvestites out on the streets that don't use drugs.

What about the term "drag queen." People in STAR prefer to use the term "transvestite." Can you explain the difference?

A drag queen is one that usually goes to a ball, and that's the only time she gets dressed up. Transvestites live in drag. A transsexual spends most of her life in drag. I never come out of drag to go anywhere. Everywhere I go I get all dressed up. A transvestite is still like a boy, very manly looking, a feminine boy. You wear drag here and there. When you're a transsexual, you have hormone treatments and you're on your way to a sex change, and you never come out of female clothes.

You'd be considered a pre-operative transsexual then? You don't know when you'd be able to go through the sex change?

Oh, most likely this year. I'm planning to go to Sweden. I'm working very hard to go.

It's cheaper there than it is at Johns Hopkins?

It's $300 for a change, but you've got to stay there a year.

Do you know what STAR will be doing in the future?

We're going to be doing STAR dances, open a new STAR home, a STAR telephone, 24 hours a day, a STAR recreation center. But this is only after our bank account is pretty well together. And plus we're going to have a bail fund for every transvestite that's arrested, to see they get out on bail, and see if we can get a STAR lawyer to help transvestites in court.

In the meantime if anyone wants to write to STAR for information, what address should they write to?

211 Eldridge Street, Apartment 3, c/o Marcia Johnson, vice president, STAR, New York, N.Y.

What's that thing going to be?

What thing?

That thing you just made.

It's a G-string. Want to see? This is so that if anybody sticks their hand up your dress, they don't feel anything. They wear them at the 82 Club. See? Everybody that's a drag queen knows how to make one. See, it just hides everything.

If they reach up there, they don't find out what's really there!

I don't care if they do reach up there. I don't care if they do find out what's really there. That's their business.

I guess a lot of transvestites know how to fight back anyway!

I carry my wonder drug everywhere I go—a can of Mace. If they attack me, I'm going to attack them, with my bomb.
Did you ever have to use it?
Not yet, but I'm patient.

IV.
GAY
PEOPLE
VS.
THE
"PROFESSIONALS"

LESBIANS AND THE HEALTH CARE SYSTEM

Radicalesbians Health Collective

Introduction

When a group of us got together to write this article, we found that medical doctors, including gynecologists, knew little about women's bodies. They neither knew nor cared about lesbianism. Psychologists, likewise, seemed more interested in the fact that we did not fulfill the heterosexual woman's functions than in how we lived our lives and fulfilled ourselves as lesbians.

When one of us expressed emotional or physical pain not even related to her sexuality, the medical doctor or psychologist told her, "It's all because you're a lesbian." We are put in a non-human category through doctors' ignorance of us.

The road to health is always seen as becoming heterosexual. Especially psychologically, to be well means to have a good relationship with a man. Our problems are not human problems; they are made into lesbian problems which would go away if we became heterosexual.

Heterosexual doctors seek out our problems, not our strengths. They fit the evidence to their assumptions. Analysts tell lesbians, "You're looking for a mother"; why don't they tell heterosexual women, "You're looking for a father"?

It is the responsibility of the health professions to admit when they have no knowledge about us and therefore are incapable of treating us.

There are real pressures in lesbians' lives. These pressures are not in our heads. Any therapy that is honest must validate our anger. We have a right to be angry because there are things wrong with this society and our position in it.

The health system as it is now postulates superior-inferior relationships where the professional knows everything and the lesbian patient has no right to speak for herself. What we need is advice and support from people in an equal relationship with us.

The health system is geared to serving the heterosexual nuclear family not the personal family made up of people we love. One lesbian said, "Under the usual health plan my father can receive blood if he needs it but my friends and lovers can't. If these people needed help I would be unable to sign legal papers to admit them to a hospital. My friends and lovers are not considered my 'immediate family.'" Lesbians are considered "single," as opposed to "married," and are discriminated against.

Instead of the current health plans there should be mutual concern contracts which groups of three or four persons could sign.

We demand that health "professionals" stop destroying our lives by teaching that lesbianism is a sickness that should be cured or abolished. They perpetuate and give validity to a society where lesbians are forced to hide. We are emotionally and economically punished when our lesbianism is known. If we work for the government we must sign forms that say we do not engage in any "sexual perversions." We answer, "No," knowing that our life style is considered a perversion by this society. In fact, no matter who we work for and in almost every aspect of our daily lives it is assumed that human = heterosexual. Laws and institutions that discriminate against us must be changed or abolished entirely.

It is the responsibility of the medical and psychological professions to educate themselves to the validity of lesbianism as a life style. Stop negating our existence. Affirm it.

Personal Testimony

D: I was in therapy for about ten months (two or three times a week) at the post-doctoral clinic of one of the country's most prestigous clinical training programs. This clinic has a reputation for "liberalism" and my shrink considered himself a left-liberal. Understanding his inability to help me, the way he further confused me in so many areas, is to get some insight into the failure of liberalism as an ideological perspective.

My shrink agreed that women are oppressed. (He gave verbal assent to my women's liberation talk.) However, the focus of my therapy was how I contributed to my own oppression. Once, I was talking about a guy I knew that I wanted to know better. I felt that I couldn't say to this guy, "M., I'd like to see you." I felt dependent on M. making the first move. Dr. X told me, "You know, you do have other options." I asked what they were and he told me, "Well, you can flirt." I was furious. One, I know that. Two, any man that I'd like to know would be someone I wouldn't want to flirt with. And, three, that's like telling me I can shuffle. "I know I can shuffle," I said, "I've been a woman for 24 years." Then he asked why I was so angry at his response. He implied that if I was really together about women's liberation I wouldn't have gotten so angry. Later, when I left him I realized that if I was really together I would have gotten ten times as angry, but at that time I almost swallowed his analysis.

Sometimes, Dr. X. would be real understanding of my anger. He would say, "It's all right to be angry." But he wouldn't say my anger was Right On. And that's the difference between a liberal and radical approach to psychotherapy. I need my anger validated. You have to see the reality of my oppression. His thing always was, "Why do you *feel* so oppressed." (The answer is, "Because I am.") In some ways he made me see how much of the female role I'd internalized. But he never helped me to understand that I'd internalized it because of real coercive pressures. Being intelligent and aggressive, wanting always to "speak my piece," there were tremendous pressures on me to conform. I just wasn't going to get love and approval being who I was.

During the spring I began talking to my shrink about my feelings toward my roommate. A. was the first woman I'd met who took herself as seriously as I took myself, who took me as seriously as I wanted to be taken. When A. and I began talking about our sexual feelings for each other I took much of my conflict and confusion to Dr. X. In spite of the fact that this person really loved me, that she was the closest person in my life and that our communication was the most effective I'd ever experienced, I never felt Dr. X in any way validating or authenticating the love. Rather, he encouraged me to get in touch with all my ambivalencies about the love, without ever clarifying where those ambivalencies came from. He thought it was "normal" and "healthy" to be hesitant about a homosexual relationship, so he'd validate all my fears.

In April A. and I made love for the first time. It was after much talking about all our feelings. I got very scared and withdrew right away. I was terrified of being a "lesbian," but Dr. X didn't see that. I had rationales that he didn't see beneath because they're the same rationales every "straight" person uses to avoid sexual contact with someone of the same sex. "Well, I wanted to try it, I thought it was nice but it's just not for me." It was because of my tremendous love for A. and her insight into my feelings that I began to re-examine what my withdrawing from a sexual-love relationship meant. I knew no women who were relating to women; A. and I were totally isolated. Dr. X never in any way suggested that my fear might grow out of my isolation, out of real pressures from the world out there to conform, that they could be anything but intra-psychic conflicts.

After the May strike my political feelings really blossomed. I was involved with a man who validated both my feelings toward A. and my anger toward Dr. X. I decided that "therapy" wasn't helping me much and I wanted to leave. But you're not supposed to leave "therapy" until the therapist decides you're ready. Any expression of self, any assertion of self that isn't according to their cues or formulas is seen as "defensiveness."

I didn't show up at my sessions for a week. Dr. X called and I told him my decision. He asked me to come discuss it with him. I wanted to meet for coffee, or in the Student Center—anywhere we could talk as people rather than as doctor-patient. He refused. I finally agreed to meet him in his office. We talked about why I was leaving and I asked him to explain to me why he thought I should stay. He gave me three reasons: "You have a tendency to doubt your own judgment. You have a tendency toward submissive relationships with men. And you have unexplored homosexual feelings." At first I got really frightened by that list, I thought, "He's really got me, maybe I really do need therapy." Then I realized those statements could apply to almost any woman in our society. Submissiveness and self-doubt are nurtured in women. It's ironic that Dr. X thought I'd be cured of these problems by continuing in my submissive relationship to him, doubting my own judgment about myself and the situation we were in, and accepting his. The implication that my "homosexual" feelings were part of my problem and that they could be dealt with in a one-to-one relationship with a man is astounding.

I don't think women should be in therapy with male therapists. Women who have conflicts should try to resolve them in women's groups. If that's not possible they should see women therapists with gay and feminist consciousness.

A. and I are now lovers. I feel more authentic, more in touch with myself, more productive than I ever have. More of myself has been validated, supported, helped to grow and change than in any relationship I've had.

F: I wasn't going to talk about my relationship with my analyst but I will. First, there was never any support for my relationship with any other woman. There was always something wrong with it and the best I could get out of her was, "Well, maybe if you work very hard it won't be too bad." Also, there was never any equality between us. She used to call me by my first name and I never called her anything. One day I asked her if I could call her by her first name and she said, "You can not. I'm Miss X to you." That was almost the last time I saw her.

She was a woman of about 45. She was having a very hard time because she was breaking up with her boyfriend. She used to come in twenty minutes to half an hour late. Once she missed the appointment completely. And I used to say, poor X. One day I was five minutes late and she said, "Why are you so late?" So I said, "Well, traffic is heavy." She said, "Did you really want to get here?" I said, "What do you mean? You've been late for weeks." She said, "That's not relevant." I got mad and I said to her, "You've been having such a hard time, but if I have trouble it's always because I'm a lesbian. If my job is too hard for me today it's because I'm a lesbian." Maybe if I struggled very hard I might manage to come up to a low level of human existence.

This is a woman that I genuinely like. She said some things I believed. But there was always this tearing down at the root of her analysis. Everything was because I was a lesbian and it was always negative. One time I was talking about women's liberation and she said, "How do you know? You're a woman but you don't act like one." The fact that I could hold a good job seemed to be the one really acceptable thing about me. One day I came in a dress. She looked me up and down. She seemed to be thinking, "I see you can look acceptable."

All the time she said I couldn't call her by her first name, that I wasn't in a personal relationship with her, she let me see that she was miserable about her breakup. One day I said, "Well, it's obvious that you're having a hard time in your personal life." She said, "How can you be so insensitive as to mention that to me." She was saying, how could you be so insensitive as to bring up the fact that I'm not functioning perfectly. I met her at a play and she was with a man. She was sitting directly in front of me. Throughout the play she spent the whole time looking at this man. She could not enjoy herself although she seemed to like the play because the man was bored by it. She spent the whole time looking at him for approval. I couldn't reconcile this. She kept putting down women's liberation—"It's just a matter of temperament."

D: Why did you initially go to see her? What did you think this therapy situation would do for you?

F: I needed someone to talk to. I developed a lot of affection for her. I see that she's suffered. She's an attractive woman, but there's not one thing about her that she was born with. I told her this one day and she told me even her contact lenses were tinted. I found a great deal of value in specific things she said to me that no one else would have said—it's sometimes very good to have your mind put on different trains of thought—and if I was in great distress and had no place else to go I'd trust her and go back, yet in her whole philosophy she expected all kinds of human consideration for herself and her failings but there was very little for the patient. There was no support. There was just, "You're very lucky that you haven't committed suicide because you're a lesbian." From there, there might be hope for you.

D: Did she want you to be straight?

F: She suggested, "Well, I think that there might be some hope for you. Why don't you be straight?" I said, "I don't want to be straight," and she kept saying, "Well, I can't force you." There was a put-down of the women that I loved. "If it wasn't for these women your life would be so much better—if you were straight." It happens that I only have one male friend who is straight. I told her that many of the things she was putting down women for were duplicated in this man's personality. I felt that she had linked herself in some way with me and was supporting her own life by putting mine down. I think that may be what a lot of gay people come up against when they see an analyst no matter how well-meaning. Just the fact that you're gay and they're straight makes them better and they can keep pushing themselves up and you down.

D: They haven't explored their own gay feelings at all and they're just threatened by you.

F: I was not a full human being because I was not straight. There was no way to move the philosophy of the analysis beyond this despite the fact that I ended up trying to counsel her and there was an emotional rapport between us. I stopped seeing her around December 15 and by January 1 I felt a great release of energy that I think I was pouring into the analysis. I was always exhausted when it was over. Whether I could have used that energy in the same way if I had not had analysis, I don't know.

Now I'm going to talk about what I had intended to talk about. I have a wonderful woman gynecologist.

D: It's so hard to find a woman doctor, whether she's good or bad. How long have you been going to her?

F: About eight years. I had a vaginal infection that she couldn't cure. She said, "Maybe you have diabetes. Go to your regular doctor and he'll give you a test." I had a medical doctor for about three years whom I "inherited" from a woman doctor. He was her doctor and she retired. I went to him and told him I had this infection and that my gynecologist suggested he give me a diabetes test as well as check any other condition that he thought I might have. He asked me about my sex life and I told him that I was a lesbian. He looked at me and said, "Well, what do you expect?" I said, "What do you mean?" He said, "You engage in lesbian sexual activities and that leads to infections." Then he said, "Women just have these infections and that's all there is to it. You're a woman and you have to suffer." He literally said that. I said, "What do you mean? You haven't made a study of this. You belong to a very big hospital and there must be some doctor who made some study and knows something." He said, "No. Women just have to suffer. Maybe if you lived in an old fashioned way and didn't have much sexual contact and douched often then it would be better. Otherwise, you just have to suffer. And I think since you're a lesbian I'm going to give you a venereal disease test." I said, "No, you're not." By this time he had already taken my blood for the diabetes test because I was so stunned that I let him take my blood in the midst of this discussion. I was desperate to get rid of this infection and the whole thing was too much for me. He said, "Now that I have your blood I'm sending it for a venereal disease test." I said, "You are not." He said, "You're a lesbian and how do you know who you consort with?" I said, "I'm very sure of these things. My life is very definite. I don't want my blood going for this test." Meanwhile, he had my blood. I couldn't grab it out of his hand. I said, "You're not treating me in any way I expected you to or any way you ever treated me before. All of a sudden I've turned into an outcast, a pariah that deserves to be sick. There's no cure for it because after all women have to suffer." He said, "I have no time to talk to you any further. I have another patient and you must leave immediately." He pushed me out the door. I left and I called him from the corner because at that point the rage had built up. I said, "You've treated me in a way you wouldn't treat anyone else. You cast all kinds of aspersions on my personal life suggesting that I don't even know who I had contact with, that I have venereal disease. Of course, what else would I have because I'm so sexually depraved that I don't even know what I'm doing? I don't want you to do anything with my blood." He said, "You're a very sick young lady and it's not my problem. Take it up with your analyst." He hung up on me. He never sent me any notice about tests or any bill. I never tried to contact him. I respect the woman who sent me to him. He was a perfectly ordinary and capable doctor. He turned into a monster the minute sex of any sort was mentioned.

I never had the courage to admit to my gynecologist what happened. She would ask me if I had the blood test done. I would say, "Not yet." I was ashamed to tell a woman I thought so highly of—what would she think of this story?

She found out about some tests that were being done on this particular infection and got me medicine that seemed to be successful at a great deal of trouble to herself. She had to look up many records and accounts of experiments. I know that if I had to depend on any variation of the mentality of the medical doctor for my gynecological care I would still be sick. It was only through the good will of this woman who really believed that women don't have to suffer that I am well. There's no provision in medical science to cure these things. It was obvious that she single-handedly went through papers and files and talked to doctors.

Q: Did you ever tell anyone about this doctor? Did you try to report him to anyone?

F: I told my analyst and she said, "Of course he was acting improperly." It just goes around and around. You put your mental and physical life, especially your physical life, in the hands of people who have no concern. They really think you're condemned to suffer. The minute that you say you're a lesbian, whatever minimum sympathy, interest or concern was coming through is immediately shut off. It's transformed into clinical interest—you're all right as an exception to the general rule of lesbians as long as you act nice. I'll treat you if you act nice, take everything I dish out and don't complain. When I went for the diabetes test it was obvious before he could show me what he was thinking that I was at a low ebb. I was very desperate, I was in a lot of physical pain. This was his response to someone who was desperately frightened and who had given up hope.

A: I want to talk about a shrink I went to a year ago. I'd gone to a lot of shrinks and they were all men. I was so male identified at that time that I preferred a man, thinking they were more intelligent and more perceptive. When I went to this shrink I was involved with a junky who was also a psychopath. I was in such a bad way that however the shrink treated me helped. He was a hypnotherapist and a behaviorist. I thought for a long time that he saved my life. He helped me get away but the way he did it was evil—he built me up as an object and ultimately as a sexual object for men in terms of his own preferences. He told me I was attractive, intelligent, charming—to make me see how I appeared to men. There was hope for me, I could have a happy life. I started dressing up and men noticed me on the streets. It was such a contrast to the life I'd been living that I really enjoyed it. I was brainwashed. When I was under hypnosis he told me, "You're going to start wearing skirts." I never asked him to tell me that. But I really liked it. When men noticed me it was positive reinforcement. I wouldn't wear pants. I identified sanity with wearing skirts. I became the attractive young uptown woman who had lots of boyfriends and went out. At first it made me feel better to have affection, to be wanted—but the affection lacked human feeling. Men would take me to dinner, be nice to me, have a good time in bed. Then I became acquainted with the women's movement. I saw through this creature he had made of me because of my terror and the really bad place I had been. Shrinks are in that kind of position, especially the men, having woman going to them with trust. They're really damaging because they're taken so seriously.

D: What you said before about the equation between sanity and femininity is a beautiful analysis. On some level, all our shrinks did it.

A: Last summer was the last time I wore a dress—it was sort of like a trial. The way I felt walking down the street, I could have sworn I had pricetags attached to my legs and breasts. I wanted to run home and change. I wondered how I could have been so willing to expose myself. I saw men looking at me—it was the ugliest thing.

Another shrink I saw when I was eighteen was a Reichian therapist. I don't feel I've ever fully recovered from some of the Reichian axioms. Sanity is equated with the ability to experience orgasm which is defined heterosexually. One of the goals of the therapy is to have the patient in a fully adjusted heterosexual relationship. The shrink I went to told me I was all woman. I accepted that view of the world. Men and women were made for each other. This was the natural order. One of my main goals was to find a male mate. I went through a lot of sexual experiences. That was the main material the therapy dealt with—the quality of that sexual relationship. The sane expression of a woman is to have vaginal orgasms. Reich makes no distinction between a clitoral and a vaginal orgasm but says most women do not experience full orgasms because they're armored, which means they have muscular tensions which are blocking their life energy inside their body. It wouldn't be just male ignorance of a woman's body, it would be some kind of tension in herself. I believed there was something wrong, because I didn't have full orgasms or any at all for a while. When I finally started having orgasms, I believed I was healthier. I never connected it to more physical knowledge of my body—I was getting more clitoral friction. It's a totally sexist way of seeing the world to say that a woman's role is to relate sexually to a man.

I trusted Reich's theories because his healthy male model was not macho at all, he was gentle. Both male and female were to be open and giving. I never questioned the heterosexual system because he didn't put men in a controlling role. Someone told me that at Summerhill, with a free environment, the women turned out to be more aggressive and the men were more gentle. But A.S.

Neil, the founder of Summerhill, took over Reich's assumptions and put down homosexuality. Neil's only analysis of homosexuality is that it's some kind of perversion of the natural order.

W: There's a question and answer section in Neil's book, *Summerhill,* and one question asks: Do you think certain ways of touching are wrong? Neil said anything done in a loving spirit is fine. But when he got to homosexuality, he called it mutual masturbation.

S: And we all know masturbation is bad!

W: He said about homosexuals, "These people are sharing their guilt over masturbation."

A: Reich accepts Freud's heterosexual bias and builds on that. He did discover a lot of valid things about people but he took over that assumption and, working from there, can only have the conclusion that any homosexual experiences are a perversion of one's natural direction. I question that.

D: Did you feel guilty because you couldn't find the ideal man?

A: My Reichian therapist said men were more armored than women and couldn't open up to a soft, open woman.

D: Right on. But he didn't know what the next step after that is.

A: That's true. I had to continue in this difficult search for this rare man that didn't seem to exist.

F: Talk about the scandal about your second analyst, the behaviorist, not having any credentials. People are conditioned to put so much trust in medical doctors or analysts. Then you find out what they really are after you have tortured yourself because you weren't living up to their dictates.

A: The behaviorist had created a reputation for himself. He built himself up in the eyes of his patients. He mentioned he had cured cancer patients.

F: Of what?

D: Homosexuality!

A: He had aborted women. He had cured patients of cancer through hypnotic suggestion. He was arrested recently because his claims were uncovered as false. He had been training some ex-patients as hypnotherapists and they were supposed to get a certificate from a university. One of them checked and found it never existed. That led to other questions. The hospital he was supposed to have worked at said they never knew him. He never was trained by the therapist he said had trained him.

Many of his patients were young women college students who found him attractive. He went to bed with many of his women patients. Even with me, he tried to build up love. He would half-jokingly say when I was under hypnosis, "When you come out of hypnosis you'll fall in love with me." Through hypnosis he got a lot of things he wanted from women. Probably other therapists do similar things just because of their position and have affairs with their patients.

S: Something the gay community is talking about now is that behaviorists use shock treatment to stop gay people from having gay feelings. They take a gay man and show him a picture of a man and give him electric shocks. They show him a picture of a woman and don't give him the shocks.

A: He fully supported that therapy. He marvelled that it was used so effectively in Russia that they had no homosexuals; they cured all of them through this shock treatment—aversion conditioning, I think it was called—associating something painful with a stimulus. This doctor asked me if I would pose for some pictures which would be positive reinforcement for a male homosexual patient he was trying to cure. I have to say this: He didn't tell the patient what was wrong with him. The patient went to him saying, "I want to be cured of homosexuality," and he took over from there.

S: He wouldn't try to find scientific means to turn a black person white. Only someone who already believes there is something wrong with being gay would do something like that.

D: One of the things about behaviorism and a lot of liberal psychology—it pretends to be value-free when it's not. It is anti-homosexual, it is anti any real liberation for women.

F: Did you talk about your homosexuality with him?

A: This was before I had any gay experiences or gay consciousness.

S: I've known about my feelings for women since I was about twelve. But I never had anyone to tell them to. I always was alone in those feelings. I knew that I couldn't tell it to my family doctor because there's a basic heterosexual assumption coming from the medical profession, from everywhere. I remember when I was about eighteen asking my family doctor for birth control and he blushed. He gave me some Cequin, which later turned out to be one of the most dangerous brands. He walked out of the room for me to read the label and came back and said he wouldn't tell my mother. The reason I was getting it wasn't even for birth control, it was so I would have less pain from menstruation. I knew I couldn't tell him anything.

When I was about sixteen I was seeing a psychologist who was very good and was a feminist. She was a white liberal very active in the civil rights demonstrations then. She didn't get married until she was about 29. She was the first person I spoke to who was a model for me other than my family where the women got married when they were fifteen. She was going for her second PhD. She was married to a gynecologist who she told off for expecting her to be a housewife. One day I told her that I didn't understand why when I was on the subways I found myself gazing at women. She asked me, "When you look at women, what do you fantasize?", and I told her I fantasize making love. She said, "Do you imagine having a penis?", and I assumed the answer was yes. So I said, "I think so," and she said, "Don't worry. That means you're going through a late adolescent stage that you'll outgrow. It's something that thirteen-year-olds usually go through when they're going through puberty wondering about what the opposite sex is feeling." I never outgrew it. Luckily. But what that did to me was that I kept waiting to outgrow it. I kept feeling that that was part of my childishness and this childishness was a bad thing.

I joined the movement after that and because I'd had horrendous experiences with psychologists and medical doctors, I started going to movement doctors, people who were trying to break down the whole hierarchy of professional and patient. I started seeing this dermatologist because I didn't have any money for a mononucleosis test and he was going to take me free. He had me come when his nurse wasn't there. He was a young doctor. All I was getting was a shot in the finger to test for mono. I walked in and he said, "Take your clothes off." I took my clothes off. He pricked my finger and took the test and told me to get dressed and come back next week. I was angry but I couldn't deal with it because he was a doctor—I was intimidated. I found out the people who recommended the doctor were into free love. They had met him in a clinic in one of the major hospitals and while he was examining the woman they fucked, and they hadn't bothered to tell me that was why he was so groovy. I felt there was something wrong with me that I felt funny about getting undressed. I got sick but was so intimidated by doctors that instead of going to get cured I spent a month in bed hemorrhaging from ulcerated colitis.

Finally, I went to a radical woman doctor. She doesn't charge anything. One of the Gay Liberation Front women was referred to GLF by her. Even in this good context she was filling in a form and one of the questions she asked me was, "Do you use birth control?", automatically assuming that every woman is heterosexual. My reaction was to say, "No, I have relationships with women." She took it very well. We didn't know whether I had a general vaginal disorder or gonorrhea. She knew that if it was gonorrhea I couldn't have sexual intercourse if I was straight. She said, "Abstain from sexual relationships until we know." I asked her, "Do you mean from intercourse or do you mean from oral sex or do you mean from touching?", and she didn't know the answer. She had to call a research friend to find out how it spreads and they didn't know. The whole medical profession ignores homosexuality. They don't know. They ignore sexuality. What she was saying was: because I don't know you can't have sex for six weeks.

I freaked out during the summer and I needed someone to talk to. Since I joined the women's movement I found I didn't need a therapist. Most of the things people need a therapist for are people to talk to regularly, people to take their pain to, and in consciousness-raising the group provides this and also an analysis of the real causes of the pain. But I needed a more individual thing. I found a good therapist through a lesbian organization. It's a different kind of therapy than with men therapists. I had tried six men therapists and walked out crying. From a lot of reactions she has I think she's either gay or bisexual. Until the time we don't need therapists anymore—I think that's going to happen when consciousness-raising groups, communes and collectives, and different definitions of relationships can take over that function—the only thing I can see is gay people helping gay people. She can't come out and say that she's gay because of all the oppression that she would face in the psychiatric profession. She would probably be fired and then she couldn't help. The kind of support I get from her is that she makes no demand that I should relate to men. It's perfectly valid for me to be relating to women exclusively. A lot of shrinks go on a bisexuality trip. She doesn't talk about it even in terms of, "As long as you have a sickness we might as well make the most of it." I can say things to her. She asked me in the beginning of therapy, "Did you date men when you were younger?", and I said, "Yeah, I went out and dated because that was what I was supposed to do. No one ever told me that I could not date. No one ever told me that I could be gay." She said, "Oh, God, I know." The kind of things she says are the kind of things only someone gay or someone really open would say. Psychology and the whole medical profession the way it is now with its heterosexual assumptions can only mess over gay people's heads. What's needed is a whole new kind of psychology. There's the whole professional situation—me being too intimidated to call her by her first name; her not really being able to be open with me. She's a psychiatric social worker, which is part of why I think I can talk to her. She's not a psychologist, she's not a medical doctor, she's a human being who wants to help people.

In order to see her I had to see a male psychologist in the same clinic. I was depressed so he gave me anti-depressants. My reaction was to fall asleep so he gave me something that would keep me awake, which made me nervous so he gave me tranquilizers. I kept saying, "I don't want to take any pills at all. I don't want to get dependent on pills." He kept saying, "You don't know what you need. I'll decide." One time when he went out of the room I read what he had written about me: "Patient has trouble with her feminine identity." My woman shrink made sure I didn't have to see him anymore. It lasted once every two weeks for about two months. In order to see her I had to see him and he was also helping me stay on welfare. He said, "We can't force you to take the pills but if you're not going to listen to me what's the use of your being here?" They have the power. They can write the notes for you.

W: I felt that I was gay since my early childhood, somewhere around the age of five. I wanted information on lesbianism because as far as I was concerned I had invented it. I eventually found psychology books that "explained" homosexuality to heterosexuals. Lesbian lives were treated as case histories. The idea of two people of the same sex loving each other was considered a disorder. It was assumed that we tried to imitate male-female sex when we made love.

When I was sixteen my mother told me I should see a psychologist because I couldn't get along with her. I thought, "This will give me an opportunity to talk about my feelings about women." In the back of my mind was the idea, "I'm still young enough to be cured so I won't have to have this life of misery." My mother had gotten a form to submit to a clinic saying why I wanted to see a psychologist and I wrote an extra page telling about my lesbian feelings. I got an interview with an old man. He said, "You've written all this about lesbianism. You really shouldn't worry about that. You're much too young. Why don't you take a trip to Israel? Go live on a kibbutz. Chop down trees and you'll forget all about it."

He sent me to a woman therapist. I talked to her about my lesbian feelings. Some of the things she said were: "Pleasure is like candy. You really shouldn't take too much of it or you'll get yourself sick." "You have to learn to deny yourself so you can become mature. There are so many other things in life." "A woman can never make a home for another woman. When my husband comes home at night I can make a home for him. You can only make a home for a man."

When I first went to see a gynecologist I had a vaginal infection. I was about twenty. She asked me about my relationships with men and I managed to say I was a lesbian. She said, "Oh, you play around with women." One time when she was examining me she asked me something to which I answered again that I was a lesbian. Just at that moment she was taking the vaginal clamp out of the cabinet where it is sterilized and it fell on the floor. She picked it up and used it anyway. I felt she did that because I was a lesbian and it didn't matter that something she used on me wasn't sterile. When she handed me medicine at the end of my visits, she actually laughed at me.

I went to see a woman psychologist this year. I'm 27 now. She had a tremendous amount of sympathy for me. At first I felt this as support because I was very unhappy. A long relationship with a woman I loved had just ended. But Dr. X had so little understanding of homosexuality that it was as if she had blocked the whole subject out of her mind. At one point I said, "I feel that a lot of gay women have the same look on their faces." I was about to describe what I meant when she said, "They have a look of guilt." I said, "That was the farthest thought from my mind. Actually, they're nervous because they're afraid they're going to be found out. It has to do with self-preservation." I realized that she was not my friend, she was not neutral, and I was seeing her out of desperation.

J: The first time I went to a psychiatrist I was nineteen. My mother had just died and I was upset and there was nobody in my family I could talk to. I paid $35 a session.

He told me that all my problems would be solved if I found the right man, got married and started a family of my own, since my present family was incomplete. He pointed out that it was time for me to grow up. One of the things that was still keeping me a little girl was my virginity. I would become an adult by falling in love with the right man and fulfilling myself sexually. I happened to be dating a man of 22 named M. on a casual basis. The psychiatrist encouraged me to fantasize about falling in love with M. and marrying him until I finally believed I loved him and was ready to marry him. We became engaged and then Dr. X encouraged me to have sex with M., insisting this would counteract my feeling of loss over my mother's death and would make me feel like a real woman. I felt frustrated because M. and I had not yet become intimate sexually. I had been brought up to believe that as a woman I couldn't initiate a sexual relationship. I was still depressed despite my romance, which didn't change my feelings of loss over my mother's death.

Dr. X told me to take a vacation. I went to a hotel with my aunt. When one of the hotel employees made a pass at me I jumped at the opportunity and had sex with him even though he was a total stranger. I believed I was helping myself grow up and reach womanhood. I returned home and told Dr. X the story. He approved of what I did. He encouraged me to talk about the experience. I pointed out that I was actually very bored sexually. I had felt no sexual arousal during intercourse. I didn't reach orgasm at all. I wanted to find out what was wrong with me. I mentioned to Dr. X that I had been made love to orally by a previous boyfriend and I had no trouble reaching orgasm. I wanted to know why this was.

I was fifteen and sixteen when I was made love to orally and Dr. X used my age against me. He said that when a girl is younger her sexuality is located in the clitoris and I was young enough then to reach orgasm that way. Now that I was older my point of sexual arousal should be in my vagina. I had grown past the phase where my clitoris would provide me sexual pleasure. He said because my mother had died I was attempting to regress to the years when she was alive and one of the things I wanted to do was return to the clitoral orgasm. He said that the way I could get over my depression was to sever my little-girl ties with my mother and start having vaginal orgasms. He said, "Keep away from the clitoris. Don't play with it too much, it's not good." I became upset because when I masturbated I always satisfied myself by stimulating my clitoris. I never touched my vagina. When I went home after the session I tried to arouse myself vaginally from every angle and it didn't work. For the next few weeks I tried to arouse myself clitorally almost to the point of orgasm and then I would stop and put my finger in my vagina and see if I would have an orgasm. All that happened was that I stopped feeling anything. Meanwhile, my sorrow over my mother's death wasn't being dealt with.

I was seeing Dr. X three times a week and when I wanted to go less often he said I was afraid to grow up too fast. I actually believed for a long time afterwards that my body hadn't grown up yet sexually and wasn't ready to have sex with other people. I would masturbate to satisfy myself and feel stupid about it. Dr. X told me that the clitoris becomes permanently enlarged if you touch it too often and people would know I masturbated.

I started to have vaginal intercourse with M. and I still didn't have an orgasm. Dr. X told me it would take time, only therapy would help to take away all the years of concentration on the clitoris. Soon he started to ask if I had sexual dreams or day-dreams about him—he would sit there and pluck his red mustache—it had never crossed my mind. He had tried to hug me goodby from the first visit and I shrugged him off. He asked what I was afraid of and I said I didn't like to be touched like that. When I would say, no, I didn't want him sexually, he would accuse me of lying either to myself or to him. He said I was repressing those fantasies. I tried not to repress them but I still didn't have them.

Dr. X suggested that what I really wanted was to have sex with him. The only way to stop repressing this was to actually have sex with him so I could deal with my feelings. When I said I didn't want to, he said I was still hanging on to my dead mother. At that point, I broke my engagement with M. and stopped seeing Dr. X. But I went crazy for years afterward trying to figure out where my sexuality was.

The next time I saw a psychiatrist I was 23. I'd had a bad drug experience during which I thought I saw and talked with my mother. My old conflicts came back and I had a breakdown. I had come out as a lesbian about ten months before this. Even though I went to the psychiatrist to talk about my mother, he dwelled on my sexuality. He was much better than my first psychiatrist. He really did help me in some ways, but he would say things like, "Well, about your homosexual tendencies—." I would say, "They're not tendencies, they're realities." He would go on, "About these tendencies—." He wasn't blatantly anti-lesbian. It was just that he had no knowledge of lesbians. When I tried to describe my relationships with women he would make comments like, "Oh, you sleep in the same bed?" He was shocked that lesbians had interests beyond their sexuality. He seemed surprised that I and a woman I made love with were also painting her apartment together.

I feel that I came out at this point in my life because there was a movement that helped me come out. My feelings about women would have directed me to be a lesbian for my whole life, except that I was programmed to be a heterosexual. This psychiatrist suggested that I came out now because I had a new feeling of sorrow over my mother's death and was looking for a mother-substitute. He said, "I think you're a lost little girl looking for your mother."

P: When I first went to this psychiatrist over five years ago he said I wasn't gay, the problem was with my mother. He told me to have sexual experiences with men. He thought he would help me out by having sex with me. So we had sex about five or six times during therapy sessions which I paid for. He insulted me when I wore slacks or jeans or anything that didn't seem feminine. Sex was just a mechanical act and I didn't think it would cure anything because it didn't help me relate emotionally to a man. He was shaving during about 80 percent of my sessions. He seemed bored, uninterested. I need affection from men and women and he gave me that affection except I had to be good in order to get it, I couldn't be hostile. I said, "I bet you do this (the sex) to all your women patients," and he said, "If you're going to talk that way you can leave." When I mentioned I was going to see someone else he said, "I bet he charges more than I do," and called me a sneak because I didn't tell him beforehand that I was going to do it.

I have mixed feelings because I might want to go back to him. I need affection. He kissed me and hugged me every session and was tender. I paid about $15 a session. It's hard to say if he did something wrong. Freud would think he was doing the right thing.

W: You saw this psychiatrist for five years?
P: Yes.
W: When did he first suggest that he have sex with you?
P: Around the second year.
W: How did he suggest it?
P: It was a gradual thing. First we were kissing and making out, taking my clothes off, taking his clothes off. It made me happy because I had nothing else. He hinted at having sex—how would I like it? He put it into my fantasies. I wanted it. I didn't want to be a virgin. I wanted to get over my fear of sex.
W: He did this in his office?
P: Yes.
W: How did he decide you had problems with your mother and weren't really gay?
P: Because I've always had crushes on older women.
W: He didn't come to this through talking about your mother? It was through talking about your feelings about older women?
P: Yes. We didn't talk much about my mother until later when I brought it up. At first I talked about my problems with my father.

Conclusion

We want every gynecologist we go to to know all aspects of lesbian sex with relation to gynecology and not to say, "I don't know. There haven't been any studies." We demand that every doctor or psychologist know those facts about lesbianism that are relevant to his or her specialization. The prevailing myths thrive on ignorance.

We demand that doctors know all aspects of society's pressures on us and stop enforcing those pressures themselves, so that they can no longer find the most ordinary details of our lives shocking, ("Oh, you take walks together?"), or ask us insulting questions, ("How does it feel to hold hands on the street?"). We demand that no analyst dare treat homosexuals or lesbians only on the basis of textbook knowledge—some of it ancient, some of it invented in heterosexual men's imaginations —without human contact with us and without having homosexual experiences themselves. Psychologists must stop trying to redirect our energies toward heterosexuality.

We demand that doctors and hospitals acknowledge our lesbian friends and lovers as our true family when it comes to hospitalization or emergencies. Trust the people we trust and allow them to help us.

Women doctors should be encouraged to be gynecologists. Up to now, the field that is closest to our bodies has been treated by men who don't know what it is like to have female genitals or to experience menstruation. Why must we ask men questions about ourselves?

We lesbians must have the full health field open to us without stigma. Women are frightened away from caring for other women's genitals because of taboos on lesbianism. Our genitals most of all belong to men. Must it be a male privilege to inspect a woman's body and tell us how to care for ourselves? We can never honestly ask men our questions because they can never honestly answer them.

There should be neighborhood women's clinics to deal with women's problems. Women should learn to transmit preventative medical care. At present, little information on genitals is transmitted in this society. Care for women's bodies should not be limited and defined by the heterosexual functions of pregnancy and birth control. Sexuality and reproduction should not be linked. Sexuality is emotional; reproduction is a medical/physical fact.

We demand the right to preventative medical care as well as effective treatment for specific ailments, administered to all persons equally without irrelevant discussion of our life style.

We demand the right to obtain psychological help, often needed for problems other than our sexuality, without automatically having our entire lesbian life style questioned.

HEALTHY LESBIAN MINDS IN HEALTHY LESBIAN BODIES!

We would like to hear your experiences with the health care system. Write to us and let us know what your group is doing to organize around lesbian health care issues.

Radicalesbians Health Collective
Women's Center
243 West 20th St.
New York, N.Y. 10010

GAY LIBERATION MEETS THE SHRINKS

Gary Alinder

Walking into the enemy's inner sanctum is an enlightening experience. In the summer of 1970 gay liberation invaded the National Convention of the American Psychiatric Association in San Francisco. We found out how tuned out the shrinks are.

The main convention meeting looked like a refugee camp for Nixon's silent majority. It was 99 and 44/100 percent white, straight, male, middle-aged, upper-middle class. They are the insulated ones—separated in their immaculate garb, cars, country clubs, planes, expensive hotels—protected from emotional involvement by a gibberishy vocabulary which translates humanity into "scientifically" quantifiable and "objective" terms.

Oh yes, psychiatrists come in different stripes; some are right-wingers, many are liberals, a few radicals. But they seem with few exceptions to be caught up in a sense of their unusual importance. They expect to be listened to. They have no qualms about male chauvinism, they've never even thought about it.

And so they couldn't imagine what the woman was getting at when she took the microphone to say: "I want to know what room the women can have to meet together in, and I want to know now." The chairman went on to the next speaker. Another woman got on the microphone: "I don't believe you heard, we want to know what room we can have and we want to know now."

A week after Kent and Cambodia, the psychiatrists had come to discuss business as usual. A caucus of radical psychiatrists described what business as usual would be: "...a panel about American Indians which concentrates on suicide by them rather then genocide by us...learning about aversion treatment for homosexuals—but not considering whether homosexuality is really a psychiatric 'disease'...hearing about drugs, new drugs and old drugs—but not the way drugs are used to tranquilize people who are legitimately upset . . . hearing about psychiatry and law enforcement but not about how our society uses police to oppress people and prevent change...discussing sexuality and abortion—but not the way sex roles are used to oppress women."

I've read psychoanalytic writing on homosexuality. They have a million theories about its "causes" and "cure." As a homosexual, it occurs to me that the shrinks don't know their elbows from their assholes.

I don't so much mind people playing intellectual games. (How many angels can dance on the head of a pin?) But psychiatrists hold power to inflict their games on people.

As a young homosexual you feel alone, you need answers but there's no one to talk to. So you read books or end up under the "care" of a psychiatrist. You find out how sick you are. The reactionaries want to cure you through brainwashing, shock treatments or castration. The liberals just want you to be "happy." Of course they know homosexuality is an inferior way of life, but they have little faith in cures and encourage their patients to adapt to the "deviation." A minority of shrinks say that homosexuality falls within the "range of normality." Those with the latter view kept coming up to Gay Liberation people after the sessions: "We agree with you, so what's your complaint?"

One of our replies was: "You do? Why don't you tell the world? Silence is also a crime."

One of the worst mind-pigs is Dr. Irving Bieber, Professor of Psychiatry at New York Medical College. Listen to Dr. Bieber: "A (male) homosexual adaptation is a result of hidden and incapacitating fears of the opposite sex...frequent fear of disease or injury to the genitals!...frequently includes attempts to solve problems involving the father.... The combination of sexual over-stimulation and intense guilt and anxiety about heterosexual behavior promote precocious and compulsive activity.... By the time the son has reached the preadolescent period, he has suffered a diffuse personality disorder. Pathologically dependent upon his mother and beset by feelings of inadequacy, impotence and self-contempt.... Mothers of homosexuals are usually inadequate wives. They tend to dominate and minimize their husbands and frequently hold them more or less openly in contempt.... Often there is a sense of identification with a minority group which has been discriminated against. Homosexual society, however, is neither 'healthy' nor 'happy.' Life within this society tends to reinforce, fixate and add new disturbing elements to the entrenched psychopathology of its members." (Irving

Bieber, *Homosexuality: A Psychoanalytic Study of Male Homosexuals.)*

When we heard that Bieber and company were coming to the American Psychiatric Association convention, we knew that we had to be there. And we were—on the convention floor microphone:

"We've listened to you long enough; you listen to us. We're fed up with being told we're sick. You're the ones who are sick. We're gay and we're proud"—bearded Konstantin running around in a bright red dress.

Andy laying it on the twenty shrinks who show up for a Gay Liberation workshop. Gay guerrillas in the balcony sailing a paper airplane down to the convention floor when the delegates voted for a two-year study of violence.

Bieber is almost too good a target. His views are grotesquely reactionary; personally he is old, with a pinched face and nasal voice. A few days later we dealt with Nathaniel McConaghy of Australia. Young, charming, sympathetic. ("I've gone on television urging an end to discrimination against homosexuals.") He reported his "research" as part of the program entitled "Issues on Sexuality."

From a summary of his paper: "With apomorophine therapy, the patient was given injections of apomorophine after which he viewed slides of males while experiencing the resultant nausea. With aversion-relief, the patient received painful electric shocks after reading aloud phrases describing aspects of homosexual behavior. Following a series of shocks he read aloud a phrase describing an aspect of heterosexual behavior, and this was not followed by a shock..."

The Veterans Memorial Auditorium is nearly full—about twenty women's liberation people, fifteen gay liberation people scattered through the 300 psychiatrists as McConaghy begins his paper. Shouts of "vicious," "torture," "get your rocks off that way?" McConaghy stops, apparently he'd expected trouble. "If you'll just listen, I'm sure you'll find I'm on your side." Intermittant heckling continues, but he completes his paper. Five minutes of discussion and the chairman announces it's time to go on to the next paper. "We've listened to you, now you listen to us," we shout. "We've waited 5,000 years." The chairman responds, "Can't you just wait a half hour longer?" "We've waited long enough, we've waited long enough," comes our chant. With two papers still unread, the chairman announces, "This meeting is adjourned."

We are in a room of enraged psychiatrists. "They should be killed," shouts one. "Give back our air fare," shouts another.

Maria DeSantos reads from a women's liberation statement: "Women come to you suffering from depression. Women ought to feel depressed with the roles society puts on them.... Those roles aren't biological, those roles are learned.... It started when my mother threw me a doll and my brother a ball..."

Michael Itkin reads the gay liberation demands. Anarchy. Knots of people talking loudly all over the room. Shrinks coming up asking us what we want. Finally, some discussion.

Dozens of gay brothers and sisters have told me what awful experiences they've had with shrinks. "I was in and out of mental hospitals for three years. I know how to talk their language, and they're motherfuckers," a brother told me. Another said, "When I was about nineteen, I read Bieber's book; that set me back two or three years. Then I went to a psychiatrist who took Bieber as gospel; finally after a year I stopped."

Rather than dealing with a sick society, the shrinks deal with the individual members of that society. Conform, fit in, straighten up, the shrink tells us. "Something's wrong? It's in your head." And for the privilege of getting such advice, we pay them $30 an hour, and more.

One of gay liberation's demands to the convention was the abolition of psychiatry as an oppressive tool. The more I think about it, the more I favor the abolition of psychiatry, period.

"We've known 4,000 years of violence, don't fight us, fuck us; don't shoot us, suck us."

Bruce heckling the man in a booth selling shock treatment machines. He demonstrates a machine which shows slides of nude males during which the male patient is painfully shocked; the next slide is of a female, the patient receives no shock.

Finally we found Dr. Bieber on a panel. (Transsexualism vs. Homosexuality: Distinct Entities?) By this time I'm really angry: "You are the pigs who make it possible for the cops to beat homosexuals: they call us queer; you—so politely—call us sick. But it's the same thing. You make possible the beatings and rapes in prisons, you are implicated in the torturous cures perpetrated on desperate homosexuals. I've read your book, Dr. Bieber, and if that book talked about black people the way it talks about homosexuals, you'd be drawn and quartered and you'd deserve it."

Bieber answers; "I never said homosexuals were sick, what I said was that they have displaced sexual adjustment." Much laughter from us: "That's the same thing, motherfucker." He tries again, "I don't want to oppress homosexuals; I want to liberate them, to liberate them from that which is paining them—their homosexuality." That used to be called genocide.

A LEAFLET FOR
THE AMERICAN MEDICAL ASSOCIATION

Chicago Gay Liberation Front

From its outset, the gay liberation movement has identified establishment psychiatry as a basic institution involved in the oppression of homosexuals. On Aug. 24, 1970, the *New York Times* published a front page report entitled "Homosexuals In Revolt," in which it chose to give a considerable amount of space to the psychiatrists' view of the gay movement. One of the shrinks, Dr. Lionel Ovesey, a professor of clinical psychiatry at the Columbia University College of Physicians and Surgeons, told the *Times*; "Homosexuality is a psychiatric or emotional illness. I think it's a good thing if someone can be cured of it because it's so difficult for a homosexual to find happiness in our society. It's possible that this movement could consolidate the illness in some people, especially among young people who are still teetering on the brink." The following analysis of the oppression of homosexuals by establishment psychiatry originally appeared on a leaflet distributed by Chicago Gay Liberation to doctors attending the convention of the American Medical Association in 1970.

The establishment school of psychiatry is based on the premise that people who are hurting should solve their problems by "adjusting" to the situation. For the homosexual, this means becoming adept at straight-fronting, learning how to survive in a hostile world, how to settle for housing in the gay ghetto, how to be satisfied with a profession in which homosexuals are tolerated, and how to live with low self-esteem.

The adjustment school places the burden on each individual homosexual to learn to bear his torment. But the "problem" of homosexuality is never solved under this scheme; the anti-homosexualist attitude of society, which is the cause of the homosexual's trouble, goes unchallenged. And there's always another paying patient on the psychiatrist's couch.

Dr. Socarides claims, "A human being is sick when he fails to function in his appropriate gender identity, which is appropriate to his anatomy." Who determined "appropriateness"? The psychiatrist as moralist? Certainly there is no scientific basis for defining "appropriate" sexual behavior. In a study of homosexuality in other species and other cultures, Ford and Beach in *Patterns of Sexual Behavior* conclude, "Human homosexuality is not a product of hormonal imbalance or 'perverted heredity.' It is the product of the fundamental mammalian heritage of general sexual responsiveness as modified under the impact of experience."

Other than invoking moral standards, Dr. Socarides claims that homosexuality is an emotional illness because of the guilt and anxieties in homosexual life. Would he also consider Judaism an emotional illness because of the paranoia which Jews experienced in Nazi Germany?

We homosexuals of gay liberation believe that the adjustment school of therapy is not a valid approach to society.

We refuse to adjust to our oppression, and believe that the key to our mental health, and to the mental health of all oppressed peoples in a racist, sexist, capitalist society, is a radical change in the structure and accompanying attitudes of the entire social system.

Mental health for women does not mean therapy for women—it means the elimination of male supremacy. Not therapy for blacks, but an end to racism. The poor don't need psychiatrists (what a joke at 25 bucks a throw!)—they need democratic distribution of wealth. OFF THE COUCHES, INTO THE STREETS!

We see political organizing and collective action as the strategy for effecting this social change. We declare that we are healthy homosexuals in a sexist society, and that homosexuality is at least on a par with heterosexuality as a way for people to relate to each other (know any men that don't dominate women?).

Since the prevalent notion in society is that homosexuality is wrong, all those who recognize that this attitude is damaging to people, and that it must be corrected, have to raise their voices in opposition to anti-homosexualism. Not to do so is to permit the myth of homosexual pathology to continue and to comply in the homosexual's continued suffering from senseless stigmatization.

A psychiatrist who allows a homosexual patient—who has been subject to a barrage of anti-homosexual sentiments his whole life—to continue in the belief that heterosexuality is superior to homosexuality, is the greatest obstacle to his patient's health and well-being.

We furthermore urge psychiatrists to refer their homosexual patients to gay liberation (and other patients who are victims of oppression to relevant liberation movements). Once relieved of patients whose guilt is not deserved but imposed, psychiatrists will be able to devote all their effort to the rich—who do earn their guilt but not their wealth, and can best afford to pay psychiatrists' fees.

We are convinced that a picket and a dance will do more for the vast majority of homosexuals than two years on the couch. We call on the medical profession to repudiate the adjustment approach as a solution to homosexual oppression and instead to further homosexual liberation by working in a variety of political ways (re-educating the public, supporting pickets, attending rallies, promoting social events, etc.) to change the situation of homosexuals in this society.

Join us in the struggle for a world in which all human beings are free to love without fear or shame.

SURVIVING PSYCHOTHERAPY

Christopher Z. Hobson

Through such actions as the disruption of the American Psychiatric Association convention in the summer of 1970, the gay liberation movement has focused attention on psychiatrists' treatment of homosexuality. Some writers have criticized Freudian and neo-Freudian theories of homosexuality; others have exposed barbaric clinical practices such as the use of electroshock "therapy." Little has been written, however, about the experience of psychotherapy.

My own experiences were not dramatic: I never had shock treatment, I never even encountered the gay analogue of the hair-raisingly male-chauvinist statements reported by some women's liberation activists who have had psychotherapy.

My therapists—there were three over the years—were all intelligent, somewhat sensitive men. I cannot even claim that they tried to convince me that homosexuality was an illness; the product of an orthodox upbringing, I was convinced before I ever consulted them. All I can claim is that their treatment contributed nothing to my awareness of myself and even retarded it; that this was connected to their view of homosexuality as an illness; that my self-understanding eventually grew from quite different sources.

I first applied the term "homosexual" to myself when I was

fourteen. If I wasn't then an irreversible homosexual, I was fast becoming one: almost all my sexual inclinations were toward males, virtually none toward females. I sought psychotherapy when I was seventeen, basically because I desperately wanted to be heterosexual. I was in therapy in my last year in high school and for four years in college. Nothing changed—though I did gain insight into various personal and especially family relationships. For two years after college I was a teacher; then I was fired for a homosexual affair with a student. Beginning graduate school, I began therapy again and continued for five years on a once-weekly basis.

In my teens I tried actively not to be homosexual. Even when I stopped trying, at 22, I didn't accept being gay—I merely decided to express it *until something changed,* because I realized that in trying not to love men, I was losing the ability to love at all. Not until I was 25 did I begin to see homosexuality as something that shouldn't be despised, and not until I was 28—only one year ago—did I "come out" in the sense of beginning to live openly as a homosexual. Only then, moreover, did I actively step into gay life and begin to meet other gay people. During those fourteen years I had almost no sexual contacts and was, naturally, unhappy, frustrated and confused. If my entry into gay life seems unusually late, I am convinced this isn't so: while manning a gay liberation telephone in recent months, I have talked to many like myself.

During those fourteen years of waste and unnecessary grief, my psychotherapists exposed none of what was really wrong. Please note: this means *what I now believe was really wrong.* Biased, yes—but true in my experience; I will stand on my judgment and on that standard so regularly invoked by psychotherapists themselves, success. In my opinion, I am healthier now.

I was not the happy homosexual who doesn't enter Dr. Socarides' office (and doesn't enter his statistics). There I was—in my teens, guilty about masturbation (my only form of sexual expression) and about homosexuality; occasionally thinking suicide; drawn into passionate friendships with "straight" males and either guilty about the sexual element or blind to it; infrequently but regularly revealing the truth (in conversation, in the most non-sexual way) and sometimes, very infrequently, making tentative sexual advances—usually rejected. In later years, fewer self-revelations (I had control of myself now, achieved with the aid of my therapists: I never told anyone unless it was necessary) and more frequent advances.

In therapy, I looked for the factors which had caused my

homosexuality. It did not occur to me that no one asked what caused heterosexuality, or that the two questions stood on a par. None of my psychotherapists ever pointed this out. When discussing my urge to self-revelation, my therapists and I explored the dynamics of this "Dostoevskian" manifestation—guilt, eagerness for punishment combined with eagerness for acceptance, etc. All of this, I must make clear, was true—I *was* guilty, eager for punishment, and eager for acceptance. But while exploring this (and, as I mentioned, helping me master the urge) none of my therapists exposed to me the simple, blinding underlying truth that in a society which condemns homosexuality and hence forces it to be secret, the homosexual will wish to break out of the secrecy by telling someone, and hence, that the urge itself was not sick at all. I had to figure this out for myself, at 28. Still less did any of my therapists ask why I *told* my friends rather than making sexual advances, or explore with me the question why I didn't seek gay society where I could make advances without risk.

My other psychotherapeutic experiences, or non-experiences, were like this. Twice while in therapy, I met homosexual acquaintances with whom the possibility of a real relationship existed, and shunned them. A therapist might usefully have explored why I was so guilty, even urged me to overcome this guilt; instead, these occurrences became evidence that I did not really want to be homosexual (which we already knew) and since my not wanting to be gay was implicitly a sign (perhaps my only sign) of health, these occurrences were not examined critically. Similarly, my therapists spent much time trying to discover why my relationships with straight friends were so passionate—rather than asking me why I formed these passionate relationships *with straights*. Similarly, after the homosexual affair which lost me my teaching job—a very warm relationship which continues, intermittently, to this day—I brought to my next therapist the datum that while in bed with my lover, I felt completely harmonious and "natural," not "sick" at all and not even guilty. Although this contradicted the very basis of the feeling which led me to psychotherapy, my therapist never took the initiative in exploring this contradiction.

This all might be thought to result from the "non-directive" quality of psychotherapy, or some psychotherapy. But elsewhere, my therapists *were* "directive." Very late, actually while I was "coming out" through gay liberation, I had a sexual affair with a woman (also, a warm one, interrupted only by circumstances). To this my therapist's response was positive: with a little smile, "Well, I see *something* has 'come out.' " The therapist's cues revealed clearly enough the idea of a repressed heterosexuality which *should* be "brought out," and though Freudian theory assumes an inborn bisexuality (an assumption I don't share, not regarding *any* particular form of sexuality as inborn), this theory assumes that repressed *homo*sexuality *shouldn't* be brought out, but should be sublimated. Thus psychotherapy, in my case, was directive indeed.

Rather than from "non-direction," the omissions of my therapists seem to me to have resulted from their assumption that I was, by definition, sick—that homosexuality (but not heterosexuality) is a pathology. It did not occur to them to "direct" me in ways which might raise in my mind the idea that I was *not* sick. But how can I complain of this? Didn't I know this was their theory, and didn't I myself share the assumption?

The point is simply that the therapists *failed to help me understand my situation*—to overcome my own *lack* of understanding. Even from a viewpoint of assuming homosexuality to be a pathology, it would remain true, I think, that my urge to self-revelation was *in fact* related to my *social* isolation as a homosexual. But my therapists never helped me to understand this. Even from the viewpoint that homosexuality if "incurable" should be accepted, it might have made sense for me to explore the possible relationships with my two gay college friends. But my therapists never tried to make me focus on this. Similarly, if I hadn't already been moving away from psychotherapy, after my heterosexual affair (if it had occurred at all) my therapist would have encouraged me to mull over that experience, to try to cultivate my heterosexual impulses, and to waste another ten years on top of the fourteen I had wasted already.

Basically, the therapists' theory made them incapable of viewing my situation as I now view it. If I understand it, their view was that the conflicts in my mind about accepting homosexuality indicated a very strong heterosexual impulse being checked subconsciously. In my view today, they indicated a very strong socially-conditioned rejection of being gay, combined with certain patterns—such as the tendency to be attracted to straight men—which were related to the inability to think of myself as gay and which created impossible (and, I would now add, unnecessary) conflicts between my sexual impulses and my need for ordinary friendship. (Only in the last year has this conflict become unnecessary: until now, gay people have had either to repress their gay nature while with straight friends, or to make their entire social life among gay people. I wonder how many therapists, exploring this conflict with thousands of gay patients, have tried to expose the *socially-conditioned* nature of this conflict.) In short, psychotherapy could not help me to understand my situation because it did not—and given its theoretical basis, *could* not—encourage me to think of my conflicts as resulting from social conditions.

How did I come to do so? Although therapy helped me understand many side issues, my understanding of being gay comes from social movements. My first step toward health—oh yes, I was sick: I was unable to view myself as I was—came when I was 22, in my determination to find love where I could. This step of simple self-preservation, never suggested by any psychotherapist, left me still viewing myself as an inferior creature. The first suggestion that homosexuals were unhappy not because we were sick but because we were oppressed, came from an acquaintance, who *not* coincidentally was a revolutionary socialist, who influenced me as I got deeply into the student radical movement at the late and lucky age of 25.

My first real understanding of my oppression, however, came as the women's liberation movement grew. Some of my closest acquaintances were very active in it. The critique of the social stigmas attached to being a woman, of the myths of female personality type, of the role of social factors in producing the *real* personality disfigurations women suffered—and most of all, of the treatment of all this by psychiatry as personal neurosis demanding personal therapy rather than as social oppression demanding a collective struggle—all this seemed true of myself as well. Further, my fear and dislike of women, which my therapists and I had spent much time discussing, began to change as I saw—from the movement, not from my therapists—that I was *not* expected (any longer) to relate to women primarily sexually, something I had always felt unable to do. Simultaneously I began seeing women and myself as human beings.

Finally gay liberation...but it shouldn't be necessary to describe how this changed my view of myself. It did, however, change the direction and content of my life.

My break with psychotherapy came gradually. Women's liberation made me take seriously the critique of psychiatric theory as regards women, but this was tangential to my own therapy. Very late, relations with my therapist became strained when, discussing my mother and her ambitions for me, he referred to her using me as "her penis." I saw that what women's liberationists had been saying was true: my mother's ambitious and successful life, in which she had always had to struggle against the limits placed on her as a woman, was to my therapist a manifestation of the desire for a penis rather than a rebellion against constraints which warred against her great abilities. Had it not been for the women's movement, I might have accepted this view—and found a new, apparently analytical way to despise my mother, rather than coming to understand her.

Instead, I asked myself how this theory, which regarded women so barbarically, regarded me. And I asked my therapist. His reply, which covered several sessions and touched on both women and homosexuals, was roughly that homosexuality could be regarded as a pathology (and heterosexuality could not) because in this society (he said "culture") the norm for the family was that of a male occupying a dominant position, a female in a subordinate position, and the reproduction of these roles in the young. We agreed that in terms of these roles both an "aggressive" woman, such as my mother, and a homosexual child were deviant cases. We differed in that he insisted that this deviance be viewed simply in terms of its psychic determinants, a position which I maintained, and he denied, was equivalent to refusing to question the psychic costs of the dominant pattern. I insisted that if no positive value were placed on the dominant pattern, then the deviant manifestation had to be viewed not as a psychopathology, but as a manifestation of a pattern which might in the absence of social pressures, be as fulfilling or more fulfilling than the dominant one, but which was socially disapproved. Thus a woman or a homosexual should be encouraged to see social norms as part of his or her "problem." This my therapist denied.

In the midst of this argument I traveled to another city. Since I was now active in gay liberation, I asked the person I was going to see to ask around if a gay liberation group existed there. None did, but as a result of his queries, I was telephoned at his house by a man who said he was gay, asked about gay liberation, but refused to come to see us. He also refused to give his last name, but he told me his profession—psychologist.

It was clear to me that a profession whose homosexual members had to conceal themselves could not adequately counsel homosexuals. Returning home, I related the incident to my therapist. His reply was that my caller had been a psychologist, not a psychoanalyst. Suppose he had been a psychoanalyst? My therapist replied that there were no homosexual psychoanalysts. In fact, he repeated this three times, as I literally could not believe he had said it. Some psychoanalysts occasionally "decompensated" and became active homosexuals, he said—but they "stopped being psychoanalysts."

You and I both know that this isn't true. At most, it may be true that psychoanalysts publicly identified as gay are forced to give up practice. But my therapist had claimed much more, and the conclusion I was forced to draw was that his theoretical outlook had so stereotyped his perceptions that he was incapable of correctly perceiving reality.

This particular incident made me terminate therapy, but in fact I had been moving in that direction for years—every step I took toward living my life as a homosexual, toward being less concealing, toward being, finally, openly and proudly gay, was a step toward ending a "therapy" which encouraged none of this. Even during the few weeks in which I was making the decision to contact gay liberation, my therapist, while not actively discouraging this step, cautioned me about it—it was another of my comrades in the revolutionary movement who, viewing my condition as one of oppression, urged me toward this step.

I, of course, chose on the basis of my inclinations, and I have only my life to offer as evidence that my choice was correct. The last year has been, not just one of the happiest of my life, but one of the *few* happy years of my life. I do not mean I have found bliss—quite the contrary: I have enough problems to convince me that my happiness is not founded on thin ice. I do not believe that this happiness would have been predicted by my therapists. (Similarly the experience of several gay liberation activists, who "came out" as homosexuals for the first time *after* several years of well-adjusted heterosexual life, would not have been predicted by psychoanalytic theory.) And all over the United States there are thousands in psychotherapy, and millions more under the pervasive social influence of psychiatric dogma, who never will make this step until they are reached, not by doctors, but by the winds of social protest. As Trotsky said of his comrade Adolf Yoffe, several years in analysis and later an outstanding Bolshevik diplomat, "The revolution healed Yoffe better than psychoanalysis of all his complexes."

THE ORDERLY

Robbie Skeist

These are some scraps of writing I did connected with homosexuality while I was working as an orderly in a private mental hospital in Chicago. I changed the names so the patients and the staff won't get hassled.

The French Kiss and the Pinch

Today's crisis came when Lenny, a patient around 15 years old, gave me a French kiss. Just before, Michael—who was discharged from the Army when they caught him making love (not war) with another soldier—had smiled, hugged me, and given me a smack of a kiss on my cheek. I thought Lenny was about to do the same, but instead he went for my mouth.

His lips were wet. He put his tongue in and moved it around. It was a good kiss and I couldn't tell him to stop. Still, the head nurse was standing about seven feet away watching, quite surprised, so I couldn't respond. I stood there. He kissed me. After a while, maybe four or five seconds—delicious, anxiety-filled seconds—the nurse came running out and screamed, "Lenny! Stop that!" I think she pulled his arms from around me and scolded him. He asked if she would be as upset if he were kissing a woman. She muttered something about "You know the rules."

Three hours later, Mr. Waller, a licensed practical nurse, pulled me over and said he was told to have a "fatherly talk" with me. The head nurse told him to tell me she was upset that I had just stood there when Lenny kissed me. I told him I was stunned so I didn't react, which was misleading because I didn't explain how nice the stunning kiss was. Mr. Waller said if it happens again, I should push Lenny away and insist that he stop.

At the end of his little lecture, Mr. Waller gave me a little pinch on the side of my stomach, gathering a little roll of my fat between his large thumb and forefinger. It felt good.

Holding Hands and the Confession

Jacob is a social worker who cracked up and committed himself. He wanted a rest and some therapy. They're giving him insulin shock treatment—a procedure which scares me and which none of the staff want to explain to me.

Yesterday they gave him shots, drained out some blood, put him in a coma and got him out of a coma. Today he was sweating and tired and scared. He was strapped to his bed and looked like a cornered puppy. They had to give him another shot to return some essential fluids to his blood stream, but he was fighting them off and the doctor had scratched him twice with the needle.

They called me in to hold him down and they were going to call the other orderly, too. This was upsetting me and I gave them a line about "You just leave me alone with him for a few minutes and I'll get him ready for you." They agreed to let me try.

For ten minutes Jacob and I held hands; his deep brown eyes

pleaded with me. I told him that no matter how much he disliked the insulin shock treatment he needed that particular shot to recover from the last few hours. We sat quietly. The nurse and the doctor came in and easily gave him the shot.

I stayed in the room, sitting on Jacob's bed, holding his hand, talking quietly. All sorts of things came out. He put down the hospital, cried for his parents, talked about his girl friend, blurted out "Sometimes I'm a little queer," squeezed my hand.

Today, two nurses and an orderly told me not to spend so much time in a patient's room, not to sit on a patient's bed, not to hold a patient's hand.

Shaving and the Unexpected Mole

I'm 23. I'm 80. Harold's 80 and I just helped him shave, just shaved him, and it took a while. It took two hours or maybe 23 minutes. Twenty-three minutes out of 23 years. I'm 23. I'm 80. Harold's 80 and I just helped him shave, just shaved him, and it took maybe 23 minutes.

He's an old man. An old Jewish man. An old Jewish lonely man. An old lonely Jewish man named Harold. A man named Harold Foner. An old lonely Jewish man named Harold Foner. It's quite clear in my memory and in my fingers that I shaved him.

I could hold my life together with a little string of holy acts like that. The place does him no good. He gets lonelier and more confused.

Yesterday, at the side of his bed, the right side near the foot, as he lies on his back, I saw on the floor there he had his left shoe and his right slipper. Or perhaps it was his right shoe and his left slipper.

Shock, hurt, why choose a word. He didn't like it. I found the other shoe and the other slipper on the floor in the TV room where the teenagers sit and smoke L&M's and play old 45's. Harold didn't know how they got there (the shoe and the slipper *or* the teenagers).

Well, today he was having trouble shaving. The way to say it is it was impossible. He just couldn't do it.

From one way of looking at it, shaving is really an unnecessary activity. But at that moment, from what his eyes, little sounds, and twitches told me, it was the focus of whether he would survive or give up.

It took a long time. Maybe an hour—did I say 23 minutes a while ago? His skin sags in many places, it has wrinkles and folds. And whiskers. The hairs were grey—whitish grey, plain grey, brownish grey—a lot of hairs. Tough, strong, wire-like. I used water mixed in the lather, it was better. I did it patch by patch. A few times he bled.

One unexpected time was caused by a mole the same color as his skin, near the left end of his left nostril.

Morning, and Harsh First Words

Welch, when I woke you that morning, I put my hand gently on yours, cupped your hand in mine and gently squeezed it. Your sunshine eyes were clouded over, grey and stormy. When you woke, it was with some shock and the words came harshly, "Why did you touch me like that?"

The Rumor

One morning I got to work at 7:02 A.M., stepped out of the elevator and started walking down the hall to put my coat and purse in the staff closet. I had a Gay Alliance newsletter and the February issue of *Gay Sunshine* from San Francisco Gay Liberation Front in my bag to give to Michael.

I passed Welch, the patient (or prisoner) I was closest to, and his eyes were upset, his forehead was scowling. Have your heard? Heard what? You haven't heard? Heard *what*? Dr. Schmuenbacher says you're going to be fired. The shrink had told the patients I would be fired.

I was scared. I picked up a few rumors from the dust and the corners—the doctor found out I had brought gay liberation literature to Michael a few weeks ago. A patient's mother I spoke to on visiting day told the doctor she was afraid I might molest some of the younger boys. The nurse didn't like my hospital corners. I didn't keep discipline. I was "too personal" with the patients. I had held Jacob's hand.

A shiver ran through me. I remembered Gay Liberation Front literature about how gay people who take a step or two outside their closets lose their jobs. "Their" jobs? *My* job. I knew I wouldn't starve, could find another job...still, "No more paychecks" was a shock. I knew a lot of people thought that one guy who touched another is a sex fiend...but *me* a child molester? I knew there were "proper ways" for orderlies to act, but couldn't they see how I had calmed Jacob by holding his hand and talking softly that afternoon? I hadn't worn any buttons, I had just tried to act as though I and the "patients" were human. I felt dizzy, a little wobbly, a little scared.

Angry, too. But that took a while. It helped when Welch told me he argued with the shrink that I had helped him. I called Renee, who is a lawyer, and she gave me some advice and reassurance that I won't forget.

Will I be fired? Well, I was called to the office twice and Mrs. Fiend sent the message that she didn't have time to talk with me.

. . . And My Departure

I wasn't fired. Some of the staff, certainly the doctor, gave me looks that hurt. I guess they were short-staffed and decided to keep me, or else an orderly is so unimportant to Mrs. Fiend that she forgot—it slipped her mind that she was going to fire me.

A couple of weeks later I stopped going to work. I was exhausted. I had problems at home, too. I had trouble waking up at 5:30 A.M., more trouble than before. One of the patients kept bugging me evey day with quotes from the Bible about how only heterosexual sex is O.K. I was hurt, scared, tired, and I just lay in bed whimpering for a few days and realized I couldn't go back.

Regrets? Of course. Maybe next time I'm at a place like that you'll be there, too, and we'll help each other survive.

THE ANTHROPOLOGICAL PERSPECTIVE

The Red Butterfly

A. Is Homosexuality Natural?

The anti-homosexuality statutes in America are full of such phrases as "unnatural intercourse," "unnatural crimes," and "infamous crime against nature." The concept that all homosexual acts are unnatural is a part of the prevailing myth system or ideology of our society, and most people would probably agree, at least publicly, that homosexuality is unnatural.

Yet, within the perspective of greater human society, the belief that homosexual acts are unnatural has no more validity than the once prevailing belief that the earth is flat. On the contrary, the findings of all relevant and intellectually respectable social research support the conclusion that *homosexual acts represent natural, completely human forms of behavior.*

What is meant by defining particular acts as natural or unnatural? It should be made clear, first, that by "natural" we do not mean "in a state of nature" or apart from the conditioning influences of human society. Humans are distinguished from all other animals by the relative size of the cerebral cortex: consequently we speak of human beings as the "learning animal" and the "social animal." Occasionally individuals are found who have grown up apart from any human companionship. These individuals are referred to as "feral," or wild, and fail to exhibit the characteristics we regard as essential to being human.

Vastly more than for any other animal, human behavior is the result of learning rather than instinct. And this learning takes place in a social context.

Therefore, we will consider homosexual acts to be natural if they represent behavior which (1) may be expected to occur (and has been observed to occur) in a great variety of human societies; which (2) occurs with substantial frequency within specific societies; and which (3) may be inferred to have a biologic basis as evidenced by studies of closely related animal species.

1. *Studies of varied human societies.*

The United States condemns any and all forms of homosexual behavior for males and females of all ages. This is not a middle-of-the-road, but an extreme position; it differs from the majority of human societies. Other peoples condone some forms of homosexual activity, particularly during adolescence. A third group of societies actively enforces homosexual relations upon all male members, usually in connection with puberty rituals.

Typical of the third group are the Siwans, an African people:

...males are singled out as peculiar if they do not indulge in these homosexual activities. Prominent Siwan men lend their sons to each other, and they talk about their masculine love affairs as openly as they discuss their love of women. Both married and unmarried males are expected to have both homosexual and heterosexual affairs. [1]

Another people which encourage homosexual activity are the Keraki of New Guinea. In their puberty rites every boy is initiated into sexual activity by the older males, who universally practice sodomy.

It is misleading, by the way, to refer to such societies as "primitive." Although underdeveloped from a technological standpoint, these societies may be highly evolved with regard to other aspects of culture: laws, language, kinship systems, art forms, etc. Conversely, a critical examination of our own society—its foreign and domestic policy, the misuse of natural resources, the allocation of the national budget, the distribution of

1. C.S. Ford and F.A. Beach, *Patterns Of Sexual Behavior,* N.Y., Harper & Row (Perennial Library, paper), 1970, p. 139.

income, the treatment of minorities, the forms of entertainment
—indicates that our society may be considered primitive by the
standards of a truly human society of the future.

2. *Incidence within the United States.*

Despite the severe legal and social sanctions against
homosexual relations, homosexual activity does take place
among American men and women to a much greater extent than
usually imagined.

Kinsey, Pomeroy and Martin interviewed more than 5000
American men, using a study design of extreme sophistication.
Following are some of their findings:

50% of American males have been conscious of specifically
erotic responses to other males.

37% have had at least one homosexual experience leading to
orgasm.

30% have come from being given a blow job by another male.

18% have had at least as much homosexual as heterosexual
experience for at least a three-year period between the ages of 18
and 65.

These findings are absolute dynamite. Think about them! They
mean, considering the conformity and pusillanimity of the
American male, that the man on the street must have conscious
homosexual desires. For every active gay man, how many others
simply lack the courage and know-how? The button slogan, "Face
it, we're all queer," is no exaggeration.

Kinsey and his associates followed up with a similar study of
almost 6000 American females. It would appear from their
findings that homosexuality is less prevalent among women than
among men, and the general anthropological picture agrees with
these findings. Among the total sample of American women:

28% have been conscious of specifically erotic responses to
another female

13% have reached orgasm from at least one homosexual
experience.

There is one important qualification to stating that the incidence
of female homosexual behavior appears to be less than half that
of male homosexual behavior. Between 14% and 19% of the
unmarried women and 1% to 3% of the married women were
classified as not responding erotically to either heterosexual or
homosexual stimuli, whereas almost no men fell into this

category. The implications of this sizable "asexual" category among women may depend upon further research employing the techniques of depth psychology.

At any rate, male homosexuality has historically been a matter of much greater social concern in Anglo-American culture than has female homosexuality. Male homosexuals were commonly put to death in ancient and medieval history, whereas female homosexuals rarely were. Homosexuality laws are frequently enforced against men, but almost never against women. It is almost always the male homosexuals who are murdered and blackmailed by police and other criminals. This is not to say that gay women have been better off—rather, it reflects differences in the specific ways sexual chauvinism operates against male and female homosexuals.

3. *Animal studies.*

Animal species below humans exhibit homosexual behavior, and it is particularly frequent among the infra-human primates (apes and monkeys). Descriptions of monkey sex are not only fun, and quite human sometimes, but also enlightening as to the genetic bases of our own behavior.

Bachelor baboons who have restricted opportunities for contact with females sometimes strike up homosexual friendships, and for a time a masculine pair remains constantly together. Immature males often join full-grown bachelors and engage in sexual activity. Prepuberal and adolescent males show a wide range of sex responses. They display the feminine sexual presentation, masturbate, and mount one another. They also mount and are mounted by adult members of their own sex. And they engage in manual, oral, and olfactory genital examination with other males of their own age. [2]

Our little cousins can also use sex for social manipulation and ulterior reasons:

There are, however, many advantages to be gained by a smaller and younger male who submits to a more dominant partner. Aggressive adults tend to protect their homosexual favorites from assault by other monkeys, and the favorites soon learn to seek this protection. In such a relationship the socially

2. *Ibid.,* p. 143.

inferior partner often adopts the sexual presentation when his dominant partner starts to take food away from him and the procedure is often effective.[3]

A true homosexual liason has even been observed between two male porpoises. One partner was removed from the tank for three weeks. Their reactions upon being reunited are described in this lovely passage:

No doubt could exist that the two recognized each other, and for several hours they swam side by side rushing frenziedly through the water, and on several occasions they leaped completely out of the water. For several days, the two males were inseparable and neither paid any attention to the female. This was in courting season, and at other times the two males seemed bent only on preventing the other's copulation with the female.[4]

In addition to the three examples just offered as proof, mention should be made of one-sex groups (prisons, religious orders, athletic groups, boys or girls schools, military services, etc.). In all one-sex groups, homosexual acts tend to occur spontaneously, often among a majority of the group members.

Estimates have been made that 80-90% of the inmates in certain prisons actively take part in homosexual activity, which is only to a minor degree the result of physical coercion. Jane Alpert wrote in *Rat* newspaper, "Anyone who spends a month or more in the House of D. learns to be bisexual, and the hard-core butches are some of the most together and respected women in the jail."

It might be argued that the prisons do not constitute a natural situation. True. Neither does a repressive society outside prison. The point is that many types of "straight" men and women can enjoy gay sex and can form romantic attachments that go far beyond mere convenience.

However, a particular culture may delineate sex roles for its members, the overall perspective is the great malleability of human nature and the variety of human experience. No more explanation is required for homosexual acts than is required for heterosexual acts; neither is more instinctive or natural than the other.

3. *Ibid.*, p. 144.
4. A.F. McBride and D.O. Hebb, "Behavior of the captive bottle-nose dolphin, *Tursiops truncatus.*" *J. Comp. Pysiol.*, Vol. XLI, p. 121.

Essentially this viewpoint is expressed by the anthropologist, Clellan S. Ford, and the zoologist, Frank A. Beach. They sum up the relationship between homosexuality and culture as follows:

Men and women who are totally lacking in any conscious homosexual leanings are as much a product of cultural conditioning as are the exclusive homosexuals who find heterosexual relations distasteful and unsatisfying. Both extremes represent movement away from the original, intermediate condition which includes the capacity for both forms of sexual expression. In a restrictive society such as our own a large proportion of the population learns not to respond to or even to recognize homosexual stimuli and may eventually become in fact unable to do so. At the same time a certain minority group, also through the process of learning, becomes highly if not exclusively sensitive to the erotic attractions of a like-sexed partner. ...human homosexuality is not basically a product of hormonal imbalance or 'perverted heredity.' It is the product of the fundamental mammalian heritage of general sexual responsiveness as modified under the impact of experience. [5]

Let us conclude by returning to the anti-homosexuality statutes. Clearly these laws are based on false premises. Therefore, they must be null and void. In addition, any society which so far departs from fairness and rationality in one area must be subject to the most exacting scrutiny in all of its aspects!

B. The Individual and Culture

The individual who finds his way of life in conflict with the culture he lives in may respond in various ways. He may attempt to deny his own nature and to adopt the prevailing behavior patterns, even if they are alien to him.

Two other courses, however, are open to him. He may learn to view his differences from the cultural model objectively, and to seek support from alternative models, such as other societies or subcultures. He may then be able to function adequately, and with self respect, within the existing society.

A third course is to examine the existing culture critically, to understand its defects, and to struggle to change that society. We believe that true gay liberation will follow this course, which must involve fundamental change in the structure and material base of this society.

5. Ford and Beach, *op. cit.*, p. 263.

The conflicts between a gay person's needs and the condemnation of this society would strain anyone's vitality. Often the results of this conflict are identified with a person's homosexuality, whereas this would not be the case in a more human society. Certainly most of the psychiatric literature on homosexuality is reactionary in that it transfers the blame from an unfree society to those who are among the victims of that society.

The great anthropologist Ruth Benedict makes a plea for a cross-cultural, or comparative, psychiatry. This is how she describes "tradition," with America particularly in mind:

Tradition is as neurotic as any patient; its overgrown fear of deviation from its fortuitous standards conforms to all the usual definitions of the psychopathic.[6]

People who represent, in extremes, the prevailing values of the society are not regarded as abnormal. On the contrary, they are generally the cultural heroes of the epoch. Think about the cultural heroes of America, the "normal American," as related to this passage from Benedict:

In our own generation extreme forms of ego-gratification are culturally supported in a similar fashion. Arrogant and unbridled egoists as family men, as officers of the law and in business, have been again and again portrayed by novelists and dramatists, and they are familiar in every community. Like the behavior of Puritan divines, their courses of action are often more asocial than those of the inmates of penitentiaries. In terms of the suffering and frustration that they spread about them there is probably no comparison. There is very possibly as great a degree of mental warping. Yet they are entrusted with positions of great influence and importance and are as a rule fathers of families. Their impress both upon their own children and upon the structure of our society is indelible. They are not described in our manuals of psychiatry because they are supported by every tenet of our civilization. They are sure of themselves in real life in a way that is possible only to those who are oriented to the points of the compass laid down in their own culture. Nevertheless a future psychiatry may well ransack our novels and letters and public records for illumination upon a type of abnormality to which it would not otherwise give credence. In every society it is among this very

6. Ruth Benedict, *Patterns Of Culture*, N.Y., Mentor Books, p. 235.

group of the culturally encouraged and fortified that some of the most extreme types of human behaviour are fostered.[7]

We intend to change our society, going down to the roots of the system. May we achieve a society where the normal man can be a helper to Man; where cooperation, not competition, is the virtue.

C. The Family

Just as the forms of human society have undergone historical changes—from slave societies to feudalism, then capitalism, and now a world straining towards a higher form—the family also has changed. Older forms of the family, matriarchal and communal, have been superseded by the patriarchal, monogamous family of today. The extended family, which was common in the 19th century, is largely replaced by the nuclear family (man, woman, and children). Each change in the family structure correlates historically with a change in the forces of production, illustrating the materialist position that the institutions and social relations of a culture are determined, in the final analysis, by the economic base of the society.

Gay men and women are undoubtedly oppressed to a large extent because their choice of love falls outside the model sanctioned by society: the family. And not only gay people, but perhaps the majority of the people are kept down by pressures to conform to the present family structure.

Nuclear families seal off little groups of people from the rest of humanity. Women are possessed and oppressed by their husbands, and children, by their parents. Children are brought up with only two people to serve as basic role models, with resulting authoritarianism, ignorance, and hostility towards other people. Psychic life of family members becomes morbid from taking place within such a closed arena. Domestic work is done wastefully. Why should 50 families have 50 separate kitchens, when communal eating arrangements would free women from this alienated labor? The family, owning and transmitting private property, is the basic social unit of a society of class domination. Within the present family structure can be seen, in embryo, the basic contradictions of the entire system.

We certainly are not out to destroy existing families (we hardly have power to do so), or to deprive anyone from enjoying the domestic arrangement of his or her choice. On the contrary, what gay men and women, as well as others, should demand is

7. *Ibid.*, pp. 238–239.

freedom from being forced to mold their lives after a rigid, and strictly historical, family structure.

When the leap has been made to a freer and more human society, the old family structure will wither away. And there will be no other motive left for the attachment of two people (or more) than that of mutual inclination. When a new generation of women and men have grown up, who have never known the curious prejudices and regulations of this time, they will make their own practice. What forms this will take will be determined by the freedom of the future.

(This section has necessarily been sketchy because of space limitation. We hope to develop an extended analysis of gay liberation and the family. Relevant reading can be found in Frederick Engel's *The Origin Of The Family, Private Property, And The State;* Wilhelm Reich's *The Sexual Revolution;* and the literature of various women's liberation groups.)

GAY BUREAUCRATS: WHAT ARE THEY DOING TO YOU?

Mike Silverstein

At the last school where I taught, the most universally detested member of the administration was Dean Grey. Grey was the administration's hatchet man, in charge of all the really nasty business like firing faculty. Most of the hostility came out in dirty jokes about the fact that Grey was such an obvious old queen. He was the standing snicker of the school. He must have noticed that he had no friends, but he never let on; he was totally loyal to the administration. I believe he was grateful that they pretended not to notice what he was, at least to his face.

Historians, writing about the decadence of the Chinese and Persian Empires, always make a point of the connection between despotism and the rise of eunuchs to positions of power. The eunuchs were generally totally isolated from their fellows, having no family and generally being held in contempt by their colleagues. Thus their only security and position came from absolute loyalty and commitment to the despot.

They always played the roles of toadies and lickspittles. Sometimes they became quite powerful because of their usefulness to their rulers, but they were always held in universal contempt, and for this reason were absolutely dependent on their patrons.

Dean Grey held exactly that position, the Chancellor's private eunuch, his private vassal, and the focus of all the hostility and contempt of the rest of us.

The college at which I now teach has Dean Greys all over the place. I don't know if they are all gay, but I do know that this is a pretty common role for the gay bureaucrat to find himself in. It's one of the ways bureaucracies find us useful. It's not always that bad, of course. Maybe you get along better in your job. Maybe you are treated just like everyone else. Perhaps. But I believe we are systematically exploited in institutions. Further, this exploitation goes on especially where they appear to be "treating us just like everyone else."

We all know about blackmail. We can't be hired for "sensitive" work because "our peculiar private lives" make us susceptible to blackmail. Well, we are susceptible to blackmail, that's what makes us so useful to our organizations. Dean Grey was being blackmailed—that's why he did the shit work nobody else would do and was grateful for the opportunity. He was being blackmailed—by his organization. How many of us are in the same boat?

Our bosses know we're gay. We all really know that. At least they know we're not married, we don't talk about our private lives much, don't mix with the other office people off the job. They probably tell the same jokes about you that they tell about Dean Grey behind his back.

But our superiors and our colleagues pretend not to notice and treat us just like one of the guys anyway. For this we are profoundly grateful, as we are expected to be. We show we're worthy of stupid shit work that doesn't seem to fall to our straight co-workers. We do all kinds of embarrassing nasty little hatchet jobs for the boss, so he'll treat us like a regular guy.

In return for this it's amazing what those stupid straights won't notice. You can swish around the office and camp it up, and nobody will say a thing to your face—as long as you do your work well—and then some. In fact if you've got a fairly high level job, they'll even send the company lawyer down to bail you out if you get busted in a tea-room, and still not notice a thing. And you'll be grateful for life—you damn well better be.

Is all of this true? Well, look around you at your gay co-workers, and yourself. Bet you never saw a more grateful bunch, so thankful to be treated just like everyone else that they'll work their ass off without a thought of reward. Now ask yourself just what

Gay Liberation takes over a conference

From John Roper
Medical Reporter
Bradford

About 50 members of Gay Liberation groups took over the congress on psychosexual difficulties for two hours at Bradford University yesterday.

The chairman of the day's sessions, Mr Justice Waler, a judge of the Queen's Bench Division, and Sir John Peel, chairman of the Board of Science and Education of the British Medical Association, both o fwhom were due to sum up the three-day meeting; left as a result of the demonstration.

Dr J. B. Randell, consultant psychiatrist at Charing Cross Hospital, London, who was to have spoken on transsexualism and transvestism, withdrew his paper, and another paper on homsexuality by Dr Donald West, reader in clinical criminology at Cambridge, had to be curtailed.

The Gay Liberation members who had occupied the main lecture hall ,pushing past the university security men well before the meeting was due to begin left only after Dr Edward G. Edwards, vice-chancellor of the university, had talked to them and had undertaken to provide free facilities for a conference which they would call on a date to be arranged ; an had agreed immediately to provide a room for their discussions while the congress programme continued.

The Gay Liberation move was wel organized, Not only the Bradford group but members of London groups and also the Campaign for Homosexual Equality, Manchester, the Bristol Icebreakers and the National Transvestite Group, Cardiff, supported the demonstrations. On the first day of the meeting they claimed that although some members had applied to atend the conference as delegates, their applications had been refused.

When doctors ,social workers and educationists arrived yesterday they found the 50 men and women Liberationists in occupation. For half an hour an ordered debate between Dr H. B. Milne, the Bradford consultant psychiatrist largely responsible for initiating the conference, delegates and Liberationists took place on their demand to sit in and have a dialogue instead of lectures.

Dr Milne called for a vote and by a large majority it was agreed that the Liberationists should remain.

Liberationists, naming themselves only by names such as Steve, Don, Julie and Niki, took part in a general debate which, apart from hissing of one or two doctors' contributions, was conducted intelligently and smoothly. Some points by the Liberationists were accepted by the delegates and others spoke in support of some of their claims.

aid the motion concealed matters
that should be brought into the
open. The vision of Europe and
the administrative structure of the
EEC must be clearly distinguished.
Liberals must not put the admini-
rative structure first.

Miss **Muriel Burton**, prospective
candidate for mid-Oxon, said
Labour should be cooperating with
the European Parliament. The public had a right to elect directly
their own European MPs.

Mr **Rodney Smith**, financial vice-
chairman of the Young Liberals,
wanted to delete the clause on
the promotion of aid by the EEC
to the third world. Many deve-
oping countries were totally dependent on the export of a narrow range of primary commodities,
he said. Britain should have been
ashamed to exploit the sugar-
producing countries for cheap
sugar. Yet the country apparently
faced a sugar crisis because it was
going to have to pay a fair price.
The developing countries should
have free access to our markets
and a fair price for their com-
odities.

The amended resolution was
agreed to.

Leading article, page 15

TIMES 14.9.74

ndiscriminate
growth rejected

A resolution from the environ-
ent and economic growth com-
ission, which was carried,
rejected the goal of indiscriminate
economic growth as measured by
crease in gross national pro-
uct. It also rejected the idea that
the improvement of society could
be measured by the monetary value
of goods and services produced,
and stated that the assessment
of the effects of economic activity
ust take into account social and
vironmental factors.

The farmers' crisis of today was
the housewives' crisis of tomorrow.
They faced further shortages because farmers, in order to live,
had been selling their best breed-
ing animals. Farming had been
brought by the Conservative Government up to February to the
brink of disaster. The Labour
Party had seen livestock farming
go over the brink and had done
nothing about it.

A stage had been reached where
the interests of consumers and
farmers coincided as never before.
Housewives should be marching
the streets in support of the
farmers.

Mr **Alan Butt Philip**, prospective
candidate for Wells, moved an
amendment, accepted by Mr
Hooson and carried by the
assembly, condemning the Government for introducing food subsidies to all consumers, thereby
worsening the food supply situation.

He said that the £700m being
spent on subsidies could be used
to raise family allowances, including making the allowance payable
for the first child and by directly
helping pensioners

Mr **Clement Freud**, MP for the Isle
of Ely, said the relationship between the Government and the
agricultural industry had never
been worse. There had never been
such contempt and distrust among
farmers for Westminster, where
they were entitled to have someone
they could trust.

Sugar beet farmer received
£111 a ton while the Minister
of Agriculture went off to
Guyana and paid £140. It was
iniquitous that while the world
price for sugar was £350,
farmers should be getting £111
and did not know what was
going to happen.

There was no less sugar in
the country than last year but
it was in larders and cupboards.

you have to be so grateful for. Suppose they stopped pretending you weren't gay. Who would that hurt—you or them? It would still be hard for them to fire you, especially since your gratitude has made you such a loyal and hardworking employee. They wouldn't know how to treat you, they'd be embarrassed. It's so much easier for them to pretend not to notice. They pretend you don't exist as a gay person for their sake, to save themselves the embarrassment of dealing with you as who you are—this is what you're expected to be grateful for.

If you don't believe this, try telling them you're gay. You'll find they still won't notice. They don't want to know. In my case I made a speech to a student rally about gay liberation, had a story about it in the school paper, and wore a gay liberation button around the office. My sociologist colleagues—students of minority groups, social movements, deviant behavior—never noticed. When I bring the subject up as relevant to my work they change the subject. When I asked my colleagues' opinion of a paper I wrote on camp roles, they returned it to me with a note saying I shouldn't have shown it to them, it's a personal document and they don't want to know about my personal life. The only time they ever broached the subject was when they fired me; they spent fifteen minutes explaining that the fact that I was one of the, uh, gay people, had nothing to do with it. This experience isn't unique to me. A friend of mine who teaches history wrote a couple of papers on gay identity. He told me how tactful his colleagues have been in never mentioning it. He's very grateful. (He also lost his job for entirely unrelated reasons.)

They don't want to know about us. They don't want to know who we are. They refuse to confront us as persons. They have made us invisible and totally depersonalized us. For this they expect us to respond with undying gratitude and unswerving loyalty. And we have. No more! Enough! They are not our friends, they are using us. They are destroying our souls and making us thank them for it. Like the Jews in the concentration camps that were forced to dig their own graves, we pay the price of our own degradation as gay people, and are grateful for the opportunity. They use the self-hate they teach us to feel, and the need for concealment they create to get a lot of cheap dirty work out of us. Stop playing their game, stop being grateful, and find out just who needs who.

So our bosses are using us. They use our self-hate, and they use our gratitude to get all their nasty little jobs done, and doing this ensures the contempt and hostility of our fellow workers, especially our underlings, giving us nothing to cling to except the support and approval of our superiors. But for us to be really useful, with no other support but the bosses, it's also necessary that we be kept entirely isolated by being made to hate and fear each other. This is taken care of quite efficiently. How many of us have heard about the department that's dominated by fags, the office the queers have taken over, the division where the gay boys have it all their own way. "They're everywhere, those queers, always bringing in more of their own kind. They're taking over the music business, the ad agencies, the theatre art department, Broadway. They've ruined interior decorating. If you're not one of them you don't have a chance." Somehow the department we work in never seems to be like that. Maybe there's another gay person or two in the office, but you hardly know each other; in fact, you avoid each other. If people saw you with him too much, they might suspect you were up to something. And you know as sure as hell, no gay sister or brother ever helped you get where you are. If anything the opposite is true. In fact how many of us know of an office with two gay executives who hate each other, two gay English professors in the department who are bitter rivals, the gay personnel director who avoids gay applicants like the plague. We all know that just to be on the safe side it's not a good idea to get involved with any gays on the job. Even the straights notice this, and they have an explanation right at hand. Those queers are so neurotic they can't even stand each other.

Well, that's the way it's always been with groups which the people on top have wanted to use, and at the same time keep away from any real power. The myth of the close-knit conspiracy of outsiders has been used to keep Jews divided, to keep women divided, and to keep us divided. We have to prove we're not a conspiracy, not a homintern, by staying away from each other. If we don't keep each other at arm's length we open ourselves up to the suspicion of being friends, of helping one another. We have to hate each other to prove our loyalty to our bosses. Our co-workers and underlings hate us because of our subservience. We have no one left to turn to except the boss, and he has us available for the dirty work of keeping the rest in line. We're the boss' pet, the dirty little snitches, trusted by no one, trusting no one—especially each other. We have no one to be grateful to except our boss and he can make us grateful for every little crumb.

It's time to stop. Time to declare our freedom, our self-respect, our love for one another. Other people have been treated this way—women, blacks, they have been used against us and we have been used against them. This whole rotten society is based on people being used against each other, not able to trust each other, cutting each other's throats. Well, blacks and women are learning not to cut each other up, to trust each other and work together. It's our turn now. It's time for us to stand up and demand our freedom, demand our rights as human beings, demand our right to love each other. If we are proud of ourselves and help each other, it will strengthen us, not weaken us. What have we to lose—invisibility, isolation, the contempt of straights, other gays, ourselves? Together we can win our humanity back.

What can we do? Well, think about it. Is it true? Why not discuss it with the other gay girl or guy in the office, that you've never had anything more than polite chit-chat with? What does she or he think of it? Perhaps she or he feels it too? Has felt it all long? Maybe you can be friends and you're not as alone as you thought you were. Make gay friendships, caucuses. Let us help each other, let us trust each other. Let us be ourselves, free and together. We have our humanity to win. How can what we pay for it be more than what we are paying now?

PHOTOGRAPHS BY ELLEN SHUMSKY

170 /Out of the Closets: Voices of Gay Liberation

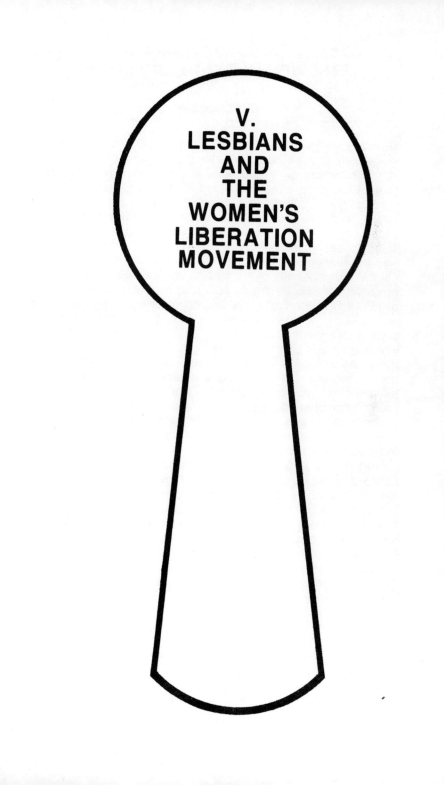

V.
LESBIANS
AND
THE
WOMEN'S
LIBERATION
MOVEMENT

THE WOMAN-IDENTIFIED WOMAN

Radicalesbians

What is a lesbian? A lesbian is the rage of all women condensed to the point of explosion. She is the woman who, often beginning at an extremely early age, acts in accordance with her inner compulsion to be a more complete and freer human being than her society—perhaps then, but certainly later—cares to allow her. These needs and actions, over a period of years, bring her into painful conflict with people, situations, the accepted ways of thinking, feeling and behaving, until she is in a state of continual war with everything around her, and usually with her self. She may not be fully conscious of the political implications of what for her began as personal necessity, but on some level she has not been able to accept the limitations and oppression laid on her by the most basic role of her society—the female role. The turmoil she experiences tends to induce guilt proportional to the degree to which she feels she is not meeting social expectations, and/or eventually drives her to question and analyse what the rest of her society, more or less accepts. She is forced to evolve her own life pattern, often living much of her life alone, learning usually much earlier than her "straight" (heterosexual) sisters about the essential aloneness of life (which the myth of marriage obscures) and about the reality of illusions. To the extent that she cannot expel the heavy socialization that goes with being female, she can never truly find peace with herself. For she is caught somewhere between accepting society's view of her—in which case she cannot accept herself—and coming to understand what this sexist society has done to her and why it is functional and necessary for it to do so. Those of us who work that through find ourselves on the other side of a tortuous journey through a night that may have been decades long. The perspective gained from that journey, the liberation of self, the inner peace, the real love of self and of all women, is something to be shared with all women—because we are all women.

It should first be understood that lesbianism, like male homosexuality, is a category of behavior possible only in a sexist society characterized by rigid sex roles and dominated by male supremacy. Those sex roles dehumanize women by defining us as a supportive/serving caste *in relation to* the master caste of men, and emotionally cripple men by demanding that they be alienated from their own bodies and emotions in order to perform their economic/political/military functions effectively. Homosexuality is a by-product of a particular way of setting up roles (or approved patterns of behavior) on the basis of sex; as such it is an inauthentic (not consonant with "reality") category. In a society in which men do not oppress women, and sexual expression is allowed to follow feelings, the categories of homosexuality and heterosexuality would disappear.

But lesbianism is also different from male homosexuality, and serves a different function in the society. "Dyke" is a different kind of put-down from "faggot," although both imply you are not playing your socially assigned sex role—are not therefore a "real woman" or a "real man." The grudging admiration felt for the tomboy and the queasiness felt around a sissy boy point to the same thing: the contempt in which women—or those who play a female role—are held. And the investment in keeping women in that contemptuous role is very great. Lesbian is the word, the label, the condition that holds women in line. When a woman hears this word tossed her way, she knows she is stepping out of line. She knows that she has crossed the terrible boundary of her sex role. She recoils, she protests, she reshapes her actions to gain approval. Lesbian is a label invented by the man to throw at any woman who dares to be his equal, who dares to challenge his prerogatives (including that of all women as part of the exchange medium among men), who dares to assert the primacy of her own needs. To have the label applied to people active in women's liberation is just the most recent instance of a long history; older women will recall that not so long ago, any woman who was successful, independent, not orienting her whole life about a man, would hear this word. For in this sexist society, for a woman to be independent means she can't be a woman—she must be a dyke. That in itself should tell us where women are at. It says as clearly as can be said: women and person are contradictory terms. For a lesbian is not considered a "real woman." And yet, in popular thinking, there is really only one essential difference between a lesbian and other women: that of sexual orientation—which is to say, when you strip off all the packaging, you must finally realize that the essence of being a "woman" is to get fucked by men.

"Lesbian" is one of the sexual categories by which men have divided up humanity. While all women are dehumanized as sex objects, as the objects of men, they are given certain compensations: identification with his power, his ego, his status, his protection (from other males), feeling like a "real woman," finding social acceptance by adhering to her role, etc. Should a woman confront herself by confronting another woman, there are fewer rationalizations, fewer buffers by which to avoid the stark horror of her dehumanized condition. Herein we find the overriding fear of many women towards exploring intimate relationships with other women: the fear of her being used as a sexual object by a woman, which not only will bring no male-connected compensations, but also will reveal the void which is woman's real situation. This dehumanization is expressed when a straight woman learns that a sister is a lesbian; she begins to relate to her lesbian sister as her potential sex object, laying a surrogate male role on the lesbian. This reveals her heterosexual conditioning to make herself into an object when sex is potentially involved in a relationship, and it denies the lesbian her full humanity. For women, especially those in the movement, to perceive their lesbian sisters through this male grid of role definitions is to accept this male cultural conditioning and to oppress their sisters much as they themselves have been oppressed by men. Are we going to continue the male classification system of defining all females in sexual relation to some *other* category of people? Affixing the label lesbian not only to a woman who aspires to be a person, but also to any situation of real love, real solidarity, real primacy among women is a primary form of divisiveness among women: it is the condition which keeps women within the confines of the feminine role, and it is the debunking/scare term that keeps women from forming any primary attachments, groups, or associations among ourselves.

Women in the movement have in most cases gone to great lengths to avoid discussion and confrontation with the issue of lesbianism. It puts people up-tight. They are hostile, evasive, or try to incorporate it into some "broader issue." They would rather not talk about it. If they have to, they try to dismiss it as a "lavender herring." But it is no side issue. It is absolutely essential to the success and fulfillment of the women's liberation movement that this issue be dealt with. As long as the label "dyke" can be used to frighten women into a less militant stand, keep her separate from her sisters, keep her from giving primacy to anything other than men and family—then to that extent she is controlled by the male culture. Until women see in each other the possibility of a primal commitment which includes sexual love, they will be denying themselves the love and value they readily accord to men, thus affirming their second-class status. As long as male acceptability is primary—both to individual women and to the movement as a whole—the term lesbian will be used effectively against women. Insofar as women want only more privileges within the system, they do not want to antagonize male power. They instead seek acceptability for women's liberation, and the most crucial aspect of the acceptability is to deny lesbianism—i.e., deny any fundamental challenge to the basis of the female role.

It should also be said that some younger, more radical women have honestly begun to discuss lesbianism, but so far it has been primarily as a sexual "alternative" to men. This, however, is still giving primacy to men, both because the idea of relating more completely to women occurs as a *negative reaction to men,* and because the lesbian relationship is being characterized simply by sex, which is divisive and sexist. On one level, which is both personal and political, women may withdraw emotional and sexual energies from men, and work out various alternatives for those energies in their own lives. On a different political/psychological level, it must be understood that what is crucial is that women begin disengaging from male-defined response patterns. In the privacy of our own psyches, we must cut those cords to the core. For irrespective of where our love and sexual energies flow, if we are male-identified in our heads, we cannot realize our autonomy as human beings.

But why is it that women have related to and through men? By virtue of having been brought up in a male society, we have internalized the male culture's definition of ourselves. That definition views us as relative beings who exist not for ourselves, but for the servicing, maintenance and comfort of men. That definition consigns us to sexual and family functions, and excludes us from defining and shaping the terms of our lives. In exchange for our psychic servicing and for performing society's non-profit-making functions, the man confers on us just one thing: the slave status which makes us legitimate in the eyes of the society in which we live. This is called "femininity" or "being a real woman" in our cultural lingo. We are authentic, legitimate, real to the extent that we are the property of some man whose name we bear. To be a woman who belongs to no man is to be invisible, pathetic, inauthentic, unreal. He confirms his image of us—of what we have to be in order to be acceptable by him—but not our real selves; he confirms our womanhood—as he defines it, in relation to him—but cannot confirm our personhood, our own selves as absolutes. As long as we are dependent on the male culture for this definition, for this approval, we cannot be free.

The consequence of internalizing this role is an enormous reservoir of self-hate. This is not to say the self-hate is recognized or accepted as such; indeed most women would deny it. It may be experienced as discomfort with her role, as feeling empty, as numbness, as restlessness, a paralyzing anxiety at the center.

Alternatively, it may be expressed in shrill defensiveness of the glory and destiny of her role. But it does exist, often beneath the edge of her consciousness, poisoning her existence, keeping her alienated from herself, her own needs, and rendering her a stranger to other women. Women hate both themselves and other women. They try to escape by identifying with the oppressor, living through him, gaining status and identity from his ego, his power, his accomplishments. And by not identifying with other "empty vessels" like themselves, women resist relating on all levels to other women who will reflect their own oppression, their own secondary status, their own self-hate. For to confront another woman is finally to confront one's self—the self we have gone to such lengths to avoid. And in that mirror we know we cannot really respect and love that which we have been made to be.

As the source of self-hate and the lack of real self are rooted in our male-given identity, we must create a new sense of self. As long as we cling to the idea of "being a woman," we will sense some conflict with that incipient self, that sense of I, that sense of a whole person. It is very difficult to realize and accept that being "feminine" and being a whole person are irreconcilable. Only women can give each other a new sense of self. That identity we have to develop with reference to ourselves, and not in relation to men. This consciousness is the revolutionary force from which all else will follow, for ours is an organic revolution. For this we must be available and supportive to one another, give our commitment and our love, give the emotional support necessary to sustain this movement. Our energies must flow toward our sisters, not backwards towards our oppressors. As long as women's liberation tries to free women without facing the basic heterosexual structure that binds us in one-to-one relationship with our own oppressors, tremendous energies will continue to flow into trying to straighten up each particular relationship with a man, how to get better sex, how to turn his head around—into trying to make the "new man" out of him, in the delusion that this will allow us to be the "new woman." This obviously splits our energies and commitments, leaving us unable to be committed to the construction of the new patterns which will liberate us.

It is the primacy of women relating to women, of women creating a new consciousness of and with each other which is at the heart of women's liberation, and the basis for the cultural revolution. Together we must find, reinforce and validate our authentic selves. As we do this, we confirm in each other that struggling incipient sense of pride and strength, the divisive barriers begin to melt, we feel this growing solidarity with our sisters. We see ourselves as prime, find our centers inside of ourselves. We find receding the sense of alienation, of being cut off, of being behind a locked window, of being unable to get out what we know is inside. We feel a realness, feel at last we are coinciding with ourselves. With that real self, with that consciousness, we begin a revolution to end the imposition of all coercive identifications, and to achieve maximum autonomy in human expression.

REALESBIANS AND POLITICALESBIANS

Gay Revolution Party Women's Caucus

Recently within the women's movement there has been some recognition of the fact that lesbianism is a central issue in the struggle for liberation. Since publication of "Woman-Identified-Woman" and the Lavender Menace action at the Second Congress to Unite Women in the spring of 1970 (a zap in which the movement was confronted with its sexism by realesbians), consciousness on the lesbian issue has expanded to the degree that at present the spectrum of opinion within the movement is very wide. One position on the question of lesbianism is that it remains a "side issue" of a "special interest group" and serves as a continuing source of embarrassment to the movement. This was the rationale for the absence of a lesbian speaker on the schedule at the August 26 Women's Strike in the summer of 1970. More drastic actions based on this false consciousness were taken within NOW in the winter of 1970–71 in the form of a lesbian purge. Beyond the more blatant sexism of neglect and purges is found the liberalism of straight guilt of others in the movement, who say it's OK to sleep with women, but that one should not become a "lesbian chauvinist" and fancy oneself in the vanguard of the revolution.

So how has the women's movement been dealing with this issue on a day-to-day, personal level? Specifically, how are its participants relating to each other and to men? (1) There are considerable numbers of women who are continuing to live with and/or struggle with men either in mixed communes and collectives or in couples. These women apparently believe that men can be educated out of their sexism, or "reconstructed." (2)

Many women stopped relating sexually to men and have settled into a state of comparative asexuality: they masturbate a lot. (This is not to say that masturbation is not something that every woman must be able to do, like changing a tire, defending herself, or picking locks, as the publication *Rat* suggests.) (3) Other women have not only stopped relating to men in a fairly comprehensive way but consider themselves politicalesbians. This means that their full commitment as they see it is to women and the movement, but most of them do not have sexual relations with their sisters. Within this group are found women who are interested in having a "lesbian experience" or who consider themselves bisexual. Another segment among the politicalesbians are women who quite sincerely want to become gay-feminists but feel that only a realesbian can bring them out. Frequently, politicalesbians have expressed fear of being "dominated" by a lesbian, while other criticisms include sexism and role-playing among lesbians.

Women in the movement who are still relating intimately to men seem to believe that through their attempts to create "new men" they will liberate themselves. Enormous amounts of female energy are expended in this process, with little effect; sexism remains the overwhelming problem in the most "liberated," "loving" heterosexual living situations, and women are still dealing in the politics of housework. Straight women remain throughout this struggle fundamentally isolated from each other and the dissipation of their energies in this way is far out of proportion to the degree of apparent success attained. In seeking a personal solution to a political problem, these women have produced a new variant of sexist male. The "reconstructed man" is a more subtle creature, but still very much a man: the imbalance of power remains.

This latter point is recognized by some women who have ceased having heterosexual relations in hopes that "their men" will "get better." Like Lysistrata and her followers, they are in a state of sexual siege, witholding from the man. They extoll the pleasures of masturbation but will not take the next step in relating to themselves—to lesbianism. While the ability to relieve tension through auto-erotic manipulation is essential to woman's sexual autonomy, the emphasis in masturbation is heavily genital and orgasmic, rather than sensual. In women who classify themselves as "asexual" there is a tendency towards self-denial and defensiveness.

Among politicalesbians are found women who consider homosexual relations "right on" and politically correct but who themselves abstain. Somewhat guilt-ridden, they offer such explanations as these: 1) "I can't because that would mean I was 'self-identified,' that, in fact, I understand what my own nature could be so with that I could truly relate to another of my kind." 2) "Masturbation is just as good and besides I don't want to get emotionally involved and lose my autonomy." The first statement implies that self-identification and affirmation are solely a head trip, when, in fact, a woman can never comprehend herself in sensual isolation. It is only through sensual communication and association within her sexual peer group that she can hope to do this. The process of physical and psychic self-affirmation requires full relation with those like oneself, namely women. As to the second statement, masturbation is *not* just as good, and fear of emotional involvement, while valid enough in itself, cannot serve as reason for inactivity. It is simply non-struggle. Personal autonomy is not attained through denial of erotic involvement, aloneness, or the sublimated coziness of straight-defined "sisterhood." Women can become autonomous beings only through constant struggle with their equals, and it is a cop-out to refrain from sensual relations and thus not to deal with sexual passivity that is one of the role functions assigned them by the oppressor. The basis of feminine passivity is the suppression of female sexuality, which was so necessary to the creation of the man/woman caste system. As long as women continue to accept (and promote through their personal-political lives) this suppression of their erotic energy, they will not become liberated.

Another variety of politicalesbians is the straight-identified woman who is interested in having a "lesbian experience." Necessary to this is an "experienced lesbian," to whom the woman comes on as a potential sexual object, laying the male trip on the lesbian. This is the most oppressive of all women's movement routines to the gay feminist, who is personally diminished (to the state of "manhood") and sexually objectified. In this process, the lesbian is required to function in a service role, that of the "butch." Sexual initiative on the part of a woman does not result in direct physical gratification, as it does in a man. The equation, therefore, of "butch" and male is false. In this relation the lesbian is oppressed by the straight-defined woman in the same way that women are oppressed by straight men. Very often after this false lesbian experience, women return to straight men and to privilege without having developed self-definition or gay pride. In the end, to them, women are an *alternative* to men.

The claim to bisexuality is commonly heard within the movement, and while bisexuality is not physiologically impossible, the term cannot be used to characterize a stable socio-sexual orientation. Because no heterosexual relationship is free of power politics and other masculine mystifications, women who assert that they are bisexual retain their definition by men and the social advantages accruing from this. Bisexuality is a transitional stage, a middle ground, through which women pass from oppressive relationships to those of equality and mutuality. It is a struggle with privilege and fear, and not all women come through it to their sisters on the other side.

Fortunately however, there are increasing numbers now of previously straight-identified women who seem to be truly committed to becoming gay-feminists. The only problem seems to be a shortage of realesbians to bring these politicalesbians out. At a recent women's liberation conference a woman from a rural, mixed commune expressed enthusiastic interest in "this gay thing" and told about a visit to the farm by a group of realesbians (—"they were just like us!"—) from Boston. The impression lesbians got from this and other sources within the movement is that the common belief is that a woman should have her first Lesbian Experience with a real one, an Experienced Lesbian. These women are often puzzled and hurt by the realesbians' general unwillingness to deal with them, because they fail to understand why lesbians are so wary of straight-identified women. Lesbians have been used and fucked over many times by straight women and as a result many of them are quite bitter. But the real solution to this difficulty can come only through recognition of the sexual passivity of straight-identified women and their lack of political-emotional-sensual integration. They are still too straight and must become gay by confronting their passivity and bringing each other out.

Movement women often criticize lesbians on the alleged grounds of role-playing, sexism, and desire to dominate, without realizing that their straightness severely limits their perception of lesbians' potential to get beyond these things in equal, reciprocal relationships. Although none of us has ever been educated in the conduct of relations of roleless equality, lesbians can come closer to this achievement than others because none of the sexist role-playing training everyone receives helps make their relationships work. Role-playing gets them nowhere, because the "butch" gets none of the male sexual, social, or economic rewards while the "fem" does not have a man to bring home a man's wages or to protect her from other men's attacks. Similarly, sexism profits men, not lesbians, and it is clearly in the interest of lesbians to become feminists. But what about lesbian behavior that is characterized by straight-identified women as sexist? There exists within the women's movement a tendency toward puritanism, which classifies almost all sexual activity as sexism. Obviously, puritanism is itself rooted in sexism, where female sexual and emotional needs are suppressed for the higher goal of child-bearing, family, and service to the man. Lesbians, on the other hand, are non-productively sensual and sexual beings, having largely reclaimed the erotic potential of the female, which she was deprived of in the process of development of the man/woman caste system. Fear of "dominance" by lesbians is equally unfounded. Men have been much more highly educated in this than any women and it is likely that the generally passive straight-identified woman will project this on any woman who is more integrated and self-defined than she is.

Such myopic criticisms of lesbians indicate the degree of resistance which most women in the movement have in respect to total physical affirmation of themselves. In denying their sensual and sexual needs they have accepted the oppressor's delimitations of a crucial aspect of their physical and emotional existence, and it is therefore of little consequence that many women no longer fuck the man. Women's "right of control over their own bodies" cannot mean simply contraception and abortion but, most importantly, erotic liberation. With the best intentions in the world, the women's movement has shouldered the burdensome cultural myth of woman-as-breeder, through continuing emphasis on birth control and child-care. (More appropriate, if they must be straight a little while longer, would be mass education in oral-genital sensuality.) This does not mean that lesbians will not continue to support efforts to deal with the consequences of straight sex (we get raped too —), but rather that the women's movement must cease being a reformist head trip (politicalesbian plot) and get on to real revolution.

COME OUT!!

A LETTER FROM MARY

Mary

TO MY SISTERS:

We have all said it in our leaflets, to our friends, in our screams in the night: what we want is equal, open, loving relationships where each person can see the other as an individual human being, not a member of some mythic group, where each person loves and wants the other instead of needing her for some quality he does not himself possess. So why when I affirm all this, do you see me with strange eyes? Why when I love my sisters wholly do I make you uneasy? Why, if I talk of my feelings, do you look away or, if you listen, at the end relax as if to say: "Well, I guess you had to do that...it's probably very healthy that you brought your secret out into the open...but now that's over and we don't, thank God, have to talk about it anymore." And after that, every remark I make is filtered through the label "lesbian."

We all realize how terrible it is to be fragmented as women are in this society, split into roles, having secret identities, split mind from body. I know this. I could not stand being torn to pieces trying to love with my body men who could not even hear my voice. And now you tell me that I must do this? Now you tell me my body is to be an organizing tool, winning men away from their contempt of me, a reward for understanding an obscure point in our literature? I may love my sisters with my mind and heart, but my body belongs still to men or to no one? Or you say it belongs to me, but the love I express with it must be limited, by tacit command. "You may 'love' your sister...you may not make love with her. If it really can't be helped, we won't totally shut you out, but of course you understand we can't have you speaking for women's liberation anymore...your feelings are too uniquely your own, too personal. In short, you are the second-class citizens we need to keep us from hitting bottom, to keep us from completely losing men's approval...you are our women, every movement needs some so that it can be political."

The irony of it all is that I probably would never have discovered my homosexuality without women's liberation. You have helped to create what you now despise or fear, the incarnation of the sisterhood which was to be a lovely ideal, a sentiment of pure girlhood. Why does my body, which you claim should not be alienated from me, make my love for my sisters suddenly something furtive, something lower, something which is somehow wrong? Would that be too much of a separation from straight society, from men? But weren't these the questions we asked ourselves when we first thought of a women's movement and we were afraid of taking ourselves, our feelings, our oppression seriously? Or do you think that I will attack or seduce you, that loving other women somehow makes me a man or one of those "oversexed niggers and queers"? The accusation of being a movement of lesbians will always be powerful if we cannot say, "Being a lesbian is good." Nothing short of that will suffice as an answer.

This wasn't meant to be totally bitter, because at least some of you know how I feel; after all, I was brought up to be a heterosexual too. My mother never even mentioned homosexuals until the other day, when she spoke of them the way the Sunday sermons used to speak of lepers. I didn't even know they were possible until I was in college. I can remember the terrible desperation I felt when I began to realize that I wasn't going to be able to communicate with men. My immediate reaction was to go out and get screwed by the first guy that came along. I worked terribly hard on that relationship; I guess I felt it was my last chance. I explained myself hour after hour, sometimes articulately, sometimes incoherently, but always with kindness and sweet reason. I was driving myself crazy trying to love someone who wanted a woman, not me. I began to avoid him, not to be home after I had told him to come over, to sleep with him to shut him up, to be silent out of exhaustion, to take tranquilizers and do yoga for hours to relax. And I couldn't even see how much more I hated him for making me hate another person. And all this was after I had been in women's liberation for nine or ten months. Before women's liberation, I had always conveniently disappeared after a relatively short time with a guy, as soon as I realized that they couldn't even see through the games I was playing or that they only wanted a particular one of my roles. But I had learned: men are people too. If you wish them to be honest, love them as friends. Wow, had I learned. I was honest and loving and I was rapidly being torn into shreds.

After a couple of months of this I was beginning to believe that celibacy forever was the only thing that would save whatever was left of me, which was not much. And then I found myself loving another woman. And I was scared, so scared that I might have said nothing if she had not let me know she loved me. What I was afraid of was not social ostracism or the power of the name lesbian, because I already thought homosexuality was necessary to our liberation. I was simply afraid to find out that this too was a fraud and be left with nothing. But somehow my love was greater than my fear. I was clumsy and ignorant of how to make love to another woman, but the first time we slept together I did not mind being these things. I had never felt so completely joyous. I was one individual whole person and she was a different individual whole person and we were loving without trying to obliterate that integrity through possession or control. I was no longer an outside observer watching my body go through the motions. My mind was with my body, was with my heart.

I've learned so many things from my loving. I've learned that mutual tenderness and sensitivity are not myths. I've learned to be more easily affectionate and open with myself. I don't have to hate myself for the fact of being a woman, for being the opposite of all I was taught to love and for being unable to communicate with the people I'm supposed to love. Because I love another person, and many other people who are women. I love these people for who they are and I can love them because they can see me and hear me, as I can see them and hear them. I don't have to fight to keep from hating men, because I don't hate them. I no longer have to resent them for my need of them and I am much freer to see them as people instead of tormentors/lovers, and most of all, judges of my validity. Not having that particular resentment gives me more strength to fight against male supremacy as an institution. A desperate need is hostile, resentful. It drains our energy and keeps us from knowing what we want. To want another person as a whole individual whom one likes rather than to need someone as the representative of a valuable group or the possessor of things one wishes one had, is to affirm self love and to begin to really love other people. It also means that as men learn they are not needed for their maleness, but instead wanted if and only if they are nice people, they might have to learn to be nice people. If we swear undying loyalty and heterosexuality, they may never learn. Power is not given up unless it is obviously hollow and self-destructive. As long as women do not accept as a real alternative, as a real personal possibility, the end of sexual relationships with men, that power is strengthened and we are trapped into negativism. Affirmation of a new reality is making that kind of power irrelevant. It is speaking in new voices, new words; it is liberation from old categories and myths.

It's really hard to write process, because you end up speaking of ends as well as means and you can sound really visionary. I know homosexual relationships can get messed up by the dominant culture, by being repressed, by playing man-and-woman. I have a thousand million hang ups left, but the important thing is that I would have even more than that if I weren't a lesbian. Women's liberation needs lesbianism. Lesbians need women's liberation. We are all sisters.

My love for my sister, for my sisters, was and is good and beautiful. I don't see how it can be ignored if women are to talk about liberation. This does not mean we all have to leap into bed with each other, now or ever. It does mean we can't make homosexuality the one thing we won't talk about honestly. It means we must really accept such love as a positive good, which I think we can do by dealing honestly with our feelings about it and each other. We can't afford to be afraid of these feelings or of our sisters.

Love,
Mary

TAKE A LESBIAN TO LUNCH

Rita Mae Brown

Women's tragedy is that we are not defeated by hybris, gods or our own passion but by society, a society controlled by insensitive men. We are not the masters of that social organization and so it towers over us just as Moira, fate, towered over the mythical chauvinist, Oedipus. Women began to fight that corrupting, anti-human, anti-life structure. This beginning is known as the Women's Liberation Movement.

However, before there was a WLM there were always a number of women who questioned the system and found it destructive to themselves. Those women became women-identified. The male culture's word for this kind of women is lesbian. This is a narrow definition so typical of the male culture's vulgar conceptual limitations—the term applies only to sexual activity between women. To us, to be a lesbian means much more. It means you move toward women and are capable of making a total commitment to women.

The male party line concerning lesbians is that women became lesbians out of reaction to men. This is a pathetic illustration of the male ego's inflated proportions. I became a lesbian because of women, because women are beautiful, strong and compassion-ate. Secondarily, I became a lesbian because the culture that I live in is violently anti-woman. How could I, a woman, participate in a culture that denies me my humanity? How can any woman in touch with herself participate in this culture? To give a man support and love before giving it to a sister is to support that culture, that power system, for men receive the benefits of sexism regardless of race or social position. The higher up they are on the color line and the salary line the more benefits they receive from society but all men benefit from sexism.

Proof of the pudding is that the most rabid man-haters are heterosexual women, and with good reason, for they are directly oppressed by individual men. The contradiction of supporting the political system that oppresses you and the individuals who benefit by that system, men, is much more intense for the heterosexual woman than for the homosexual woman. Lesbians are oppressed by the male power system but not by individual men in the same intimate, insidious fashion. Therefore, we lesbians are the ultimate insult to the sexist male and the world he has built up around his weaknesses. Why? Because we ignore him. Heterosexual women are still caught up in reacting to him. Because we ignore him, because we are the ultimate insult, we pay and we pay heavily. Following are some instances of how a woman pays for lesbianism in America. The examples are from my direct experience.

In 1962, when I was sixteen, a schoolmate's father threatened to shoot me on sight. He had found love letters that I had written to his daughter. He literally locked the girl up. He drove her to and from school. She couldn't go out at night, and she couldn't receive phone calls unless he screened them. He went so far as to go to the administration of the school and have her transferred out of the classes we had together. I also got kicked off the student council, thanks to his moral purity. Naturally, our classmates were surprised at my getting bounced and at the sudden ending of my friendship with this girl. Many of them vaguely figured out what was happening. The result of this sleuthing was that our friends split over whether we were lesbians or whether we weren't. Our closest friends hotly defended us by saying we weren't lesbians—that we couldn't possibly be such horrible creatures. Our not-so-close friends smacked their lips over the scandal, and in a short time it was all over our high school as well as every other high school in the city.

The gossip was shortlived as I flatly stated that I did love the girl and if that was lesbianism I was damn glad of it. The gossip stopped and so did the friendships. My closest friends nearly trampled each other in the rush for the door. My civics teacher and student council advisor, a pompous, pasty-faced asshole who proudly proclaimed his membership in the John Birch Society, declared as he canned me, that I was unhealthy. I was sick all right, but not in the way they imagined—I was sick of all those dirty looks, snickers and outright fights I was having with everyone who crossed my path.

The next year I went to the state university. I had won a scholarship, which was a good thing because my family's total income for 1962 was $2,300. The university had around 15,000 students, if not from the state itself, from neighboring southern states. Everything was fine until I became mildly involved in the just-beginning civil rights movement. I had been seen on the black side of town. One of my friends called me into her room to talk about my sudden change for the worse. I told her I thought just the opposite about my behavior. She upbraided me for mixing with those people—blacks and Jews (who were behind it all, of course—can you believe it?) I told her I didn't give a flying fuck about race or sex. As far as I was concerned, it was the person that counted, not pigment, not sex. At that time, I believed that.

Within three hours of that conversation I was called into the office of the Dean of Women, guardian of morals and the flowers of Southern womanhood. This cheery-faced, apple-cheeked, ex-Marine sergeant offered me a cigarette with a tight-lipped smile and then blasted me with, "Now what's this I hear about your relationships with other women?" She went on to accuse me of seducing the president of Delta Delta Delta, of seducing numerous innocents in the dorms and, sin of sins, of sleeping with black men. She threw in a few black women for good measure. If I had kept such a busy schedule, I think I would have been too exhausted to walk into her office.

She hinted in heavy tones that in addition to my numerous sexual perversions that I was also a communist and was "stirring up the nigras." In a burst of anger I cracked her with: "How dare you accuse me of lesbianism when you are a lesbian yourself? You persecute me to protect yourself, you broad-assed sow." Rational discourse collapsed. She put me under house arrest, and I couldn't leave the dorms at night. I was also checked out hourly by the resident counselor in the dorm and had the pleasure of reporting to the university psychiatrist once a day, and if I didn't, the campus guards went out looking for me. My psychiatrist couldn't speak good English, but he was a whiz at Turkish. I couldn't speak Turkish. He had, however, perfected one English phrase with remarkable enunciation: "You sleep with women?" He had a habit of embracing me after our half hour of international exchange. I question whether those embraces were part of my therapy since he always had a hard-on.

All of this happened during exam period. One night I was busy cramming for a physics exam when a self-appointed contingent of physical education majors burst into my room. It was quite a shock since no one had been speaking to me since the beginning of this mess, but they didn't exactly speak to me, either. Frightened past reason, these wild-eyed women informed me that if I even hinted that they were lesbians or that any of their beloved faculty fell into that damned category—they would kill me. Nothing like a little melodrama to spice my misery.

The next day, I was treated to an example of how sexism kills minds. I walked into my exam, and silence fell over the crowded auditorium. When I would try to sit in an empty seat, the student next to it would inform me that it was taken, that I should drop dead, that it was broken—plus a few I don't remember. I took my exam sitting on the floor, and I know I got an "A." I had a 99 percent average before the exam, and the exam itself was easy. When the grades were reported, my average was 61 percent. No explanation, just 61 percent.

Southern hospitality does not apply if you are a lesbian, and if you dared to wink an eye at civil rights. I couldn't get a job. My scholarships were suspended, so I couldn't go back to school. In other words, I couldn't go home again. And so, after a long series of adventures, I arrived in New York City. I felt as though I were in the hanging gardens of neon. Home now was an abandoned red-and-black Hudson automobile near Washington Square. I lived in the back seat, with another orphan, a kitten named Baby Jesus. The front seat was inhabited by Calvin, a South Carolina homosexual. Calvin had suffered many beatings from his heterosexual black brothers because of his homosexuality. Our pain was a common bond: Nobody wants their queers. We stayed together a short time until Calvin found someone to keep him.

Eventually, I got a job as a waitress. I had to wear demeaning clothes, and put up with passes that ranged from the tragically transparent to the truly creative. I saved money by living in a cold-water flat, without stove or heat. I wore few clothes and saved money until I could enroll in New York University. Finally, I earned a scholarship and finished my education.

During the week I would sometimes go into gay bars. To avoid paying for drinks, I grabbed the first empty glass in sight and went to the bathroom where I filled it with water. If anyone asked me what I was drinking, I said "gin." The women I met were interesting. Many were tied into establishment jobs and others were secretaries trying to look like the women tied into the establishment jobs.

New York's old gay lesbian world has as many rules as the tsarina's court. Most often I was struck by the isolation the women enforced upon each other. Oppression runs deep, and among our own we act it out on each other with as much viciousness (sometimes) as the very culture which produced the oppression. It was in gay bars that I learned that a world of women can only work if we destroy the male value system, the male pattern for human relationship (if you can call it human). These methods employ role play, economic exploitation, dominance and passivity, and material proof of your social rank—they can only keep people apart and fighting with each other. As long as you work within that system you can never really know anyone—least of all, yourself.

When the rumblings of the just-born women's liberation movement reached me, I was filled with hope. I thought women's liberation could conquer sexism once and for all, but what I found was that sexism exists even between women in the movement and is just as destructive as the sexism between men and women.

I came to women's liberation via a political homosexual group, the Student Homophile League, which was male-dominated. Homosexual men (with few exceptions) are like heterosexual men in that they don't give a damn about the needs of women. So I left the group for the National Organization for Women. I went to a few business meetings where the women conducted themselves in a parliamentary manner and generally behaved like good, white, middle-class ladies are supposed to behave. I was hardly enamored of the bejeweled and well-dressed women. I heard vaguely of more radical groups, but I couldn't get in touch with any of them. It was almost like prohibition days—you had to know somebody who knew somebody in those groups. I didn't know anybody, so I gritted my teeth and stuck it out with the golden girls. I sat at the general meeting and said nothing. Eventually a woman did talk to me. I questioned her on the lesbian issue, and she bluntly told me that the word "lesbian" was never to be uttered. "After all, that is exactly what the press wants to say we are, a bunch of lesbians." She then went on to say patronizingly: "What are you doing worrying about lesbians; you must have lots of boyfriends." OK, sister, have it your way!

Finally NOW had a rap session for new women, and I attended. The women bitched about job discrimination, the pill, and so on. Although I had been silent until now, I am not generally a silent, retiring woman. I had kept silent up until this meeting because I was unfamiliar with the organization, because I was born poor, and because now I was surrounded by privileged, well-spoken women, who took food, housing, and education for granted. Lastly, I did not want to jeopardize other lesbians.

By this time I had had a few months to review the political issues at stake and to come up with the firm conclusion that NOW was, to make a long story short, full of shit. A women's movement is for women. Its actions and considerations should be for women, not for what the white, male media finds acceptable. In other words, lesbianism definitely was an important issue and should be out in the open.

I stood up and said something that went like this: "All I've heard about tonight and in the other meetings was you women complaining about men, in one form or another. I want to know why you don't speak about other women? Why you deliberately avoid lesbianism and why you can't see anything but men? I think lesbians are ahead of you." (At that time I believed the lesbian politically superior to the heterosexual woman. I still do although now I recognize there are such gaps as apolitical lesbians and political heterosexuals.) What followed my short remarks resembled a mass coronary. One woman jumped up and declared that lesbians want to be men and that NOW only wants "real" women. This kind of thing went on for a while. Then the second wave set in—the sneaky, sly curiosity that culminates in: "Well, what do you do in bed?" (I paint myself green and hang from the rafters.)

After approximately one hour of being the group freak and diligently probed, poked, and studied, these ladies bountiful decided that, yes, I was human. I even looked like what young women in their early twenties were supposed to look like. (I had long hair and was in a skirt. Now I have short hair, and if I wear pants, I'm told I look like a young boy. You figure it out.) There were other lesbians in the room, and they too looked like what women are supposed to look like. The difference between them and me was that I opened my mouth and fought the straight ladies. I was even angrier at my silent lesbian sisters than at these incredibly rude, peering, titillated heterosexual wonders. Lesbian silence is nothing new to me, but it never fails to piss me off. I know all the reasons to be quiet in front of the straight enemy. They cut no ice with me. Every time you keep your mouth shut you make life that much harder for every lesbian in this country. Our freedom is worth you losing your job and your friends. If you keep your mouth shut, you are a coward. The women in that room were cowards. They thought they would pass for straight, but in the last three years since that meeting, every one of them has been brutally purged from NOW!

In that room somehow, a few women got past the label "lesbian" and tried to see me as a person. At the next general meeting, some of them came over and talked. They were trying to break down the barriers between us. The NOW leadership was another story. They would in no way recognize the issue of lesbianism as relevant to the movement. Secretly, a few of them called me and "confessed" to being lesbians themselves. They were ashamed of their silence, but their logic was, when in Rome, do as the Romans do. They were very busy playing straight because they didn't want to lose their positions in the leadership. They asked me not to reveal them, and there were hints that I could have a place in the leadership if I would play my cards right (shut up). This kind of buy-off is commonly known as being the token nigger. They got a real bargain with me, because not only was I a lesbian, I was poor, I was an orphan (adopted) without knowledge of my racial/ethnic origins.

At the time, I saw the co-optation, but I had nowhere else to go, and it didn't occur to me then to start a whole new movement. I became editor of New York NOW's newsletter. From that I moved up to being the administrative coordinator for the national organization—an appointed post. It sounds good if you care about titles, but what it really means is that you do lots of boring labor, like collating, stapling, and mailing.

Everything was fine as long as I did not bring up the lesbian issue. After all, the issue was solved because I was in the power structure, and I was a lesbian. Being the token lesbian, I also helped take the heat off the hidden lesbians. It wasn't right, but I couldn't figure out how to fight it. I still couldn't get in touch with the radical groups, and when I mentioned my interest in these groups, a woman on the executive board told me they were all a gang of unclean girls who hated lesbians and who talked about their personal hang-ups. I asked her if she had ever been to a meeting and she said that she hadn't. However, she assured me that she had heard this on very good authority.

As women began to be comfortable with me and see that I was a fairly decent human being with no obvious defects, they began to turn on to me. It was very painful for me because when they experienced warm, or sexual feelings, they began to treat me as a man. All these women knew was men, and I was getting the old seduction game we learn in preschool sex-role training. I can't respond to that kind of thing anymore. Some of the women were hurt, some angry, and some vicious. Then there was the most manipulative woman of all, the one who was going to liberate herself on my body. She could then pass herself off as right on, new-wave feminist because she had slept with a woman. It was pretty confusing.

As you can see, the women still thought of lesbianism as a sexual activity only. This is the way in which men define it. The women couldn't understand that lesbianism means a different way of living. It means, for me, that you dump all roles as much as possible, that you fight the male power system, and that you give women primacy in your life—emotionally, personally, politically. It doesn't mean that you look at girlie magazines or pinch the bottoms of passers-by.

Difficult as all this was, worse events were to follow. A NOW national officer of much fame made a clumsy pass at me. Not only do I not want to make passes at other women, I don't want women to make passes at me. It all sounds like a football game. Needless to say, I did not respond to the woman. Within an amazingly short time I was relieved of my duties at the national office for lack of funds. While the leadership was nervously casting its eyes about for someone to take on the burden of the newsletter, I decided to go down fighting. I put out the January, 1970 issue of the newsletter with a blast at the leadership for its sexist, racist, and class-biased attitudes. Two other NOW officers who were fed up with the back-room politicking and high-powered prison guarding helped with the issue and also publicly resigned their offices.

By this time, I had discovered some of the other groups. I went to Redstockings, an organization which pushed consciousness-raising and the pro-woman line. Redstockings was not too pro-woman when it came to lesbians. They could empathize with the prostitute, support the housewife, encourage the single woman, and seek child care for the mother, but they wouldn't touch the lesbian. I became the token lesbian once more, and I became more and more depressed. At least I had enough insight to realize that this was not my personal problem. It was and still is the crucial political issue, and the first step toward a coherent, all-woman ideology. But when there is just one person pushing an issue, that one person becomes the issue until others see it; she becomes a Cassandra of sorts.

Lesbianism is the one issue that deals with women reacting positively to other women. All other issues deal with men and the society they have built to contain us. The real questions are: Why are women afraid of one another? Why does the straight woman throttle the lesbian? Why do women keep insisting this is a bedroom issue and not a political issue, when in fact, this issue is at the bottom of our self-image? If we cannot look at another woman and see a human being worth making a total commitment to—politically, emotionally, physically—then where the hell are we? If we can't find another woman worthy of our deepest emotions, then can we find ourselves worthy of our own emotions, or are all commitments reserved for men, those that benefit by our oppression? It is clear that men are not reserving their deepest commitments for women. Otherwise, we couldn't be raped, butchered on abortionists' tables, jeered at in the public streets, and denied basic rights under a government that preaches equality. We are taunted in the streets, in the courts, in the homes—as though we are nothing more than walking sperm receptacles.

A few Redstockings tried to deal with these issues. They received no support from the other women. By this time I was too tired and too wise to spend much energy on the straight ladies. I left the group with recriminations and blow-ups. Those women from the group who have become lesbians have also left.

The next move was to the Gay Liberation Front. It supposedly is for men and women, but I was wary because of my previous experience in the SHL. Some of the women there had gay consciousness but little women's consciousness, and I thought that introducing the idea of consciousness-raising to them would be a positive step for them as well as me, as I needed to be among other lesbians. If these lesbians could connect their two oppressions, it would be a new ball game.

There are good reasons why many lesbians have no political consciousness of woman oppression. One of the ways in which many lesbians have protected themselves from the pain of woman oppression is to refuse to see themselves as traditional women. Society encourages this view because if you are not a traditional woman, then you must be some kind of man. Some lesbians do assume a male role (become imitation men) but never get the man's political and economic privileges. Other lesbians feel themselves to be women, know intensely that they are not imitation men but stay away from women's liberation: They know from direct experience that straight women cannot be trusted with lesbian sensibilities and sensitivities.

Many of the women in GLF fell into that group. They would rather work with male homosexuals and endure the chauvinism than expose themselves to a more obviously hostile element—the heterosexual woman, who is more hostile because lesbianism forces her to face herself with no social props, more hostile because inside she knows and hates herself for her fears.

When I suggested consciousness-raising to the women in GLF, they were suspicious. They thought I was a Pied Piper, wooing them into women's liberation instead of fighting homosexual oppression by working through GLF. They didn't bother to ask me much: If they had, they would have found out that I went that route in 1967-68.

In spite of their suspicions, they did form consciousness-raising groups. A sense of woman oppression was developed, and many were well along the way because of their increasing anger over how the gay men mistreated them. They saw that lesbian oppression and male homosexual oppression have less in common than they formerly thought. What we have in common is that heterosexuals of both sexes hate and fear us. The similarity stops there because that hate and fear take on vastly different forms for the lesbian and the male homosexual. As the months rolled by, a few of the homosexual women began to see that, yes, I was human, etc. Through the work of those original consciousness-raising groups, a new phase was started in the war against sexism. Women who love women came together. We are no longer willing to be token lesbians in the women's liberation movement nor are we willing to be the token women in the Gay Liberation Front.

The first explosion from this new growth came at the Second Congress to Unite Women when the lesbians (40 in number) confronted the women there. For the first time, straight women were forced to face their own sexism and their complicity with the male power structure. The lesbians are moving and have grown enormously since the Congress, which was in the spring of 1970. As the lesbians have grown in number and in revolutionary ideology, the backlash has increased until it has become clear to all revolutionary lesbians that straight women work for The Man and are not to be trusted. They don't want to lose the privilege they gain by being heterosexual. Out of the lesbian/heterosexual split has come a clearer politics, and the terms heterosexual and lesbian mark the difference between reform and revolution. It is the woman who loves women who will make the revolution. It is the woman who sells out to men who will betray her. And time decides who wins. Or will we all be destroyed by The Man's next filthy war?

I'd like to be expansive and say that the last four years in the Woman's Liberation Movement weren't all that bad. I'd like to be generous and say that I didn't resent the reaction of the women in the Gay Liberation Front. I'd like to close this article with glowing phrases of sisterhood and coalition fronts. But I can't. My experience has taught me that sisterhood is for straight women to use to cover up their dirt. My experience taught me that straight women do not love other women. It taught me not to trust the straight woman because she cannot build a solid politics. I have learned from my experience and will build on the bones of my life rather than phrases snatched from former revolutions, revolutions made by heterosexual males that fucked the women over who gave themselves to those revolutions. I know there can be a revolution, and I know it will be made by women who are women-identified.

This article is critical of a movement that has already been co-opted by the media: I mean women's liberation. Co-opted because greedy reformists and egotistical writers have used it to advance themselves in the white male world. For those who build toward a new world, women's liberation is a dead movement twitching its limbs in the vulgar throes of establishment recognition. It can now join hands with the male left and black capitalism as the unholy trio of sell-outs—take what goodies you can from The Man and let the people fend for themselves.

Women-identified women will not sell out. Neither will we go around making loud noises about killing pigs and blowing up the Capitol. Talk is cheap, and violent talk is the cheapest of all. We are not taken in by the easy politics of violence just as we are not taken in by the more clever politics of reform. We have no instant formula that will dazzle reporters and media vultures. We have mountains to move, and we have, today, only our hands to move them with. But every day there are more hands.

HANOI TO HOBOKEN,
A ROUND TRIP TICKET

Rita Mae Brown

Why the persistent enthusiasm for far away places and distant struggles with imperialism? Why travel to Hanoi when you can go to Hoboken and see the same show? Granted, the costumes are native, the accents New Jersey; the exotic touch is missing and you won't get napalm for an encore but the plot is still the same: Oppression.

There are a number of reasons why Hanoi fascinates so many women in our movement and why Hoboken is definitely a drag. Visiting Hanoi or Havana and writing articles on such a visit is one way to legitimatize our movement through participation in those areas that the white, middle class, male-left movement has designated as legitimate. It shows that we women are reaching out beyond what the male left defines as "women's issues" to what they define as the "important" issues. Women's issues are not important. It is inconceivable to think of a male left heavy going to Hoboken to study how lack of child care facilities oppresses poor women.

I am not for one minute announcing that U.S. imperialism is not a concern of the women's liberation movement. The struggle of our Vietnamese sisters is anything but frivolous, but the way in which many American women approach that struggle is both imitative and frivolous.

When our Vietnamese sisters throw out the invader they will have yet another war on their hands, the war against sexism in their own society. But right now those women are fighting for their lives. Here in Amerika many women are also fighting for their lives. There are no bombers, but the struggle is just as relentless and deadly—we are the poor, the black, the Latin and the lesbian. We aren't exotic and we aren't remotely glamorous. The male left is not concerned with us although it will make token statement for the benefit of black males concerning racism (the black woman is supposedly incorporated in the black male). By flying to Hanoi, you win the attention of the male left. By working in Hoboken you attract no attention at all, and by working with lesbians you are quickly dismissed as irrelevant and sick.

Another reason why Hanoi is such a beacon for revolutionary moths: you can return to the U.S. and rip off the liberals with speaking tours, books, movies, etc. on your experiences there. That's not to say that all who go to Hanoi are rip offs, nor are all who go eager for male left approval, but enough are to make it a problem. Unfortunately, poverty and woman oppression are not so lucrative a profession despite recent attempts by the establishment media to cash in on these oppressions.

If you worked in Hoboken, who would be grateful but the women in Hoboken—women who have no power to bestow prestige or money on anyone?

What I am getting at is this: It's easier to worry about far away problems than our problems here at home. Not only is it easy, it's comfortable because the problems here at home might possibly be cleared up if we worked at clearing them up. How far would Ho Chi-Minh have gotten if he had run all over the globe to witness other forms of imperialism? By concentrating on imperialism abroad we use quantities of energy that could be used here, like setting up health clinics. In other words, the priorities of the anti-imperialist women are ass backwards. For example, *off our backs*, a feminist newspaper, ran a special issue on Women and Imperialism on December 31, 1970. Most issues of this paper (after the initial six issues) carry some article on the subject of women and imperialism. Has there been a special issue on lesbianism? Articles in most issues? Plain, flat, ugly, No. What about black women? Latin women? Poor women? It's not fair to single out *off our backs;* most of the other papers and magazines are the same. Our feminist media are young and wobbly and because of that many of the articles in the big city papers such as *oob* and *Rat* have been in those areas that male politics has considered important. The other papers and magazines not contaminated by male left politics confined themselves to heterosexual interests. The media are simply a reflection of the white, middle class, straight bias of the women's liberation movement itself.

Imperialism begins at home. The best place to fight imperialism is at its center. Let's stab the monster in its heart rather than slapping its fingertips.

Imperialism, racism and the attendant disregard for human life (change that to all forms of life) spring from sexism. Way back in the dim mists of prehistory when man beat down, degraded and enslaved women he clearly showed his career preferences. In degrading woman he degraded himself. Once the initial inhumanity was committed it was a simple matter to progress step by step to today. History is man remembering the subsequent degradations of other men over time. He degraded us at such an early age that he has practically forgotten it and derives little satisfaction from it in a political sense although he gets a great deal out of it personally. The real glory is in shitting on other men. To fight The Man we don't need to go to Hanoi, we fight him right here.

Let's be clear in our priorities ideologically (pragmatics will follow later in the paper) and focus our energies on the destruction of sexism rather than scatter our energies all over the globe on the latter stages of sexism known as imperialism. By fighting here, which is the current international center of the latter stages of sexism known as imperialism, we help our Vietnamese sisters. Any attention we can draw away from our sisters gives them more time to breathe. In practical terms, we cannot do more. We cannot launch an armada to join them in combat. We can express solidarity, which we have done, and we can do our best to keep in communication with our Vietnamese sisters, relating their experiences and struggle to Amerikan women and vice versa.

It does us and the Vietnamese women no good if we join the male left in desultory protest. Women have tried that for a number of years and the government's response is the dreary, well known, no response. Uncle Sam knows how to ward off anti-imperialists, after all he's had nearly 200 years' experience. But he's not so ready for anti-sexists. While he's got his arms up fighting the NLF abroad and protestors at home, let's grab him in the crotch and make him howl.

Vietnamese women understand that howl. They told Charlotte Bunch when she visited Vietnam in 1970 that Amerikan women must exercise power. The cruel irony is that the Vietnamese women take us more seriously than we take ourselves. And isn't that the key to woman oppression: We have internalized The Man's definition of women and do not take ourselves seriously. Neither do we take other women seriously so we shit on the lesbian who in many cases does take other women seriously. We write a lot and we talk a lot and we cry a lot. Unless I am completely without perception, I don't think writing, talking and crying have yet produced a mass movement of political power.

I'd like to present what I believe are the first steps to political power. Since I am only one woman I can hardly present this as a comprehensive program in the first phase of our revolution. If this remains my idea then it isn't even a first step, it's a retreat from responsibility. If the ideas spark further ideas in your head and you share it and build with other women, then we will all get somewhere.

I: Work Projects

Women with economic privilege, whether straight or lesbian, black or white or Latin, should organize to meet the survival needs of women without economic privilege. This means food distribution centers, child care centers, health care centers, self-defense programs and halfway houses for women in transition or without adequate housing. If you have special skills such as editorial abilities, mechanical or medical knowledge, anything, set up a teaching program and share it. These projects will take time and work as well as patience and self-understanding. The women whose needs you will be meeting may have no feminist consciousness at all. Don't look down on them. It's hard to have consciousness of anything when you are hungry. You will need a great deal of patience with yourself to really get in touch with this kind of oppression and why you have ignored it in the past.

Together with these work projects goes structured, disciplined consciousness-raising. This process helps women get in touch with their distinctive oppression. The black woman learns to understand racism in a political sense rather than just in a personal sense. She can begin to see the intimate connection between racism and sexism through testimony with her sisters. The lesbian recognizes lesbian oppression from the male culture and from heterosexual women. She begins to understand how this supposed individual trait, choice of sex partner and life style, is an attack on the Amerikan political structure. And so it goes, each woman learns from another woman how her particular life is a reflection of and a response to the dominant, white, rich, male culture and after that the sub-culture she herself lives in. Each woman learns that her life is a political life and by examining that life each woman learns the mechanics of oppression. Once you know how something works you can begin to fix it or fight it.

II: Re-education

This is partly done through consciousness-raising but it must be transmitted on a large scale through the feminist media. If we are serious in our work, we can only trust our own feminist media and we can relate only to that media. That media needs to be expanded. Each city needs its own newspaper. We also need other forms of media—films, slide shows, music, etc. If you start a paper, concentrate on your locality. Local news is immediate. Women can identify with what happens in their own city and in the lives of people like themselves. Be local and serve the needs of your women if you want to touch their lives. If you carry articles of international feminist events, be sure to help your readers see how this affects their own lives.

III: Lesbianism

Before our movement can advance as a political force with a coherent women's ideology (not something borrowed from the male left) we need to completely analyze lesbianism. This is the touchstone of our self-image, the mirror of our oppression, and is such an intense experience that it cuts across racial and class barriers. Living communes hinge on this issue as does all subsequent feminist analysis of sexism.

Lesbianism is the one issue that deals with women responding positively to other women as total human beings worthy of total commitment. It is the one area where no male can tread. It is also the one area that demands deep self-criticism. To hide from this question is to hide from yourself. To hide from this question is to doom the movement to a pale imitation of existing leftist ideologies—ideologies that may have served the needs of dedicated men in Russia in 1917, in China in the 40s, but which cannot and do not serve the needs of women today.

Lesbianism is important structurally because confronting it will help us develop techniques we can use to deal with other differences. Every woman can confront the issue of lesbianism because she has the potential to be a lesbian. It is more difficult to confront class and racial differences because there is not that commonality. One does not transcend race and class—you can only come to a clear understanding of those differences in your own life and then use that understanding in conjunction with women from different classes and races to build a solid politic. Lesbianism is the great gut issue, it touches every one of us. If we learn how to deal with such an explosive issue constructively (which we are in the process of doing) then we will have the tools to deal with the other two explosive issues: Race and Class. Lesbianism will provide us with the individual and group skills for constructive confrontation, for struggle, for progress. In other words, we need a foundation to build our house upon and this issue gives us our ideological and technical foundation. We cannot unify unless we deal with this issue first.

Those three steps make up what I see as the first phase toward seriousness and toward real change in the lives of all women. Many of us can see beyond this first phase, but we must accomplish these goals before we can move on. They aren't easy goals, maybe that's why we are tempted to concentrate on distant places. The first step involves nothing less than meeting the survival needs of all women. But we must do this or the women's liberation movement is destined to stay a white, middle-class, heterosexual movement—physically and psychically. If you want to see what comes of that, visit the Women's Party at 144 Constitution Ave., Washington, D.C., the graveyard and the shrine of the last great wave of white, middle-class, heterosexual feminism.

To advocate other goals at this time, like world wide revolution, is to slip from the serious and pragmatic to the imagined and fantastic. We can have women united across the globe but we must start somewhere and that somewhere is with the above mentioned measures, unglamorous though they may be. If we do not commit ourselves to this serious work, if we indulge ourselves in "right on" rhetoric, we create a preposterous lie and its twin, cynicism. The only people capable of living with that kind of unreality will be our self-ordained leaders who have need of the illusion to inflate the ego, who have need of the liturgy for a grim, old form revolution and its heavy death wish. We must begin to achieve concrete results with our energy or we will, as a movement, lapse into disbelief in our own capabilities and our political effectiveness will be limited to a few, self-indulgent media stars trotted out by the male establishment in an orgy of tokenism.

We must begin to achieve these concrete ends in order to test ourselves. We will learn a great deal from these early projects—self-reliance, pride and organizational skills. If the management of the state were in our hands tomorrow we would not be ready for it. We must train to handle political responsibility for our own lives and other lives through these kind of outreach projects. You learn by doing. Do it. We will all do it together. This first step is the hardest because we have so few models or examples for it, another reason why it is so crucial.

So we have a lot to learn from a visit to Hanoi; we learn we have to come home to Hoboken. Let's take ourselves seriously and seriously support our sisters in Vietnam who do believe in us. Let's begin the slow and tedious labor here in our own backyard that will eventually change the world.

LESBIANS AND THE
ULTIMATE LIBERATION OF WOMEN

Gay Liberation Front Women (New York City)

Gay Liberation Front women welcome all women. In meetings and activities we maintain a flexible way of doing things to encompass our sisters of different social, economic, racial, religious, and political interests, and to permit individual freedom in actions and activities, both inside and outside of GLF.

We provide an opportunity for women to relate to other women—through political activities and community social activities, beginning with dances and moving out into new forms of socializing and communicating with our sisters.

GLF was the first group in New York to come together specifically to fight homosexual oppression. GLF Women, a caucus of GLF, are lesbian activists fighting oppression on two fronts: As homosexuals, we work with our gay brothers to fight oppression based on society's exclusion of individuals who love members of the same sex. As women, we work with women's liberation to fight the oppression of all women.

Our strongest common denominator and greatest oppression

lie with society's injustice against us as homosexuals. We are discriminated against as women, but lesbians who live openly are fired from jobs, expelled from schools, banished from their homes, and even beaten. Lesbians who hide and escape open hostility, suffer equal oppression through psychic damage caused by their fear and guilt. With this understanding, we focus on gay liberation, giving priority to gay issues and gay problems. We are part of the revolution of all oppressed people, but we cannot allow the lesbian issue to be an afterthought.

GLF Women are dedicated to changing attitudes, institutions, and laws that oppress lesbians, using all or any methods from reform to revolution. Actions and consciousness-raising achieve this goal. Gay liberation is a movement and a state of mind challenging history's basic legal and social assumptions about homosexuality. Openly proclaiming ourselves lesbians is a revolutionary act and a threat to the prevailing society, which excludes people who live outside the norm. We work for a common understanding among all people that lesbianism is the most complete and fulfilling relationship with another woman and a valid life style.

Gay consciousness-raising is a primary interest:

1. So that our lesbian sisters understand our oppression and fight against it. To be effective the lesbian movement must be a grass roots effort. We denounce the fact that society's rewards and privileges are only given to us when we hide and split our identity. We encourage self-determination and will work for changes in the lesbian self-image, as well as in society, to permit the "coming out" of each gay woman into society as a lesbian. The new self-image or "gay consciousness" refers to our sense of pride, unity, life-style, and community.

2. Raising consciousness of people in all movements—to be aware of their sexism.

3. Raising the consciousness of our sisters active in women's liberation to openly acknowledge and actively support lesbians, with the attitude of solidarity and not reciprocity. We denounce the use of the word "lesbian" to divide us from our sisters, who should be united with us in our common struggle for the liberation of all women. We feel that the core oppression of women is the lesbian's oppression and the ultimate liberation of women is through the liberation of lesbians. Real freedom for lesbians will mean the end of all oppressive relationships based on male dominance and the compulsion women feel to seek male approval and support.

Women's liberation groups must undertake consciousness-raising on lesbianism. They must accept among their leadership admitted and publicly known lesbians. They must make explicit their acceptance of the lesbian life-style now implicit in their analysis.

a) Feminists speak of rejecting role-playing, but fail to see the pressures in society during children's formative years to love men over women.

b) They say that women should be free to govern their own bodies, but fail to grant freedom of sexual preference.

c) They denounce stereotyped male and female attitudes and characteristics, but fail to accept as natural the so-called masculine female and so-called feminine male.

d) They talk about being independent from men, but do not see that the lesbian life style is the ultimate form of independence.

e) They talk of love among women, but do not include physical expression of that love.

4. Education of the public to recognize homosexuals as an oppressed minority and to destroy stereotyped images based on and perpetuated by society's hostility. To fight prejudice with reason and love. *Gay is Good*. Sexuality is basic to all human beings, and homosexuality is as natural as heterosexuality. To teach children from the earliest years about homosexuality without bias.

To effect change, we advocate an open media policy, with media defined as lectures, demonstrations, leaflets, consciousness-raising, dances, and rapping in bars, as well as the press.

**VI.
CUBA:
GAY
AS
THE
SUN**

THE CUBAN REVOLUTION AND GAY LIBERATION

Allen Young

The struggle against sexism—women's liberation and gay liberation—is part of a long historical process to create a society based on equality and justice. In an earlier part of this century, standard-bearers of equality and justice found themselves fighting as workers against bosses, or as lovers of democracy against fascism. At that time, that was all it meant to be for socialism or communism, to be a leftist or a revolutionary or a progressive. These were political realities I found easy to understand as I learned them as a small boy in my home. It was easy to see the injustice in a system, the capitalist system, in which bosses who did no work became rich from the labor of others. The evils of fascism, with its racism, militarism, and near enslavement of masses of people, were not hard to grasp. Surrounded by adults who were either members or sympathizers of the Communist Party, I also learned to admire and defend the Soviet Union as the leading force against capitalism and fascism. I never heard a negative word said about the Soviet Union, except from the people who defended capitalism or fascism.

By the late 1950s and early 1960s, a new political force emerged in the world—the people of the Third World. The origins of that term the "Third World," are often forgotten, but they are significant in understanding the political growth of myself and the current generation. The "First World" was that of the wealthy nations of the capitalist world, such as the U. S., Britain and Australia. The "Second World" consisted of the newly comfortable nations of the socialist world, such as the Soviet Union and Czechoslovakia. Both the First World and the Second World were equipped with nuclear weapons. The term "Third World" began to be applied to a new, third grouping—the poor nations of Asia, Africa and Latin America, lands inhabited primarily by non-white peoples. As people in the Third World nations began to fight for national independence, and in some cases for socialism (the sharing of wealth and labor), U.S. imperialism emerged as a primary enemy. (If you are reading this, and you don't think that

U.S. imperialism is the enemy of people seeking freedom, then you should seek out the facts about the Vietnam war, or about the role the U.S. plays, day to day, around the globe.)

Critics of the U.S.S.R.—many of them from Third World nations—said that it was abandoning its historic role as a center of revolution by becoming wrapped up in international power politics. From within the U.S.S.R. itself, the truth about Stalin's purges and the death of democracy there became known. It was also charged that the U.S.S.R. had stopped building socialism and was creating a bureaucracy, a privileged elite of individuals (not so different from bosses) who obtained economic advantage but did no work. In some Third World countries, such as Cuba and Algeria, the people were fighting against considerable odds to overthrow colonialism or neo-colonialism, but local communist parties, whose members were the staunch supporters of the Soviet Union, played little or no part in the struggle (or even tried to cool it off).

Cuba, in particular, carried out a revolution whose most famous leaders—Fidel Castro and Che Guevara—showed a commitment to political independence, a desire to build a political and economic system which would be just but which would not depend upon the dictums of the Soviet Union. During the same period of time, the Chinese people were establishing an independent road to socialism, while in Vietnam and a dozen other countries, workers and peasants picked up the gun in wars of national liberation. While these guns were often of Soviet manufacture, the political scenario was not built in Moscow. Soviet citizens (and especially Soviet bureaucrats) were prepared to co-exist with the U.S. while millions suffered extreme poverty, ignorance and disease in the underdeveloped world. But the peoples of those underdeveloped countries were showing less patience.

For young Americans such as myself, Cuba, 90 miles from home, provided the first and the clearest example of a people fighting with considerable unity against U.S. imperialism. The speeches and writings of the Cubans—the Second Declaration of Havana is perhaps the best example—provided the clearest explanation of what U.S. imperialism means for the people of the Third World. As a North American already concerned with political change and social justice, I found myself studying the Spanish language and Latin American history and otherwise making my own life relevant to what by then seemed to me the most meaningful and significant conflict in the world. It didn't take long for me to feel a deep love, an emotional as well as intellectual commitment, to the people of Cuba and the rest of Latin America. I became involved in arguments with the detractors of Cuba. I learned about the Cuban government's successful efforts to wipe out illiteracy, to provide free medical care for the whole population, to mobilize the people collectively to do the hard work that could bring about an improved living standard for all. I felt strongly that as a North American, much of my comfort was due to my white skin and to my citizenship in an exploitative nation. So I felt an obligation to work to support Third World people who were opposing the military power and the racism of the U.S. I felt this was essential to my own humanity, and I still do. In general, however, politics was something outside of myself. My own suffering—as a faggot—would go untouched by all this.

Before long, with this perspective on life, I carved myself a more or less comfortable niche in the established New Left, specifically as a member of Students for a Democratic Society (SDS) and an editor for Liberation News Service (LNS). People other than myself, most of them women and gays who did not have such a niche, launched the movement against sexism. Women's liberation and gay liberation—or gay feminist revolution as we sometimes call the combined efforts of women and men against sexism—takes politics to its most elemental level, to the source of power relations among humans. It presumes the justice of the proletarian struggle against the bosses and the Third World struggle against imperialism, seeing manifestations of male power in both the bosses and the imperialists. Gay feminist revolution became and is my cause because it is the only way I can successfully fight against exploitation and oppression of all kinds. What's more—and this is where so many people fear to go along—gay feminist revolution is the cause of all revolutionaries, because only by ending sexism will the root cause of oppression be destroyed. Most important, gay liberation means dealing with the politics of personal relations, and as such is the path to personal fulfillment and joy, which proletarian revolution and Third World revolution cannot promise by themselves.

The Bolshevik revolution in Russia began the process of building socialism, but the process became distorted, scarred, moribund. This failure was due in part to the male ego of one man—Stalin. In fact, one of Stalin's crimes (usually forgotten by even his most vehement critics) was to reverse progressive measures designed to destroy the nuclear family and accept homosexuality. (Such measures had been approved by earlier Bolshevik governments.)

Cuba's revolution is younger, and it is not possible to pass judgment on Cuba the way one can on the Soviet Union, where bureaucratic minions are entrenched and capitalist values restored. In Cuba less than a decade ago, measures were taken to prevent the growth of a privileged elite; by now there are still both good and bad tendencies.

The fact that Cuba's leadership is sexist should be no surprise, and should not prevent us from applauding the accomplishments of the revolution, especially the ouster of the dictator Batista. Cuban society was sexist before the guerrillas came to power. What is a surprise, or at least is disturbing, is that dynamic change through struggle over sexism is not occurring in Cuba. Worse, in mid-1971, at an important Congress on Education and Culture, the Cubans saw fit to reiterate overtly anti-homosexual policies and to totally ignore the problem of *machismo* (male chauvinism) which, in private conversations, Cuban communists admit must be eliminated in order to bring about equality for Cuban women.

Cuba, then, is a country which has been in the front lines of combatting U.S. imperialism and of trying to eliminate the scourge of underdevelopment. It is also a country whose political leadership, asserting male power and drawing upon a sexist cultural background, is preventing vital new revolutionary developments from occurring in certain areas. What it means for me is that I experience contradictory emotions—love for the Cuban government's courageous opposition to U.S. dominance, hatred for the same government's cruel oppression of my gay sisters and brothers.

My first visit to Cuba took place in February and March of 1969. I arrived in Havana well-prepared for this visit, better-prepared, I might say immodestly, than most North Americans arriving there. I spoke the language well, and had done considerable reading on the history of Cuba and its revolution. I had been a graduate student at Stanford University's Institute of Hispanic American and Luso-Brazilian Studies, where I closely watched Cuban events and read the Cuban press as part of my work on the monthly Hispanic American Report. I was familiar with Latin culture, having lived for three years (1964–67) in Brazil and Chile, where I did free-lance newspaper work and traveled widely, taking advantage of scholarships I had won. This experience also had brought me in close contact with the political and economic reality of underdevelopment. I had seen the arrogance and racism of North American tourists in Rio de Janeiro. I had seen the slums of Santiago, Chile. I had seen the downcast passivity of people who lived under decades of Stroessner's fascism in Asuncion, Paraguay. I had seen impoverished peasants in Brazil's drought-ridden Northeast.

I was prepared to like Cuba, and I did. I felt that the people there had acquired a new sense of dignity and were at work improving their lot. This was a people who had defeated the giant Amerika. The tourists were gone, and with them prostitution, the narcotics syndicates and the gambling casinos. Slums were being torn down as quickly as possible. Most of all, I saw a people who seemed to be mobilized and active in a process of social and political change. The positive spirit of Cuba during this period has been written about at length in several books, and my purpose here is not to provide an overall analysis of Cuba. (One of the best of these books is *The Youngest Revolution,* by Elizabeth Sutherland, who, by the way, includes criticism of Cuba's anti-homosexualism.)

One of the most important facts about my first visit to Cuba was that my homosexuality was a secret, "a deep dark secret" with all the weight of that cliche. That wasn't so unusual in those days. Or even in these days—statistically and logically speaking, it's a good guess that there's at least one person on the Central Committee of the Communist Party of Cuba who has that same secret. But I knew that I was gay and I knew, even before I arrived in Havana, that I would be able to meet gay people there. I knew I would want to meet gays—partially for sex, partially for the closeness I can have only with gay people, and partially to find out what it is like to be gay in revolutionary Cuba. I also knew that I would be able to find out something about straight official Cuban attitudes toward homosexuality simply by raising the question. My hosts seemed to be amused, confused, surprised and sometimes annoyed at the concern so many North Americans have shown over the status of women and gays in Cuba.

As for the general position of homosexuals in Cuba, I quickly determined that the Cuban government had a semi-official anti-homosexual policy, and that this policy was rooted largely in the male chauvinist, anti-gay attitudes of generations of Cuban people (fostered by Roman Catholicism and Latin culture). As far as I could determine, the issue was not the legality of homosexual acts. The oppression was not through sodomy laws, but rather through a commitment to creating a society which would have no homosexuals. Cubans involved in the Communist Party were most articulate in explaining Cuba's anti-homosexual position, though it has not been possible to find this position in public writings and speeches of the Cuban leadership. I was told that homosexuality was an aberration produced under capitalism, that the future generations of Cuba would be free of homosexuals if only the youth of the country could be kept from having contact with acknowledged homosexuals. They admitted that in an earlier period (1965, to be specific) homosexuals were interred by the thousands in special work camps known euphemistically as Military Units to Increase Production (UMAP). But, they said, the brutality which marked these camps was a "mistake," and the camps no longer existed. Instead, measures were taken to insure that homosexuals were excluded from contact with the youth. In practice, this meant constant purging of homosexuals from schools, including the universities, and from many work centers. No one who is gay, for example, may be employed in any division of the Ministry of Education, though enforcement is not perfect. One member of the Cuban Communist Party told me how about a dozen homosexuals of both sexes were quietly asked to leave their posts in the Foreign Ministry. This action was justified, he said, because these homosexuals could not be trusted since their loyalty to the revolution was weakened by the fact that the revolution was opposed to homosexuality. He tried to convince me that this action was taken humanely—"we transferred them to less sensitive positions in other agencies," he explained.

One Cuban army officer I met told me that the worst thing that could happen to him would be for him to discover that his son was a homosexual. (Remaining silent after that was perhaps the most difficult part of my entire Cuban visit.)

The subject of homosexuality came up unexpectedly during a visit I made to an encampment of an elite youth corps known as the Followers of Camilo and El Che. One of the "followers" was proudly telling me how the entire campground could be mobilized in just three minutes in case of emergency. I asked him if such a mobilization had occurred (conjuring up images of CIA-trained exile invaders), and he said that it had. I asked him the circumstances. He got a slightly embarrassed look, and then proceeded to tell me how one young man had been caught in a homosexual act, so a mobilization was called to expose him in front of the entire population of the camp. When I asked how come only one person was expelled, I was told that the other person was "only testing" him. (You know how it's OK to get a blow job from a faggot, how you can still be a real man after that!) I felt free enough—despite my closetry—to challenge high-ranking camp officials the next day about this cruelty. Oh, yes, they quickly said, that was a terrible thing. But I soon found out that it was the method of expulsion, not the expulsion itself, which they viewed as wrong. They would have expelled the homosexual, too, only they would have done it more quietly. After all, they said, the Followers of Camilo and El Che represent the flower of our youth. "Could a homosexual become a leader of SDS?" I was asked. (I

can't remember exactly what I said in answer to that question—
probably something like "maybe." The fact is that no openly gay
person functioned in SDS.)

One night I went cruising on 23rd Street, the main drag of
downtown Havana, which ran past the Havana Libre Hotel, where
I was lodged. I knew the street (known as La Rampa) was cruisy
by watching the people there, and it didn't take too long before I
exchanged glances with a young man. We talked for hours. Afraid
of being discovered, I said I was a visiting Canadian. He
complained at length about the government's infringement on his
comforts and individualism (many of his complaints seemed petty
to me and I was depressed), and then we talked about going
somewhere to have sex. He lived with his parents; I lived in the
security-minded hotel (no visitors allowed in rooms, largely a
measure against renascent prostitution). So we ended up
exchanging blow jobs at 2 a.m. on the stairwell of an apartment
building on Linea, one of Havana's main residential avenues. In all
fairness, I can't put all the blame for this oppressive situation on
the Cuban government. It can be hard in any country for gay
people to find a place to make love. In the U.S., thousands of
homosexuals do it every day in public rest rooms. In any poor
country an acute housing shortage is a major economic fact. In
Cuba, cultural and economic factors keep people living at home
with their families. Even heterosexuals have trouble finding
privacy. But let's face it, straight Cuban lovers do not end up with
the indignity of a stairwell. The alienation and depression that I
and my Cuban gay friend experienced that night was a strictly
homosexual experience.

My second Havana contact with a gay person was with a young
man who works in one of the cultural institutions. We talked at
length about the pervasive anti-homosexualism of Cuba. He said
that change would come slowly. Basically he felt himself to be a
part of the revolution. He rigorously did militia duty (he was an
excellent marksman) and he gladly did his share of volunteer farm
labor. He told me he could never hope to join the Communist
Party, just because of his homosexuality. He was a very nice
person, though he seemed to be sad most of the time and he
drank a lot. We made love one morning in his family's house
around 10:30 a.m., as this was the only time we could have
privacy there.

I met another gay person—we caught each other's eyes the
way gay people have been doing for I don't know how long—at a
Havana theater. We talked about the arts and the educational
system and we spent three days in a fruitless search for solitude.

One arrangement failed because a lesbian friend of his had company from out of town (her husband's relatives), and another arrangement failed because an older, single gay man he knew decided at the last minute that we couldn't go to his place because he was afraid the busy-bodies of the Committee for the Defense of the Revolution (CDR) would ask too many prying questions. Friends of Cuba have long praised the CDRs (block committees) for their role in elevating political awareness and mobilizing neighborhoods for immunization programs, volunteer labor, neighborhood clean-ups, and other worthwhile projects. Gays in Cuba can't help but see these committees as interfering in basic personal freedoms. (If the above sounds like a brief catalog of pick-ups, that is only because that was the way I expressed myself as a closet gay.)

It was apparent to me, as a result of my observations and experiences as a gay person, that the Cuban Communist Party's hope—to free their nation of homosexuals in future generations —was based on incredible ignorance. The natural presence of homosexuality in a considerable portion of Cuban youth was somehow invisible to them, or explainable only in terms of "bad family background" or contact with older homosexuals. I realized that their understanding of homosexuality was based on very little knowledge, and on a lot of male power. The Cubans saw themselves as having a compassionate view—homosexuals should not be brutalized, but rather isolated like contaminants. They totally accepted Freudian and other bourgeois psychological notions about the "origins of homosexual behavior." One Cuban official told me that it was necessary to put down homosexuality because Cuba needed to promote a fighting, aggressive image of manhood in order to successfully combat imperialism. The image of the Cuban militiawoman, briefly projected by the revolution, is now played down, and in fact women play a very minor role in the armed forces of the nation. Most professional soldiers see the army as a male institution, with female participation valid only on an emergency basis. The Cubans seem to believe that homosexuality is limited to the visible homosexual—in particular a group of campy transvestites who hang around a certain street corner, as well as the known gays in the cultural fields. (When police photographers came to film the drag queens in their usual setting, they camped it up for the cameras!) The straight Cubans also argued that homosexuality was in large measure connected to a style of life which had dominated old Havana (though this argument has little relevancy so many years after the revolution). Purging Cuba of homosexuals was seen as integral to ridding the country of vice, including prostitution, gambling and narcotics. This point of view was based entirely on the oppressive anti-homosexual reality of pre-revolutionary Cuba. Needless to say, Batista's Cuba was no paradise for homosexuals. True, there were gay congregating places, such as bars (where, on January 1, 1959, gays joyfully welcomed in the New Year and the victory of Che, Fidel and the rebel army). But to be a *maricon* (that's Spanish for faggot) was to be the scum of the earth, automatically part of an underworld. It was precisely in a corner of this underworld in Havana, where croupiers, dope-dealers, prostitutes and pimps catered to the needs of American tourists, that open homosexuals could obtain some employment. Other gays— teachers, doctors, fishermen, taxi drivers, actors or whatever— were invisible as gays by definition in a sexist society dominated by blind straight men. It was straight men, of course, who ran the underworld and garnered its profits.

Now, open homosexuals in Cuba have no underworld to go to—except perhaps to join the segment of alienated youth who feel that the revolutionary process has excluded them. But more of that later.

On New Year's Day in 1969, just a few weeks before my arrival in Havana, Fidel Castro made an important speech announcing the plans for the ten-million ton sugar harvest. Several North Americans there, members of a delegation from Students for a Democratic Society, proposed to their Cuban hosts that a brigade of North Americans visit Cuba for a given period to help with the cane harvest. By the time I arrived, the proposal had been OKed at the highest levels (presumably by Fidel himself). I and a few other New Left North Americans who were in Cuba met frequently with Cuban officials to work out the details for the organization of the brigade. I had been invited to Cuba as a representative of Liberation News Service and I was a member of SDS, which meant I had "good politics" in the eyes of the Cubans. My homosexuality was a secret, and the Stonewall uprising which marked the birth of gay liberation was five months away. I did my part to build the cane-cutting brigade, which I was convinced was a good idea.

I returned to the U.S. an enthusiastic supporter of the Cuban Revolution, rarely even discussing my doubts about such things as the Cubans' *macho* attitudes toward women and prejudices against homosexuals. One women in SDS who knew I was gay was my sole confidante about those experiences.

By the beginning of 1970, I had become active in the Gay Liberation Front of New York City. Finally, I had a political context in which I could begin to understand my experiences as a homosexual, and the experiences of Cuban homosexuals. I was still involved in the activities of the Venceremos Brigade; in fact, Senator James Eastland of Mississippi was on the warpath against the brigade and I and others were risking possible prosecution under the "trading with the enemy" act or espionage statutes for our pro-Cuba activities.

When I told my former roommate, a straight man active in the New Left's North American Congress on Latin America (NACLA), who had traveled to Cuba with me, that I was gay and involved with GLF, one of the first things he said was, "The Cubans won't like that, will they?" I don't think he liked it either, but in any case, he was right. I still hoped that a choice would not be necessary, that it would be possible to work with GLF and defend the Cuban Revolution at the same time, that the contradictions could be lived with. A gradual process then began which made the contradiction between Cuba and gay liberation sharper and sharper.

One Sunday night in the spring of 1970, at a regular GLF meeting, a young man named Ron, just back from the Venceremos Brigade canefields, proposed to GLF that he and some friends come to a GLF meeting to talk about Cuba. I couldn't believe my eyes and ears—a gay person was on the brigade! My heart leapt. I had been thinking about making such a presentation about my own experience even before this, but I was afraid and confused. Ellen, a lesbian and GLFer who was in Cuba in the summer of 1968 with the European Fifth of May Encampment, was going through similar mixed feelings about her Cuba experience and her new identity as a gay liberation person. The GLFers at the meeting agreed to hold the Cuba forum, although I anticipated conflict. The five participants were myself, Ellen, Ron, Guy (an SDS colleague I'd known for years and previously presumed to be straight), and Richard. (I remember how scared Richard seemed to be about even attending a GLF meeting. He preferred to call himself "bi-sexual" rather than gay; Richard is now living in a gay collective in Brooklyn and has been active in several gay groups.)

Ron, Guy and Richard had participated in the brigade—as had, we found out in the coming months, many other gays—as closeted homosexuals. Of the five of us, only Ellen had lived as an openly gay person in Cuba. The returned brigadistas wanted to tell GLF about how wonderful Cuba was, about the accomplishments of the revolution, and their excitement about the collective process they were a part of. The GLF membership was decidedly hostile to such an approach. They already knew that the Cuban government, like governments everywhere, was overtly anti-homosexual—and they wanted to hear about the reality of being gay in Cuba. I felt the security blanket of the New Left right-on revolution slipping away from me; I could see that my involvement with gay liberation was going to challenge many of my previous political notions. I got my first chance to react to this new contradiction when I read an article by Martha Shelley about the GLF-Cuba forum, published in the *Liberated Guardian*. I found myself strongly motivated by years of conditioning to defend Cuba above all. One sentence in that article particularly angered me: "'Marxist,' schmarxist, get off our backs!" Martha had exclaimed to the world. The label "Marxist" was sacred to me, and I blanched. Of course, Marxism provides a valid framework for all of us to fight against economic exploitation. But that is simply not enough. Before long I came to embrace Martha's sentiments. Why should a label be sacred if it is used—as in Cuba—to justify oppression?

The last week in June of 1970, a few months after the GLF-Cuba forum, was Gay Pride Week, the first anniversary of the Christopher Street uprising, gay liberation's first birthday party.

At this point, I was still working for LNS, still working with Venceremos Brigade people (many of whom didn't know yet that I was gay), still uncomfortably new to gay liberation—strongly sensing that somehow my gayness didn't fit into the accepted patterns of what it meant to be a "revolutionary." Suddenly, I found myself in an awful conflict. *Gay Power* (a now defunct movement paper) and the Venceremos Brigade had both engaged the Elgin Theater for midnight benefit showings on the same day. The management had made an error. Both groups had publicized their events (though as it turns out neither group attracted much public), but a choice had to be made and the management chose the Venceremos Brigade. After all, the Cuban revolution is better known than the Stonewall Riots. The gay people argued that since this was Gay Pride Week, and we are an oppressed people launching our struggle, the Brigade should yield. But the Brigade didn't. Movies about Vietnam and Cuba were to be shown instead of the Gay Power film program *Brand X*, which is, incidentally, a sexist movie, but then again, our movement was so new we didn't have anything better to show. The evening was, for the most part, an angry dialogue between the gay people and the Brigade people. I was confused, straddling the fence between my familiar Brigade comrades and my new-found gay sisters and brothers. I still felt that the "international communist revolution" was somehow more valid than gay liberation—I couldn't yet see the connection between the two. A lot of the gay people despised me for my fence-straddling, and I can't really blame them. The next day, at a Gay Pride Week workshop at Alternate U, Ken Pitchford read a poem he had written after hearing about the confrontation with the Brigade. When he read that poem, "The Flaming Faggots," I got chills down my spine and tears in my eyes and I knew his righteous anger was more correct than my own confusion, more solid than my own futile attempts to grasp tightly to a New Left that was really not so new and not so left as it pretended to be. I found out later that my identifying myself as gay at the Elgin shocked some of the Brigade organizers, and helped them to open their minds up on the question of homosexuality. In the following months, a group of gay people, including myself, met with the Brigade leadership, and it was agreed that activists from the gay movement would join in the third contingent of the Brigade. (Some of their experiences are related elsewhere in this anthology.) Cuban officials and Brigade bureaucrats became very up-tight about the gay liberation issue after the Third Brigade. It was all right as long as gay people stayed in the closet and worked for "the revolution," but there was discomfort, if not disgust, at gay people fighting for their own liberation. By the time the fourth contingent of the Venceremos Brigade went to the Caribbean—in February 1971—many of the gay people and feminist-oriented women were told they had been cut. For the gay people on the Fourth Brigade, the experience was even more difficult than for those in the Third Brigade. It seemed almost a certainty that Cuban officials and their brigade organizers would strive to eliminate gay liberation activists from future brigades.

I left the staff of LNS in September 1970 to work full time in the gay movement. I maintained close contact with LNS, however, and a few months later I was invited as an LNS representative to attend the Seventh Congress of the International Organization of Journalists, meeting in Havana in January 1971. By this time, the Cubans knew I was a homosexual, and I could determine that my invitation to the Congress was specifically a result of the Cubans' efforts. (The IOJ has been basically oriented toward the views of the Soviet Union and its loyal friends in other countries, and I did not fit into that scheme.) On one level, at least, the Cubans were prepared to have a homosexual like me as their friend, but within a day or two after my arrival, I realized that the Cubans did not understand what my commitment to gay liberation meant. When I gave out gay liberation literature, along with things such as LNS packets, the *Guardian* and *Rat* to IOJ delegates, and openly identified myself as a homosexual, the Cubans were very unhappy. They asked me to stop giving out anything about homosexuality, saying, "We invited you because you are an anti-imperialist journalist." Cubans were forced to defend me against several delegates who thought it was terrible that there were "homosexuals" (I'd become pluralized, instantaneously) infecting their congress. (One Peruvian, conversing with me on an Aeroflot jet taking us to Havana from Moscow, said it was "disgusting" when I told him the significance of the gay liberation button I was wearing.) But the Cubans defense of me was based on my anti-imperialist credentials, certainly not on any affirmation of my homosexuality.

Although I was willing to do my part as an "anti-imperialist journalist" at the conference, I soon discovered that the event was characterized by rhetorical speeches and back-room haggling which seemed quite inaccessible to me. Besides, I felt incredibly out of place in this roomful of people, nearly all of them men with closely-cropped hair dressed in dark suits and ties. I felt mistrust for the Soviets and their Eastern and Western European friends, and although I felt tremendous warmth and solidarity towards revolutionary journalists from Asia, Africa and Latin America, the bureaucratic, formalistic nature of the gathering made meaningful human contact almost impossible.

I responded to this situation quite naturally by talking about gay liberation informally to as many Cubans, gay and straight, as I possibly could. There were scores of Cubans at the congress aside from the official delegation—translators, guides, and the reporters and writers and artists for the Cuban media. Many of these people knew me personally from my first trip, or by name or reputation, since there is a great deal of interest in the North American New Left. They also all knew of my affiliation with gay liberation. Word quickly got around, and many asked for gay liberation literature. Many of them had had contact with GLF people in the Third Venceremos Brigade, and now they were interested in continuing their discussion of the gay topic with me. All of the Cubans I met inside the halls of the congress were identified as "straight," though of course it is safe to assume there were closet gays among them. I discovered that I was a sought-after personality! And more often than not, it was the Cuban friend who brought up the subject of gay liberation. I think it is fair to say that they were very anxious to talk about it. I had the impression that homosexuality was, by and large, a forbidden topic, one which could more easily be discussed with me, a foreigner, than among Cubans.

The overwhelming majority of these Cubans I spoke to were in sympathy with the ideas and goals of gay liberation and women's liberation. They seemed to agree that sexism was a serious political and cultural problem of their country and that change was necessary. They were also pessimistic about the possibility of such change, suggesting that it could not happen for many years. They told me that many of their colleagues were very anti-gay. One man who worked for a radio station told me about a colleague of his who said that all homosexuals should be shipped out to sea and then the boats should be sunk, or, as an alternative, all homosexuals should be put at the bottom of a big pit, and the pit should be filled with oil and set afire. One man responded very warmly to me during our rap, and I was disappointed to find out later from a co-worker of his that he was always telling fag jokes at work. I identified this behavior as typical of the closet case, and I wished him no ill. Only a few Cubans—those who were members of the Communist Party or the Union of Young Communists —seemed to have the prepared rap on the subject, namely that homosexuality was a "degeneration" and that protecting Cuba's youths from known homosexuals would eventually create a generation free of the scourge. But even the most friendly of the straight Cubans said that outward manifestations of homosexuality (such as effeminacy in males or public affection between two people of the same sex) was offensive to them.

Much of my time was spent outside the halls of the congress. I met some two dozen gay people in Havana. The love and solidarity I experienced with these gay brothers and sisters (unfortunately, I met only a few lesbians) is unforgettable, and is still very much with me. (Sex was not a factor in most of these relationships.) We hear a lot about such concepts as nationalism and culture and class, and these are real divisions among people. But I found (given one's ability to overcome the language barrier) that our shared gay experiences as homosexuals gave us a feeling of unity that is so powerful as to be almost mystical. Some people, straight and gay, think that gayness is defined by what you do in bed, but my contact with Cuban gays taught me in myriad ways how gayness is shared experiences based on the uniqueness of gay love plus the struggle to resist the oppressions of a sexist society.

I am unable, at this time, to give a detailed account of the different gay people I met, for fear that this may bring harm to them. I am forced to generalize, and beyond that, to admit that I did not go outside of the capital city. My friends who went on the Venceremos Brigade told me that they found many gay people on the streets of Santiago (Cuba's second largest city), and, in any case, we are everywhere! It has always been easier for gay people to affirm their identity as such in large cities. It would have been harder for me to meet gay people in the Cuban countryside, but that is only because gay oppression is more severe in rural settings.

I felt that the gay people I met could be divided into two categories, generally, though by doing that I don't mean to take away anyone's individuality. First, there were those gay people, most of them in their late 20s or in their 30s or 40s, who were successfully employed in the various cultural fields, such as the theater, the dance, cinema, art and literature. These are people whose creative abilities have enhanced the prestige of the Cuban revolution around the world. They struck me as incredibly dedicated, energetic people who loved their work to the point of unbelievable self-denial. This group of gay people defined themselves as "revolutionaries," which, as I interpreted it, meant that they were committed to socialism and internationalism and recognized the current situation as an improvement from the Batista dictatorship (under which many of them had suffered persecution). Many had fought in the underground movement against Batista, or were active as sympathizers. Now, they were incredibly grateful to the revolution for the support it has given them in their cultural, artistic endeavors. While not allowed to join the Communist Party, most of them worked at voluntary labor and militia duty. As for the fact that they were not accepted as homosexuals, there seemed to be a mixture of bitterness and hope. All of them told me that it was in no way possible for them to raise the issue within the context of the internal politics of the nation. A meeting, for example, is out of the question—they would probably end up in jail. The only time that they knew of homosexuality being discussed at a Communist Party meeting was during the 1965 round-ups, when members of the Cuban Union of Writers and Artists protested against the incarceration of homosexuals in camps. This protest was part of an overall successful effort to close these camps. Still, these gay brothers and sisters hoped for change, and, in fact, they saw my presence and the presence of gays in the Venceremos Brigade as a hopeful sign. They were very interested in the gay liberation literature and told me they would try to translate it and pass it around. One man told me disconcertedly just before I left Havana that he had at first planned to do a translation of the pamphlets and mimeograph them up, but subsequently decided that he was unwilling to take the risk, since this would be illegal. Only one gay man I met seemed hostile to my presence and the idea of gay liberation. ("I just meet a North American and I assume he's a CIA agent," he told me.) This man was a bundle of contradictions. He was black, 40 years old, married with two children, and was the lover of an army officer. Before the victory of the revolution, he shined shoes and worked in the urban underground movement. "I relate more to being black and being lumpen than to being gay," he said, adding that "ninety percent of these faggots you meet in Havana aren't worth anything." He told me about his experiences cutting cane and noted that no matter how good you are, you're still nothing more than a *maricon* in the eyes of the straight revolutionaries. Despite this, he insisted in effect that the only way for gays to gain dignity for themselves in Cuba was to out-*macho* the *machistas*.

The other type of gay person I met was younger (age 16–25), and almost totally alienated from the revolutionary process. When asked if they were revolutionaries, they said things like, "I'm for Che's revolution, but not Fidel's" (a 17-year-old lesbian), or "I'm revolutionary, but in my own way. What we have here is not the kind of revolution I want to fight for" (a 20-year-old black student). Most of these sisters and brothers were students or had artistic or clerical jobs. They immediately put on the gay liberation buttons I gave them (the older gays had discreetly put them away). They wanted to know everything about gay liberation, and beyond that, what it was like to be a rebel youth in the U.S. today. They had an incredible understanding of sexism—in fact, they used the term *machista* as an epithet against their oppressors. They despise the *verdes* (the green ones), members of the Cuban army, who often hassle them in the street. Gays, by the way, are not allowed in the army. I heard many stories of gay oppression—gays being expelled from school, gays losing their jobs, gays being embarrassed before assemblies (the love letters of two lesbians at the dance school were read before a public assembly called together for the purpose of expelling them), gays denied admission to the university, gays in medical school afraid they'd be discovered, gays rounded up, photographed, interrogated, gays mocked for their long hair and/or shorn by force, gays with no place to make love, gays in jail for trying to swim to Guantanamo Naval Base in order to leave Cuba. The more I heard, the more I became confused, hurt, scared, the more my categories fell apart. I knew that the Naval Base had no business even existing on Cuban soil—it was the result of U.S. military conquest. And I had learned to have contempt for the *gusanos*—Cuba's right-wing exiles. But I certainly could understand the desperation that would drive two young men in love with each other to try to swim away from Cuba even to end up in such a place as the U.S. My Cuban gay friends made it clear to me that they, too, despised the *gusanos.* I also heard that Cuban revolutionaries put down *gusanos* by telling them that there is only one thing worse than being a *gusano*—being a *maricon.*

My gay friends told me that they had many straight friends who also felt alienation from the revolutionary process. They said many young people were not anti-gay, that anti-gay attitudes were a product of the older generation. Yet the Cuban press has been used, on a number of occasions, to promote hostility and mockery toward homosexuals. Some examples: 1) a news report on two U.S. servicemen who left Guantanamo to seek asylum in Cuba, but were shipped on to Europe when it was determined they were gay ("we don't want their kind here," said *Granma*, the leading Cuban daily); 2) a report on Britain's legalization of homosexual acts among adults, describing such legislation as an example of the further decadence of the British empire; 3) a feature on U.S. astronauts impugning their masculinity; 4) a column in *Bohemia,* the nation's most popular magazine, making a total mockery of a gay liberation march in Los Angeles; 5) a feature article making fun of U.S. homosexual churches and accompanied by an absurd cartoon showing a bearded man in a wedding gown; 6) publication of the anti-gay statements of the Congress on Education and Culture. So I felt that it was hypocritical for Cubans to blame past generations of anti-homosexual attitudes on current attitudes when only anti-gay material appeared in the current press.

(I do not have time to explore fully the question of women's liberation here, but despite some steps toward the emancipation of women, especially as regards education and jobs, sex roles as such are enforced and justified as necessary and desirable. When I visited the physical education school on the outskirts of Havana during my first visit to Cuba, my host pointed out the elaborate beauty parlor installed there for female students. "We like our women to be feminine," he said, "and you know how sports can tend to make women more masculine." It was easy to see beyond the euphemism to his true meaning: we want to give women a chance to play sports, but we sure don't want them looking or acting like dykes. I knew that before this school was built, before the revolution, women were by definition excluded from sports. So this was a fantastic change, and on some level the women of

Cuba must have welcomed not only the physical education facilities but the beauty parlor, too.)

Young gay Cubans in Havana somehow manage to live with their difficult oppressive situation. For example, it is common for two gay males and two lesbians to go out together. To the uninformed, the foursome is two straight couples on their way, say, to a lovers lane. In the dark solitude of a park, however, the couples re-form and the gay lovers can finally be together!

The official Cuban wish—that homosexuality will go away—seems more absurd every day. One Cuban official confessed to me that they are very worried about the "homosexual problem." He even asked me if I thought the "problem" would get better or worse, and all I could say to that was that his problem as a *macho* was what worried me. In the declarations of the Congress on Education and Culture, it was said that "homosexuality should not be considered a central problem or a fundamental one in our society, but rather its attention and solution are necessary." This wording, and my experience, convinced me that the straight Cubans are freaked out and baffled by widespread manifestations of homosexuality—often where they least expect it. One official mentioned to me that there were a number of "cases" of homosexuality in the Centennial Youth Column, one of the revolution's prestigious work-study programs involving young people of varying backgrounds from all over the nation. The Youth Column represents an assault on the nuclear family—people leave home to join the column—but current housing programs indicate that the Cubans have no plan to abandon the family structure or work against it as a long-range goal. Either way—by trying to maintain the nuclear family by force or by breaking it up—Cuba will find itself with new generations of gay people. Will this change their minds? I doubt it. In the Soviet Union, where homosexuality is also considered a degeneration, where its disappearance was part of "communist" planning, gay people live as they do under capitalism—as deviates, pariahs, outcasts who somehow never go away.

I went home elated at the beautiful experiences I had had with my Cuban gay friends, but generally shaken by their pessimism. When 1,700 Cuban teachers and political cadre met in Havana in late 1971 for the First Congress on Education and Culture, they didn't even mention the problems of *machismo* and racism—clearly among the most important cultural questions the nation has to face. Instead, following a course mapped out by this leadership, the congress issued an angry blast at "cultural imperialism," focusing its collective anger on European intellectuals and other outsiders who had criticized Cuba. Specifically, homosexuality was denounced as a "social pathology." Long hair, certain unspecific fashions and "extravagant behavior" were also denounced at the congress. When the statement was read on Cuban TV, Cubans and many of the North Americans watching at the Venceremos Brigade campground thumped the tables enthusiastically like collegiate jocks—with North American gay liberationists looking on in anger, pain, dismay and, certainly, fear. This was the first printed statement on homosexuality which bears the official stamp of the Cuban Revolution. It is printed elsewhere in this anthology.

I later determined, from friends who visited Cuba later on in 1971, that the behavior of U.S. gay liberation people in Cuba, including myself and brigade people, was considered to be part of the "cultural imperialism" denounced by the congress. Some weeks before the congress met, gay liberation people in New York received an anonymous letter from Cuban gays discussing the repressive conditions for gays in Cuba. This letter was eventually published by the gay press and, in edited form, by LNS, and it was picked up as a news item by the Associated Press. My friends who went to Cuba were told that this was an "international scandal." I firmly believe that the letter from Cuban gays was not written by the people I met and knew in Cuba, but in any case, the ire of straight Cubans has less to do with my transgressions and more to do with the fact that they are threatened. That letter was written by gay people speaking out against their oppression—how can it be wrong for such a letter to exist and to be publicized through revolutionary media? (The fact that AP picked it up is incidental.) For the crime of publishing this letter, LNS was excluded by the Cubans from a gathering of radical media people held in Havana in early 1972.

I have some straight North American friends who are working in Havana "for the revolution." One, for example, is a script-writer and announcer for Radio Havana. These friends all claim to support the ideas of gay liberation. They think the Cubans are making an "error" in insisting on their anti-homosexual path, and they think it is only a matter of time before the Cubans rectify the error. In the meantime, they think I should shut up and say nothing bad about Cuba (except maybe in private). Anticipating, perhaps, my ire at the congress's declarations, they wrote me long analytical letters in defense of "The Revolution." I received another long letter in a similar vein from a woman active in the radical movement on the West Coast who was in Cuba with me on both occasions. Other straight radical friends returned to Cuba to report that the Cubans were unhappy with my January visit and with the behavior of gays on the Venceremos Brigade. These people make the following arguments:

1) Cuba's declarations about homosexuality are a mistake. Be patient, change will come in due time.

2) Gay liberation is already a part of the U.S. revolution and justly so, but it is "cultural imperialism" for North Americans to expect Cuba to adopt the principles of this movement.

3) Cuban gays and friends of Cuba elsewhere who wish to criticize Cuba should do so "within the revolution" as to not aid the enemy, U.S. imperialism, which is constantly threatening Cuba.

4) Cuba and the U.S. are at a different time and in a different place historically, and this must be recognized. We shouldn't expect Cuba at this historical moment to put an end to sexism.

5) It is unfair to scrutinize and criticize Cuba on the question of how homosexuals are treated there, glossing over the issue as it pertains to other socialist countries, such as China, Vietnam and Korea.

In my correspondence with these friends, I have tried to make the following responses to each of these points:

1) The anti-homosexualism of Cuba is not an error, but the rational policy of a male power structure which enjoys being on top. These policies are part of an overall pattern of permitting only minor or temporary changes in sex roles and the nuclear family. Cuba's leaders justify their unwillingness to launch a major assault on male chauvinism because they fear it will "divide" the nation. Their desire for unity is premised on squelching internal contradictions and protecting their power, though they verbalize other rationalizations.

2) Gay liberation is by no means a certainty in the North American revolution, whatever that is. The overwhelming majority of those who call themselves Marxists or socialists or revolutionaries in the U.S. do not embrace the political views of gay feminist revolution, but in fact seek to oppose this growing political tendency. I and other gays are frankly afraid that one day these straight revolutionaries may decide to eliminate us! Gay militants in the U.S. are constantly asked by Marxists to validate themselves by doing the proper amount of work for the anti-war movement—this is one way that these so-called radicals invalidate the gay struggle. Wars are produced by straight men, and gay liberation *is* anti-war movement. The charge of cultural imperialism, when placed in the context of Cuba's total reality, is a total farce. It is, after all, the imposition of Roman Catholic religion

and bourgeois psychology by imperialism on Cuba that is, in large part, responsible for the anti-gay attitudes found there today. Catholics in Cuba have freedom of assembly, while gays do not! Male power or *machismo*—certainly not gay liberation—reigns in the seat of empire, the U.S.A. Imperialism exists only where there is power—and gay people in the U.S. are powerless.

Cuban youths who wish to grow long hair or Afros, who like rock music, who engage in "extravagant behavior," who want to use psychedelic drugs, who want to wear hippie-style clothing (whatever that is)—are said to be victims of "cultural imperialism." I say that youth in many parts of the world want all of these things for the same valid reasons—a desire to be more free and more natural and to be in constant rebellion against the old and the outdated. The CIA may exploit this desire, but that doesn't make the phenomenon a CIA plot, as some people charge. I can think of many things I saw in Havana which I see as real examples of cultural imperialism and extravagant behavior, things which should well be the targets of such a cultural offensive.

I am thinking of rape, a crime which occurs less frequently than before the revolution, but which is not at all uncommon. Interestingly, rape is rarely or never reported in the press, presumably because its political nature is not recognized.

I am thinking of the existence of bell-hops and chambermaids in the hotels of Havana. Although they are supposedly serving revolutionaries, and workers on vacation, there is every reason to believe that these jobs are by their very nature servile and are totally unnecessary, reminiscent of a kind of human relationship we no longer need.

I am thinking of such accepted notions of fashion as white gloves for military men on dress parade, tuxedos for waiters in fancy restaurants, suits and ties for men who want to look their best, high heels and make-up for the "attractive" woman.

I am thinking of the time that one of my hosts, a respected member of the Party, whistled at a woman on the street.

I am thinking of laws, historically originating in Washington, D.C., which put Cuban pot-smokers behind bars.

I am thinking of a Cuban psychologist advising one of my hosts (a married student) that he and his wife should not go ahead with their plan to be naturally nude in front of their children, because, even if it is correct, it would traumatize the children when they discovered that their friends' parents behaved differently. This incident is an example of how change coming naturally from the people is resisted by conservative professionals and bureaucrats.

Perhaps it seems that there is some arrogance in my judging

the Cubans in this way. I think I am motivated less by arrogance than by anger—anger at how uncritical Cuba's friends in the U.S. have been, anger at how the youth of Cuba have so far been robbed of their right to take this beautiful and once joyous revolution to its next stages.

3) Gays are not allowed to criticize anti-homosexualism "within the revolution" because they are by definition excluded from the Communist Party and the entire political process. Lasting strength against U.S. imperialism will not come from a people who are divided by oppression, or from a country whose internal contradictions are not on the road to resolution.

4) It is of course true that Cuba and the U.S. are in different historical stages. But things don't always occur the way they are supposed to historically. It was the Russian workers, not the British or the French, as Marx would have had it, who successfully fought for socialism in 1918. There is no real reason that Cuba cannot learn from the women and the gay people and all the rebellious youth of the advanced capitalist country which lies to the north. Certainly our experience under affluence, an experience which gave rise to our consciousness about sexism and other problems (such as ecology), is valuable to the Cuban people. Why shouldn't that kind of knowledge about human relations be just as valuable and sought after by Cubans as, say, knowledge developed by U.S. physicians, chemists and computer engineers? Besides, we live in a shrinking world, where time and distance are not what they used to be.

5) It is not unfair, but only natural and logical, that we North Americans should have a unique relationship with Cuba. The concepts of nationhood cannot be turned into an abstraction— Cuba is only 90 miles away, and it functioned virtually as a U.S. state for 50 years. That may be a despicable fact, but our recognition of the evils of imperialism cannot wipe away 50 years of history. Cuba's language, Spanish, is familiar to us, while the languages of Asian countries are not. The cultural and human contact between North Americans and Cubans has been considerable. Much of it was perverted contact, the result of militarism and tourism. But that is not the whole story. If it is only natural and logical that there have been thousands of sympathetic North Americans travelling to Cuba and praising it, then the same holds true for gay liberation people and others who feel some affinity but also feel the need to criticize. Cuba's proximity is such that more of us have been inspired by Cuba than, say, by China or Korea. (Vietnam is a special case because of the war.) If we can be more readily inspired by Cuba, then we can also be more

readily warned by Cuba, warned about the ways that sexism can retard and perhaps even destroy the revolutionary process that has begun. The youth of France will naturally know more about Algeria, the youth of Japan will look to China and Korea, and the youth of North America to Cuba. These special relations are a natural result of geography; it is faulty logic to charge "imperialism" because the particular march of empires also depended upon geography. As for China, Vietnam and Korea, when the revolutionary successes and failures of these countries are fully understood, a consciousness about sexism there will be essential to that understanding, too. Our challenge to straight radicals is: when will you engage in honest, open criticism of the Third World nations you have so romantically idealized for years?

There is no valid separation of the political and the personal. If you are engaged in a struggle for liberation, you must work to free yourself. If you want to bring joy to suffering masses, you must be engaged in the process of bringing joy to yourself. Otherwise, the whole thing is an abstract game, and the revolutionaries might as well shut their mouths and stop printing their newspapers. This is the part of gay liberation which I find hardest to put across to so many of my straight friends (like the ones who wrote me those letters).

I hesitate to use a phrase like "I fell in love," because it seems like such a holdover from the worst romantic movies. But anyway, when I was in Cuba in 1971, I fell in love. Our love was very beautiful and I knew it was good. All around me, Cuban communists were telling me such love was bad. How can I call them my brothers?

ON THE VENCEREMOS BRIGADE

A Forum

Editors' Note: In the late summer of 1970, a small group of gay people openly identified with the gay liberation movement joined several hundred young North Americans in the Venceremos Brigade, violating State Department restrictions, to travel to Cuba's Isle of Youth to help with farm work. When the gay brigadistas returned, several of them spoke about their experiences at a forum held at the Alternate U in New York City.

The following is excerpted from the transcript of a tape recording made at the forum.

MICHAEL: I come from Kansas, and I went out to Los Angeles in June to go on the brigade, and I was there for two months before the brigade left. While I was in L.A., a Gay Liberation Front was formed in my town in Kansas, and one of the men who I'd been living with became very active in it. And the week before I left for the brigade he came out to L.A. to see me off, and that was the first contact I had at all with any idea of GLF. I didn't know anything about it. He told me that there would be a guy on the boat that had my name and would look me up. (Laughter.) So with that in mind, I went to an L.A. GLF meeting, and it was a business meeting. I got totally turned off to that, but I tried to see it in perspective. When I got to the boat—I think maybe it was the second day on the boat—all these people were coming around saying, "Some guy from GLF is looking for you." (Laughter.) They were all these people from the bus. We came across country together—for four days—and I pretty well knew them all. We had had some cadre work together. So all these people from L.A. that knew me were saying that this guy—Step—is looking for me, and they kind of wondered about me, because Step was very out then. So Step found me and I was very defensive—it was incredible. I began going to meetings and things. Richie talked to me. There was a brother from L.A. who was also gay, but he was not out. It was a big struggle for me whether to come out or not, and I guess by the end of the boat trip, two days before we docked, I had come out and I was wearing a GLF button. That was really heavy for me because I'd never been open, and all the people that knew me from the boat and on the bus, they all related to me entirely differently as soon as I wore that button. When they talked to me, they looked at the button, they wouldn't look at me. (Laughter.) It was incredible. That was really hard for me to deal with. The whole two months in Cuba was like an encounter thing every minute. I went through so many changes on the boat, not just in gay consciousness, but in general political consciousness. It was really heavy.

RICHIE: One of the problems that we had as soon as we got on the boat—and this was our fault—was that we did not have a political statement. What this means is that black people were already in caucus, Latins were already in caucus, women were already doing that; but white people in general were not, and GLF was not. We were torn, white people and white GLF, because to get together around your whiteness, was considered racist by some people, both blacks and whites. And then at the same time they wanted you to organize so that they could have a structure to deal with. As a group all we really had as experience was consciousness-raising groups. I think we had learned not just to talk about black oppression, Latin oppression, and women's oppression, but to talk about our own. And what this meant was becoming identified on the ship again as not totally political people but as people who were only interested in their private little thing. So one day we had our first consciousness-raising session on the boat because we did not really know each other very well. Nancy was there, and she had not identified herself as homosexual, but as someone who was interested in the movement and had a lot of homosexual relatives (laughter) and just knew a lot about what was going on on the West Coast and could help what we were doing. We started and were talking about sexuality and about homosexuality. Then people started joining. We saw some black faces, some Latin faces, and just people in general coming around: "What is being rapped on this big tarpaulin?" There were sort of centers of activity on the ship, and we became one of them that day. Then questions were asked: "What is the material base of your oppression?" "What do the communists say, what do the socialists say?" And luckily we had Earl along, and he answered many of those questions with a lot of political aplomb. People didn't know what to do with all of that, because we're still gay and we're still fighting for something they did not quite understand. So that's one of the things that has to be settled, this whole political organization, how to present ourselves as individuals and as a group, as a political functioning body with an anti-imperialist stand.

STEP: Just about as soon as we left harbor, people started caucusing. There was a women's caucus, and a Third World women's caucus, and a Latin caucus and so on. And the formation of these caucuses was causing a lot of tension. For example, a lot of men didn't understand why women were caucusing, and there was tension between the white women and Third World women, and so on. Tensions were building. Then on about the second evening, in the men's dorm, a discussion started among some of the men. They were talking about the caucuses, and about racism and some of the other issues. The discussion got bigger and bigger, and some other people joined in, and then the way it developed was just a few men started taking over the whole discussion themselves and started haranguing the others. All these men who were standing around were completely intimidated. The only men who got up to oppose what was said by one of the haranguers were three gay men. Someone called Nixon a faggot, and Earl spoke out: "Wait a minute. Nixon is a straight man and don't you forget that."

RICHIE: One of the men who was talking was a black man from the mid-West, who was eloquent and witty and had the whole group either intimidated or entranced, depending on your prejudice. Eventually he got around to talking about how these white women come into our neighborhood, and there was a lot of that stuff about abortion, and forcing black women into using abortion measures. A statement was made about fags, I raised my hand—I opened my mouth, you couldn't raise your hand—and I said: "Don't you have anything from your own women? Can't they make their own decisions? Who are you to boss them around?" It was just a statement on the independence of their own women as human beings.

After the meeting was the good part. You see, two or three of the gay men who spoke up were white. First of all, white men came up to me afterward and said, "Thank you for speaking out. You know, we didn't know what to do. Our tongues were tied." People are still afraid today, no matter what their consciousness is, of being accused of being racist. They can't deal with an idea. They have to see where it's coming from first, rather than being able to deal with a statement and say something to that statement. So a few men came up to me and said, "Wow, I'm glad that happened." The dynamic for black and Latin men was, "Wow, why were the only men who had enough guts to speak gay men?" So subtle things happened in that meeting, and opened up the idea of "we're going to have to deal with this."

EARL: It was both fortunate and unfortunate. Something that was very unfortunate was that there were Third World gay people on that trip that were not open about their homosexuality, even though everyone knew who they were. The pressures were very heavy and they weren't open; they were sometimes anti-homosexual in their statements. The only white groups who were semi-organized, or had some sort of thing to be related to, were women and gay people. And so all the resentments and all the racial tension, all that energy, were directed at gay liberation and women's liberation. And they were identified as white movements. And for some reason, we were declassed, de-everything. It was made out as if a homosexual was some kind of being that lives in...space, I guess. That made for more difficulty. Beyond that there was a great number of people who just couldn't deal with homosexuality, or even sexuality. So homosexuality was in the air constantly. The topic was always there, and people were into digs at each other. Like, the men would allude to homosexual tendencies, or question each other's masculinity, or things like that.

In the dormitory, when we got to Cuba, by the end of the first week, I thought that I was ready to kill, because I would try to go to sleep at night and people would be hollering: "Oh, there's homosexuals trying to get into my bed!" (Laughter.) One time after work, I came in and this guy was sitting on his bed and he said, "I need some homosexual repellent." And he kept screaming this thing about homosexual repellent, so I got really furious and said: "It's in your blood." (Laughter and applause.) I also said: "You're revolting to us just as you are!" (More laughter and applause.) That was the only way to deal with the thing at that time. We had to be spontaneous, and we turned into almost vicious creatures, just to show this fury, and for me, at any rate, it started to quiet down. In my presence, they would no longer do things like that.

ELAINE: After I got on the ship, the situation wasn't what I expected. There were, I soon found out, four men from GLF there, but no women. I assumed that there were other gay women on the trip, but I didn't know exactly how to find them. So I had another decision to make, and I thought it through for a while. I felt it was a necessity to come out in order to make this union between my personal and political life, at least to make it possible. I decided at that point it was both a personal and a political decision. On the political side, it looked to me that it was very important that GLF not be all men. That's one of the things about being a woman and being a lesbian—you're invisible in two different ways. It was fairly important that right from the beginning GLF not be identified as an all-male thing, bad enough that it was an all-white thing. On a personal side, I was pretty scared, because I had never come out really, except to close friends. Even that was a production! And here I was going to Cuba where I understood it wasn't going to be really cool, and besides that I was supposed to be with 405 other people, living in close quarters for a length of time and I could fantasize about how much problem there might be. So finally I decided I just was going to try it. And, as I think Step put it very aptly, one time I came screaming out of the closet (laughter) into the hold of the ship.

I can remember the very beginning. I was sitting around up on the deck of the ship, and a lot of people were sitting around talking—all women—and I don't even remember what was in the conversation that led me to this particular use of words, but I remember saying, "Well, how does that apply to me? I'm a lesbian." And there I was. So from then on, on the ship, it was just a constant barrage. There were a couple of semi-planned consciousness-raising groups. It seems like that was the content of most of my conversations. As soon as people would find out, they'd come over and have questions, and we'd start another group. And we'd have a lot of individual conversations. After a week of that on the ship, I was pretty freaked out. I had never had anyone relate to me as a gay person, and all the assumptions that are connected to that—all the things they were talking about before; questions like "Do you relate to Third World struggles?" "Can you?" All those kinds of things. And on top of that, I had to constantly fight a sense of paranoia in looking for people to look down on me. And the third factor, which I didn't really begin to understand until later on in the trip, was the fact that I didn't have a very highly developed gay consciousness. I didn't know what was happening in the various organizations, how they were organized, what their history was, and all those things. Basically all I could talk about was my own experience and some intellectual things I had worked on in my own mind, and some conversations with others, and articles I had read. The only thing that could come out of my direct experience was a very personal kind of thing, so I got a lot of criticism about dealing too much on a personal level because I didn't have a complete Marxist-Lesbian analysis. (Laughter.)

The last night on the ship (we were supposed to get into Havana the next day, and I had been through this for a week) I was pretty freaked out and very homesick. And I just lay there in bed trying to imagine who I could go and talk to. And two women came to mind, but I wasn't ready to do that. The interesting thing is that those two women became some of my closest friends, later on in the trip. I really felt that I was both setting myself apart from the other women on the trip, and that I was *being* set apart from them. And it seemed like a curious contradiction: the fact that I could love a woman completely separated me from other women. So I just cried most of that night. But when we arrived in Havana the next day, it was just such an up, that...all that didn't disappear, but I was so overwhelmed upon arriving in Cuba—the amazing welcome that we had—that a lot of my fears blew over. And it wasn't so bad after that night.

MICHAEL: Elaine started talking about the Marxist-Lesbian analysis and all that. I was in the same position; I had no gay consciousness, and really, the whole time we were in Cuba we had to prove ourselves as revolutionaries to all the other North Americans. We spent all our time, it seemed, trying to prove ourselves to people. On the boat, actually on the whole trip, I was always the quiet one. I never said much in meetings. Thank God Earl was there; he had all the analysis and all that. The only way I could deal with things was out of my personal experience. That was all I could talk about. People would say, "That's personal, we can't talk about that." It was incredible, so many people could not connect personal things with ideology and rhetoric. If I were to give a rap on what I've come out of, you could clearly make all the connections. So I was always criticized in the caucus for not really talking, but I didn't have all that much to say.

RICHIE: This is in a way a talk about Cuba too, and not just ourselves in Cuba. We were well taken care of on the ship. We were guests, very special guests, all of us North Americans and Puerto Ricans, gays, straight, white, black, yellow, the whole gamut. When we sailed into the harbor...Well, there was a lot of music. Cubans use music as a way to express joy and also as a mind-deadener. It's a combination. It was a very exciting, joyous arrival. Our band was playing and we were all singing and the harbor is very beautiful. You go past an old castle or a prison kind of fortress structure. The whole shore was all lined with people. They were all shouting and waving, and there was a brass and conga steel band on the shore overwhelming the little band we had on board, and everybody was yelling and screaming, the noise and the horns. And everybody was ecstatic, and everybody was holding on to each other. It was a kind of rare moment when divisions were not obvious, when we were all revolutionaries going to Cuba to share the Cuban experience—blacks thinking there might be racism, gay people knowing there was going to be anti-gay sentiment, women knowing that the women's role in Cuba was pretty bad, and yet at the same time, there was a connection, a real live connection.

EARL: The relationship with the Cuban people who were on the ship was a little freaky, but it was also encouraging. First of all, we had these various gay liberation buttons, and the Cubans love American political buttons. And everyone wanted buttons. We were wearing these gay liberation buttons. (Laughter.) Like "Out of the closets and into the streets." Cubans would ask for them, and we would explain what they meant, and they still wanted them. Far out, you know! There was also one Cuban man who I spoke to about GLF and so forth who was very sympathetic, and I translated the statement that Huey Newton had made from the Black Panther paper into Spanish, and he took it and had it mimeographed and sent that all around Cuba, which was another encouraging thing. But most of the Cubans on board were very young people, sixteen and seventeen years old, and by our standards not very sophisticated about a lot of things. Not the way people are here. They were just coming from a different experience. There was no communicating almost. Most of them were polite but distant or cool or nervous or intimidated or shy or didn't really know what to do….

JESSE: In my work brigade, the thing I experienced most was complete oppression. I was the only gay person, and there was a lot of anti-gay feeling among a lot of people. There were a series of words that were used indirectly toward me—this was by North Americans—such words as *mariposa, gavillota, maricon,* there's a few others, I forgot them, and high voices and whistling. Those were things that I was constantly running into. I also ran into physical threats. One time I was threatened that I was going to be thrown through a wall. The most revolutionary thing I could do, I was told, was to confront my homosexuality and change it and become a man, and that if I was really proud of being a faggot I should stand up and punch this guy in the mouth. He said, "Punch me in the mouth." I didn't do that, so then he went away and the whole dorm started applauding his little speech. So I started really internalizing a slave mentality, in the sense that I was very intimidated in a lot of ways, and the feeling of being an oppressed person became very clear to me, and I really started seeing what a slave mentality means for any oppressed people. I didn't find any mechanism for confronting them, because it was so prevalent.

I think the oppression I felt was not as strong as what was experienced by the Third World gay people on the brigade. Like, there were, I would think, six gay men who were Third World, or at least four, and there were two gay women who were Third World. And they didn't come out, because homosexuality was called a "white man's disease" by certain people. The Third World gay people stayed in their respective communities and related to each other. So in terms of the other brigades, I can say that Third World gay people are the only gay people who can communicate to Third World people. The strongest oppression that I felt came from Third World people, and a lot of times, I don't think it was anti-gay as much as it was, you know, intense feeling about being from the mother country.

STEP: Another thing on Third World people and gay liberation. There was a black man who took a pretty great interest in gay liberation. He identified himself as straight and he came to just about every discussion, every rap session on gay liberation, but he always maintained that he was straight. Because he was open about his interest in gay liberation, he took a lot of crap from other people, particularly Third World men. Like one time, we were about to have a rap session, and I put a sign on the door of the dormitory which said, "Tonight, consciousness-raising, gay liberation," and throughout that day people would make comments to him, like, "Hey, did you see the sign on the door?" And "Hey, don't forget to go to your meeting tonight." And he started to get really pissed off, and he didn't just take it. When people would make comments, he tried to talk to them about how they were being foolish. But there never was enough feeling of support within the Third World group for the Third World gay people to feel that they could come out without having to suffer really serious consequences. One remedy for this is that on future brigades there be Third World gay liberation people as well, of course, as more gay women.

RICHIE: For the first time I identified as a gay person in public. And there was oppression. People you hadn't known before but who you could say hello to, when they knew, they suddenly didn't see you when you walked by, you're like an invisible person. And you feel that, you know, it means something. To live your life that way, it must be horrible, it must be a tremendously alienated feeling.

At the same time, I saw the whole trip so differently, as tremendous support in a lot of ways. Earl had something with a Puerto Rican guy in the dormitory who had been yelling about fags and disease. The guy—his name is M.— had been a prostitute, and he pulled himself out of that moral degradation, that whole business. Well, Earl went up to him, and they started talking about politics, yelling politics. M. got out of his bed and started to be threatening, and was talking to Earl in a loud voice, and Earl just stood there and yelled right back and looked him in the eye and, when it ended, M. was like the extreme case of irrationality toward homosexuality. Nobody had ever encountered somebody like him, and everybody on the brigade knew that he was irrational. A whole lot of people in the dormitory were listening when this went on, and they started saying, "Wow, it really is fucked up to be anti-gay in that way." And when Earl sat down, Earl and gay liberation had made a lot of friends. Right after that, we sat down with five or six men who had been listening to the whole thing, white men, and had a session right there on the floor in the dorm, three steps away from M., who was muttering into his breath, since he had not intimidated Earl. And the feeling was, yes, how can anybody believe that kind of thing, how can anybody ever verbalize in such an irrational way all that was happening? So I went to a lot of groups and I found a lot of support, people who were willing to argue. I could just sit back and listen, because they were together on sexuality.

JESSE: There's something that you said that has to be analyzed. M. was a hustler and had been fucked over by gay bourgeois people. In a sense M.'s whole life is a classic example…. Well, there were a lot of Third World people there who had gay experiences in prison and hustling, and their gay experiences related to the economic oppression, and like his view of homosexuality was not the way we view homosexuality. His view is that there are rich white people who buy and exploit Puerto Ricans. He viewed homosexuals as that. The Third World men I spoke to who had been in prison had a totally different view. They thought that homosexuals in prison were like low grade. Somehow not being Third World I don't understand it, but I understand that anti-gay Third World people had a totally different experience, and when they would call me a faggot it didn't mean the same thing as when a white person would say it, because I somehow embodied the whole system to them. The white individuals who would say things like that were more or less threatened, their masculinity was threatened, whereas the Third World people weren't having their masculinity threatened as much as they were attacking a whole thing. It's both things, but it can get very racist when you start describing M., because M. wasn't totally irrational. M. was coming from his oppression. We were coming from ours. A lot of time you would come out of your oppression toward a Third World person, and you would be called a racist, because you were. Like the way I would criticize someone for being sexist, was racist, and there was always this pow, pow, pow, and it was really very heavy to deal with. I just really became convinced that Third World people are a different community, and white people are a different community. White people were easier to deal with because they are our community, we speak the same language. Does anyone have questions?

QUESTION: I'd like to know how the people from Vietnam and the other Latin American countries related to you.

STEP: One experience which was really Jesse's, I'm stealing it from him…he was talking to a Vietnamese woman, and the Vietnamese, often as an opener in conversation, would say, "And what group are you from?" So she asked Jesse this and Jesse said, "I'm from Gay Liberation Front," and she said, "Wha'?" (Laughter.) And he said, "That's an organization of revolutionary homosexuals." And her response to that was, "Ah, yes, homosexuals are also oppressed under imperialism." You see, and this really reveals a whole lot about differences in political concepts between Vietnamese and Cubans and United States people. Like, the Vietnamese and the Cuban understanding of the movement in the United States is completely different from our understanding of it. Like, one kind of gross simplification is that whereas we view male supremacy as divisive, they might view women's liberation as divisive. It's like viewing it from two different ends. And the statement about "Ah yes, homosexuals are oppressed under imperialism," I thought that was especially ironic hearing that on Cuban soil, on socialist soil.

EARL: The week the Vietnamese and Laotians were with us really, oh, it just changed so many things the week they were there, they were like this incredible influence. It was like humanity returned to the camp. When they asked what organization we were from, I explained we were from a homosexual organization, and then I tried to find out about homosexuality in Vietnam. And I really couldn't find out anything at all. Some of them evidently didn't know that word in Spanish or in English, and some said, "We don't have it," but I really don't know what that meant either. It wasn't something that they had thought about very much, but there was a distinct difference that I noticed between them and Cuban men. Like most of the Cuban men, with the exception of three that I know, are physical with each other in their own particular fashion, and were also physical with the North American men there when they were being friendly. But they were noticeably not physical with us, with the gay men. (One man in the group objects.)—Well, maybe they were with you; they weren't with me. (Laughter.)—They weren't with most of us, at any rate. Well, there were a few who were, but with most of them I really felt, you know, I felt different. But with the Vietnamese and the Laotian men, who knew I was homosexual, I didn't feel the least bit different from anybody else. And the way that they related to each other: they're constantly hand-holding—and they don't just hold your hand like a dead hand, there's always squeezing, and you know, it's a cultural thing, it's a human thing, touching, it's spiritual. The one thing they did say about the gay movement in the United States was, "Good!" You know, anything that will help to stop American imperialism is right on in their eyes, and their support of gay liberation would be without reserve.

STEP: I disagree that it would be without reserve. Whenever I talked about gay liberation, I would always have to break it down. I would say we oppose the United States government and its imperialist policies, and we also fight against the oppression of homosexuals. And I think that if any Vietnamese expressed support for gay liberation, it was for the former part of our position rather than the latter.

NANCY: I think that as a woman the important thing for me to talk about is the position of women in Cuba. I heard that on the other two brigades the women's liberation people were always talking about the fact that the Cuban women would go out to the field wearing curlers or wearing make-up. You know, when I first heard that, it blew my mind. I don't know how people can be so stupid and culturally blind. I'd been to Spain, I was in Spain about four years ago, so I know something about Latin culture, and I now live in New Mexico, so that I'm also around a lot of Latin culture. The position of women in Cuba has just gone forward in leaps and bounds. The women in Havana used to not be able to walk around in the streets wearing pants. Now there are women all over wearing pants. There are women in uniform, women in the militia, there are women learning how to handle rifles. The thing that's important to realize is that before the revolution, open sexuality—just open heterosexuality—was not acceptable. A woman especially was not allowed to express any sexual desires before she was married, or before she was engaged, and she was not allowed to go out with a man without a chaperone, and the man always had to be approved by her parents—from our standpoint, rather archaic. All of these attitudes are changing, and we just can't expect a cultural revolution on the level of, say, the sort of phony cultural revolution that is taking place in the United States.

ELAINE: There are many different opinions among the people that came back as to how severe the oppression of gays in Cuba is. I think that anyone here will definitely agree with this statement: it's not going to be a place where homosexuals are going to feel free very soon. It's not going to be a place where, at this point, there will be no social stigma or whatever. It's not going to happen very quickly. But there are things in process in Cuba, the effects of which will have a big effect on the whole cultural revolution there. And some of them are very basic to women's liberation, obviously, in getting women out of the home. At this point, there is a big push to get women out of the homes and into different things. Educational opportunities have been opened up. Institutional structures which separate sexes are being broken down. Women are becoming engineers. Women are becoming doctors. So that for adults or young people at this point, those kinds of things have opened up. The cultural things—there's a lag there, obviously, and that'll take time to work out. And a lot of inter-personal things have to be worked out. Divorces at this point in Cuba are very high, because of that whole process. To me, the real thing to focus on in terms of this cultural change in Cuba is the breakdown of the nuclear family to some extent through the child-care centers, through boarding schools, semi-boarding schools for kids, the fantastic accent on education. It's really important to understand that Cuba is an underdeveloped country in every possible way. It's underdeveloped economically. It's underdeveloped culturally in terms of education. There are splits and differences in culture, say, in the cities, as opposed to way back in the hills. But all those things are being dealt with, not on the basis of, "Well, we've got to solve social relationships between men and women," not on the level that we have to break down the nuclear family. They're dealt that on the level that at this point, for basic survival and sustaining life in Cuba, every person has to develop to the fullest potential just in order for their country to survive. That means that every effort is made at this point to start children as young as possible, get them together, get them to learn to play together, learn things collectively, to work collectively. This carries all through the society. Each one of those children is considered a very valuable human being. Each one of those people has potential in them, whether they're male or female. That potential is to be explored or expanded as far as possible. You can see this in the child-care centers, you can see this in the schools. The long term effect that this will have on changing social and cultural realtionships seems very clear to me. Although all these problems aren't going to be resolved very quickly, as women begin to assert themselves more, to develop themselves completely, all these kinds of things will change. And I have a fantastic amount of optimism. I can see these things happening in Cuba.

EARL: I want to add one thing to that, just to explain something, because this thing is really real, the development of the collective consciousness that's going on with the children and the way that they are being encouraged to relate to their own peer group. In Cuba, you would never hear them say that they are going to smash the family, like we say here. But at the same time, that is precisely what they're doing. You see, if they would say to people: "We're going to smash the family," the reaction would be incredible. But instead, all of these child-care centers are there. It's a convenience for the people. It's seen as a positive thing. What they will say is that these child-care centers are the policy of the revolutionary government, and the schools are the formative cell of the individual. That's about the clearest statement they'll make about what's going on. So what you have to understand is that while they may not say something in the way we do here, they share many of our concerns about culture and are really doing something about them.

QUESTION: I don't think there's any necessity to assume that the changes that are going on in Cuba will in fact bring about the sort of improvement that people talk about. I have two reasons for saying this. The first is that in the first few years after the Russian Revolution, there was this same apparent breakdown of the family, the same apparent emancipation of women, the same setting up of child-care centers, etc.; and fairly soon after this, the policy was reversed. Now I'm not saying that Cuba is the Soviet Union. I'm not saying that a Stalin is going to rise in Cuba. I am saying that there's no necessity that things have to get better, and that the historical parallel of the Soviet Union should at least make us consider the possibility that these things can be reversed.

The other thing that I wanted to say is I think more important. Everyone is talking about the attitudes towards homosexuals as if they exist in Cuba because there's a hangover from the traditional Latin Catholic culture. But as far as I know, Communist Parties in most countries today, and I think I'm right in including the United States, hold that homosexuality is a bad thing, and it's a product of the capitalist system, and it will vanish as capitalism is eradicated. Now if this is so, then I'd suggest the Cuban Communist Party is going to take the same sort of attitude. There's no real possibility therefore that things will get better for homosexuals. They might decide not to put them in camps. I assume that has all sorts of defects as a policy, anyway: it's a very expensive thing to do. But I don't see why we should assume that as the traditional values of the society die out, they're necessarily going to be changed in a direction that we'd like. The Communist Party of Cuba is just as likely to force a total end to homosexuality for the same sort of reasons that other socialist countries have tried to do it. I'd be interested in hearing your comments on that.

STEP: Some things were pointed out about better developments for the Cuban homosexuals, like what somebody said was the breakdown of the nuclear family. I think that there are also a lot of forces at work in Cuba to keep homosexuals down, and that's a part of the Communist Party's position on homosexuals. The Communist Party rules Cuba, and I really disagree with the statement that was made before that there are no laws against homosexuals. There might not be laws in the sense that we know them, in the sense that they're legislated by a house of representatives or a senate, but there are policies that exist and are enforced. Like the way open homosexuals can't be teachers and can't be in the Communist Party. This is enforced right down the line, and if you want to call that a policy or a rule or a law, the truth remains that it's made to work and it has that effect. As a part of the Communist Party's position, there's even a word for it; they call it a *peligrosidad,* which means a dangerous thing, or a danger to the society. And because of the way the Communist Party or the government operates in Cuba, there is a policy that once the government takes a position on something, or determines that something is a *peligrosidad,* such as marijuana or homosexuality or whatever, then it's considered to be a closed matter, in the sense that people cannot propagandize or agitate for a position that's in opposition to the position that the Communist Party has taken. Of course, somebody was very careful to point out to me that that doesn't mean that somebody can't talk about it—people can talk about marijuana, can talk about homosexuality—but I don't think that's a very big concession. If homosexuals in Cuba get together, decide to work from the bottom up, to agitate or propagandize in their own behalf, if they want to organize as homosexuals to oppose homosexual oppression, there is no doubt in my mind but that they will be severely repressed by the government. For example, if they try to put out a leaflet talking about homosexuality not as a disease but in the way that we in gay liberation think of it, or a leaflet advocating a real change of the status of homosexuals in Cuba, it will not be tolerated. This leaflet just won't be able to be distributed, unless you do it underground. The government, I feel, would actively seek out the source of these leaflets and act in a really repressive way.

JESSE: We made a presentation to the Venceremos Brigade about gay liberation, and in arranging it (this goes along with what Step was saying about *peligrosidades*), we were somehow informed by the people in the camp, the Cubans, that Cubans would not be coming to the presentation, and that we could not make the presentation to the Cuban delegation. There was no explanation given for why we couldn't talk about our organization. However, if you take that position about the *peligrosidades,* it somehow fits in that a group of Cubans coming to hear a discussion about a *peligrosidad* would be bit of a contradiction. But we didn't understand it at the time.

ELAINE: I think it's important to realize that at this point in Cuba, unity is the most important thing. There are other situations where people right now would be discouraged from starting up a separate group on any level. This can be traced back to the Sino-Soviet split, when Cuba was having a lot of her own problems. During this split, there were some groups of Cubans who were handing out leaflets and having discussion groups and whatever, getting materials from the Russian Embassy in Cuba, and there were other groups who leaned toward the Chinese and were working from the Chinese Embassy. And for a while everyone was talking about the Sino-Soviet split and not talking about concrete things that had to be done in Cuba at that time, and it was felt to be a divisive thing, that it was dividing Cubans. So since that time there has been kind of a policy that rather than form separate groups when new issues come up, they should be treated through mass organizations that don't divide the people into factions. And that doesn't work out very well at this point in terms of changing things about homosexuals.

The other thing I wanted to point out is that we really have to look at the situation in the United States and in other countries as relatively separate. What happened in Russia, for example was that the intellectual leaders after the revolution did have very utopian kinds of things that they wanted to institute right away. There wasn't any organization of homosexuals in Russia, and there wasn't any in Cuba when their revolution came about. So that we are practically an historical first as revolutionary homosexuals in the world, and I think that's an important thing to understand.

RICHIE: To go back to the question of reasons for optimism. First of all, Cuba has learned from Russia—that's one reason why it'll be different. Cuba has learned from Russian mistakes. Cubans have seen what it means to repress a whole class like artists; Cuba does not do that. The leaders in Cuba are not the Russian leaders. Cuba is a very tiny country. That means that everybody can feel each other almost physically. It's not a place that has to be centralized. Fidel has said Havana is much too big for Cuba. If you go to any capital anywhere in Latin America, you find that the capital has nine-tenths of everything, no matter what the size of the capital. Havana is one-quarter the size in population of its country, and maybe it gets a half of everything. It gets a lot. But in no sense is it the one centralized place for all the goods and everything else. The Communist Parties in other countries have functioned as an intellectual unit, as a power structure. The Communist Party in Cuba works in the same way right this minute, but every time that there's a decision to be made—and it goes one step at a time, as Elaine said—it does not impose a whole superstructure that the people have to reject, the way a body rejects a new heart that's been transplanted into it. So they're very sensitive to the people. Fidel knows what it means to have callouses. He knows what it means to work in a 100-degree sun.

That's completely different. I don't think that's ever happened in a revolution, where your revolutionary leaders have had that kind of gut feeling for the people. And this is going to make a difference in the future. Day-care centers and those sort of things are not going to be ended, because they are an economic necessity. Cuba's so underdeveloped as a country that the women will have to work for a lot of years before the country gets things together, and those things are going to go on their own way and develop a people. This isn't to say they're solving all the problems, but the only reason it would go backwards is if outside people like us push things that the Cuban people would have to reject. The Party doesn't push. It may be aware of homosexuality as a force, or it may not. It doesn't matter. But they know well enough not to push it. The state is pragmatic. There are homosexuals teaching, I'm sure, that may even be recognized as homosexuals. There are homosexuals in the artistic community who are recognized as homosexuals. But that is not how they are identified for the people. They are identified as people who are helping the revolution. They are going to stay there. That pragmatism—taking advantage of whoever's work you can—is a necessity, and that's why I have optimism.

JESSE: I don't think Cuba is any more anti-gay than the United States. I don't think it's any different than living in Ogden, Utah. And being in a mental institution in Cuba is the same as being in a mental institution in the U.S. if you're a homosexual. All I'm saying is that in terms of GLF, like Elaine said, we're a first. It's a total affirmation coming back from Cuba and knowing what struggle means, from the Vietnamese, because they've lived their whole life in struggle. And I just feel more convinced that we must struggle. I don't have optimism or pessimism. I just know that the struggle must increase.

LETTER FROM CUBAN GAY PEOPLE TO THE NORTH AMERICAN GAY LIBERATION MOVEMENT

Sisters and Brothers:
By chance, we got a copy of your publication with the statement of Third World Gay Revolution (*Gay Flames* pamphlet No. 7).
We believe it is our duty to inform you of our situation as homosexuals in Cuba, as people who experience discrimination in

a country which presumably is involved in a revolution and is committed to the creation of the "new man." This revolution is struggling against the traditional injustices that all Cubans have suffered as a result of economic exploitation and a class society. The vestiges of this class society still bring us suffering. We wish to inform you, however, of a series of events which fundamentally deny the postulates of the social and political movement in Cuba. In fact, our country is in a state of increasingly greater crisis, quite in contradiction with the success stories told abroad.

If in a consumption society, run by capitalists and oligarchs, like the one you are living in, homosexuals experience suffering and limitations, in our society, labeled Marxist and revolutionary, it is worse. Since its beginning—first in veiled ways, later without scruples or rationalizations—the Cuban revolutionary government has persecuted homosexuals. The methods range from the most common sort of physical attack to attempts to impose psychic and moral disintegration upon gay people. In theory, at least, the Cuban revolution holds that homosexuality is not compatible with the development of a society whose goal is communism.

Here, the homosexual is attacked in such a way that he or she becomes the victim of a series of formulas to make invisible what the authorities judge to be an aberration, a repudiable fault. One formula is for homosexuals to marry and pretend to live a "normal" life. Another has been the confinement of homosexuals on farms where they are brutally treated. This happened with the concentration camps of the UMAP, which, for the uninformed, were simply "military units to increase production," a place where people did farm work and youths received military training, the sort of thing that might take place in any civilized country. This situation provoked an international scandal, and subsequently the UMAP camps were eliminated as a branch of obligatory military service—but there still are prison farms exclusively for homosexuals.

On the street we suffer persecution, aggression, and a constant abuse of authority. We are asked to produce I.D. cards. We are arrested for wearing certain clothes or using certain hair styles, or for simple get-togethers. This is a violation of freedoms guaranteed by the Declaration of Human Rights, freedoms which, contradictorily, are more respected in societies that are called fascist than in ours—though Cuban society has been seen as a model for the solution of the problems of individual and collective freedom.

Methods of psychological repression, social isolation, control by districts, neighborhoods, work places and schools, always with the aim of negating us, are commonly used by this regime. It can be said that there are many homosexuals, some of them intellectuals, some not, who live apart from this situation. In the first place, they are very few in number. To the extent that such persons exist, they know that they cannot cross the limits of behavior that have been outlined for them, and that in the case of opposition, there is only the risk of exile or the response of a dictatorial system which can lead to the worst consequences.

It is not possible to advocate freedom, respect and justice for homosexuals throughout the world without taking into consideration the situation of thousands of individuals in our country. There must also be protests for the treatment they are given, and the search for an effective solution, not a theoretical one, to such problems.

We hope in future communications to give plenty of details and to shed light on many situations which you do not know about in this uncertain and chaotic pseudo-socialist system.

(Note: to protect ourselves, we have given a false return address.)

DECLARATION BY THE
FIRST NATIONAL CONGRESS
ON EDUCATION AND CULTURE

Excerpted from *GRANMA*, daily organ of the Communist Party of Cuba

The social pathological character of homosexual deviations was recognized. It was resolved that all manifestations of homosexual deviations are to be firmly rejected and prevented from spreading. It was pointed out, however, that a study, investigation, and analysis of this complex problem should always determine the measures to be adopted.

It was decided that homosexuality should not be considered a central problem or a fundamental one in our society, but rather its attention and solution are necessary.

A study was made of the origin and evolution of this phenomenon and of its present-day scope and antisocial character. An in-depth analysis was made of the preventive and educational measures that are to be put into effect against existing focuses, including the control and relocation of isolated cases and degrees of deterioration.

On the basis of these considerations, it was resolved that it would be convenient to adopt the following measures:

a) Extension of the coeducational system: recognition of its importance in the formation of children and the young.

b) Appropriate sexual education for parents, teachers and pupils. This work must not be treated as a special subject but as one falling into the general teaching syllabus, such as biology, physiology, etc.

c) Stimulation of proper approach to sex. A campaign of information should be put into effect among adolescents and young people which would contribute to the acquisition of a scientific knowledge of sex and the eradication of prejudices and doubts which in some cases result in the placing of too much importance on sex.

d) Promotion of discussion among the youth in those cases where it becomes necessary to delve into the human aspect of sex relations.

It was resolved that for notorious homosexuals to have influence in the formation of our youth is not to be tolerated on the basis of their "artistic merits."

Consequently, a study is called for to determine how best to tackle the problems of the presence of homosexuals, in the various institutions of our cultural sector.

It was proposed that a study should be made to find a way of applying measures with a view to transfering to other organizations those who, as homosexuals, should not have any direct influence on our youth through artistic and cultural activities.

It was resolved that those whose morals do not correspond to the prestige of our revolution should be barred from any group of performers representing our country abroad.

Finally, it was agreed to demand that severe penalties be applied to those who corrupt the morals of minors, depraved repeat offenders and irredeemable antisocial elements.

Cultural institutions cannot serve as a platform for false intellectuals who try to make snobbery, extravagant conduct, homosexuality and other social aberrations into expressions of revolutionary spirit and art, isolated from the masses and the spirit of the revolution.

RESPONSES

1. Gay Revolution Party

The statement on homosexuality issued in Cuba by the First National Congress on Education and Culture, which was attended and endorsed by the leaders of the Cuban government, is openly reactionary. It is a threat to the lives and freedom of gay people because of the "severe penalities" demanded for "repeat offenders" and also because it encourages individual physical violence against homosexuals. It is also a threat to gay people throughout the world because of Cuba's reputation as a revolutionary nation.

We, the Gay Revolution Party, condemn the statement of the First National Congress on Education and Culture. We demand of revolutionaries everywhere that they join us in this move initially by the printing of this statement or their own comments.

The fight of the Cuban and other Third World peoples against the imperialism of the U.S. and its lackeys cannot be won by maintaining the attitudes of cultural and sexo-economic systems which support and are nurtured by sexism, male individualism, capitalism, and imperialism. It is necessary that cultural as well as political and economic revolution occur, and that this revolution destroy the sexist roots of exploitation.

As long as anti-gay attitudes persist, not only will gay people suffer, but the exploitation of women by men will be normal, competition among males will be the rule, and true communism will be impossible. We are socialists. We have come to understand that the destruction of straight social patterns (i.e., those modeled on powerbased, role-playing heterosexuality) and the creation of gayness (i.e., mutuality and equality of human relationships based on the model of free homosexuality) are inherent to the development of a true socialist society. Thus, the only way to ensure a straight Cuba is to re-establish capitalism. A people struggling toward socialism can, due to an incorrect ideological superstructure, kill, relocate, or isolate individual gay people, but they cannot help but create conditions favorable to gayness.

Gay people are not one more group struggling for liberation. We are, and have always been, considered the scum of the earth, but we are you; we are everyone. The gay revolution is basic because it will destroy the sexual and social roles which are at the bottom of all exploitation, establishing mutuality of relationship between all people.

We do not call upon any straight male government to change its policy or reform its laws, whether it is in Cuba, the United States, or the Soviet Union. We call instead upon all people who seek freedom and an end to domination to examine straight relationships and to realize with us that it is the roles and attitudes inherent to the maintenance of these relationships that prevent revolutionary change.

Cuba's reactionary policy cannot defeat us. It will only strengthen our resolution to fight collectively until the gay liberation of all people.

Turn it out!

Gay Revolution Party

(Note: translated into the straight idiom for the benefit of those not yet gay)

2. Gay Committee of Returned Brigadistas

We, as gay North Americans who have identified with and supported the Cuban revolution and our gay sisters and brothers in Cuba through our participation in the Venceremos Brigade, denounce the anti-homosexual policy formulated at the recent Conference on Education and Culture and endorsed by the Cuban government.

We have seen the struggle of all Cuban people and gay people all over the world as a common struggle; we have supported the progressive economic policies of the revolution and have been excited and encouraged at the indications of a developing cultural revolution toward the liberation of women in all areas of life.

Inherent to socialism and socialist practice is the equalization of power among all people. People cannot seize control of their own lives unless they see themselves historically and analyze critically the culture and institutions which have formulated them. Centuries of sexist attitudes inculcated by all the institutions of "western civilization," especially the church, have served to solidify today's sexist superstructure which places straight men at the top—defining their masculinity by the amount of power they have over gay people, women, and other men. It is each person's revolutionary responsibility to be critical, to be critical of the racist and sexist institutions which perpetuate divisions among us. There can be no real revolution, no truly socialist society until we remove the walls of self-hatred that separate us from ourselves and other people.

Gay people owe allegiance to no nation. The anti-homosexual policy of the Cuban government does not simply fail to include gay people in the revolutionary process—it *specifically excludes* them from participation in that process and the right to self-determination. We have been told that it is reactionary for us to criticize and condemn our oppressors when they call themselves "revolutionary" or "socialist." A policy of ruthless and incessant persecution of gay people is contradictory to the needs of all people, and such a policy is reactionary and fascist. All sexist policies and practices are counterrevolutionary and evidence the efforts of a ruling class to crush the people's cultural revolution when it threatens the ruling class (or caste) position of privilege.

Also, we denounce the national committee of the Venceremos Brigade as the agents of a sexist hierarchy. They, in their liberalism, have not engaged in critical relationship with either the Cuban people or with revolutionaries here.

We call upon all progressive people to join in our protests against this reactionary policy and to make their feelings known by writing to the Cuban Prime Minister and First Secretary of the Communist Party in Havana.

Turn it out!

Venceremos!

Gay Committee of Returned Brigadistas

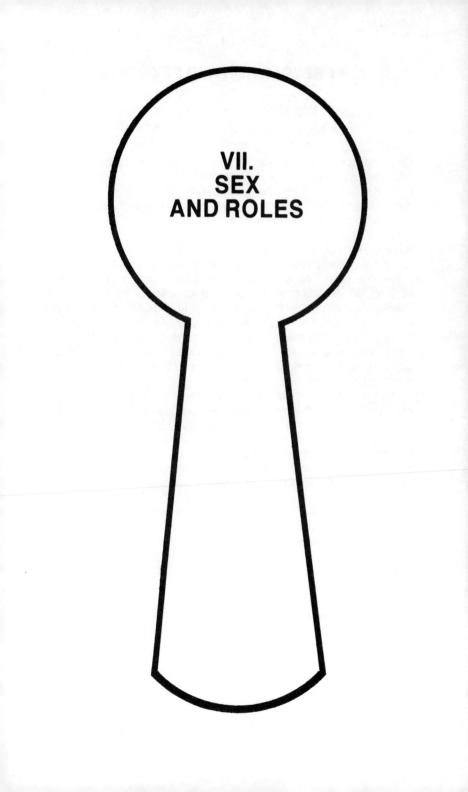

VII.
SEX
AND ROLES

GAY REVOLUTION AND SEX ROLES

Third World Gay Revolution (Chicago) and Gay Liberation Front (Chicago)

Gay liberation is inherently revolutionary. Most of homosexual oppression, and of the oppression all society receives as feedback, grows from the assumption that people are inborn heterosexual. That is acknowledged as false by even the most pig shrinks by now—now that sexist societal structures are no longer dependent on the assumptions that bore and nurtured them. They have created a life of their own, and a justification of their own: sexism is necessary to protect the structures built on it.

On that postulate of inborn heterosexuality is based the next step in the invention of homosexual illness: homosexuality is a misdirection of natural heterosexuality. (The homosexual doesn't really dig those of her or his own sex, you see; he or she hates or fears the opposite sex.) Growing from the same postulate is the weird idea that to be homosexual one must identify with the opposite sex. Some pig mentalities even build on both these contradictory fantasies.

With the assumption of inborn heterosexuality come the assumptions of whole package deals of inborn traits of women and of men. Everyone by now recognizes these as programmed role-playing. The recognition hasn't much weakened their rule. If you challenge their tyranny over you, you're "confusing gender identity." (No normal person would question his or her normal roles, so your failure to adjust is latent homosexuality—keep your place!) To maintain sex roles, heterosexual standards had to manufacture artificial definitions of male and female. A "real man" and "real woman" are not so by their chromosomes and genitals, but by their respective degrees of "masculinity" and "femininity," and by how closely they follow the sex-role script in their relationships with individuals and society. Heterosexual "normality" demands all-or-nothing outlines of "masculine" and "feminine" and denial of half the self.

Sex roles are so institutionalized that "normal" heterosexual relationships are so unequal, so exploitative, so possessive, so noncommunicative, so manipulative, so competitive, so nonrespectful, so tied up in power struggle and with fulfilling roles that a ridiculously unloving standard of love is accepted. Through what Shulamith Firestone calls "privatization," society isolates people, coopts them into believing it's all a matter of individual solutions and into futilely trying to build less inhumane variations within the anti-human institutions. So one believes that her or his frustration, insecurity, and alienation from his or her body and emotions and from other people are due to her or his own personal failure rather than to universal oppression that reaches to the roots of experience and consciousness. Our society restricts love to sexual and parental "love," actually judging it by the degree of its exclusiveness and possessiveness (the "virtue of monogamy"). This makes love cruelly competitive and, by channeling one's need to love as narrowly as possible, isolates people. It forbids touching without sexual overtones. It enforces as "morality" fear and disgust toward the body and physical sensation, and the divorce of sexuality from the rest of being. Through competition toward a uniform beauty (especially for women, a commodity whose value is determined by physical appearance), it denies the magnificent, uncompetitive beauty innate in everyone's individuality. All this and more were built from the sex roles and necessary to maintain them, whose origins were in reproductive functions and in the ancient requirement that all sexual activity to be channeled into reproduction. It grew with a religious tradition tailored—for an ancient, barbaric society—to keep stability of a family-tribal structure, thus of a primeval class-caste structure, thus of the power structure. The sex roles constructed a blueprint for modern oppression: a family structure defining children and wife as property of a head male; an economy based on competition, power struggles, inequality, exploitation, and isolation, whose patterns of caste and competition were extended to build racism and other chauvinisms; a culture which places crucial value on "masculinity" (translated into possessions, force, domination, and ultimately militarism and imperialism) which determines the ruling class of the sex-class system (and ultimately of the economic class system); a society in which people must perceive each other as threats, believing that they cannot have something without its being denied to someone else, and vice versa (which is made reality in the economic system.) Genuine love is dangerous to an economy based on people destroying one another.

Sexist oppression has become so integral to society that it has to protect structures from those who threaten it. Among these threats are homosexuals, whose oppression is used as a weapon against other rebels. ("You don't dig rape? You must be a dyke.") The sexists define "normal family environment" as what they fantasize produces heterosexual children. The children of a family that "fails" (to conform) might at best turn out "maladjusted" to roles or to the regimentation and dehumanization of the larger class society. (Notice that once you've gotten this far, you can forget the false initial postulate of inborn heterosexuality. In fact, recognition of sexual orientation as learned and acquired comes in handy here: look how easily you can fuck up and make your kid queer! Watch your step and know your place!) Hetero-chauvinism has not only proclaimed homosexuals inferior, it has refused to believe that a love-sex relationship (or love) could exist between human beings of the same sex. (Hence the myth of "gender confusion.") So it tried to *ensure* they couldn't exist—in the process ensuring that virtually *no* love could exist at all. Society protected sex roles from homosexuals not only by quarantine, not only by open persecution. It also enforced on homosexual relationships the same inequality and role-playing, the exploitation and non-respect it made the norm for heterosexual relationships —so that no *truly homosexual* relationships could be. (Some have anyway.)

Homosexuals, like other oppressed minorities in pre-liberation consciousness, long accepted subhuman status as deserved. They dutifully imitated heterosexuals—their relationships crippled by that and by the projected self-contempt of the oppressed—and accepted heterosexual values, which have created the infamous homosexual misery and self-hate.

A gay person who accepts straight standards will associate "masculinity" with men and "femininity" with women. He or she will accept definitions of "real man" and "real woman" by that and by their proper relationships to the proper sexes. She or he will accept labeling of many of his or her feelings (which have nothing to do with being gay—just being human) as characteristic only of the opposite sex. He or she will accept that there are only the straights' two alternatives—mutually exclusive "manhood" and "womanhood." Thus has sexist brainwashing actually *created* a correlation between homosexuality and transsexualism. Though "gender identity," being entirely artificial, has little to do with sexual orientation, this is another way gay oppression is used to keep people in line. Anyone should be allowed to do anything with his or her appearance. Everyone should be allowed to integrate his or her personality. But, by straight standards, a person cannot like certain modes of appearance for their own sake, or give rein to some aspects of her or his personality, without violating her inborn sex-determined tendencies toward different appearances, interests, emotions, etc.; and therefore identifying with the opposite sex, and therefore being homosexual and therefore sick.

The oppression of women and that of gay people are

interdependent and spring from the same roots, but take different forms. Women and children are oppressed by *how* they fit into the sex-class structure. Gay people are *persecuted* because we don't fit into that structure at all. Every effort has been made to exterminate us. (This is not to say that gay people are more oppressed than women or vice versa. It is counterrevolutionary to try to rank oppressed peoples in the order of the viciousness of their oppression, or to claim that one liberation movement is more important than another.) It was simpler in the times when deviation of many kinds was "sin." Past societies did not kill deviates for amusement or because they were less enlightened than modern societies which persecute nonconformists with the label "sick." (This was made easier after Freudian psychoanalysis started explaining "normal" behavior in terms of the "abnormal.") Heretics are persecuted today for the same reason they were fifty centuries ago: they are a threat.

But individuals refusing to keep their places do not equally threaten a class structure (whether it be of economic class, sex, race, or whatever.) It can easier afford to allow an individual from a lower stratum to try to enter upper strata than vice versa. This reinforces the preeminence of the ruling group and keeps the oppressed divided and competing. For he or she must concede the superiority and desirability of the upper stratum. He or she must "work within the system," thus acknowledging the validity of the system. He or she must gratefully acknowledge being generously permitted to work *up* from her or his inferiority, not being unjustly pushed down (that's called "bootstraps"). And she or he must reject identity as one of the oppressed, blaming the *oppressed* for their (and his or her) oppression ("I made it—why can't they?"), and presenting herself or himself as the superior *exception* to them. (These qualifications distinguish the Uncle Tom who is climbing from the "uppity nigger.") Role-transcend-ence that does innately threaten a hierarchy is a member of the *higher* strata descending. This denies the superiority and weakens the position of the ruling group, and represents its loss of key domination—psychological—as does the greater threat of solidarity and pride among the oppressed.

This principle is related in a complex way to the anti-sexist revolution. Although women have less freedom *within* their roles, men have less freedom to *transcend* their roles. Individual women have gained progress in the "man's world" (whether business, the arts, or the male pseudo-movement) by accepting male values and goals, and disowning their sisters—by being exceptions. Women have been more effectively divided than any other oppressed people. Instead of sharing exclusion from the dominant culture, women are psychologically isolated from each other, intensifying the division of the competition and projected self-hate of the oppressed. Kept individually dependent on men, women have no culture or ghettos as a framework within which to build autonomous self-identification. Women are suspended between blatant discrimination and the anesthetizing dehumanization that Robin Morgan calls "patronizing pedestalitis." The proper being for a woman is as an appendage (as ornament, toy, alter ego, parasite, burden, or slave) to an individual of the oppressor class—her identity defined by that relationship. Women are "both marginal and fundamental," in Juliet Mitchell's words—marginal in participation in real life, and fundamental to social structures. In effect, women are assimilated, without the concessions given when assimilation is a defense measure. Women are ignored and invisible outside specific realms; homosexual women, as anomalies within the mass of women, could also be ignored. For sexism had separated homosexual women from the rest of womankind —partly by the scare value of the label "homosexual" and denial of the "definitions" of femaleness to homosexual women. Anti-homosexuality is necessary not only to keep women in "women's place," but to keep women divided and self-denying —and thus down. For lesbianism is self-affirmation.

But sexism trapped itself into much greater vulnerability to the *very existence* of male homosexuality. Sexism has sought to keep the sex-role structure, like other class structures, vertically one-dimensional. It was to conform to this, to keep the structure rigid, that the confusion of homosexuality with transsexualism (i.e., changing class) was necessary. Lesbianism can hardly be called "working within the system," and it doesn't tend to raise a person's status. Yet male chauvinist fantasy considers lesbianism women's trying to be men (or sour-grapes after rejection from or failure in the sex-role structure). This somewhat neutralizes the threat to male supremacy that homosexual women's not needing men represents. Male homosexuals, however, have partly relinquished male privilege (though it wasn't voluntary, which is why male supremacist values still infect some homosexual men). So homosexual men are actively, openly persecuted by straight male-society—the persecution a magnification of straight men's insane reactions to fear of their own homosexuality—and of anything else within them, such as the "femininity" they attribute to homosexual men, that might imperil their power and privilege. Sexism's vertical one-dimensional class structure is also why *any* deviation from "normal" interests, feelings, etc. for one's sex is often attributed to transsexual tendencies (thus homosexuality). This is a major reason for the personality-typing of gay people. It is also why, for example, women's liberationists are accused of wanting to be men, and why terms such as "faggot" are thrown at a boy who doesn't suppress his "feminine" interests or characteristics. A "feminine" male threatens other males by in effect partially renouncing privilege, and thus threatening their own privilege, not only by mirroring a suppressed part of them but by weakening male-ruling-class position. So, as a defense of male position, he is separated from his maleness—"not a real man." Male supremacy is directly responsible for the more active persecution of male than of female homosexuals and transvestites.

The dependency of male privilege on "masculinity" and male role-playing is the means by which sexist "normality" requires men to "prove their masculinity" by obsession with possessions and with power, whether on the level of the sexual or the international. Male values are societal values in a male-dominated society, and "masculinity"-tripping is the anti-human values of the death culture. So it's even more important for society to compel men than women to suppress half of themselves. And it's even more crucial to keep men than women divided—to keep men from loving anyone, especially themselves and each other. (This is why it has been a key part of homosexual oppression to keep homosexuals from *loving* themselves and each other. Sexual relations don't ensure love. But the *prohibition*, among a given group, of physical relations—to the point of attaching guilt and shame to touching—effectively *prohibits* love.) Without sexism's isolation and anti-love, there would not be the emotional insecurity and self-hate that necessitate ego-tripping, power-tripping, and money-tripping. No other ruling class depends on division among itself. For *all* oppression (starting with that of women) depends on division among *men*—on *men* fearing, hating, seeking to dominate and trying to destroy each other—which in turn depends on male supremacy.

Gay liberation cannot be achieved internally while male supremacy and other sexist values remain within gay people, nor can it be achieved externally while sexist institutions remain intact. The extent to which a gay liberationist is unaware of sexism in society—or in gay liberation—is the extent to which he or she is ineffective as a gay liberationist. For to that degree has he or she accepted and assimilated the all-pervading sexism as natural, right, and deserved—made it his or her own. To that extent, he or she cannot be a revolutionary gay liberationist—merely an advocate of gay rights who is incidentally pro-revolution. For gay people have evolved an apparently independent oppression—as another victimized minority, in psychological and geographical ghettos, seemingly isolated from the role-imprisoned society yet both imitating and feeding it. So she or he can fight for gay rights—no more job discrimination, relatively fair trials, no more police harassment, etc. It's possible to gain such things within the system, which can make concessions (painkillers for the oppressed) to protect itself. So that's a potentially productive front to work on, but gay liberation won't be achieved there. And gay liberation doesn't depend on our public relations job with straights. To get some rights *granted* by our oppressor is not gay liberation. To persuade society to tolerate a bit more unhassled deviation *within* the framework of sexism is not gay liberation.

Gay is good if we declare it so. Gay can be a force for everyone's ultimate liberation if *we* recognize it as such. Though to us as individual gay people gay represents potential for love with equality and freedom, that's only the first level of gay is good. After all, the imprisoning, artificial labels of gay, straight, and bi would be meaningless without the sex roles and "correct gender identification" and isolation and channeling and antihumanism that sexism imposes. (As Judy Grahn said, "If anyone were allowed to fall in love with *anyone,* the word 'homosexual' wouldn't be needed.") A higher level of gay is good is as a tool to break down enforced heterosexuality, sex roles, the impoverished categories of straight, gay, and bisexual, male supremacy, programming of children, ownership of children, the nuclear family, monogamy, possessiveness, exclusiveness of "love," insecurity, jealousy, competition, privilege, individual isolation, ego-tripping, power-tripping, money-tripping, people as property, people as machines, rejection of the body, repression of emotions, anti-eroticism, authoritarian anti-human religion, conformity, regimentation, polarization of "masculine" and "feminine," categorization of male and female emotions, abilities, interests, clothing, etc., fragmentation of the self by these outlines, isolation and elitism of the arts, uniform standards of beauty, dependency on leaders, unquestioning submission to authority, power hierarchies, caste, racism, militarism, imperialism, national chauvinism, cultural chauvinism, class chauvinism, adult chauvinism, human chauvinism, domination, exploitation, division, inequality, and repression as the cultural and politico-economic norms, all manifestations of non-respect and non-love for what is human (not to mention animals and plants)—maybe even up to private property and the state. For sexism was the founding oppression—the original inequality, the original domination, the original isolation, competition, and division among people, the original relation to people as property, the original rejection of humanness. And sexism has remained within people to fuck up their efforts to build collective societies, both abroad and in America's own communities. The individual's relationships with other individuals, in the erotic sphere and in other areas, creates her relationship to the world. The society's relationship to love and to sexuality and to all human interaction builds the patterns for the economic system, the political structure, and the culture—which in turn set patterns for individual self-relations and relations to other human beings. The personal is the political, the economic, and the cultural. Gay is the revolution.

SMASH PHALLIC IMPERIALISM

Katz

Sex is an institution. In an oppressive society like Amerika, it reflects the same ideology as other major institutions. It is goal-oriented, profit and productivity oriented. It is a prescribed system, with a series of correct and building activities aimed toward the production of a single goal: climax.

It's also a drag. For women, in a culture based on our oppression, heterosexual sex is a product we have had to turn out. To encourage us, we are given two minutes of this, a few moments of that, a couple minutes at something else . . . all aimed towards the Great Penetration and the Big Come. There is great pressure to have an orgasm. Sex without orgasm is a failure, it's a drag, it's incomplete, and very very sad. (Just like marriage is not real until it is "consummated.") Because of phallic imperialism built upon Freud's ignorance of the female body, orgasm is supposed to come from intercourse. That's just terrific for boys, but since our orgasm-producing organ is the clitoris, external to the vagina—contradicting capitalist sexist physiology—many women don't produce the appropriate orgasm through heterosexuality. By that criteria, they are frigid.

I'm a lesbian. A lot of people can't figure out "what we do," how we make love without a penis around for the final consummation. A lot of boys have these ideas of dildos and bananas. Sex as an institution is so totally tied up with the penis and its goal that boys assume there must be some poor substitute for their noble item.

I always hated sex with men. The pressure of the goal, the rigidity of the process and ends was always totally unsatisfactory. Whenever I hear the word "sex," all those shitty experiences I had with men come to mind. I cannot separate the word "sex" from the phallic tryanny I suffered from for so many years.

For me, coming out meant an end to sex. It's dead and gone in my life. I reject that institution totally. Sex means oppression, it means exploitation. It serves the needs of boys. It has little to do with pleasure for the greatest mass of oppressed people: women.

Physical contact and feelings have taken a new liberatory form, and we call that "sensuality." The women's movement in general, especially at the beginning, and gay feminism now is a fantastically sensual experience for me. I love my body and the bodies of my sisters. Physicalness is now a creative non-institutionalized experience. It is touching and rubbing and cuddling and fondness. It is holding and rocking and kissing and licking. Its only goal is closeness and pleasure. It does not exist for the Big Orgasm. It exists for feeling nice. Our sensuality may or may not include genital experience, that may or may not be the beginning or the ending of the experience. It may be anywhere, or nowhere.

To make good love with women, I don't want to have to "produce" anything. Except pleasure. And that should be at whatever level or in whatever form seems comfortable for that time. Lesbian sensuality works toward solving the contradictions between my mind and my body by transforming all politics with the energies of our woman-love. If we feel good in a group we may have a pajama party, which would be called an "orgy" inside the institution of straight sex. It could mean a lot of things from hugs to climax to cuddling to back-rubbing. It could be a genital thing or not. We are free to act without pressure. There is no set physical goal to our sensuality. There is no sex.

The whole language is oppressive. It is white male-oriented and heterosexual. One word that must go is "sex" because that describes a way of being physical that can only draw up the very bad memories for a lot of us. We must use it only in referring to that oppressive institution, not to any new forms we are developing. Having sex means accepting a set of criteria for "success" that we did not set up and develop among ourselves.

Sensuality is formless and amorphous. It can grow and expand as we feel it. It is shared by everyone involved. It isn't something one puts out for another. Sex with boys was like doing alienated labor so that one with power could make good profit off of my surplus labor. Sexuality with women is a collective experience growing out of our struggle.

Smashing the notion of sex, getting away from these concepts so intimately tied up with the penis, helps us destroy roles. It helps us to destroy those heterosexual categories which have polluted our own culture. It has allowed us to develop a variety of combinations and forms in which to express ourselves: some of us are involved in monogamous, one-to-one relationships; some of us are brazen floozies, sharing sensuality with a variety of sisters; some of us are celibate; some of us are involved in "monogamous" threesomes.

Sensuality is something that can be collective. Sex is private and tense. Sensuality is often spontaneous. Sex is something you want power and territorial rights over. Sex is localized in the pants and limited by that. Sensuality is all over and grows always. Sex is pinpointed in the pants because the penis is there and the penis is, if not the material source, the material basis for power in Amerika. If you don't have one you are fucked over by those who do. If you don't have capital you get fucked over by those who do. Unless you attach yourself to someone who has it so that you can serve them in exchange for protection (known as marriage). Sperm is coin. And that whole system of exchange necessarily excludes us as lesbians. We can't pretend that those few flaps of skin that make up the masculine apparatus are just a few objective ectodermal gatherings. That stuff is the proof of a right to have access to privilege. Some boys reject that privilege, but they always have the possibility of whipping it out in an emergency and asserting their privilege.

We are building a revolution which isn't based on such drivel. And we must have a new language and aesthetic to describe it. Lesbianism is not a sexual perversion: it has nothing to do with sex. It is not another way to "do it": it is a whole other way to have contact. Sex is a phallic term and we are involved in building a humane world. It's like when people talk about being bisexual it blows my mind. It's like saying that if you have an apple and an orange you have two apples because they're both fruits.

Heterosexuality and lesbianism are two forms of physical contact. But that's as far as the similarity goes. I sleep with women, make love with women, am a woman, a lesbian. But I don't have sex with anyone. If I had sex, I could have it with a boy, but that would be a whole other trip from what I am feeling about my gay sensuality. It would be another experience altogether, not a different form of gay sexuality. I would be reentering an institution the structure of which is inherently oppressive to me, although particular experiences might be of reasonable fun. But radical lesbian sensuality is a form which I myself am helping create. It is not an institution existing outside of me, like sex is. It is me, us, as it comes out of our new consciousness.

ON SEX ROLES AND EQUALITY

N. A. Diaman

Total liberation demands the reevaluation of all existing institutions in our society. What may have served us in another time and place may very well oppress us now. The validity of any institution is determined by whether it truly serves our human needs presently in a meaningful and fully satisfying way.

Marriage and the nuclear family are two of the most heavily defended institutions in capitalist American society, promising personal satisfaction for people trapped in an economic system which provides them with shoddy goods while continually exploiting their labor. The rising divorce rate alone suggests there is something wrong. Then there is the bearing and raising of children within these traditional institutions, a matter which seems poorly managed, if one can judge by the myriad problems adults trace back to their childhood.

At first glance it would seem that these are things which only concern heterosexuals, but most of us are born into families, regardless of our sexual orientation, and are taught the dubious values of these institutions. Many gay people even use them as models for their own relationships, either advocating or proclaiming gay marriages. We should take every opportunity to develop something better.

Both gays and straights perpetuate the myth that heterosexuals have long and happy relationships which homosexuals can never achieve. Straight couples often just hang together because it's easier than breaking up, which is hardly the sign of a positive relationship. I personally don't know anyone, either gay or straight, who is involved in a really beautiful, creative, lasting monogamous relationship.

The search for the one perfect mate re-enforces our feelings of alienation and keeps us apart from others who fall short of the ideal we imagine. And people merely bound together by legal and economic pressures, unable to relate to each other at a deeper level as fully realizing human beings, begin to hate themselves and each other because of the frustrations which follow the failure to satisfy all their needs within a narrow world of two.

We must begin to improve the quality of our lives. To develop the full range of our being, whether we be biologically female or male. We must realize that we are born equal. It is our indoctrination into the present society which downgrades women and raises men to the positions of power, all the important decision-making being done by men. And all of us ultimately suffer because of sexism when we are expected to become caricatures of our gender instead of complete individuals able to explore both our femininity and masculinity.

As lesbians and male homosexuals, we are put down by straights because we are not real women and real men, but we are certainly one step ahead of straights in realizing how artificial and limiting those categories are.

Unfortunately sexism is not unique to heterosexuals, but pervades homosexuality as well. This is especially true with male chauvinism, which all men must struggle against. Sexism is also reflected in the roles homosexuals have copied from straight society. The labels might differ, but it is the same unequal situation, as long as roles are rigidly defined, as long as one person exercises power over another. For straights it is male-female, master-mistress. For gays it is butch-femme, aggressive-passive. And the extreme, in either case, is sadist-masochist. Human beings become objectified, are treated as property, as if one person could own another.

I believe in equality all along the line, including sexual equality. Even in bed. Especially in bed! This does not mean that two people must do exactly the same thing, in the same way, at all times. What it does mean is that whatever one person does may be done by the other if she/he wishes. That no person is treated merely as a sexual object but as a human being. This involves respect and concern for others as well as ourselves. Love for ourselves as well as others.

If marriage and the family, as we know it, are unable to meet the demands put upon them by our changing consciousness, then these institutions will have to be abandoned. Many gay women and men are already exploring the viability of living collectives. Hopefully, liberated people of the future, no longer divided by gender, sexual orientation, age, race, etc., will be able to come together to experiment further with revolutionary concepts of life that will better serve their needs for companionship, love, sex, all that is humanizing. Without the liabilities of hierarchy and roles.

Cooperation replacing competition. All people living full lives within a caring community.

CRUISING: GAMES MEN PLAY

Perry Brass

The games people play go on and on and on. This is especially true of that cruelest of human games known as cruising. In cruising, the hunt is on and the hunter becomes the hunted. Eventually the tension becomes so high that the whole aspect of meeting someone with the prospect of an evening, a week, or even a lifetime of satisfaction, or even pleasure, becomes lost in this confrontation of wills. Cruising is one of the great male chauvinist games: I can be tougher than you can be. I can hold out longer than you can hold out. I don't need you. I can't open up to you until you open up to me.

Most men try to set up their own roles in the first moments of this contest of wills. Whether the playing ground be some street in the Village, one of the avenues. or any bar or beach, there are always the same roles, often enough being played by the same men only wearing different faces. We could begin with the extreme caricature of masculinity who believes that it is below his masculine dignity to ever approach anyone else. He will usually stand like the steadfast tin soldier for hours on end, wondering why this isn't his particular night.

Next to him is the aggressive animal, the tiger stalking his way through the situation, looking at everyone but not looking at anyone. He is really looking for that perfect fulfillment of some adolescent sex fantasy (referred to as his "type") who was possibly his first love at the age of twelve (his first "type") and whom he expects to walk by momentarily.

There is also the verbal bully who thinks the best way to captivate his latest is to out-man him (voice three octaves below normal) or outwit him (except that you've heard it all before) or out-talk him (most of which you've heard even before he tried to outwit you).

And there are of course also the always-with-us clothes queens (nothing below Bonwits), size queens, body queens, height queens (nothing below six feet), race queens, blonde queens, chicken queens, astrology queens (his sign always agrees with yours), drug queens, campus queens (world's oldest frat men), muscle queens, and even queen queens.

There are the "numbers" guys who have to announce to you that you're going to be their first of the evening or the week or whatever. They also have to constantly tell you what the cruising report is for every port between here, San Juan, and Dubrovnik. In other words, this is to make you feel like another swell number in his address book. If you're lucky.

And the put-up artist who has to first off embarrass you with how you're the most beautiful thing he's ever seen since the last most beautiful thing he has ever seen.

Or the put-down artist who thinks he has to shake you up to get you out.

There are the fantasy creeps who stare at you all night until you walk over to them and then they walk away. They'd rather not know you too well.

All of these men add up to a frightening lack of self-understanding and self-confidence. They cannot face up to a situation without the roles pre-defined, the definitions roled out. We are all too afraid to find out that that certain gorgeous "number" over there is just like we are inside: afraid and alone. Trapped in the role that he has learned how to play very successfully, but has outgrown years ago, whether it be the gorgeous "number" role or the twittering little boy of thirty.

Gay roles are designed by fear. Just as we act in straight society out of fear that they will discover us, we react with each other out of fear that we will discover ourselves also.

It is no small wonder that from out of this self straight-jacketing, many gay men develop a real hatred for men, just as many straight men hate women because of the roles they must act out. Because we are forced to live in a society that condemns us as half-men, many of us feel that we must become men-and-a-half. This means to shut out all of the real tenderness and sensitivities associated with femininity. Gay life is a gay drag when it forces a man to reject most of himself and only leaves him a shell or role he must show in order to live with the reality of our situation: that we are all outcasts.

We must reject what straight society has straight-jacketed us with and form our own life as real people, not merely imitating the old male chauvinist roles left over from a dodo society. It's very simple, men. It's just a matter of getting together or falling apart.

THE FAIRY PRINCESS EXPOSED

Craig Alfred Hanson

It used to be that when most male homosexuals came out of their closets they headed straight for that gay fairyland somewhere way over Judy Garland's rainbow and set up housekeeping as fairy princesses. The gay liberation movement has been an escape from the old fairyland, and Judy Garland, and from the traditional gay subculture. The philosophy and way of life of that old make-believe world has been called the "princess syndrome" by Los Angeles Gay Liberation Front founder Morris Kight. "Princess syndrome" is a good name because it sizes up the fem-identifica-tion, the fantasy imagery, the egocentricity, and the cultural conservatism of the tired old gay trip.

Fairyland is still alive and well in Hollywood and for most of those half-decloseted gays over 30, and I don't think most of our older brothers will ever escape from it. Those aging princesses will simply linger on unto death as past relics of a bygone era in their fantasy world of poodle dogs and Wedgewood teacups and chandeliers and all the fancy clothes and home furnishings any queen could ever desire; but it is a world of would-be princes and princesses living on a shoestring; a phony world of countless impersonators of Judy Garland, Bette Davis, Mae West, and of plastic midnight cowboys from Brooklyn cruising Times Square. And it is that same tired old fantasy world peopled by bitchy male hairdressers, snobbish antique dealers, and effete ballet masters, a sham world of egophilic actors turning women on before the camera and turning tricks over behind the camera.

We did not really create our fairyland; the hets did. But we had no other place to go after we came out of our closets. It was reserved just for us as our very special place to live our very special way of life, and it provided laughs for the hets when we appeared on the balconies of our fairy palaces and waved our wands at the world to make the het women "beautiful" (so their men thought) and decorate and glamorize their lives. Despised as we were, we were still their pampered pets in gilded cages.

I suppose we have been their decorators and beautifiers ever since Christianity captured the Western World. As Emory said it in *Boys in the Band*, "It takes a fairy to make something pretty," and making things cute and pretty was our social function. We slavishly imitated and served the wealthy, and we went down with them during the French and Russian Revolutions, the grand couturiers of a bankrupt *haute couture.*

We were conservative, and in some ways more conservative than our masters, but we were conservatives of a very different sort than the American Gothic with his grim and narrow-minded Protestant Ethic. I suppose one would call us cultural conservatives who fed luxury to the establishment; and we were selfish, petty, and vain little men who dedicated their lives to preserving the past and serving our masters, the rich. We called ourselves "artists," but greatness in art depends on innovation, not repetition of the old. For that reason, if none other, the fairy princess is an evil demoness because she stifles and smothers those creative urges deep within us.

The fairy princess creates a romanticized, egocentric, and spurious inner world—fairyland—set against outer reality because he lives a frustrated life of emotional deprivation and isolation due to feelings of inadequacy and worthlessness in the real world. These feelings of inferiority come from the heterosexuals who after centuries of practice have developed hatred for gay people into a fine art. In attempting to escape the emotional pain, the princess flees to a past, more perfect, quasi-mythical era where he believes he would have achieved status and success if he had only been born into it.

Because they cannot rationalize why they are gay (except in context of sin or sickness), gay traditionalists tend to believe that mysterious forces quite beyond their immediate control rule and guide their lives. The centuries of persecution and discrimination by the Christian Church and other forces of social control have mesmerized them into believing that they are thoroughly rotten sex degenerates, a class of perverted half-men doomed to live a living hell and beyond the scope of humanity. They are unable to imagine that gay is good.

This faith that he is the predestined victim of determinism explains why gay traditionalists are drawn towards astrology, the occult, and superstitious ideas of every sort. They desperately want to be heterosexual, but they believe the hand of cruel fate is set against them. Some become believers in reincarnation, hoping to be reborn "whole" in the next generation. Others join any number of the many phony religious and bogus "scientific" cults in an ever-seeking search to find meaning in their lives. Victims of the princess syndrome probably account for a large proportion of the male membership in the manipulative sects and cults which flourish in the Hollywood area.

Since the fairy princess cannot explain his life rationally, he tends to view everything irrationally, and irrationality and superficial emotionalism and sentimentality become a hallmark of the princess. Rather than using reason, he emotes, and he emotes on stereotype and ceremony because these produce order and certainty in an otherwise disordered, irrational world. He simply refuses to either accept or understand science because it demands that rational and ordered mind which would cause chaos in his egocentric world.

The fairy princess lives in romanticized and traditional settings, and he tends to romanticize past class and sex role differences. Above all, his is the egocentric imagination of one living in a make-believe fantasy world, a world where some young, handsome, and masculine prince clad in white will ride up on his noble steed and sweep him up in his strong arms; and he sometimes imagines he is both prince and princess, a duality which reflects on the gender identity confusion of the princess.

Therefore, as he flees from reality, the princess acts out his life, and sees himself as a symbol of ceremonial achievement in a role cast by fate or accident of birth rather than real personal achievement. His fairy palace is hung with a thousand magic mirrors which, at his every turn, remind him that, indeed, he is the fairest of them all. The princess basks in the mirrored reflection of his own imagined glory, and this glory comes, so he believes, from his real or fancied association with the great and famous. He imagines that by acting like or knowing Bette Davis or Mae West he is Bette or Mae—their personalities have entered him—but in reality he is only burlesquing a grotesque caricaturization of those symbolic motion picture actresses of a Hollywood past.

The prince is a parody of the princess in male drag, and the cowboy and leather images common to the American gay scene are really hypermasculine expressions of that same spirit of romanticism, which creates the two-bit impersonation of Bette Davis. Japan too has its special tradition of masculinized gay romanticism—the samurai image—and, like his American cowboy counterpart, the gay samurai relives an era long gone. There are special Japanese bars where the participants gather in full eighteenth century samurai drag, swords and all.

Perhaps there are those who are altogether opposed to the image fantasy, but we must remember that fantasy has always been a basic part of the human experience. After all, fiction and drama are really dignified expressions of this same human urge. The danger with fantasy is that the participant may become the image he attempts to project to such an extent that he moves from conscious make-believe to a fantasyland where he is unable to separate the real from the imagined, and the fairy princess really thinks he has become a real fairy princess.

There is another danger with role playing, a danger which profoundly affects all humanity. Because the fairy princess identifies with the heroic, the wealthy, the noble, and the romantic, he becomes an authoritarian, for these real or fancied image figures come to rule his life. There is always the danger that he will identify with a misanthropic Hitler. So far, the most America has been able to offer has been an endless parade of motion picture and sports figures.

In many ways the gay traditionalist is victim of his material possessions, a captive of his own fairy palace. Material goods are probably the most important things for the fairy princess. They lend credence that his fantasyland is real, and that he is a real prince or princess, for here is concrete proof that fairyland exists. But these are only self-aggrandizing rejections of the real world and a substitute for real human relationships.

The gay princesses are prone to exaggerate their personal wealth, mode of living, and achievements in desperate ego-serving attempts to bolster feelings of self-rejection and inferiority. Naturally, these internal self-rejecting attitudes result from oppression by the heterosexual and his institutions. We tend to find the princesses' homes and apartments done in an over-decorated decor which could only be called "homo-baroque." Because of real poverty, the furnishings are more apt to be of cheap plaster, paper, or plastic than marble, velvet, or crystal. Then again, the decor may be the real thing. I know of one old queen whose life has been devoted to collecting Wedgewood china, and another, a really ancient individual, whose dank and dismal Italianate villa in the Hollywood Hills is lined with rows of musty chairs from a medieval Italian monastery.

We cannot really expect most fairy princesses to rip down their chandeliers, smash their plaster statues of David, kick their poodles out, or flee from fairyland to reality. Most are simply too old for that. But we should expose our Princess Floradora Femadonna so that our younger brothers will not fall into the lavender cesspool and be swept down the sewers of fantasyland. We must make our gay brothers realize that the princess trip is a rotten one, a self-deluding flight into a past that never was, an artificiality, and an escape from reality. It is a selfish, self-serving, irrational and materialistic journey which shuns real human relations for past images and things material, and human relations are what being gay is all about.

THE POLITICS OF MY SEX LIFE

Mike Silverstein

All my life, the emotions that have controlled me have been feelings of isolation and loneliness, fear and mistrust of others, and a need for their love.

Most of my life I was too scared to have any sex life at all, except jacking off to pictures of pretty boys like I saw on television and in the ads, and I went around feeling like shit all the time, since that's the way you're taught to feel, if you don't have a sex life. It got so bad that I just wanted to die, so bad that it was even worse than my fear of associating with a bunch of filthy faggots and silly queens, even worse than my family and friends finding out what I really was. So I came out.

There was another reason I came out when I did. Gay liberation came along. I had been in the bars a few times, enough to know I was a loser there. I wasn't pretty enough to get the sexy guys to sleep with me. But gay liberation was made up of people like me; they sat around and argued and discussed things. This was the game I could win at. So I came out, talking. Inside of a few months I was pretty well known as an active participant in all the debates, a leading theorist, and I was doing pretty well for myself. A surprisingly large number of pretty boys were willing to go to bed with me—probably because I was movement "heavy," or because I sounded like I knew what was happening, and they were looking for someone with answers. (Maybe they went to bed with me because they liked me, or even because they thought I was sexy: these reasons were less likely to occur to me, because I didn't like me much, or think I was very sexy.) In any case it never really occurred to me to wonder why they did what they did or that they were people at all. It's not that I just saw them as sexual objects: I was too romantic and sentimental for that, too nice a guy. I really liked them, really wanted to help them, and they really needed my help, so they would really be grateful and love me. It's a common enough fantasy, not as cruel as many, though cruel enough. It let me feel dominant and benevolent at once. I could give a lot to a person—money, advice, "love"—and never let my guard down for a minute, never show a weakness. And although I would never reduce anyone to a sex object, this fantasy attached itself mainly to young pretty boys.

It never worked. Most of the boys I went to bed with wanted to be recognized as people, and since I was unable to do this, unable to even be aware of their desire for it, they didn't last long. Occasionally I met a boy who really wanted to play this game, really wanted a father-protector. Then I discovered I couldn't play that too well either. Oh, I could play it really well at a distance. As a teacher I could really make it with my students. I never had a class where four or five of them didn't think I was the grooviest guru going. Perhaps this is the main thing that kept me going for the last few years. But once I got into bed, I couldn't play my role any more; I didn't believe in the game. I needed something from them, I wanted them to love me, and I showed it. I came off as too weak to support anyone, and they freaked. Either way I lost, though for awhile I thought I was getting something just by getting my rocks off with them.

Meanwhile, as I got more and more into gay liberation, I began to unlearn the lies I had been taught about filthy faggots and silly queens, and started really seeing the people about me. At first I was relieved—they were just men—like other men. Then I started to panic. My God! They really were other men—competitors, rivals, not to be trusted. We could go to bed together—sex between men works fine—but how can men love each other, how can we get to know each other, when we always have to be on our guard?

So when I tried to get close to a man whose love I needed, we always started a contest, a game of roles. Perhaps we were even playing different games. In one game, I was playing master and he the disciple; in this game, I was on top. In another game, he was playing beautiful young innocent and I the rich old seducer and this time he was on top. No wonder we never made contact with each other.

So after six months out of the closet, as a reasonable success in the gay world, that is, having a fair amount of sex with relatively desirable guys, I discovered I was as lonely and isolated as ever. Then I started to freak. My cover started to fall off, my game playing got ragged around the edges, and finally what I was always afraid of happened. People could see what I was really like. All my needs, fears, and weaknesses were out there for everybody to see—all my friends, all the other men. They could all see that I needed them, I wanted them to love me, I wanted them to go to bed with me to prove it. And I wanted them to do it even if I had nothing to offer in return.

I had always been taught never to reveal myself like this, that to do so would only drive everyone away. I had been taught correctly, that's exactly what happened. My friends, the other men? If they might have been interested in me for sex, how could they value someone who rated himself of so little worth? If they really liked me, they were scared of the intensity of my demand. They had all they could do to keep themselves afloat, and they had little psychic energy left over for me. Even if they liked me they couldn't show it in the way I demanded, by going to bed with me. Only pretty boys have a right to ask that as an indication of love. (But of course it's just pretty boys who learn most quickly how little the sex they are offered has to do with the love they need.)

So for a year I put all my life into gay liberation, and at the end of the year I felt as bad as I had before. I had no lovers, no friends I really trusted, and was being stripped of all the symbols of success I had had before, as their meaninglessness became increasingly obvious. I couldn't be a teacher any more because I could no longer pretend to be strong and self-sufficient. It was too late to put the mask back on. I couldn't pretend to be a man anymore.

You can't do more than pretend to be a man if you are gay. To be a real success you have to do your share in the fucking of women. That's how the straight man in charge defines things, and he runs the show. Of course we can pretend to be like the straight world. We can divide ourselves into imitation men who do the fucking, and imitation women, who get fucked over, and play all the games straight men play with their women. But even straight people (even some straight men) are beginning to realize these games aren't good for much, even being a "real" man isn't worth shit. But for us gay men we couldn't even pretend to be gratified by masculine powers very much. Straight society likes us to play their butch-femme game of dominance-submission because we acknowledge their superiority by attempting to imitate them as much as possible.

But usually when two gay men get together, both want to be men, and ball together like men. Men can ball together fine, and as long as things are kept casual gay men can partially avoid the power games that characterize straight sex, but there is still no place for a deeply committed love between two equal human beings. To the straight world, and ultimately to themselves, gay men aren't "real" men. I used to be afraid of this concept, but now I know it's our only hope for survival, as "real" men drive themselves to extinction. But we're too much like men: we're male impersonators. Like men we haven't learned how to love each other.

Every man in capitalist Amerika is lonely, isolated, mistrustful and in desperate need of love. And everybody in Amerika is taught to hide his or her unhappiness at all costs. Unhappiness is the stigma of personal inadequacy, since if you're unhappy, it's your own fault. So from grammar school we're taught to walk around with smiles on our faces all the time, and every man seeing all the other men smiling hides the secret shame of his own unhappiness, his own inadequacy. Lately millions of people are wearing buttons with smiling faces. Perhaps it's too much for people to keep up the false smiles anymore, the best they can do is buy a painted-on smile for a dime.

We gay men have a harder time than most hiding this from ourselves. For us our needs are so up-front, so unsatisfiable by the stupid games this society teaches us to play, that we are almost forced to acknowledge them. It's no use for us to pretend we give a shit about the kind of success this society offers, no use to pretend we're winners, no use to pretend we're happy. This is what gay liberation is about, this is what it's done for me. It has stripped us naked, of all our rationalizations, all our sublimations, all our successes, and left us standing uncovered before each other, in all our despair, all our need for one another, all our fear of one another. If gay men survive the suicide of imperial Amerika it will have been in part thanks to this purgation.

Of course, it's all right to admit you're unhappy if you also admit it's your own fault, and try to help yourself economically, or cure yourself psychiatrically. All the force of the culture has been used to tell us and make us accept the fact that we were sick, neurotic, making ourselves unhappy. As long as we could be kept apart from each other we might believe it. We could be manipulated like the rest of the population into protesting that we are as happy as anyone else. Maybe we are. Big deal!

Well, we're starting to drop that happiness mask too. I cannot and will not pretend to happiness any longer. I am desperately unhappy. And that is the source of the only strength I have. Revolution can only be made by desperate people who know that the cause of their unhappiness is an imperialist, capitalist, racist, and anti-human society. Desperation is necessary because we still desire and are taught to desire money, power and sex even though they are useless. Only real desperation can make us go through with their final necessary renunciation. It's dreadfully difficult to give up not only the outward signs of success, position, wealth, but even those psychological characteristics that seem an essential part of our personality—the definition of every encounter between men as a competition for power.

Well, I know that all the remedies offered to me by society for unhappiness won't help. I want to live, and I want to have a life worth living, and the only way I'll ever achieve that is not just by totally changing my own "masculine" personality, my own patterns of behavior, but by collectively struggling with others to create new ways of relating to each other and ultimately by creating a revolutionary community in which love is possible, trust is possible. A community without winners and losers, without successes, without men, a community of people capable of joy and love. Such a thing isn't possible in Amerika: Capitalism, imperialism, and racism require predatory, competitive, emotionally armored men, and submissive, ornamental, emotionally supportive women. The rulers of Amerika understand this. They know we are dangerous and they won't let us alone, won't let us go off to a farm somewhere and do our own thing. As soon as we start succeeding well enough to provide a visible alternative, they will try to destroy us, and we must be prepared to survive their attacks.

But now we can do what we like for awhile, we're still far too weak and divided to be dangerous. All of this is a hope for the future. Now there is no utopian farm, no gay liberation community, no army of lovers. There's just me sitting by myself at a typewriter, trying to figure out how I can survive, and occasionally flashing on real hope. Other gay men have told me that they feel these things too. I'm not entirely alone. That's what the man is afraid we'll find out. That's what everything he says about us—in his movies, his psychiatric analyses, in his dirty jokes—is designed to conceal. If we give up our false strength, if we give up our "successes," if we give up the pretense of masculine power, if my brothers and I can learn not to fear each other, we need not be alone.

Of course we do have a pretty efficient educational system in this country. It has done its work well, and I really am alone. Even though I know other gay men in the same situation, the same trap, even though we know we need each other to make our lives worth living, we're still too afraid of each other, afraid the other will take more than he'll get. I am still afraid of my brother's needs. He is still afraid that I'll despise him if I see how weak he feels. And it's still pretty boys that give me an erection.

A lot of us in gay liberation understand this situation, understand where we're at, how we got there, and what we need but we don't know what to do next, what the next step is, and it hurts as much as ever. Now I feel my needs all the time, and none of the things that kept me going (such as sex, teaching, or even dominating a meeting) seem to help any more. (I guess that the last crutch I still cling to is writing; it's still necessary for me to be a writer, but even that doesn't help that much.) I can't hide the desperation anymore, and it frightens people off. And the desperation of my friends scares me. Perhaps we're almost ready to start changing ourselves and making ourselves the revolution.

We keep trying new things: new analysis, new encounter groups, new affairs that will be different this time. We keep tentatively reaching out to each other, only to feel rebuffed if the response is too weak, and threatened if it is too strong. But we keep on trying. Sometimes we're too tired and discouraged to do anything for awhile, but then we get the energy to try again. And perhaps with each new try we're less likely to succumb to the patterns of game playing, less likely to objectify each other, less likely to lay trips on each other, more able to trust each other.

I'm fighting for my life, because I know this society doesn't offer me a life worth living. If I fail I'll die so I've developed the politics of my sex life. First of all, the whole idea of a sex life—separated and under different rules than a "real" life, has to go. My politics are to make a whole person of myself including sex, to combine intellect and emotion, weaknesses and strength, "masculine" and "feminine." And I know I can't do this in my own head. The core of my humanity is found in my relationships with others, and I can only recover that humanity in the context of loving, human relationships. I can only struggle toward humanity if I can find other gay men, with whom I want to try to create a new humanity.

I think some of us have found each other, and we've begun, despite many mistakes, failures, and false starts. But we must keep beginning again and trying again. There is no turning back, because we are left with no alternatives, no choices—though of course we never really had any choices in the first place. The only way we can go is forward. Pursued by the fire, we've leaped off the cliff.

Of course the major reason I've written this essay is to impress my friends, but perhaps it might help discover where we're to go.

PORTRAIT OF THE LESBIAN AS A YOUNG DYKE

Karla Jay

Perhaps homosexuals are born, not made. Even at the age of two when the little girls in the next carriage were being rolled around in lacy frocks, I was posing for family pictures in a cowboy suit. I first noticed that I was different from all the other little girls when I was five, and the horror and fear of not belonging led me even then to hide what I was actually feeling, thinking, and doing.

How could I do otherwise? Judy and Alice and Sandra were identifying with Sleeping Beauty (that emblem of passivity), Snow White (that gracious homemaker), Cinderella (that wretched social climber), and even Bambi's mother (whatever her name was). I, on the other hand, was the Lone Ranger, galloping on my bicycle across the Brooklyn plains, busy saving helpless women from their fate at the hands of all sorts of villains, dragons, and Indians. I was Superman, Peter Pan, Batman and Robin all rolled into one. Free and omnipotent on my bikemobile, I would spend my afternoons stalking robbers and murderers lurking in the wilds of Prospect Park.

Judy and Alice and Sandra were always playing house with each other and with their collections of shiny, cold, plastic dolls. They thrilled as the dolls croaked out "Mama" and wet their plastic underwear. They played nurse and washed the dolls until the paint came off. They watched TV every morning to see what kind of dolls Mattel would invent for them to give birth to next. By the age of eight, they all had little homemaker kits and had produced rubbery cupcakes and cookies to be eaten by good-natured daddies who smiled and smacked their lips even though the dry pieces got caught in their throats.

I hated my dolls, which sat alone in a corner of my pink bedroom. They remained untouched, except for the weekly dusting they received from my mother. I never tried to bake and saw no need to: all my confidence was placed in the ovens of Nabisco and Sunshine. My favorite game was veterinarian. I would doctor my stuffed dogs and cats and save them from the perils of rabies and distemper. Sometimes, I would even find a real victim on the streets—usually a cat with matted fur, one eye, numerous scars, and a rather sad tail. Grateful to find a vet, the cat would follow me home, only to be rudely dismissed by my mother, who proclaimed that she didn't need animals, she had children. The rejected patient would return to the alley, fortified by a bowl of milk, which my mother could not deny even to a cat.

After school, Judy and Alice and Sandra (they were as inseparable as the Three Musketeers) jumped rope until their arms got stiff from turning the rope. Or they would play ball, bouncing the Spalding on the sidewalk or against a building while they recited rhymes. I couldn't jump rope to save my life—a serious handicap in Brooklyn. So instead, I spent my afternoons playing stickball and punchball with the boys in the gutter. I also played touch football and could run, pass, and punt with the best of them. I wore my hair in a modified crewcut, developed broad shoulders, gave a mean punch with my left hand, and was accepted as one of the boys. I still rode my bicycle and was known as the daredevil rider who could race around the Parade Grounds with her feet on the handle bars.

Judy and Alice and Sandra laughed at me. They whispered about me and pointed me out to the other girls in the sixth grade. At first, I was hurt and stopped speaking to the other girls in the class, but then I got angry and started taking revenge by playing jokes on them. Once, I gave them raw eggs and told them they were hard-boiled. Alice wound up with yolk on her dress and Judy got egg all over her long, blond hair. I planted worms and dead fish in their desks. Even though I was a behavior problem, my marks were excellent, so the principal told me I was slightly "maladjusted" and put me in a speech therapy class. The principal was a progressivist. He believed that all problems started in the mouth and could be corrected if the speech pattern could be changed. The speech therapy class met once a week with a teacher who had a lisp. The boys (I was the only girl in the class) laughed at the teacher, who condescendingly informed us that we spoke Brooklynese instead of English, and told her that we lived in Brooklyn, not England. My classmate David shot rubberbands at her when she wasn't looking and one day climbed under her dress in order to give a wonderful, beautifully articulated account of what he saw there. The speech teacher lapsed into a catatonic state, and the class was canceled.

My parents laughed uncomfortably at the principal, at my teachers, and at the neighbors and told them with an uneasy smile that I was just a tomboy. But at home my mother would lament loudly, usually at the dinner table, about the daughter she had hoped for, a daughter who fit the description of Judy or Alice or Sandra. At eleven, I was already a failure. My mother would threateningly put a lambchop on my plate and proclaim: "You'll outgrow it!" I looked at the lambchop and realized that we had about the same chance of mutating. I ate lambchops from that day forth with love.

By the time I was twelve, I, like the lambchop, hadn't changed. Neither had Judy or Alice or Sandra, and today they are women pushing real crinoline babies through suburban parks while I whizz through midtown traffic, my cowboy boots on the handlebars.

WILL YOU STILL NEED ME WHEN I'M 64?

Ralph S. Schaffer

Gay liberation has covered a wide terrain—geographically and intellectually. We gay people have recognized our oppression and, in different ways, are dealing with it. We are also confronting our male chauvinism toward women and each other, and our racism. We are coping with gender identities and gender chauvinism.

At hundreds of gay liberation meetings in four cities, I have quietly raised my voice to speak of the youthism of gay life—the chauvinism of people (young and old) against the older gay male. People listen and move on to the next topic.

Now I'm beginning to get a little pissed. I think it is about time that gay liberation come to grips with youthism. It is the most vicious and entrenched of our fuck-ups left over from our oppression. It is tragic because it leaves half our gay people lonely, alienated, and unwanted.

Youthism is the unconscious belief that older people are inferior. We older gay men are looked upon as inferior in appearance, attractiveness, intelligence and sexual prowess. Many of us have unwittingly accepted our alleged inferiority. Consequently, we cannot relate to other gay men our age—we must pursue the eternal 18-year old Adonis.

Young people constantly use us. They use us to get a crash pad, money, food, jobs, contacts, and in return they condescend to let us do them.

All the aims and goals of gay liberation are for the young gays. Nothing is for older gays—not even those who are hip and in the movement. The young take our contributions for granted, blithely accept the advantages (draft counseling, crash pads, etc.), drop a quarter in the bucket, smile and wave goodby. I'm not saying they should lay us in return. They should SERVE EQUALLY.

Who is the older person? Well, I remember two sweet young guys complaining to me at a gay liberation dance that this dirty old man was bothering them. The "dirty old man" was 24 years old! And why is it when an older man cruises he is dirty?

We hear a lot about the gay spirit, a spirit of a special tender love. Where is it? How can you speak of such a thing when millions of gays over 30 are lonely, isolated, rejected, unloved and unwanted! In gay life we must learn to relate to each other as human beings.

I have nothing against the older man who digs younger guys or vice-versa—yes, there are some younger guys who really dig older men—but when an older man is so fucked up in his head that he can't respond to a man his own age because he's got his eye on every 16-year old, he's sick.

Why is he after the 16-year old? Because he believes the physical beauty of youth is superior to the physical beauty of older men. Phooey. I'm in better shape (at 42) than many young fellows I've seen. The oppressed older man even believes he is not as beautiful as he once was. Nonsense. If our heads were not fucked up, we would see that not all older men are pot-bellied and bald. And so what if a guy does have a pot belly? A pot belly has its own kind of beauty, if you would look for it. So does baldness, grayness, wrinkledness, etc.

The older man has a beauty that is inaccessible to youth. His life story is written in his body, in his gestures, his facial expressions. His body is the history of victories and defeats, moments of joy and moments of sorrow. We've had them all. Every man has a story to tell about life. He has visited places and travelled roads the young have not yet imagined.

The young cannot be blamed for not seeing this beauty. But older gay men have no excuse for overlooking the beauty and attractiveness of their peers.

Of course, the young overlook us too. We are not invited to the party or the orgy. Our needs are not recognized. We are supposed to have some magical self-sufficiency. We're only good for money and crash pads, the need for which suddenly brings us to remembrance.

The young person who concerns himself with the busy fate of older gays is planning for his future. But, of course, young people don't really believe they will someday be a hoary 33 years old! Believe me, it comes faster than you think.

I have quit the gay liberation movement after being extremely active for a full year. In gay liberation I've known more gay people than in all my life. I have never been so lonely. What a tragic comment on gay liberation.

Gay liberation is masturbation.

280 /Out of the Closets: Voices of Gay Liberation

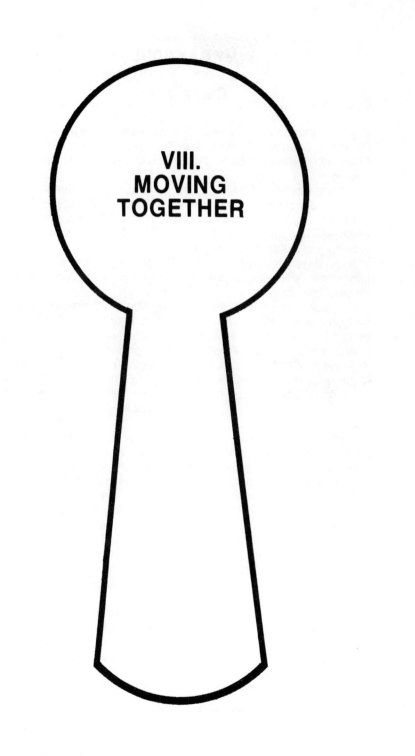

VIII.
MOVING
TOGETHER

MY GAY SOUL

Gary Alinder

A gay brother and I interviewed B.J. Beckwith, a lawyer who is sort of the Terrence Hallinan for the gay community in San Francisco—who is hired to defend homosexuals who have been busted.

I asked Beckwith if he is gay (he obviously is, but that's just my slanderous opinion—I can't prove it). He said, "If you're trying to get me to say I'm queer, I won't do it. What I do in bed is nobody's business." I wanted to scream, "Honey, I don't care what you do in bed, I just asked if you are gay."

A few days later I was in a rap with some women who are heavy into women's liberation. "You zero in on sex, you always zero in on sex," they said.

I've been told the same thing by liberal homosexuals and straights alike. "What you do in bed is your business, do your thing." They are saying that gay means SEX, nothing but sex.

Well, I am tired to the bone of being told what I am. I am gay. Yes, yes, my cock, my mouth and my asshole are gay. So are my fingernails, my big toe, my nose and my brain. I am not gay because of where I put my cock or who I sleep with. I am gay because everything about me is gay, because I am part of a gay community.

I was gay long before I admitted my homosexuality to myself, long before I ever had sex, long before I knew what sex was.

When I was ten, I played paper dolls with the girls and dug it; when I had to, I played baseball with the guys and didn't dig it.

When I was thirteen a gang of four or five guys tormented me—all through junior high school. They called me a cocksucker. I didn't know what it meant, but I knew it was the worst thing a guy could call another guy. They called me MRS. Alinder. They probably had homosexual fantasies and wanted to relate to me physically and the only way they could sense to do it was to provoke me to fight them. But I didn't. I was scared shitless. There were five of them and I was alone.

I grew up on a farm in southern Minnesota, and there you proved your masculinity in competitive athletics. I had too much self doubt to be any good in that. In high school I earned a bit of respect through journalism, theatre and art. But I was never the man I was supposed to be.

Don't get me wrong. I was not exactly a flaming faggot. I drove a tractor, plowed the fields, tossed bales of hay into the hay loft and joined the Future Farmers of America.

I went to a small liberal arts college near my home for two years. It was a parochial, superstraight middle class place, everything based on a social pecking order of fraternities and sororities. Even the lowest fraternity—a bunch of creeps—didn't want me. Did I have B.O.? Bad breath? No. I was hipper and in some ways more together than they were. But I couldn't censor myself enough. My gay self was showing through. And my gay self was me. And every response I got from the world told me my gay self was despicable. So I censored myself more, built higher and thicker walls around my soul and retreated deeper into my closet.

I had friends, other guys at the bottom. I was afraid to be seen on campus with them. I thought I would slip even lower. We were all gay, but that could never be talked about, never be acted out. We were the outcasts but we were not together.

Two years later a good friend came out. At first I played straight; finally I admitted that I was gay too. We had been friends since we were seven years old. But it was not until we were 22 or 23 that we could deal with what brought us together. Since then—although we live far apart—I've felt very close to that friend. We've been through a lot.

What separates me from the straight boy is not just the things we do in bed, but what our lives have been. When I meet an upfront gay brother, I make a connection. I already know a lot about him.

I need to be together with other gay men. We have not been together—we've not had enough self respect for that. Isolated sex and then look for another partner. Enough of that, that's where we've been. Let's go somewhere else. Let's go somewhere where we value each other as more than just a hunk of meat. We need to recognize one another wherever we are, start talking to each other. We need to say, "Hi, Brother" when we see each other on the street. We need consciousness-raising groups and communes.

Our gay souls have nearly been stomped to death in that desert called America. If we are to bloom, we can only do it together.

I need you, brother, because, brother, you are all I have.

LOOKING AT WOMEN

Fran Winant

Not knowing where to rest my eyes
where to hide my glance
If I didn't see the men on the streets
or the man behind the grocery counter
or the man in the drug store
I would not have to feel
them leering at me
their hatred mowing me down
their curiosity their triumph
at being able to threaten a woman
insult her
and still sell her something
so I learned
to look at the sidewalk
to look at the air
to look into the distance
to look away
to look at my companion
a woman
and talk about anything
so we could look at each other
I learned to opaque my face
and peek
around corners of my inattention
watching for sudden moves
waiting to be attacked openly
instead of in secret
with mumbled words
and looks that could be denied
My companion was a woman
People asked us if we were sisters
They asked us
in order to force us to lie
about our relationship
because we were constantly together

because we were lovers
because we could not protect each other
We could not protect each other
We stood by our apartment door
and listened to the neighbors
talk about us in the hall
"They'll never get married
Do you think that's right
They'll never get married"
We didn't want to go out
we wanted to stay home
all our lives
with the roaches
and the window gates
waiting for our parents to come
and drag us away
or kill us on the spot
waiting for the heterosexual gestapo
we tried to cook beautiful meals
and talk all night
and heal each other with trust
we painted the floors
and patched the plaster
that cracked again every month
we painted paintings no one saw
and wrote poems and plays
only for ourselves
we deluded ourselves that we were artists
passing through a terrible time
we went to work
in clothes we did not want to wear
and to school
where we became minds to be trained
in ancient mythology
we never learned
how to protect our bodies
how to survive and be proud
At work I thought a lot
about being a lesbian
I made love with a woman

but could never mention it
I loved a woman
but could not mention it
I lived with a woman
but I always said I lived alone
I went to the movies and the zoo
with a woman
I developed opinions together
with a woman
but I always said "I went—"
"I think—"
while the heterosexuals bragged
about their big dates
their plans for marriage
or how they hated being married
Everyone asked
"Do you have a boyfriend"
I answered
"Sure I have several"
At school I tried to make friends
with my two male homosexual teachers
but they hated women
if there were no women
all men would be homosexual
and no one would have to be homosexual
besides they were still men
and had the right to look down on me
even if the world hated them
for loving other men
and being part-woman themselves
I walked the streets thinking
All these people hate me
All these men
and the women attached to them
hate me
All these people that make me lie
that make me not exist
don't want me to exist
they want to kill me
and therefore I want to kill them

I want to kill all these people
all these men and women because
if you gave any one of them a gun
and lined up a row of people
in front of them
and told them which one was homosexual
and told them they could shoot one person
they would shoot the homosexual
so I want a lineup and a gun
and I want to know
which one of those people is heterosexual
I had read the penalties
for "deviant sex"
in every state in america
but I still wanted to know
what my crime was
Was my crime
touching a womans genitals
with my hand or mouth or body
was my crime
having another woman
touch my genitals
with her hand or mouth or body
was my crime
two women doing these things
together at the same time
My crime was
not doing these things with a man
and this crime was to be
my identity
my label
my secret
my non-existence
and the only time
I could be completely myself
I was not expected to go insane
I was not expected to complain
I was expected
to see a psychiatrist
if I had difficulty functioning

I could not expect my family
to try not to destroy my life
if I TOLD them
I had stopped
seeing my heterosexual friends
because they couldnt stop
telling me to stop
being a lesbian
My lesbian friends kept saying
I like my job
no one bothers me
Im happy
my private life is my own business
I dont look like a lesbian
although some people suspect
I keep them guessing

Womens Liberation/ Gay Liberation/
The Movement
I am told
my life-style will destroy Capitalism
Women are talking to each other
admitting what they denied
It is hard to be a woman
hard to be a lesbian
hard to be a heterosexual
hard to lie
about important things
almost impossible
to respect yourself
For a year I hardly write or speak
I join consciousness raising
go to all the gay actions
and have my face
in a thousand photographs
go to womens liberation meetings
I am told
we will work in groups
not as individuals
I am told
there are no leaders

our strength is in numbers
But I dont feel in control of my life
I see leaders everywhere
I ask them if they are leaders
and they tell me no
its my imagination
why do I keep seeing leaders
is it because
Im bitter about something
I know each of my sisters has sat
locked in a still room
with a mirror and a desk and a window
dreaming Someday I'll go out
and save that world
make it a place where I can be honest
where I can be happy
happily struggling
I understand how long
each of us was locked up with herself
how each self became godesslike
in dreams
compared to our real powerlessness
A woman looks into my face
and sees herself
I look into her face
but I do not see myself
I see her
looking into other womens faces
and seeing herself
I ask her if what I see is true
and she tells me no
Now Im looking for myself
and I get frightened because
I didn't know it would be so hard
to call myself back to reality
I thought I might be
the person I saw when I was alone
I thought I might be
the person a woman said she loved
I thought I might be
the rage that wanted to turn

and kill my murderers
I thought I might be
the shout and the explosion
that would destroy society
(not Capitalism but all societies
    in the world today)
for making
honest love between women
a crime
But I am suspicious of
any woman who tells me
she has seen her own face
knows what her voice sounds like
the shape of her body
or how her hands feel to themselves
We must all look at eachother
I must look at you
We must stare our eyes out at eachother
I must stare my eyes out
at you

LEAVING THE GAY MEN BEHIND

Radicalesbians (New York City)

The radical lesbian movement is growing and changing; coalescing would probably be the best word. Lesbians from Gay Liberation Front, Women's Liberation, the bars and the closets are beginning to get it together. Many women have been meeting informally, but regularly, for several months as a group, now called Radicalesbians.

It began during the dreary months of a dying winter. A nucleus of GLF women, with a growing woman's consciousness, began to feel the need for an all-woman's GLF dance. We had previously been working at and attending the GLF dances, which were overwhelmingly male. The oppressive ambience of a simulated gay men's bar...an overcrowded, dimly lit room, where packed together (subway rush-hour style) most human contact was limited to groping and dryfucking. Earlier attempts by both men and women at encouraging group dancing and space for conversation were nullified by the "pack 'em in" attitude of the GLF men running the dances. And there were so many men that the women were lost to each other in a sea of spaced-out men. It was intolerable to most women, but we put up with it, hoping it would change. Finally, when it was obvious it was only getting worse as the weather grew warmer, we decided to have an all-women's dance. The first dance was so successful, it was followed by several more. An environment of women rapping, drinking, dancing, relating with fluidity and grace, is beautiful. And most important, to plan and set up these dances we had to meet and work together. Weekly meetings of GLF women became routine. This provided a fine opportunity to work collectively and get to know one another.

Simultaneously with this, something else was happening. Some GLF women together with independent women from the Women's Liberation Movement had formed a consciousness-raising group. Out of our meetings two things developed: the writing of the paper, "Woman–Identified Woman" and a plan to confront the upcoming Congress to Unite Women with the issue they had been avoiding for so long—lesbianism (that ole lavender menace). The Lavender Menace action is history now. We stole the show and had an audience of 400 women relating to lesbianism as it affects the women's movement. This was followed up by two days of workshops attended by over 200 women. Our resolutions (we hope) became part of the report of the conference. WOMEN'S LIBERATION IS A LESBIAN PLOT...WE ARE ALL LESBIANS!!!

But the aftermath of the congress coup is not so well known. We called for consciousness-raising groups and 50 interested women met our call. Four groups were set up, new women from the congress action and Lavender Menace participating in each group. Many of the women in these groups were straight women who wanted to confront the issue of lesbianism and perhaps the lesbian in themselves. But a very large majority of these women turned out to be active lesbians, latent lesbians, closet lesbians, one-beautiful-experience lesbians, freaked-out lesbians, spaced-out lesbians. From the ranks of Women's Liberation, they responded.

After having related for months and years to the broader women's issues at the sacrifice of their own identity, these women were ready now to come out, to use their own energies to meet the needs of a lesbian community and to see that the concepts of primary value and commitment between women, developed in the paper "Woman–Identified Woman," were dealt with by the

Women's Liberation Movement. These sisters started coming to our weekly GLF Women meetings and as the word spread through the grapevine, more and more unaffiliated women began attending these meetings.

Finally, the various groups of women had so thoroughly merged that the name GLF Women seemed inappropriate. It was obvious we were an independent, autonomous group, and while some women in the group continued to relate to GLF, there were many from the ranks of women's liberation who felt that they could not affiliate with a male-dominated organization that was, in large part, sexist. We decided to drop the name GLF Women (we recently chose the name Radicalesbians) and begin our own treasury to relate to the needs of our sisters. The money was taken from the GLF community center fund...that portion that had been contributed by the many women who had attended GLF dances...enough to fund our first independent dance.

So a movement of radical revolutionary gay women has organically coalesced; not artificially out of rhetorical political necessity, but through the natural flow of our experience and changes in consciousness. The trip will probably be difficult but extremely rewarding. Our priorities differ. Some sisters feel themselves to be an arm of the Woman's Liberation Movement... feel that the struggle is between women and male supremacy, and experience their primary identity as women (with a difference). Others feel themselves to be in close affiliation with GLF, continue to relate to GLF and view the struggle primarily as one between homosexuals and heterosexuals. Still others see their position as unique...a struggle against sexism whatever its guise. Some women have not shaped or articulated their politics...they only know that they like to be together with their sisters and want to help. With these differences we have been meeting and working together, respecting, if not always loving, each other.

We hope our policy and ideology will assume the shape of our collective needs. We are against hierarchical structures because as women we have experienced firsthand that hierarchy is a fixed status system. (Those with power and privilege, i.e. men, assume leadership and use it to perpetuate their advantage.) We want an organization that encourages growth and fluidity. Therefore, we do not have "leaders." We experiment with forms that promote the participation of everyone in decision-making and actions. Some of these are consensus (sense of the meeting) instead of the vote, the lot system of assigning responsibilities, and a preference for meeting and rapping *with* small groups of women, rather than speaking *at* them in auditoriums and lecture halls. The quality of our exchanges with women is more important to us than reaching large numbers with stale rhetoric. We believe that we must live by revolutionary forms while we struggle against sexism, racism, and imperialism; that part of the revolution is our anti-authoritarian life style; that the revolution is process not goal. Small action-oriented collectives seems to be the direction in which we are headed.

It is important to Radicalesbians that sisters in the New York area join us in our struggle. Lesbians whose lives are a struggle against the straight patriarchal supremacy; women who desire revolutionary primary relationships with other women, relationships that offer strength, support and solidarity, are radical lesbians. Join us in the struggle to smash sexism.

Gay Sisterhood is Powerful!

NOTES ON GAY MALE CONSCIOUSNESS-RAISING

A Gay Male Group

Gay males feel pain:

You played with a ball and jacks on a sunny day and with a doll on a rainy day, all the time wondering how much longer this could go on without somebody noticing.

You're on your way home from grade school, walking naturally and thinking of nothing in particular, when the boys on the block call you "sissy" and "faggot."

You're in summer camp, and one of the boys you like goes off with one of the girls after a dance. You follow in their direction, making sure they don't see you.

You were always last when sides were being picked for any ball game, because everybody knew you couldn't stand anything to do with throwing, hitting, kicking, or batting a ball around.

You tell your older brother when you masturbated for the first time and he calls you a "pervert." You look the word up in the dictionary and see the word "homosexual"—he knows.

Your parents think something is wrong enough with you to warrant sending you to a doctor for hormone shots to bring on masculine attributes that are supposed to come with adolescence—but didn't.

You were sitting in church one Sunday listening to a sermon on homosexuality, knowing you were "going to hell" because you thought everything the preacher was saying was aimed at you.

The spiritual director at the Catholic boarding school tells you that the reason you don't get along with the other boys isn't that you have different interests than they, but because of the way you speak, the way you walk and move your hands.

You spend a whole week searching an entire neighborhood and a phone book to locate the first person you had sex with because you think you love him, and when you finally find his number and call him up he says, "Who are you? I didn't give you my number" and then hangs up.

You somehow get into a singing group in college and when the next auditions are held you have to go along with a decision to turn someone down because he's "queer" and you're too afraid to say anything.

You were so frightened by your first homosexual experience you had to stop in the middle and pretend it was because you didn't enjoy it.

The first time you go out to a place where gay males gather, you discover that in order to meet someone you're going to have to do it through your body.

You try to commit suicide because the man you fall in love with tells you he's "straight" and won't reciprocate.

You fall in love with your straight college roommate and after five months of being miserable you finally get drunk one night and tell him, crying and wanting to make love with him; but he tells you to move out of the apartment.

You're on a business trip with one of the men you work with. He constantly talks about his marriage and family, while you listen in silent pain knowing you can't talk about your relationships.

You are so uptight telling your best friend in college that you're gay that you nervously take twelve speed capsules and a tab of acid, and by the end of the evening have to be taken to the hospital because you can't make a sound.

You haven't seen your father in a long time. You meet and suddenly feel like embracing him, but have to stop yourself as he looks away in disgust.

You tell your parents that you're gay and they ask, "What did we do wrong?" Your father adds, "I always knew it anyway."

You keep asking yourself, "Why do I have to make myself look more attractive," thinking no one desires you anyway because you're a cripple.

In consciousness-raising, these and similar experiences we have kept to ourselves out of fear and shame, are shared.

Growing up as male children, we were told that the expression of our feelings was unmanly. (Don't cry, you're a big boy now; *Father Knows Best* never had any problems; Perry Mason was always in control of the situation; Flash Gordon never cried.) So we hid our feelings and suffered alone, feeling that we were different from the other boys.

In our consciousness-raising group, we relate our experiences as gay males. In this way, we are able to get back in touch with the feelings we had when these experiences took place. We then compare how we felt about those experiences then with how we feel about them now. In seeing the common root of our experiences, we begin to break down our isolation from other gay males and begin to recognize our condition in society as an oppressed class.

All this involves a particular relationship to our feelings. Men in this society are programmed to accept in themselves and express feelings considered "masculine," such as anger and hatred, but to reject and suppress feelings considered "feminine," such as fear and sadness. Struggling against this programming means that we try to get in touch with every feeling we have before we evaluate it. Women have spoken of this relationship to feelings: "Feelings are something that, at first anyway, we are *with,* that is, we examine and try to understand before we decide it's the kind of feeling to stay on top of (control, stifle, stop), or the kind of feeling to be underneath (let ourselves go with)."[1] Feelings we go with can direct us to changes we want to make and, sometimes, show us how to make them. An example of a feeling we, as gay males, may want to be on top of is the fear of being in a group because of loss of individuality. Acting out of that fear would be acting out of false consciousness. A feeling to be underneath is our loneliness, which could lead us to want to spend more time together as a group. Acting out of that desire would be acting out of correct consciousness.

Consciousness-raising is unlike therapy or encounter groups. Those of us who have been in therapy have seen it as a straight man pressuring us to think in a certain way about experiences he has never had. Therapy doesn't make clear that the relationships

1. Kathie Sarachild. "A Program for Feminist 'Consciousness Raising,'" *Notes From the Second Year: Women's Liberation, Major Writings of the Radical Feminists,* p. 78.

which cause us to have difficulties are determined by the anti-homosexual atmosphere that surrounds us.

We have been defined by the churches, by psychiatrists, by sociologists and, generally, by our sector in society which is not homosexual. Through the process of consciousness-raising, we have begun to define *ourselves.*

AN OUTLINE OF THE CONSCIOUSNESS-RAISING PROCESS[2]

I. Session
  A. *Relating experiences since the last session*
    1. Experiences of anti-homosexuality
    2. Relationships with family, women, men
    3. On-going relationships with gay males
    4. Sexual experiences outside relationships
    5. Experiences of a changing consciousness
  B. *Testimony*
    1. Choosing a topic
      a. from discussion of related experiences since last session (A. above)
      b. planning from long range series (as in suggested topic list)
    2. Giving testimony
      a. relating personal experiences; feelings about them both at the time they happened and at the present
        (1) at random (draw lots, spin a bottle, rotate in a circle)
        (2) no interruptions except for clarification, to keep from straying off the topic, or to point out inattention
  C. *Generalizing about personal testimony*
    1. Making connections between people's testimony
    2. Seeking the common root when there are different experiences and feelings
II. Discussion of relationships inside the group
  A. *Addressing feelings toward the others*
  B. *Sexual attractions and repulsions*
  C. *Changes in living situations*

2. A group's needs will determine the content of a meeting so that a group may decide to discuss relationships inside the group at some meetings and discuss a consciousness-raising topic at other meetings.

D. *Addressing power roles of one or more members of the group*
III. Projects
A. *Helping to start new consciousness-raising groups*
B. *Demonstrations; writing papers; attacking cultural phenomena; child care; starting a storefront; poster and sticker campaign*

The following is a list of topics that groups have used in consciousness-raising:
Series: Growing Up
Age 1–5
Grade School
High School
Post High School, College

Series: Sexual relationships
Coming out (first sexual experiences, acknowledging oneself as gay)
Sexual objectification
Cruising and bars
Masturbation
Sexual experiences with women
Sadism and masochism
Sexual fantasies
Monogamous relationships
Jealousy and possessiveness
Role-playing in relationships
Sex acts

Relationships with gay friends
Gay males
Gay Women
Parents
Sister and brothers

The above list was adapted from "On Our Own," an article written by a New York consciousness-raising group.

Reaction to the terms "faggot" and "queer"
Anti-womanism
Relations with straight men
Racism
Class background and prejudices

Age-chauvinism
Religious training and background

The following is a list of things we have all done which we now recognize are resistances to consciousness-raising:

Coming late to meetings or missing them with no excuse.

Unnecessarily extending the opening discussion of the past week's events to avoid choosing a topic for testimony.

Trying to direct the choice of topic so that you will not feel ashamed to give testimony.

Generalizing while giving testimony, or being abstract.

Going into irrelevant details while giving testimony, or straying from the topic.

Giving vague testimony on the pretext that you have difficulty choosing words.

Censoring testimony:
    a. By not relating bad experiences in order to look good to the group.
    b. By relating the pain you have suffered but never telling about how you have made others suffer.
    c. By not being open about your experiences on the pretext that the others in the group aren't being open.

Day dreaming or falling asleep, or allowing others to do the same, even if you are speaking and must interrupt yourself to point it out.

Distracting another's testimony by eating, laughing, talking, getting a drink, going to the bathroom, pretending to be ill, especially when the testimony is making you uncomfortable.

Remaining closed to the others:
    a. By believing their experiences to be just too different from your own.
    b. By believing yourself to be better than the others, e.g. not as sexist or racist.

c. By believing your suffering to have been much greater than the others'.

d. By having only revulsion for the experiences of others; not trying to empathize with their pain.

e. By believing your own experiences to be sufficient to generalize from.

f. By considering yourself "gayer" than the others, e.g. being "out" longer; being more open or outrageous.

g. By thinking you need peoples' attention (love, acceptance) more than the others do.

Identifying with the oppressor:
   a. By excusing straight men.
   b. By accepting straight definitions, e.g., psychiatric, religious, patriarchal.
   c. By accepting straight values, e.g., male ego, dominance, competition.

Refusing to see how you oppress other people.

Analyzing your feelings alone, being close-minded to the impressions of others.

Not discussing your relations with other members of the group:
   a. Not revealing physical attractions.
   b. Not revealing physical replusions.
   c. Hiding bad feelings without attempting to deal with them.
   d. Hiding good feelings.

Trying to impose an already-formulated political line.

Refusing to respond to the feelings, impressions, questions, or criticism of the group, saying you must have time to think things through on your own.

Not criticizing others because you want the freedom to do the same thing yourself.

Using projects as an avoidance to doing consciousness-raising.

Continual use of drugs and drink during meetings.

Thinking that consciousness-raising can come to an end
and that then the real work of the group will begin.

We have drawn up the following list of suggestions from the experiences of our group and of other groups that we are familiar with. They are not meant as rules but may help new groups establish ways of working together.

> *Groups usually have from five to nine members; smaller groups have felt the need to expand, and larger groups have been unwieldy.*
>
> *Groups generally become closed to new members after a few weeks in order to ensure continuity.*
>
> *Groups have met at least once a week on a regular night, around 7 p.m., early enough to complete the whole format in one evening.*
>
> *Meetings have rotated among the homes of the members.*
>
> *Groups haven't met when any members are absent.*
>
> *Groups have found it necessary to find some means during discussion of testimonies to ensure that each individual has an equal opportunity to speak and no one dominates the discussion. Some of the methods chosen have been:*
>
>> a. Rotating circle—someone speaks first and then the testimony continues clockwise or counter-clockwise around to each person.
>> b. Spinning a pen.
>> c. Lots—the name of each member is placed in a hat and is drawn out by the preceding speaker.
>> d. Chips—each person receives a certain number of chips. He throws one in each time he speaks and can no longer speak after he runs out until everyone else is also out of chips.
>> e. Alphabetical order.

Groups have found it important not to talk outside the group, either about testimony that was given or about relationships between people not present. This is to develop trust so that everyone can be open about themselves and express their feelings to the person about whom they are felt.

Group decisions should be made together with everyone speaking on each issue even if it is only to agree with what has already been said. This is to ensure that no one person or persons can control what happens to the group. No one should be forced to comply with majority rule if a certain suggestion is not in accordance with his needs or experience. However, the group should not allow itself to be stopped from making decisions by a person or persons never stating their opinions, expressing their needs, or making any suggestions of their own.

SOMEWHERE IN THE RIGHT DIRECTION: TESTIMONY OF MY EXPERIENCE IN A GAY MALE LIVING COLLECTIVE

John Knoebel

The first time I talked to the others about joining the 95th Street Collective was after a New York Gay Liberation Front meeting in late July, 1970. They had been together and calling themselves a collective for about a month. At the meeting Max had announced that they had lost a member and were looking for one or two new people. So after the meeting I went to talk to them.

Frankly, I was rather intimidated when they asked me why I wanted to join a collective. For some reason, I was sitting on Robert's lap while Max and Gary stood over me. I stared at the ground and said something rather lame about how it seemed a good idea to try to share things equally and how I wanted to get more involved in GLF. After all, I didn't know anything about collectives, except that they were some kind of experimental group living situation. They seemed satisfied, however. They seemed very nice, too. They suggested that I come to visit them the next night and, perhaps, spend a couple of nights sleeping there to see what things were like.

I was really excited. It hadn't been too long since I had come out. Only six months before I had been alone in New York, twenty-two years old, going to graduate school and in love with my straight roommate, whom I could never tell about it. Behind me lay

Wisconsin, my parents, five painful years in a Roman Catholic seminary, and a couple more getting my college degree. Finally, I made a few gay friends in classes who told me about their involvement in gay liberation. I had my first sexual experience with a handsome young man in Brooklyn after I had already attended a couple of GLF meetings. When I told my straight roommate I was gay, all emotional and wanting to touch him, he told me to move out of his apartment as soon as possible. Luckily, one of my new gay friends offered to let me stay with her. Everything seemed to come alive for me then, like it had never been before. I was gay! Gay! With ribbons streaming and bells ringing. It was not just the sexual awakening; I was still very shy about that. Rather it was the experience of self-validation that so excited me. As I continued to go to GLF meetings and meet gay people, I listened to what they said and saw a viable way to live as a gay person. I accepted my new identity. I had come out in the movement.

The next night I went to visit the collective for the first time. It was located in a decent-sized two bedroom apartment; like all of them, designed for a nuclear family. This forced the group to sleep in two separate rooms. They had done some painting and told me how they had bought a lot of red enamel to paint the living room. It was a nice night. We got stoned and listened to music. After a while, I went home.

The next night I went back. Robert was there alone. We played some Billie Holiday records. I thought he was attractive. We slept together.

After that, I began to stay regularly, and it was only a matter of time before I moved all my belongings in. I was a member of the collective. I didn't sleep with Robert again after that, but in my own bed in the other room where Gary slept. Sleeping arrangements never got more communal than that. Max often said he didn't want to think of any bed as his own. He wanted us to switch around all the time. But the rest of us just continued habitually to take the bed in the room where our clothes were kept. I, for one, wanted that little security: my own bed.

My first task in the collective was, obviously, to get to know the others and to find out what they expected of me.

It took a while to get to know Max. He had been active in the straight left and was always involved in making a left analysis of events. His gay politics often seemed an adaptation from the Black Panther Party. In the collective he was often rather distant, although I sometimes felt close to him. He was probably the most independent member of the collective and often received criticism for not expressing his emotions. Gary often complained that he couldn't understand Max's vocabulary or his extended syntax. For the whole length of the collective experience, Max was the least liked by the other members of the collective. I found it hard to get past the bad feelings I did have for him. This must have made it difficult for him to trust Robert, Gary, and myself and to change the things about himself that we asked him to.

Gary was easy to like. Of the four of us, he was the warmest and most outgoing. Although he could never cry about himself, his arms were always open to comfort anyone else who was feeling down. Because we shared the same room, Gary and I talked things out every night before we fell asleep. Gary liked to take care of the house, and whenever the rest of us were lax, he would end up doing the shopping, cooking, and cleaning. Gary was the youngest of the four of us and moved into the collective right out of his parent's house in the Bronx. He often talked about wondering what it would be like to live alone. Gary liked to be directive and to feel in charge of things: for example writing up lists of things to be discussed by the group, answering the phone, calling meetings. Gary felt a very strong identification with women.

Robert had dropped out of medical school. He was quiet and always uneasy when there were new people around. He was very close to his parents. Before Robert joined the collective, he had had a lover. During the six months the collective was together, Robert had a couple of rather stable affairs with men outside the collective, while the rest of us had sex only infrequently. Of the four of us, only Robert had been attending school. Because this made him absent from the collective for so much time both days and nights, the group had asked him to leave school. He considered this a just demand and dropped out.

I found out quickly enough that the others' ideas about collective living were just about as vague as mine. This was not difficult to understand: we were the first gay male living collective in the country. We were experiencing something that had never been tried before, and this meant we largely had to create it as we went along. Of course we thought of collective living as sharing everything equally: expenses, housework, ideas, and feelings. We knew from consciousness-raising that "the personal is political" and that we had to examine our experiences together in order to understand our oppression and accomplish change. We knew that changing was called "struggle." We knew that our oppression as gay people had been to live in a world totally defined by heterosexuals and that our collective would be a small world we could define ourselves. But these ideas were as yet only rhetorical and abstract. We had to test them out in the reality of gay men living together.

When I entered the collective I was told that the group had to rediscuss every decision it had made so that I could share in making them. I found little to disagree with. Some procedural items had been set up. We had collective meetings twice a week. One was a business meeting at which we discussed all aspects of the household. The other meeting we used for expressing our feelings for one another, discussion our relationships together, as well as our needs and our plan of action. Soon, one or two other nights were taken up with consciousness-raising. We also tried, when we were free, to spend nights together socially.

At meetings we tried to keep participation equal by always speaking in turn around the circle. All decisions made by the group, both inside and outside of meetings, were reached by consensus. Everyone had to speak on every issue, and nothing could be done until everyone was in agreement. These were essential structural provisions to guard against leadership in the group.

We brought every aspect of our lives to group discussion. If I was reading a good book, it was my responsibility to share it with the group, as well as my mother's letters. If I had to make a decision about something that affected me alone, like an argument with a friend, I still brought it to the group. As it turned out, almost nothing that happened to me did not in some way affect the group. Yet as this loss of individuality became part of our experience, we recognized that the need to spend time alone once in a while was legitimate and tried to provide for it.

Keeping house was an aspect of our lives together where we had to try to overcome a good deal of male programming. I, for one, did not want the apartment to look like the proverbial "bachelor's quarters." We wanted to make a home together, but, unfortunately, this endeavor bogged down somewhere. For one thing, we had different ideas about comfort, practicality, and taste; it was difficult to reach a consensus in these matters. We never had enough money to buy decent furniture, even when we agreed to buy some. Mattresses on the floor proved to be practical. The walls remained rather bare. We did have fine meals together, although not as often as we would have liked. Cooking, as well as shopping, dish washing, and other household chores were done on a rotating basis, and we kept check on each other by discussing housekeeping at every business meeting.

The problem of finances was handled in the following way.

Since at the beginning we all had about the same amount of money to contribute to the collective, whether from savings or part-time jobs, all expenses were shared equally. Whenever we spent something for the collective, we would enter it on our individual page in an account book. By comparing the running totals, it was easy to see who was ahead or behind, and we would always try to keep even. Only months later did this system change. I had run out of savings and gotten a full-time job. Max had lost his job and couldn't find another. Robert and Gary had gone on welfare. Lane, the eventual fifth member of the collective, had gotten a part-time job through me. Since our incomes were no longer equal, we began to contribute on a proportional basis. We still kept our separate accounts in the book, but those who earned more were responsible for spending a larger percent of the total. Although we discussed it, we never chose to put all our money in a common fund. One of our continual plans was to try to find a way to support ourselves together, but, this never happened, so earning money was always something we did as individuals and consequently took time away from our being together.

We were a tight group. We spent as much time as we could together and were constantly telling each other what had happened to us while we were apart. In the evenings we often took walks in Riverside Park, all of us holding hands. It was romantic, in a very different way than any of us had experienced before.

Whenever there was a disagreement between any of us, everyone would gather together. We never allowed any two members to argue by themselves. This sometimes meant getting dragged out of bed or off the phone, but it was something we all agreed to do. In the presence of the group, arguments soon turned into reasonable discussions. Everyone's opinion was solicited. Disagreements usually meant that one or both parties were asking the other to change in some way, so we always used these instances to try to get at the core of the disagreement, to understand what criticism or self-criticism was being offered. A sense of group process arose out of this. We were able to express our bad feelings toward one another as well as our good feelings, knowing that discussion of bad feelings would lead us toward working past them.

About the second week I was in the collective, I read Mao's Red Book and thought that the only worthwhile passage in the whole book were the quotations from "Combat Liberalism." I read this out loud to the group several times, and it added a great deal to our understanding of the right way to offer criticism.

One of the first rules made after I joined the collective was that if any of us wanted a visitor we would have to clear both the person and the time with the group, with the exception of those we brought home to have sex with. The intent of the rule was to provide for the group's privacy, so that we could talk about who was coming and schedule when they would come. The exception, however, reveals a lot about another state of affairs. None of the relationships inside the group were sexualized. Robert and I no longer found each other sexually attractive, nor were any other sexual attractions operative. Having no internal sexual outlet, we were forced to go outside the collective for sex, and the exception to the rule protected our ability to do so. But since we were almost always together as a group and felt our emotional involvement to be with the collective, this did not say much for the nature of the sexual encounters we had outside. For myself, I often thought it strange that living in a gay male collective in the midst of a busy gay movement, I had so little sex. I complained that I began to feel like a professional homosexual: being gay was my work, not my life.

Of course, we often discussed the need to be sexual together. This was something we did not expect to accomplish right away, as it meant coming to understand the nature of our sexuality and attempting to change our sexual programming. We tried to be physical together: holding one another, kissing each other in greeting. We learned to be naked together, around the apartment and sitting at meetings. This in itself was difficult, for it meant we had to overcome being shy and ashamed of our bodies. Several times we moved mattresses into the living room and all slept together. But we were very afraid and hesitant to do much more. We knew we should in theory, but theory was not supported by our feelings. Besides, the alternatives to the group becoming sexual were all too present. Many times we put up gay men from out of town who needed a place to stay, and this would lead to sexual encounter. Or men who came to the collective for meetings would end up spending the night with one of us. I always felt dissatisfied and slightly ashamed after spending the night this way with someone, since it always felt to me like trapping someone on my "home territory" with whom I had no intention to form a responsible relationship—and, indeed, could not without breaking my commitment to the group.

Changing our sexuality was only one of many questions of change that demanded we engage in a process of understanding who we were: gay men living in a world defined by heterosexual men, which is our oppression. In order to understand our oppression we had to examine, as a group, our experiences and get in touch with our feelings. Only then could we evaluate in a principled way what we had to change and could work toward that change. The process I have described is consciousness-raising (CR).

Robert and Gary had been in a consciousness-raising group for about six months before joining the collective. Because we thought four was too small a number to form an independent CR group and because we thought we could profit from sharing the experience of a wider range of people, Max and I joined the already established CR group. Later Robert, Gary and I became part of another CR group which called itself Fems Against Sexism, a name later dropped as embodying false consciousness. Only later still, when we added the fifth member to the collective, did we drop out of the first group and begin to do CR as a collective. We always thought that CR was about the most important thing we did together. I think it was unfortunate that we did not begin CR earlier as an independent group. Valuable as our contact was with the experience of those outside, it meant that this most important process was not focused directly on those of us who lived together but included others with whom our relationships were much less intense. If we intended our collective to be more than a group of people who lived and kept house together, and, indeed, we intended it to be more, then CR gave us the understanding to know how to proceed. Surely we saw that the homosexual experiences of each of us had consisted of long periods of loneliness, one night stands, or relationships that always ended because people were victims of their romantic illusions, clung to untenable role-playing, were irresponsible to one another, or simply failed to understand that relationships must be worked at and not assumed. All of this could be traced largely to our oppression as gay men, which we hoped, as a collective, never to accept again.

Not long after I joined the collective, we began to recognize what was to become the basic problem of the group, namely, how to focus our attention on the internal struggle of the group at the same time we were becoming involved in a multitude of gay movement activities outside of that struggle. Because we were four and we lived together, we could accomplish more than an individual who lived alone. Consequently, our collective, and another collective of men that shortly formed on 17th Street in Manhattan, assumed positions of considerable power in the New

York Gay Liberation Front that we were all part of. Whether or not we wanted that power, we began to have it because of the many responsibilities we took on for the organization.

From the very beginning, we thought of our collective as a service group. One of our very first activities was to locate space for a gay coffee house on the Upper West Side, which we found and began to operate even before we had finished painting our own apartment. Every Sunday upwards of 50 gay people, many of whom had never heard about the gay movement before, came to talk and drink coffee in an atmosphere far more pleasant than any bar. Over the months, we formed several CR groups from contacts made at the coffee house. In addition, our apartment became a kind of center for the gay movement. We housed and fed dozens of gay men from out of town. Very often our apartment was used for the weekly meetings of GLF men. At our suggestion, GLF installed a phone in our apartment listed under GLF Men so that there would be a way to contact the movement in the city until GLF acquired a community center. The telephone greatly expanded our work load. We began to feel like its slave. In addition to helping us serve as a general information center, the phone took on many other uses. There were calls from frightened high school-aged gay men in New Jersey and crank calls in the middle of the night. Many gay men called to see how they could get involved in GLF—so many that we set up a weekly orientation meeting at our apartment. We started numerous CR groups from these meetings. The phone also brought many requests for speakers from schools, churches, and the media. We set up a speakers' bureau to handle them. As a collective, we attended the sessions of the Revolutionary Peoples Constitutional Convention in Philadelphia and Washington, and for the latter we rented a truck and provided transportation for twenty-five men.

Individually, we all took on other activities. One of us started a GLF on the campus of Lehman College in the Bronx. Another started CR groups at Columbia University. Another worked on a weekly gay newsletter, *Gay Flames*. I was chosen to meet with Huey Newton of the Black Panther Party when, during a New York visit, he asked to talk to people from the gay movement. Eventually we had to add a fifth member to our collective primarily because we needed another person to help with the load—specifically to run the newly acquired GLF community center.

The error in all this activity outside the collective became increasingly obvious to us. Personal relationships within the group began to feel at a standstill; the energy we should have been directing inward was being bled off elsewhere. Because we were always so busy and always had people staying with us, the household was in a state of permanent disruption. Questions about eating together, doing the dishes and other household chores were never really solved because our lives were so irregular. We had to make a special point to eat dinner together on Thursday nights; at other meal times it was rare to find two or three of us home. Because of the people staying with us, it was necessary to start having meetings in a bedroom to get away from them. Previously, whenever the four of us were together, we talked about what we had to do, but at this point we began to have meetings that really felt like meetings. They went on interminably because there was so much to talk about. All too often our attention would be on "would we go to this or that meeting?" or "what do we think about the Panthers?", never often enough on "what are we feeling?" and "what is this collective all about?"

The analysis of this problem and the measures we took to remedy it occupied several months. Unfortunately, we felt we held too many responsibilities and could not disengage ourselves as we would have wished. One of the first steps we took was to curtail people staying with us. It was necessary to ask three people who had been with us for some time to leave. After this, we housed people only on rare occasions. Although the orientation meetings for new people were still held weekly at our apartment, we shared the responsibility for leading them with the members of our original consciousness-raising group. We decided in favor of ending the weekly GLF men's meetings held in our apartment after their purpose had become rather clouded. Gary resigned from the group that was running the gay community center.

Even before some of these measures were taken, we decided to seek a fifth member for our collective. The reason for this was twofold. On the one hand, we thought we needed a fifth person to help with all the activities we had undertaken; on the other, we thought that the addition of a new member would refocus our attention inward, since it would involve us in a major process of getting to know a new person, establishing a whole new pattern of relationships within the group, and reevaluating our commitments and direction.

I had met Lane at the Philadelphia session of the Revolutionary Peoples Constitutional Convention, had slept with him, and became very emotionally involved with him. After our short time together in Philadelphia, I telephoned him almost every day in Washington to try to get him to visit me in New York. As it developed, Lane's living situation in Washington was unstable, and he became very interested in the idea of joining our collective.

Three weeks after the convention, then, Lane arrived in New York. And to my complete shock, he felt none of the love I felt for him. His second night in New York, I had to watch him make out with someone who had come to visit, and I left the room and broke down completely. Gary held me and Robert gave me thorazine, but for several hours I couldn't stop convulsively crying and beating my fist against the wall. It was the first time in my life that I had ever so let go of my emotions for another man.

For various reasons, we chose not to accept most of the other people we had considered having join us in the collective. Lane was already staying with us and showed great interest, and he became the chief candidate. It was three weeks, however, before we made a final decision. By that time, Lane and I had begun to relate in a warm but low-keyed fashion. We had had several long discussions about what had happened between us. I felt quite sure that my feelings of disappointment and hurt could be gotten past through the group process. Besides, I realized that I would not have wanted Lane to enter the collective as my lover, since I was opposed to the idea that any two members of the collective should have an exclusive sexual relationship. With everyone's consent, Lane became the fifth member of the collective about the first of October, three months after the collective had formed.

At twenty, Lane was now the youngest member of the collective. (Max, who was 25, was the oldest.) After constantly moving around the country, over the past years, Lane looked to the collective for a stability he badly wanted. He had not been in consciousness-raising before, and he felt that there was an inequality between his slight and our intense political involvement. Of course, this fact further encouraged us to cut back on our external commitments.

Now that we had a new member, we attempted to rediscuss and redecide every aspect of collective life. But since we were already committed to some activities, like the coffee house and the formation of new CR groups, Lane's assent was really just a formality. Although it may seem contradictory, we accepted the burden of the GLF telephone after Lane joined the collective. The idea was that since the telephone would be in our apartment, it would be something to keep us at home together. Unfortunately, its effect was just the opposite: to extend us outward in so many ways.

Several days after Lane became a member of the collective, he and Robert began sleeping together every night. Gary came to me because he thought I might be upset. In fact, I was, and as the first week passed into the second, I became aware that the exclusive sexual relationship I had opposed in theory (though my feelings were, surely, elsewhere) had formed between Lane and Robert. I felt a great deal of conflict—too much, in fact, to allow me to be open about my feelings. On the one hand, I was undoubtedly jealous of Robert's and Lane's relationship. The hurt I had experienced from Lane's rejection was renewed itself. And I couldn't believe that Robert could be so callous as to get involved in this way with Lane, when he knew full well what I had just gone through and how difficult it would be for me to witness their intimacy. Robert evidentally did understand some of this because he avoided talking or being with me. On the other hand, I was convinced that my opposition to an exclusive sexual relationship in the collective was valid in principle. If the whole group was struggling, however slowly, toward being sexual together, such a relationship could only hinder that process and cause a painful inequality in the group. Those in the relationship had already achieved what everybody else desired, namely, to contain their sexuality inside the collective. The others, denied access to those in the exclusive relationship, had either to turn to one another or continued looking outside the group for their sexual fulfillment. Perhaps the most negative aspect of Robert's and Lane's relationship was that it was carried on in private and not shared with the group. Never before had two members of the collective separated themselves off from the others and spent hours behind a closed door. Max was made to feel uncomfortable about sharing the room and often slept in the living room. It began to feel like we weren't a collective anymore but, rather a pair of lovers with three hangers-on. It also became obvious that the relationship was becoming a factor in group decisions. Robert often dissented from what Max, Gary and myself would suggest on issues, and Lane was always sure to agree with him.

Despite the important conflict I felt over my motives, I began to criticize the relationship during the third or fourth week. A strange situation had developed. Prior to the establishment of the relationship, I had always felt free to express whatever feelings I was in touch with to the other members of the group. Now I no longer felt the trust to do so. I could not resist the thought that Robert had schemed all along to get Lane into the collective so that he could have this relationship. Especially since, during the discussion of whether to accept Lane as the fifth member, Robert had denied feeling sexually attracted to him. Yet within days, he had established the relationship. Lane and Robert must have felt my resentment, but I did not put it into words. Incredibly, regular process—meals, meetings, activities—went on without my saying what I felt. Max, as always, seemed too distant for me to talk to. Only Gary was in touch with my emotions, and we began to discuss the effect the relationship was having on the group. In effect, we were doing something the group had never done before, to talk about other members when they were not present. Because I did not trust Robert, whom I felt was responsible for what was happening, I did not criticize him in a good way. I was not open about what I was feeling. I had thought out several different ways to criticize the relationship and the order in which to do so. I was aware that this was manipulative. However, I thought that I ought to have been the last person to have to confront what was happening, because of my position. But Max and Gary deferred to me.

For about three weeks, then, I criticized the relationship from every angle I could think of. I talked about the effect it was having on the collective: how it was cutting Robert off from the rest of us; how it was preventing us from knowing Lane; how it was hindering the struggle for sexuality; how it was destroying collective process; how it was unequal; how Robert seemed to be playing a completely dominant role in the relationship; how, if it was going to be accepted and struggled around at all, it could not be carried on in private but, instead, would have to be completely shared with the group. This led to endless discussion, both at meetings and outside of them. Gary questioned my motives for opposing the relationship. I answered that even if part of my motives were jealousy and resentment, my criticisms were just.

Despite all the discussion, nothing seemed to change until around the end of November. By this time, Lane began to confront certain ways he felt Robert was dominating him. When they began to have arguments, Lane called the group together to discuss the agreement. Robert showed very clearly that he resented the group's interference in his relationship and was completely unwilling to discuss what was happening. During one of these long sessions, I told Robert that if he continued to refuse to answer all the criticism directed at him, the only thing I could think of was to ask him to leave the collective. He became speechless. He asked for time. He said it was too much for him to handle. For two long nights in a row, the group struggled with Robert, completely going over the situation, asking that he give some sign that he was willing to be open, willing to change. He cried but gave no positive reply to what we asked. I was very harsh because I did not trust him at all any longer. I demanded that he leave the collective. The others agreed, including Lane.

For all my previous harshness, I broke down and cried as

Robert left the apartment. I felt that I had done a terrible thing. I could not and would not go back on what I had done, but I accused myself of having been too absolute about my principles and not at all human. Suddenly, the whole fiber of the collective experience was shattered. All of a sudden it was so deadly serious. It seemed so incredible that I should have had to turn my back on someone with whom, so short a time ago, I had shared my life, my feelings, and a mutual dream about the future. I thought: what good are principles if they force people apart? Why should an action which I believed to be necessary and good, feel so shitty? It was a terrible goodbye.

The four of us began to make the adjustments that Robert's absence required. I felt the others, especially Lane and Gary, look to me for direction. And I realized then how much I had dominated the group during the last month. I began to arrive at an analysis of my own power. Hadn't I felt proud of the way I was able to criticize in the group? Didn't I see a line that went back to the time I was so eager to meet with Huey Newton and the time too that I had, unbidden, chaired the male homosexual workshop at the convention in Philadelphia? Didn't I too have a male ego that needed to be checked? Was it misuse of my power that led to Robert's expulsion from the collective? Surely, the way to deal with my power was not to continue to define for the others what the collective would do. My responsibility was to say what I was feeling. I said I wanted us to go on. It was not as if we could go back to some previous point where we had left off. We were a new collective.

The next week passed in an almost routine way: answering the phone, eating meals, having meetings that seemed amazingly calm. I was away all day at my full-time job. Max was out a lot, as usual. This left Gary and Lane alone, and they began to get to know one another for the first time. Then, one night during the second week, Max told us that he was leaving the collective. He had two reasons. The first, he said, was that Gary, Lane and I had failed to deal with our racism. He claimed there had been several instances when black friends of his had visited the collective and our responses to them had been racist. We denied it. Secondly, Max said he wasn't growing in the collective anymore and needed to experience a private life, his own home, his own friends. After some discussion of whether or not these reasons were valid, it was agreed that Max should leave. The effect this had on the collective—on me at least—was almost as if a burden had been lifted. Gary said that if we had ever confronted Max on what I called his distance and independence, he would have probably left long before Robert. I thought so too. Yet this revealed the kind of pessimism that had affected us since Robert's departure. Previously, we would never have expected anyone to leave the group. We had always talked about the future of the collective in terms of years.

Now we were down to a core of three. We decided not to be in a great hurry to add new members. We could afford to pay the rent; we could handle our work commitments, which by this time were becoming minimal: the telephone and the coffee house on Sundays. Thus we were under no external pressure to expand. We were reluctant to risk the shock of an immediate new member. We were now small enough never to have to have formal meetings. I began to get happy again. I had great hope for the future because I had a real sense that the three of us knew how to be responsible to one another.

Then Gary and Lane began to emphasize their differences. Gary complained that Lane was much too quiet, too closed off to his feelings. Lane said that Gary put too much pressure on him to be in touch with his feelings, that it was difficult for him, as yet, to express them. I began to see what was happening: the collective was slipping through my fingers and there was nothing I could do about it. I found myself one night, almost crying, holding on to Gary and Lane, saying that I still believed that collective living would work, that we could struggle, that I loved the two of them and wanted to be with them. We all embraced, and it seemed like we could be together. Several nights later, however, they were saying the same things to one another. This time, I told them that I wouldn't go through it again. I couldn't hold the three of us together. They would have to make their choice.

The next night, Lane left us a note saying that he had to be alone for a while to think, he could not discuss it with us. Gary and I asked each other: is this a collective when we can no longer talk together about what we are thinking? If it's not a collective, we shouldn't call it one. When Lane returned the next day, he had made no decisions. We held a ten minute meeting to erase the name of something that no longer existed. The collective was disbanded. We walked glumly into the living room and, for some sound, Lane put on the first record he found. The Byrds were singing, "It's All Over Now, Baby Blue." I had to take it off. We just sat in silence for a while.

It has been almost nine months since that night. I have often had occasion to think about the experience of the collective. For the past seven months, I have been in another group; different, because we are not living together, but engaged in the same kind of struggle. I do not consider the failure of the collective to work out its internal contradictions an indication that the group process itself is a failure, or that I don't have to struggle anymore to change myself. Robert, too, joined another group. I learned a great deal from what happened to me and have written this to share the experience.

PROBLEMS OF AN INTER-RACIAL RELATIONSHIP

Marlene

"I don't care if you're poor or were raised in deprivation, or if you've known Third World people all your life—you're still racist—because you're *white!*"

When Ann said this to me, I was willing to accept it in terms of "other people," but I couldn't believe it about myself. I had had close friendships in high-school and college with black women and men. All of my working years were spent with black and Spanish children and adults. But what did all that mean?

As our relationship grew, I began to see my own inbred, unconscious racism and the inbred, unconsicous racism that I had ignorantly accepted in others. Sometimes it seemed as though Ann and I were constantly battling. She would confront me on racist things I did or said, and I couldn't believe it was true.

For example, we would be having a conversation and I would correct her language, usage, or pronunciation. My educated Anglo background could not accept language that was "wrong." It took a while for me to realize that it didn't make much difference, really, as long as we could communicate. After all, that *is* the function of language.

One evening she was writing a paper, and in the midst of her activity I asked her if I could read it. She said no, and I couldn't understand why. I felt rejected, and she felt insulted. She explained to me how generally common it is of whites to interrupt and give value judgments or opinions when they are *not asked for*. If she had been white I might have waited until the paper was finished and she had asked *me* to read it. She said that a black person, because of his or her inbred inferiority, would have thought twice or three times before asking to read it. At first I thought this to be a trite complaint. The more I thought about it, however, the more I saw it as typical of the ever-present malaise of authority figures and non-authority figures—commanding "masters" and impotent "slaves."

Our confrontations reached almost every aspect of our lives. If she put the key in the door and it didn't open right away, I would reach for the keys myself, unconsciously thinking that I'm better and more intelligent and—oh brother! she can't even open a door! Angrily she would push me away saying, "You're always trying to take things out of my hands! Let me do it myself or at least discover how to!" She was right. I had acted contemptuously.

But then I began to feel that the shoe was on the other foot. If I was driving the car, she would be telling me to watch out for this or that, or drive the car this way and not that way. She would tell me when to go right or when to go left. I felt like a goddamn chauffeur. If I was building something, she would try to tell me how to build it or how to use the tools, saying, "I've had more experience with this—I have to show you first." I would get furious inside and sometimes explode, as she had done on occasion.

We pondered whether or not we were both being racist, yet somehow that explanation did not completely fit. It seemed that all of the situations could have been played out by a white couple. We realized than that our other big enemy, "sexism," was very much a part of us both. We had rejected role-playing and anything that had to do with the traditional butch-femme way of life, but we realized that our rejection had been only outward in nature. In our minds we were two aggressive, self-sustaining people and hated anyone putting us into a passive or submissive role. We then knew that it was "double trouble." We had all the problems of any white pair raised in a sexist society plus the problems of an inter-racial pair raised in a racist society.

Comprehension of the problem did not end the problem. We have been in constant confrontation with each other. But we feel that is good. We have learned to think before we speak or act and give the other person a chance. Our growing awareness of these problems has helped us in relating to each other, but then there is the outside world.

We had our own business that took us into many people's homes and put us in constant personal contact with people. Ann began to notice that our customers, mainly white, would direct all of their conversation and inquiries to me. Without hesitation, I would respond. Customers assumed right away that I was the "boss" and she was my "hired hand." Then one day we were in a home where there was a maid—a black maid. All of *her* conversation and inquiries were directed to Ann!

"You see," Ann pointed out, "the racism of our customers who completely negate the importance of my presence and the racism on your part for not even noticing it!"

From then on we decided to take turns doing the talking when we went out on estimates. When it was her turn I would stand by quietly. I even had to avoid letting the customer's eyes meet mine because when that happened they would start talking directly to me.

Once I had to do an estimate alone because Ann was ill. The prospective customer, a woman on the East Side of Manhattan, began telling me how workers in our field were now mainly black and Puerto Rican and "Puerto Ricans do such messy work."

I told the woman that the person's "Puertorican-*ness*" really had nothing to do with the quality of the job. She refuted me by saying, "Well, you should know that Puerto Ricans are just *unprofessional* people." I told her that my partner was black *and* Puerto Rican, and she was certainly professional. She said, "Well, you're just lucky." I reminded her that I had said *partner* and not *employee,* and I walked out the door.

Confrontations have reached into the realm of our social life as well. One evening at Daughters of Bilitis, I was standing by the door talking to Jean, a black sister. A white woman entered the room and began looking around as if trying to find someone. "May I help you?" asked Jean, looking directly at her. Peering right past Jean, the woman asked me if I had seen her friend. I said no and walked away very upset. The sad thing I knew was that the woman hadn't even realized what she had done. Jean knew it. I knew it. But what then? Should *I* confront the woman or should Jean or should we let it slide? No! No more liberalism! I approached Jean about what to do. She was surprised that I had noticed it at all. We decided to speak to the woman individually. Sure enough, she hadn't even realized it and she had "worked with black people all her life!"

Ann and I have been together a year now. The racism and sexism are still there but certainly not to the extent that they were in the beginning. Sure, we could have never confronted each other, and just as surely, one of us would have eventually broken and become compliant and non-resistant. Maybe life would have been easier that way, but the time for liberalism is over. We may still argue and confront each other and those about us, but at least we *respect* each other, respect ourselves, and hopefully, make other people think.

EPISTLE TO TASHA

Rita Mae Brown

The dead are the only people
  to have permanent dwellings.
We, nomads of Revolution
Wander over the desolation of many generations
And are reborn on each other's lips
To ride wild mares over unfathomable canyons
Heralding dawn, dreams and sweet desire.

ELITISM

Del Whan

In August of 1970 three women in the Los Angeles Gay Liberation Front (Virginia, June and I) decided to run an announcement for a "Women's Caucus of GLF" meeting in the *Los Angeles Free Press*, scheduled for a Tuesday evening. We were the only women in GLF and were wondering why gay women in Los Angeles were not "coming out" and relating to the gay movement. We came to the conclusion that women coming to the Sunday general meetings of GLF felt lost in a sea of men, so we decided to form a women's caucus to try and get some action going. The response was great. The first week there were about five new women, the next week we had about twelve, then close to twenty.

I was chairwoman of GLF at that time so I pretty much identified with the organization as a whole, as did Virginia and June, but the rest of the gay women's caucus didn't seem to relate to the organization at all. They seemed to really dislike the men in GLF even thought they hardly ever came into contact with any of them—very few of the women ever showed up for the meetings on Sunday. Feeling that some sort of action was necessary, I suggested in September that all the women meet at the GLF office one Thursday evening to that we could don our "Better Blatant Than Latent" buttons and trip on down to the Women's Center orientation meeting and "liberate" it, i.e. get the gay sisters there out of the closets.

That evening's encounter turned out to be very important for the future of the women's caucus of GLF because it signaled the beginning of a very beneficial exchange of ideas between women who were for women's liberation and those who were for gay liberation. Before long, gay sisters from the Women's Center were coming to the GLF office on Tuesday evenings.

In October a giant controversy arose one Tuesday evening over the alleged "male chauvinism" among the GLF men. The group took its first major step; it decided to move its meetings to the Women's Center. Late in October the *Women's Liberation Newsletter* printed the following short announcement: "New Gay Women's Liberation Office at the Women's Center. Gay Women's Liberation asked for and got office space at the Women's Center.... They are going to try to staff their office 8 hours a day, 5 days a week. This coalition marks an important step for Women's Liberation in Los Angeles."

The latter part of this statement was prophetic; it was an important step for women's liberation finally to acknowledge openly that gay women had been in the movement all along, and that now they could stop hiding their personal lives. But more important, this gain for women's liberation has to be measured against the loss to gay liberation. The women's caucus of GLF became "Gay Women's Liberation" and from that time until now has gradually moved further and further from gay liberation and into the feminist camp, even going so far in February, 1971, as to change its name from "Gay Women's Liberation" to "Lesbian Feminists."

There was—and still is—a lot of male chauvinism in GLF, expressing itself in several ways. First of all, the men predominated numerically, so naturally the organization as a whole tended to take up issues that were relevant to male homosexuals, such as draft counseling, picketing the Farm (a male homosexual bar) for not allowing touching, breaking up a behavior modification meeting on how to treat homosexuals with adversive shock, and so forth. Women took part in some of the demonstrations, but for the most part they seemed generally uneasy about not being able to think of how they were oppressed as gay women.

The men began to find the women very touchy. If a brother in GLF said how nice it was that the women "were getting their thing together," he was attacked as "patronizing." If the men just totally ignored anything having to do with issues relating to gay women (respecting the females' rights to self-determination), they were called "male chauvinists." Indeed, some of the men *were* patronizing and chauvinistic, but my rage (as I personally look back) was typical of what most women express when they discover their oppression for the first time. Quite naturally, the men drew back from me and most of the other gay women because we were always jumping on them for saying "girl" instead of "woman." And they quickly learned never to ask a woman to cook for one of the Sunday fund-raising dinners. So the men went on with their projects, the women seethed with righteous indignation, and generally each group mistrusted the other. The men felt damned if they did and damned if they didn't try to include the women.

Now, there are no longer any women in the Gay Liberation Front in Los Angeles.

In December, 1970, I kept harping at the Gay Women's Liberation meetings that we—as gay women—needed a place of our own, a gay women's center. It was becoming evident that gay women in Los Angeles had to have a place where they could meet, relax and find themselves and each other. Meeting once a week at the Women's Center was not going to solve the huge social problem that most gay women face—of feeling alone, alienated, and devalued in society as a whole. The only existing alternative to loneliness was the gay "girls' bars." But the atmosphere of a bar is not conducive to overcoming loneliness; in fact, it often reduces a person's self-respect. Many gay women have even become alcoholics, going night after night to the gay bars to find companionship, yet more often finding small consolation in pitchers of beer and shooting pool.

So some of us tried to find an old house to rent as a gay women's center, but the rent was usually over $200, and the owner required a two-year lease. Plus nobody seemed too interested in renting to lesbians. I discovered that it would probably be me who had to sign the lease, since most of the women in our group were either under eighteen years old, or unemployed, or in debt, or unwilling to sign a lease. Feeling that I perhaps did not want to commit my life to the same job for the next two years, I began to consider whether the project was worth the risk to me personally. Then I found a store front on Glendale Boulevard for only $150 and no lease; I rented it immediately without consulting the rest of the group. After doing that I realized that I could not ask the women in Gay Women's Liberation to be responsible for my impulsive act, so I determined to make the best of it. It was a way for me to be creative, to spend my time, money and energy on something that I thought would benefit all gay women, not just the activists in Gay Women's Liberation who already were coming "out of the closet" and liberating themselves.

But I was in for a big shock. What I saw as a creative act was interpreted by some of the women in Gay Women's Liberation as "elitist" on my part . . . or better yet, as an "ego trip." This caused me to really examine my motives, for I do have an ego, and I am outspoken and direct, and I am a "leader." After all, I reasoned, if three of us had not been leaders last August, we would never have tried to start a gay women's caucus at GLF, so what was the difference now? My independent action in starting the Gay Women's Service Center and incorporating it as a non-political, charitable, non-profit organization was somehow seen as a "terrible thing" by some of the other "leaders" of Gay Women's Liberation (who did not call themselves leaders, but who nevertheless led the personal attack on me).

On the first Sunday in February some of the gay women meeting at a member's house for a consciousness-raising group turned the session into a general bitch session about me *even though I was not present*. Everyone knows that it is not proper to discuss a sister in consciousness-raising unless she is present to defend herself. After that I was pretty much ostracized by everyone in Gay Women's Liberation; the weaker sisters tended to keep quiet and go along with the rhetoric of "collectivism" which the new demagogues preached. This bitter experience forced me to look behind the rhetoric of "leaderlessness" and examine the entire informal control mechanism whereby the real "leaders" actually manipulate others in a sub rosa manner.

The primary tool of manipulation is language, or rather the jargon of left wing collectivism. This states rather pompously: "Our politics are the best, our beliefs are the only ones worth having. If you don't agree with us you are full of shit." The best way to indoctrinate new people into the true faith is in consciousness-raising groups where you cram down the newcomers' eager throats all your anti-establishment, simplistic, superior knowledge that capitalism and the white male are single-handedly oppressing everyone else in the world. If anyone disagrees with you, all you have to do is laugh sarcastically, or jeer, or insinuate that she hasn't got her head together. Of if that doesn't work, you can label her "chauvinistic, egotistical, elitist, middle-class, male identified, or reactionary." Any of these will serve to get her to doubt herself and shut up so you can proceed.

Much of the rhetoric and bullshit is well-intentioned. Many sisters really do believe in their collective, leaderless path to the "revolution," but I feel that they are being either hypocritical or blind to the fact that they themselves are leading—only in a sneaky, devious, contemptuous manner which puts other sisters down if they don't conform.

A lot of articles have appeared over the past several months in various women's liberation papers describing the same issue of individualism vs. collectivism. It may even be a symptom of social movements in general, that the "individual" as such cannot exist in them. As one sister working in the left movement lamented: "We had wanted to exceed ourselves, to transform ourselves. Instead we found ourselves striving for collective salvation by individual suicide" (*Everywoman*, October 23, 1970, p. 5, article by Anna Louise Strong).

One wonders whether we are really liberating ourselves or whether we are not instead heaping up more oppression on our own heads. Unfortunately, it is common in social movements that people do not see what they are doing to themselves.

Learning theory in psychology gives us a way to understand the informal social control that goes on in gay women's liberation (and other "movement" groups). The "leaders" simply give positive reinforcement for those things they approve, and negative reinforcement for those things they disapprove. For example, if a sister says "girl" by mistake instead of "woman," she is promptly corrected. The person doing the correcting may laugh, jeer, or frown. The corrected sister quickly gets the message. This technique of socializing new members plays on everybody's need for acceptance, love and approval. New gay women who have just "come out" are very susceptible to such pressure to conform. Those who act alike and speak alike begin to form a clique, or in-group. If they all belong to the same closed consciousness-raising group, they quickly become a "group elite" or central committee in effect, since they have a monopoly on "revolutionary rhetoric" and information coming into the organization. They become doctrinal chauvinists. Very often, because of their youth, they oppress older gay sisters with their youth chauvinism and their failure to be tolerant of life styles which appear male chauvinistic. A typical example is the superiority which the Lesbian Feminists seem to feel in relation to the Daughters of Bilitis, who are generally older and more conservative, and in some cases adapted to the "butch-femme" life style.

It seems to me that lack of tolerance and lack of trust are the two major stumbling blocks within the gay women's liberation movement and within women's liberation in general. We must stop putting each other down if we really want our "revolution." How can we claim to be liberationists when we are substituting one form of oppression for another? "Revolution" to me means joy, love, creativity and freedom…not a substitution of one political system for another. I am afraid that outside influences are beginning to latch on to the gay women's liberation movement in order to grind their own ax. OK. It's great if other political movements want to relate to Gay Women's Liberation, Women's Liberation, Gay Liberation, Children's Liberation, Prisoner's Liberation, Insane Liberation, etc., but let the people within these groups define their own movement, don't superimpose socialist, communist, or anarchist, or whathaveyou rhetoric on their actions.

Finally I hope that more and more of us in the gay women's liberation struggle will start living the revolution, and start looking for new ways of liberating other sisters who are still suffering through loneliness, guilt, alcoholism, perhaps even contemplating suicide in their isolation in this sexist society. Let's not handicap ourselves by using a rhetoric of powerlessness. We must have leaders. We must start "coming out" on television, on the radio, in newspapers, in public—everywhere—especially in the professions. So when a gay sister has the courage to stand up and take self-assertive action, let's not put her down for being an "egotist," even if she is. How is her self-affirmation, her self-actualization hurting anyone? Let's stop bitching at each other and get to work.

VIEWPOINT OF AN ANTI-SEXIST MARXIST

Sandy Blixton

I joined the Los Angeles Gay Liberation Front because it was a really hot-to-trot movement in the beginning, and despite all the reactionaries and separatists, the paranoia and adverse propaganda, it is still hot-to-trot—too hot!

Now the viability of the GLF is being challenged. The elitism of GLF leaders has allowed the co-optation of the movement. From its conception, GLF "leadership" was opportunistic in trying to bring in the entire political spectrum of gay people to struggle together on a single front—gay oppression—and to *come together* on a social front. All of this was done without tying gay oppression together with social revolution and other movements. And because GLF had this wide political spectrum within its membership, the "leadership" had to utilize non-political methods in order to keep things together. That is, energy was channeled into "Funky Dances" as opposed to political *actions* or organization or attempts to radicalize gays. The impetus for the GLF is gone because we spread ourselves out into nothingness, and as usual, the committed revolutionaries are left to pick up the pieces.

We are living during the greatest age of struggle the world has ever known, when the people are desperately involved not only in making political and economic change but also a sexual revolution. (How can we liberate others unless we liberate ourselves?) Within the framework of this new revolution, radical gays see themselves as integrally aligned with the Third World struggle and furthermore finally have something tangible with which to identify in terms of our own experiences. But instead of sisters and brothers coming together in a mass-based force against the oppression, they remain conditioned and now even co-opted by sexist forces and shy away from the left—those people committed in theory and practice to total revolution; that is, fundamental change in people's relationship to their sexual, political, social, and economic identities, leading to an unalienated state of existence in harmony with nature. Or if they are on the left it is with liberal (people who may believe in revolution in theory but who are not committed enough or don't understand enough to put this theory into practice) and not with truly left political consciousness. To these liberals and pseudo-leftists, revolution means merely guns and bloody armed insurrection. They overlook or are not yet aware of the essential nature of a revolutionist—an ultimate non-sexist servant of the people who loves liberty and the peoples' natural rights above all else, and who is more than willing to carry this struggle to the very end of existence to make this liberty possible.

Yet, as gays attempt to liberate themselves, there is still sexism. We are slaves, not unlike a colonized people. Frantz Fanon has said: "National liberation, national renaissance, the restoration of nationhood to the people, commonwealth; whatever may be the headings used or the new formulas introduced, decolonization is always a violent phenomenon."

The system continues to oppress us and refuses to change the laws, and it is bullshit to believe in the liberal cop-out of "law-reform." Truly meaningful reform could only be carried out by an all-gay or pro-gay legislature—a Utopian Dream! Large amounts of capital are raised and wasted for "test case" after "test case."

But the most important thing of all is that any change must be willed. There isn't any gay person I know—whether conservative, liberal, or radical—who wouldn't appreciate the freedom of being gay that can come through change. Despite the fact that *all* gay people want change, we disagree over methods with which to achieve it, and/or tactics needed to end sexism.

One of the reasons there is such contradiction among the activists in gay liberation is that our colonization/subjugation is so well defined that we defeat our purposes by still relating to the oppressors' definition of us as abnormal. We accept their mores, their language, and their sickness: Sexism.

After years of gay struggle we had finally evolved from the old homophile sexist approach, a solely gay-identified movement which tried to make gays more acceptable by changing the homosexual designation to something more ambiguous (i.e. homophile) in order to "pass" in the straight world. In the old movement, which was based on getting acceptance from the straight world, activists failed to challenge sex roles. The male leaders, for example, wore suits and ties, while the female leaders wore dresses and make-up. In the new movement, we began to question and redefine what it means to be a "woman," or a "man." Beyond that, the Gay Liberation Front was organized not only as a means with which we could deal with our own sex-identity, but also for the liberation of the gay lumpenproletariat—the street people (including poorer gays, transvestites, and transsexuals).

There were numerous slogans, such as "Out of the Closets (bars) and into the Streets!" Yet, so-called leaders arranged to hold meetings *in* bars as they led us, with bleary eyes, down the miserable, inactive liberal path, which was not only oppressive to the politically conscious but also unbearable to the closet and street people who came to them with faith and hope in their hearts that gay liberation would end the oppressive bar situation (among other things).

Thus, began the struggle between the isolationists who argued that gay liberation should be liberal and solely gay-identified and those leftists who believed that there was reason to involve themselves with all oppressed people since it is inconsonant with worldwide struggle to have one group liberated within a structure where others remained in bondage. The isolationists claimed that we don't need straights, that they are the enemy. "We will not tolerate straights." "We hate straight people." "We don't care about all the other oppressed people."

How naive! To combat sexism, we must love all people! Must we alienate those who draw closer to touching us, loving us, having sex with us? Is gayness perhaps the ultimate threat?

How glorious is the sexual revolution! Hold the banner high! We are all one in the struggle!

Revolutionary gay sisters were the first to recognize the sexism which was running rampant in the gay liberation movement and at long last came the first breakthrough: the inevitable separation of the women from the men so they could better relate to other women and thus deal with the problems of all oppressed people. They were the ones who could see that the base of oppression was the sexism of certain men.

Many of the men resented the departure of the women and held fast to their sexist behavior. Other brothers began to deal with their own sexism and found a new revolutionary method of updating Marxist class analysis. The first method was so simple that it was actually laughed at: we merely changed the rhetoric. For example, we called the sisters "women" instead of "girls." Secondly, we saw the link between feminism and our own oppression—that is, the realization that we shared a common oppression, that women and gay men are both oppressed by sexist men. And thirdly, we reaffirmed the struggle with the straight leftists at the risk of being called "freakin' fag revolutionaries!"

Even before the sisters united and began to work together, the Marxist brothers began to encounter elitist factionalism, such as that which ripped apart the Students for a Democratic Society (SDS). The right wing began its onslaught against the left by employing the methods of "divide and conquer" with such divisionary tactics as the forming of the Gay Activists Alliance, an isolationist group which recognized that there are other valid movements for change but which states that gay people in a gay group should strive only for the rights of gay people.

Other gays allowed themselves to be deluded by the wooing of the opportunist Trotskyist Socialist Workers Party and its affiliates—the Young Socialist Alliance and the Student Mobilization Committee—thus becoming co-opted by a straight, male-dominated group. Soon after that came the dissolution of many GLF offices and the formation of certain social service agencies, founded along establishment lines, and the developing of new "alliances" and so-called action groups.

Finally, a preacher began creating a supermarket chain of "community" churches in and around Los Angeles. He claims to be a radical but has had the audacity to lead closet gays and gays who wished to have the sanctions of religion back along the homophile path. He also encouraged people to marry, to play husband and wife roles, even though the marriages were female/female and male/male. In short, the preacher was another opportunist and even worse, an ultimate sexist, who filled his speeches with such sexist phrases as: "The Lord is my Shepherd and *He* knows I'm gay!" (God the *Father,* anyone?) He and others have encouraged the wasting of money on lobbying state legislatures and giving support to opportunistic legislators who have abandoned their anti-gay attitudes in order to jump on the bandwagon of an increasingly popular movement.

Other so-called leaders have been induced down the same path and have even dared to incorporate the name "Christopher Street West"—a name that belongs to the people who fought on the streets of New York, not on television. And now these opportunists, in addition, have set up corporate organizations which imitate the capitalists who are their oppressors.

For the time being, these tactics are working, only because there are no alternatives. But there are those of us who will continue to hold high the banner of communism, for we are certain that such sexist liberalism can never smash sexist capitalism. I am sure there are many people involved in these new attempts to integrate gays into the Amerikan society whose work is to be highly praised. These people have worked long and hard, and their motives are pure. All I can say is that I am disappointed to see again the return to what looks like the tired homophile methods.

Perhaps we are all working towards a socialist society. But it seems that as long as gay liberation is a male-dominated movement, we will not be able to win the battle against sexism.

I know that I have become more liberated by working to end oppression for all people. It is frustrating to see the efforts of anti-sexists seemingly going down the drain at a time when it seems that we should be putting everything into making the revolution.

Nevertheless, I am gayer and prouder than ever before! I am gentler yet more militant, and I am more patient and much more revolutionary than I was last year. The Black Panthers have taught me, Al Fatah has taught me, and Mao and Che have taught me that only by joining the struggle against sexism and capitalism—the root causes of racism, fascism, and imperialism—do I have a greater chance for helping to build a truly egalitarian society.

I cannot fail in the struggle. I have renewed hope, for I know that I am not alone.

July, 1971

IX.
MANIFESTOS

A GAY MANIFESTO

Carl Wittman

San Francisco is a refugee camp for homosexuals. We have fled here from every part of the nation, and like refugees elsewhere, we came not because it is so great here, but because it was so bad there. By the tens of thousands, we fled small towns where to be ourselves would endanger our jobs and any hope of a decent life; we have fled from blackmailing cops, from families who disowned or "tolerated" us; we have been drummed out of the armed services, thrown out of schools, fired from jobs, beaten by punks and policemen.

And we have formed a ghetto, out of self-protection. It is a ghetto rather than a free territory because it is still theirs. Straight cops patrol us, straight legislators govern us, straight employers keep us in line, straight money exploits us. We have pretended everything is OK, because we haven't been able to see how to change it—we've been afraid.

In the past year there has been an awakening of gay liberation ideas and energy. How it began we don't know; maybe we were inspired by black people and their freedom movement; we learned how to stop pretending from the hip revolution. Amerika in all its ugliness has surfaced with the war and our national leaders. And we are revulsed by the quality of our ghetto life.

Where once there was frustration, alienation, and cynicism, there are new characteristics among us. We are full of love for each other and are showing it; we are full of anger at what has been done to us. And as we recall all the self-censorship and repression for so many years, a reservoir of tears pours out of our eyes. And we are euphoric, high, with the initial flourish of a movement.

We want to make ourselves clear: our first job is to free ourselves; that means clearing our heads of the garbage that's been poured into them. This article is an attempt at raising a number of issues, and presenting some ideas to replace the old ones. It is primarily for ouselves, a starting point of discussion. If straight people of good will find it useful in understanding what liberation is about, so much the better.

It should also be clear that these are the views of one person, and are determined not only by my homosexuality, but my being white, male, middle-class. It is my individual consciousness. Our group consciousness will evolve as we get ourselves together—we are only at the beginning.

I. On Orientation

1. *What homosexuality is:* Nature leaves undefined the object of sexual desire. The gender of that object is imposed socially. Humans originally made homosexuality taboo because they needed every bit of energy to produce and raise children: survival of species was a priority. With overpopulation and technological change, that taboo continued only to exploit us and enslave us.

As kids we refused to capitulate to demands that we ignore our feelings toward each other. Somewhere we found the strength to resist being indoctrinated, and we should count that among our assets. We have to realize that our loving each other is a good thing, not an unfortunate thing, and that we have a lot to teach straights about sex, love, strength, and resistance.

Homosexuality is *not* a lot of things. It is not a makeshift in the absence of the opposite sex; it is not hatred or rejection of the opposite sex; it is not genetic; it is not the result of broken homes except inasmuch as we could see the sham of American marriage. *Homosexuality is the capacity to love someone of the same sex.*

2. *Bisexuality:* Bisexuality is good; it is the capacity to love people of either sex. The reason so few of us are bisexual is because society made such a big stink about homosexuality that we got forced into seeing ourselves as either straight or non-straight. Also, many gays got turned off to the ways men are supposed to act with women and vice-versa, which is pretty fucked-up. Gays will begin to turn on to women when 1) it's something that we do because we want to, and not because we should, and 2) when women's liberation changes the nature of heterosexual relationships.

We continue to call ourselves homosexual, not bisexual, even if we do make it with the opposite sex also, because saying "Oh, I'm Bi" is a copout for a gay. We get told it's OK to sleep with guys as long as we sleep with women too, and that's still putting homosexuality down. We'll be gay until everyone has forgotten that it's an issue. Then we'll begin to be complete.

3. *Heterosexuality:* Exclusive heterosexuality is fucked up. It reflects a fear of people of the same sex, it's anti-homosexual, and it is fraught with frustration. Heterosexual sex is fucked up, too; ask women's liberation about what straight guys are like in bed. Sex is aggression for the male chauvinist; sex is obligation for the

traditional woman. And among the young, the modern, the hip, it's only a subtle version of the same. For us to become heterosexual in the sense that our straight brothers and sisters are is not a cure, it is a disease.

II. On Women
1. *Lesbianism:* It's been a male-dominated society for too long, and that has warped both men and women. So gay women are going to see things differently from gay men; they are going to feel put down as women, too. Their liberation is tied up with both gay liberation and women's liberation.

This paper speaks from the gay male viewpoint. And although some of the ideas in it may be equally relevant to gay women, it would be arrogant to presume this to be a manifesto for lesbians.

We look forward to the emergence of a lesbian liberation voice. The existence of a lesbian caucus within the New York Gay Liberation Front has been very helpful in challenging male chauvinism among gay guys, and anti-gay feelings among women's liberation.

2. *Male chauvinism:* All men are infected with male chauvinism—we were brought up that way. It means we assume that women play subordinate roles and are less human than ourselves. (At an early gay liberation meeting one guy said, "Why don't we invite women's liberation—they can bring sandwiches and coffee.") It is no wonder that so few gay women have become active in our groups.

Male chauvinism, however, is not central to us. We can junk it much more easily than straight men can. For we understand oppression. We have largely opted out of a system which oppresses women daily—our egos are not built on putting women down and having them build us up. Also, living in a mostly male world we have become used to playing different roles, doing our own shit-work. And finally, we have a common enemy: the big male chauvinists are also the big anti-gays.

But we need to purge male chauvinism, both in behavior and in thought among us. Chick equals nigger equals queer. Think it over.

3. *Women's liberation:* They are assuming their equality and dignity and in doing so are challenging the same things we are: the roles, the exploitation of minorities by capitalism, the arrogant smugness of straight white male middle-class Amerika. They are our sisters in struggle.

Problems and differences will become clearer when we begin to work together. One major problem is our own male chauvinism. Another is uptightness and hostility to homosexuality that many women have—that is the straight in them. A third problem is differing views on sex: sex for them has meant oppression, while for us it has been a symbol of our freedom. We must come to know and understand each other's style, jargon and humor.

III. On Roles

1. *Mimicry of straight society:* We are children of straight society. We still think straight: that is part of our oppression. One of the worst of straight concepts is inequality. Straight (also white, English, male, capitalist) thinking views things in terms of order and comparison. A is before B, B is after A; one is below two is below three; there is no room for equality. This idea gets extended to male/female, on top/on bottom, spouse/not spouse, hetero-sexual/homosexual, boss/worker, white/black, and rich/poor. Our social institutions cause and reflect this verbal hierarchy. This is Amerika.

We've lived in these institutions all our lives. Naturally we mimic the roles. For too long we mimicked these roles to protect ourselves—a survival mechanism. Now we are becoming free enough to shed the roles which we've picked up from the institutions which have imprisoned us.

"Stop mimicking straights, stop censoring ourselves."

2. *Marriage:* Marriage is a prime example of a straight institution fraught with role playing. Traditional marriage is a rotten, oppressive institution. Those of us who have been in heterosexual marriages too often have blamed our gayness on the breakup of the marriage. No. They broke up because marriage is a contract which smothers both people, denies needs, and places impossible demands on both people. And we had the strength, again, to refuse to capitulate to the roles which were demanded of us.

Gay people must stop gauging their self-respect by how well they mimic straight marriages. Gay marriages will have the same problems as straight ones except in burlesque. For the usual legitimacy and pressures which keep straight marriages together are absent, e.g. kids, what parents think, what neighbors say.

To accept that happiness comes through finding a groovy spouse and settling down, showing the world that "we're just the same as you" is avoiding the real issues, and is an expression of self-hatred.

3. *Alternatives to marriage:* People want to get married for lots of good reasons, although marriage won't often meet those needs or

desires. We're all looking for security, a flow of love, and a feeling of belonging and being needed.

These needs can be met through a number of social relationships and living situations. Things we want to get away from are: 1) exclusiveness, propertied attitudes toward each other, a mutual pact against the rest of the world; 2) promise about the future, which we have no right to make and which prevent us from, or make us feel guilty about, growing; 3) inflexible roles, roles which do not reflect us at the moment but are inherited through mimicry and inability to define equalitarian relationships.

We have to define for ourselves a new pluralistic, role free social structure for ourselves. It must contain both the freedom and physical space for people to live alone, live together for a while, live together for a long time, either as couples or in larger numbers; and the ability to flow easily from one of these states to another as our needs change.

Liberation for gay people is defining for ourselves how and with whom we live, instead of measuring our relationship in comparison to straight ones, with straight values.

4. *Gay "stereotypes"*: The straights' image of the gay world is defined largely by those of us who have violated straight roles. There is a tendency among "homophile" groups to deplore gays who play visible roles—the queens and the nellies. As liberated gays, we must take a clear stand. 1) Gays who stand out have become our first martyrs. They came out and withstood disapproval before the rest of us did. 2) If they have suffered from being open, it is straight society whom we must indict, not the queen.

5. *Closet queens:* This phrase is becoming analagous to "Uncle Tom." To pretend to be straight sexually, or to pretend to be straight socially, is probably the most harmful pattern of behavior in the ghetto. The married guy who makes it on the side secretly; the guy who will go to bed once but who won't develop any gay relationships; the pretender at work or school who changes the gender of the friend he's talking about; the guy who'll suck cock in the bushes but who won't go to bed.

If we are liberated we are open with our sexuality. Closet queenery must end. *Come out.*

But in saying come out, we have to have our heads clear about a few things: 1) Closet queens are our brothers, and must be defended against attacks by straight people; 2) The fear of coming out is not paranoia; the stakes are high: loss of family ties, loss of job, loss of straight friends—these are all reminders that the oppression is not just in our heads. It's real. Each of us must make the steps toward openness at our own speed and on our own impulses. Being open is the foundation of freedom: it has to be built solidly; 3) "Closet queen" is a broad term covering a multitude of forms of defense, self-hatred, lack of strength, and habit. We are all closet queens in some ways, and all of us had to come out—very few of us were "flagrant" at the age of seven! We must afford our brothers and sisters the same patience we afforded ourselves. And while their closet queenery is part of our oppression, it's more a part of theirs. They alone can decide when and how.

IV. On Oppression
It is important to catalog and understand the different facets of our oppression. There is no future in arguing about degrees of oppression. A lot of "movement" types come on with a line of shit about homosexuals not being oppressed as much as blacks or Vietnamese or workers or women. We don't happen to fit into their ideas of class or caste. Bull! When people feel oppressed, they act on that feeling. We feel oppressed. Talk about the priority of black liberation or ending imperialism over and above gay liberation is just anti-gay propaganda.

1. *Physical attacks:* We are attacked, beaten, castrated and left dead time and time again. There are half a dozen known unsolved slayings in San Francisco parks in the last few years. "Punks," often of minority groups who look around for someone under them socially, feel encouraged to beat up on "queens," and cops look the other way. That used to be called lynching.

Cops in most cities have harassed our meeting places: bars and baths and parks. They set up entrapment squads. A Berkeley brother was slain by a cop in April when he tried to split after finding out that the trick who was making advances to him was a cop. Cities set up "pervert" registration, which if nothing else scares our brothers deeper into the closet.

One of the most vicious slurs on us is the blame for prison "gang rapes." These rapes are invariably done by people who consider themselves straight. The victims of these rapes are us and straights who can't defend themselves. The press campaign to link prison rapes with homosexuality is an attempt to make straights fear and despise us, so they can oppress us more. It's typical of the fucked-up straight mind to think that homosexual sex involves tying a guy down and fucking him. That's aggression, not sex. If that's what sex is for a lot of straight people, that's a problem they have to solve, not us.

2. *Psychological warfare:* Right from the beginning we have been

subjected to a barrage of straight propaganda. Since our parents don't know any homosexuals, we grow up thinking that we're alone and different and perverted. Our school friends identify "queer" with any non-conformist or bad behavior. Our elementary school teachers tell us not to talk to strangers or accept rides. Television, billboards and magazines put forth a false idealization of male/female relationships, and make us wish we were different, wish we were "in." In family living class we're taught how we're supposed to turn out. And all along the best we hear about homosexuality is that it's an unfortunate problem.

3. *Self-oppression:* As gay liberation grows, we will find our uptight brothers and sisters, particularly those who are making a buck off our ghetto, coming on strong to defend the status quo. This is self-oppression: "don't rock the boat"; "things in SF are OK"; "gay people just aren't together"; "I'm not oppressed." These lines are right out of the mouths of the straight establishment. A large part of our oppression would end if we would stop putting ourselves and our pride down.

4. *Institutional oppression:* Discrimination against gays is blatant, if we open our eyes. Homosexual relationships are illegal, and even if these laws are not regularly enforced, they encourage and enforce closet queenery. The bulk of the social work/psychiatric field looks upon homosexuality as a problem, and treats us as sick. Employers let it be known that our skills are acceptable only as long as our sexuality is hidden. Big business and government are particularly notorious offenders.

The discrimination in the draft and armed services is a pillar of the general attitude toward gays. If we are willing to label ourselves publicly not only as homosexual but as sick, then we qualify for deferment; and if we're not "discreet" (dishonest) we get drummed out of the service. Hell, no, we won't go, of course not, but we can't let the army fuck over us this way, either.

V. On Sex

1. *What sex is:* It is both creative expression and communication: good when it is either, and better when it is both. Sex can also be aggression, and usually is when those involved do not see each other as equals; and it can also be perfunctory, when we are distracted or preoccupied. These uses spoil what is good about it.

I like to think of good sex in terms of playing the violin: with both people on one level seeing the other body as an object capable of creating beauty when they play it well; and on a second level the players communicating through their mutual production and appreciation of beauty. As in good music, you get totally into it—and coming back out of that state of consciousness is like finishing a work of art or coming back from an episode of an acid or mescaline trip. And to press the analogy further: the variety of music is infinite and varied, depending on the capabilities of the players, both as subjects and as objects. Solos, duets, quartets (symphonies, even, if you happen to dig Romantic music!) are possible. The variations in gender, response, and bodies are like different instruments. And perhaps what we have called sexual "orientation" probably just means that we have not yet learned to turn on to the total range of musical expression.

2. *Objectification:* In this scheme, people are sexual objects, but they are also subjects, and are human beings who appreciate themselves as object and subject. This use of human bodies as objects is legitimate (not harmful) only when it is reciprocal. If one person is always object and the other subject, it stifles the human being in both of them. Objectification must also be open and frank. By silence we often assume or let the other person assume that sex means commitments: if it does, OK; but if not, say it. (Of course, it's not all that simple: our capabilities for manipulation are unfathomed—all we can do is try.)

Gay liberation people must understand that women have been treated exclusively and dishonestly as sexual objects. A major part of their liberation is to play down sexual objectification and to develop other aspects of themselves which have been smothered so long. We respect this. We also understand that a few liberated women will be appalled or disgusted at the open and prominent place that we put sex in our lives; and while this is a natural response from their experience, they must learn what it means for us.

For us, sexual objectification is a focus of our quest for freedom. It is precisely that which we are not supposed to share with each other. Learning how to be open and good with each other sexually is part of our liberation. And one obvious distinction: objectification of sex for us is something we choose to do among ourselves, while for women it is imposed by their oppressors.

3. *On positions and roles:* Much of our sexuality has been perverted through mimicry of straights, and warped from self-hatred. These sexual perversions are basically anti-gay:

"I like to make it with straight guys"
"I'm not gay, but I like to be 'done' "
"I like to fuck, but don't want to be fucked"
"I don't like to be touched above the neck"

This is role playing at its worst; we must transcend these roles. We strive for democratic, mutual, reciprocal sex. This does not mean that we are all mirror images of each other in bed, but that we break away from roles which enslave us. We already do better in bed than straights do, and we can be better to each other than we have been.

4. *Chickens and studs:* Face it, nice bodies and young bodies are attributes, they're groovy. They are inspiration for art, for spiritual elevation, for good sex. The problem arises only in the inability to relate to people of the same age, or people who don't fit the plastic stereotypes of a good body. At that point, objectification eclipses people, and expresses self-hatred: "I hate gay people, and I don't like myself, but if a stud (or chicken) wants to make it with me, I can pretend I'm someone other than me."

A note on exploitation of children: kids can take care of themselves, and are sexual beings way earlier than we'd like to admit. Those of us who began cruising in early adolescence know this, and we were doing the cruising, not being debauched by dirty old men. Scandals such as the one in Boise, Idaho—blaming a "ring" of homosexuals for perverting their youth—are the fabrications of press and police and politicians. And as for child molesting, the overwhelming amount is done by straight guys to little girls: it is not particularly a gay problem, and is caused by the frustrations resulting from anti-sex puritanism.

5. *Perversion:* We've been called perverts enough to be suspect of any usage of the word. Still many of us shrink from the idea of certain kinds of sex: with animals, sado/masochism, dirty sex (involving piss or shit). Right off, even before we take the time to learn any more, there are some things to get straight:

1. we shouldn't be apologetic to straights about gays whose sex lives we don't understand or share;

2. it's not particularly a gay issue, except that gay people probably are less hung up about sexual experimentation;

3. let's get perspective: even if we were to get into the game of deciding what's good for someone else, the harm done in these "perversions" is undoubtedly less dangerous or unhealthy than is tobacco or alcohol;

4. while they can be reflections of neurotic or self-hating patterns, they may also be enactments of spiritual or important phenomena: *e.g.* sex with animals may be the beginning of interspecies communication: some dolphin-human breakthroughs have been made on the sexual level: *e.g.* one guy who says he digs shit during sex occasionally says it's not the taste or texture, but a symbol that he's so far into sex that those things no longer bug him; *e.g.* sado/masochism, when consensual, can be

described as a highly artistic endeavor, a ballet the constraints of which are the thresholds of pain and pleasure.

VI. On Our Ghetto

We are refugees from Amerika. So we came to the ghetto—and as other ghettos, it has its negative and positive aspects. Refugee camps are better than what preceeded them, or people never would have come. But they are still enslaving, if only that we are limited to being ourselves there and only there.

Ghettos breed self-hatred. We stagnate here, accepting the status quo. The status quo is rotten. We are all warped by our oppression, and in the isolation of the ghetto we blame ourselves rather than our oppressors.

Ghettos breed exploitation. Landlords find they can charge exorbitant rents and get away with it, because of the limited area which is safe to live in openly. Mafia control of bars and baths in NYC is only one example of outside money controlling our institutions for their profit. In San Francisco the Tavern Guild favors maintaining the ghetto, for it is through ghetto culture that they make a buck. We crowd their bars not because of their merit but because of the absence of any other social institution. The Guild has refused to let us collect defense funds or pass out gay liberation literature in their bars—need we ask why?

Police or con men who shake down the straight gay in return for not revealing him; the bookstores and movie makers who keep raising prices because they are the only outlet for pornography; heads of "modeling" agencies and other pimps who exploit both the hustlers and the johns—these are the parasites who flourish in the ghetto.

San Francisco—ghetto or free territory: Our ghetto certainly is more beautiful and larger and more diverse than most ghettos, and is certainly freer than the rest of Amerika. That's why we're here. But it isn't ours. Capitalists make money off us, cops patrol us, government tolerates us as long as we shut up, and daily we work for and pay taxes to those who oppress us.

To be a free territory, we must govern ourselves, set up our own institutions, defend ourselves, and use our own energies to improve our lives. The emergence of gay liberation communes and our own paper is a good start. The talk about a gay liberation coffee shop/dance hall should be acted upon. Rural retreats, political action offices, food cooperatives, a free school, unalienating bars and after hours places—they must be developed if we are to have even the shadow of a free territory.

VII. On Coalition

Right now the bulk of our work has to be among ourselves—self educating, fending off attacks, and building free territory. Thus basically we have to have a gay/straight vision of the world until the oppression of gays is ended.

But not every straight is our enemy. Many of us have mixed identities, and have ties with other liberation movements: women, blacks, other minority groups; we may also have taken on an identity which is vital to us: ecology, dope, ideology. And face it: we can't change Amerika alone.

Who do we look to for coalition?

1. *Women's liberation:* Summarizing earlier statements, 1) they are our closest ally; we must try hard to get together with them; 2) a lesbian caucus is probably the best way to attack gay guys' male chauvinism, and challenge the straightness of women's liberation; 3) as males we must be sensitive to their developing identities as women, and respect that; if *we know what our* freedom is about, *they* certainly know what's best for *them*.

2. *Black liberation:* This is tenuous right now because of the uptightness and supermasculinity of many black men (which is understandable). Despite that, we must support their movement, particularly when they are under attack from the establishment; we must show them that we mean business; and we must figure out who our common enemies are: police, city hall, capitalism.

3. *Chicanos:* Basically the same problem as with blacks: trying to overcome mutual animosity and fear, and finding ways to support them. The extra problem of super up-tightness and machismo among Latin cultures, and the traditional pattern of Mexicans beating up "queers," can be overcome: we're both oppressed, and by the same people at the top.

4. *White radicals and ideologues:* We're not, as a group, Marxist or Communist. We haven't figured out what kind of political/economic system is good for us as gays. Neither capitalist or socialist countries have treated us as anything other than *non grata* so far.

But we know we are radical, in that we know the system that we're under now is a direct source of oppression, and it's not a question of getting our share of the pie. The pie is rotten.

We can look forward to coalition and mutual support with radical groups if they are able to transcend their anti-gay and male chauvinist patterns. We support radical and militant demands when they arise, *e.g.* Moratorium, People's Park; but only as a group; we can't compromise or soft-peddle our gay identity.

Problems: because radicals are doing somebody else's thing, they tend to avoid issues which affect them directly, and see us as jeopardizing their "work" with other groups (workers, blacks). Some years ago a dignitary of SDS on a community organization project announced at an initial staff meeting that there would be no homosexuality (or dope) on the project. And recently in New York, a movement group which had a coffee-house get-together after a political rally told the gays to leave when they started dancing together. (It's interesting to note that in this case, the only two groups which supported us were women's liberation and the Crazies.)

Perhaps most fruitful would be to broach with radicals their stifled homosexuality and the issues which arise from challenging sexual roles.

5. *Hip and street people:* A major dynamic of rising gay liberation sentiment is the hip revolution within the gay community. Emphasis on love, dropping out, being honest, expressing yourself through hair and clothes, and smoking dope are all attributes of this. The gays who are the least vulnerable to attack by the establishment have been the freest to express themselves on gay liberation.

We can make a direct appeal to young people, who are not so up tight about homosexuality. One kid, after having his first sex with a male, said, "I don't know what all the fuss is about; making it with a girl just isn't that different."

The hip/street culture has led people into a lot of freeing activities: encounter/sensitivity, the quest for reality, freeing territory for the people, ecological consciousness, communes. These are real points of agreement and probably will make it easier for them to get their heads straight about homosexuality, too.

6. *Homophile groups:* 1) Reformist or pokey as they sometimes are, they are our brothers. They'll grow as we have grown and grow. Do not attack them in straight or mixed company. 2) Ignore their attack on us. 3) Cooperate where cooperation is possible without essential compromise of our identity.

Conclusion: An Outline of
Imperatives for Gay Liberation

1. Free ourselves: come out everywhere; initiate self defense and political activity; initiate counter community institutions.

2. Turn other gay people on: talk all the time; understand, forgive, accept.

3. Free the homosexual in everyone: we'll be getting a good bit of shit from threatened latents: be gentle, and keep talking and acting free.

4. We've been playing an act for a long time, so we're consummate actors. Now we can begin *to be*, and it'll be a good show!

GAY REVOLUTION PARTY MANIFESTO

Gay

Gay is a process of attaining mutual and equal social and sensual relationships among all human beings, which is realized only through participation in the free dynamic expression of love among people of the same sex.

Straight is the systematic channeling of human expression into various basically static social institutions and roles. The original social expression of straightness was gender: the division of humanity into the castes of woman and man on the basis of the biological sexes, female and male. In this process, females were deprived of their subjectivity and their erotic energy was suppressed, while males developed roles involving aggression and the search for power and dominance. Since gay, roleless relations acted in opposition to this process, they were suppressed.

With this caste division as a tradition and model, it was a logical consequence that the male rulers extended the caste system and placed other males (and appendaged females) into similar functional or object relationships, based either on their ethnic origin (caste) or on their personal heritage (class). This was the process in which racism, despotism, feudalism, capitalism, nationalism, and imperialism were developed. The male rulers ensured the socialization of people into this system of relationships by developing self-validating institutions such as straight sexuality, the family, the church, and the state.

Gradually these straight societies came to dominate the entire planet since their nature led them continually to seek conquest and colonialization of other peoples. Today their dominance is practically complete.

But since the nature of these societies has never corresponded to the actuality of human needs, they could never succeed in the indoctrination of the entire population. Gay people, homosexuals, are the most socially defined group of those not indoctrinated. Generally, we have been treated as an untouchable caste, "agents of Satan," criminals, sociopaths, since we act inherently to destroy the prevailing social order of straight gender.

Sometimes the reaction of societies has been to purge gay

people. Examples of this are the Medieval European practice of burning witches and faggots and, subsequently, our confinement in convents, monasteries, prisons, concentration camps, and mental institutions. Another reaction was the attempt to impose straight gender definitions on homosexual relations, as in many ancient Greek and native American groups. Generally, the practice has been to isolate gay people, deny the existence of homosexuality and increase the indoctrination.

Despite this oppression, we gay people have continued to discover ourselves. We have seen in ourselves the capability of loving each other as complete people outside the roles of straightness. We have found that humans are capable of tremendous creativity, imagination, and constant change, but that these qualities are suppressed in the process through which a child becomes a straight person.

In the past, we gay people have never been allowed to associate openly with any nation, race, ethnic group, religion, or social movement. All have denied our gayness, even while using our abilities. The result of this exclusion has been that we have had no vested interest in dogmatism, sexism, racism, and nationalism, and have been able to see the essential nature of human personhood and the restrictions placed on it by classes and castes. These factors have historically produced in gay people the desire to break down or overthrow systems of caste and class.

The isolation of gay people has, in the past, forced us into individual solutions: criminality, madness, mysticism, abstract creativity, suicide, and the conformity of the closet life-style. We have also sought solutions through directing our anti-social energies against systems of caste and class other than those of gender.

Today, conditions have changed and the isolation is breaking down. We are beginning to realize that the end of classes and castes, and even the survival of human life, depend on the total destruction of the caste system which has made women objects for straight men and made gay people the outcasts of society.

Revolution

Revolution is the method by which we will create the conditions leading to the destruction of the gender caste system and thereby to the gay liberation of all people. It will be a total change which will reach to the roots of the present social order and destroy all of its aspects which restrain freedom.

Revolution differs from reform in that it means that the

oppressed, with a full consciousness of their oppression, create social change through their own power.

Historically, revolution is the method by which one class overthrows another. Gay revolution will see the overthrow of the straight male caste and the destruction of all systems of caste and class that are based in sexism. It is on this point that gay revolution differs from past revolutions of the proletariat and Third World: it is complete revolution. Any movements seeking less than an end to sexism and total liberation will ultimately be co-opted by the oppressor. History has shown that the maintenance of straightness, female oppression, and the family system has prevented every revolutionary social and political movement from realizing its goals. Instead of destroying classes, these revolutions have produced either new class systems or a return to the previous social order with new faces. Because they retained the sexual caste system, the rebirth or non-destruction of castes and classes was inevitable.

Gay revolution will not produce a world in which women will receive "equal pay" for work traditionally assigned to their gender, nor in which they will become "equal partners" in the nuclear family. Rather, it will mean that biological sex will have nothing to do with occupation, and that there will be no families.

Gay revolution will not lead to freedom of association for gay people in a predominately straight world, nor will it lead to straight-defined homosexuality with marriages and exclusive monogamy. Gay revolution will produce a world in which all social and sensual relationships will be gay and in which homo- and heterosexuality will be incomprehensible terms.

Convergence at the point of gay-feminist consciousness by people from the gay and women's movements will be the initial stage of revolution. Gay people, first lesbians, and later males (after ridding themselves of their manhood and its privileges), will move toward becoming gayer and eliminating sexism and straightness from themselves. The straight women's movement, with its consciousness of the fundamentally oppressive nature of the man/woman caste model, will move toward sensual relations of equality and mutuality, that is, homosexuality, and from there, to gay consciousness.

At this point, increasing numbers of straight men will be forced to make a choice between becoming gay or attacking gay feminists in order to restore the previous imbalance of power. Reactionary repression is their more probable course, and it would occur both individually and through the institutions of society: government, religion, psychology, etc. The goal of this repression would be to force women back to the home and gay people back into the closet through threats of imprisonment in jails, mental institutions, and any other means that could be devised.

This reaction would then produce a collective insurrection by gay-feminist revolutionaries which would seek to end the power of straight men.

The preferable alternative to such reactionary repression would be for males to become gay in large numbers. But just as straight movement women must explore each other sensually and sexually, so also must straight males bring each other out. Gay-feminists will no longer serve the oppressor sexually or psychically.

Party

Party is the medium in which the oppressed collectivize their individual experience of oppression and develop a gay-feminist consciousness and programs of revolutionary action. A Gay Revolution Party is the means of becoming gay and destroying straight, in and around us.

A party is the specific organizational medium which effectively concentrates energies through combating individualism, power-tripping, and anarchistic self-indulgence, while encouraging commitment, collectivism, and self-discipline. This is in contrast to other organizations which dissipate our energies and to small groups which tend to become totally inner-directed.

The Gay Revolution Party is a dynamic network of small groups organized to deal collectively with specific work projects or organizational functions. Such small group functions would include: collective living, political action, consciousness-raising, political education, and sensual development. A council of representatives, acting out of the collective consciousness of their groups , will formulate party policy and coordinate action.

We will develop our structures from our own personal-sensual selves and our understanding of how to best respond out of love, not fear, to our own experience.

Our emphasis will be serving those who are sensually identified as gay. Our service will not be doing things for gays but becoming, with gays, gayer and freer gay humans.

WORKING PAPER FOR THE REVOLUTIONARY PEOPLE'S CONSTITUTIONAL CONVENTION

Chicago Gay Liberation

The following is a working paper prepared by Chicago Gay Liberation for the Revolutionary People's Constitutional Convention plenary session, held in Philadelphia, September 1970.

A. Introduction

Although we recognize that homosexuals have been oppressed in all societies, it is the struggle against that oppression in the context of Amerikan imperialism that faces us. In addition to the usual forms of oppression, we, as homosexuals, are forced to hide our identities in order to keep our jobs and avoid being social outcasts—in order to "make it" in straight Amerika. As gay liberation, we now take the position that, because of the rampant oppression we see—of black, Third World people, women, workers—in addition to our own; because of the corrupt values, because of the injustices, we no longer want to "make it" in Amerika. For to make it is to accept the oppression of others (in addition to our own). We are joining the Revolutionary People's Constitutional Convention and reject what Amerikan imperialism has to offer us. Rather we will fight for our liberation, and we will get it by any means necessary.

Our particular struggle is for sexual self-determination, the abolition of sex-role stereotypes and the human right to the use of one's own body without interference from the legal and social institutions of the state. Many of us have understood that our struggle cannot succeed without a fundamental change in society which will put the source of power (means of production) in the hands of the people who at present have nothing. Those now in power will oppose this change by violent repression, which in fact is already in motion. Not all of our sisters and brothers in gay liberation share this view, or may feel that personal solutions might work. But as our struggle grows, it will be made clear by the changing objective conditions that our liberation is inextricably bound to the liberation of all oppressed people.

This position paper does not intend to speak for the Black Caucus or Women's Caucus of Chicago Gay Liberation; we recognize that black homosexuals and female homosexuals live with doubly or triply oppressed conditions. But since anti-homosexual prejudice is rampant throughout society, homosexuals can be treated as outcasts even within an already oppressed group. Therefore this paper should speak in a general way for homosexuals as homosexuals.

B. Grievances Common to All Homosexuals

1. Employment and other economic factors.

a. Hiring: In addition to the particular discrimination against black, female and poor homosexuals, we are at a disadvantage because of discriminatory hiring practices—unless, of course, we "pass." There is a tracking system which determines the positions open to homosexuals where we are able to work in the company of other homosexuals. We often take these jobs even though we may not like them and the pay may be low, just so we won't have to worry about being found out. Our women may become physical education teachers and nurses; our men may become beauticians or ribbon clerks for those reasons. There is nothing wrong with those jobs, but the choice should be based on interest and ability. There are no "gay jobs"; there are no "women's jobs." For *known* homosexuals, *there is no employment* at all except in a few fields, e.g., theater, music, etc., which require special talents.

b. Firing: Since firing of known homosexuals is notorious, most of us hold jobs which would be closed to us if we didn't "pass." We do so at a tremendous and cruel personal cost, for we must hide what, in our hearts, we know to be important and beautiful—our sexuality. Forced to wear a heterosexual mask, we are brainwashed (without even knowing it) into believing that our sex is shameful and unnatural—this belief is usually expressed as a tendency toward compulsive promiscuity, sexual objectification of each other, and loneliness.

c. Income: The jobs into which we are tracked are often low-paying and certainly alienating. And the higher federal income taxation of "single" people—that is, those whose relationships are not recognized as legal—discriminates against us economically.

2. Political.

a. Electoral politics: As homosexuals we have *no* representation in the government, and never have had. Third World and female homosexuals are especially unrepresented, but even the white male as a homosexual has no voice. Presently there are politicians in New York and California who are trying to attract the "gay vote." But they are not homosexual and cannot represent our needs and interests. Furthermore, their political parties are corrupted by racism, sexism (male chauvinism) and anti-homosexual prejudice and are tied economically to those who are responsible, ultimately, for our continued oppression. How can these politicians be on our side, in practice? We have never had an admitted homosexual in public office, and our heterosexual "representatives" have never done anything for us although we have worked in their campaigns and given them our votes. But even if we could find spokesmen and women, they would be ineffective as part of a social system that is based on oppression, anyway.

b. The "movement": As we in gay liberation look around us to find out who are our friends and potential allies, we see that the Black Panther Party, personified by its Supreme Commander Huey P. Newton, is the first national organization to give us such warm, public support, as well as official recognition. For years, many of us have worked in radical organizations always hiding our identities, always working in the struggles of others. Some so-called "Marxist" organizations do not allow homosexual membership. This has been very oppressive to us and has kept many of us, who were potential radicals, from radicalization. These groups and individuals treat us as badly as their supposed enemy, the "ruling class'" that they are always talking about. In abusing homosexuals they show they cannot tell the difference between their friends and their enemies and are probably unable to make principled political alliances. Failing to recognize our grievances as legitimate, these "revolutionaries" and "radicals" are not only inhumane but also counter-revolutionary. We will no longer work within such groups.

3. Social institutions.

a. The law and the state: Our most immediate oppressors are the pigs. We are beaten, entrapped, enticed, raided, taunted, arrested and jailed. In jail we are jeered at, gang-raped, beaten and killed, with full encouragement and participation by the pigs. Every homosexual lives in fear of the pigs, except that we are beginning to fight back! The reasons are not that the pigs are just prejudiced (which they are) or that they "over-react," but that they are given silent approval by the power structure for their violence against us. Since our *lives* are defined as illegal, immoral, and unnatural, there is no reason why the pigs shouldn't harass us—and they are never punished for it. The law is against us, but changing laws makes no difference. That must be crystal clear; any homosexual from Chicago, where homosexuality is legal, will tell you that changing the law makes no difference. The pigs must be fought, but we must see beyond them to ultimate sources of power—an elite of super-rich, white males who control production and therefore the prevailing ideology. Their representatives may try to tempt us with reforms, "progress," divide us by class and skin privileges, buy us off with a piece of the pie or male supremacy because we have just begun to join the revolutionary and progressive people. But common sense tells us that as long as the power rests in the hands of a few and not with the people—both straight and gay—that power can be used to oppress homosexuals.

b. Housing—the homosexual ghetto: Homosexuals are frequently denied housing, much more so if they are also female or black. We avoid the anti-homosexual discrimination by "passing." But life for homosexuals is so psychologically oppressive in a heterosexual neighborhood that we tend to live in homosexual neighborhoods which take on ghetto-like characteristics. These conditions should not be confused with the immiseration and oppression in the black, brown and poor white ghettos, but there are some similarities. No sooner is it established that a neighborhood is "gay" than rents and real estate prices rise. Those that exploit us as consumers know that we will pay through the nose, even when we aren't well off, for the psychological comfort of living among "our own kind." Most of us probably live outside of these communities, but ghetto institutions are still part of our lives. We neither control nor own the institutions which we use. These bars, shops, movie-houses, etc., are owned by businessmen who serve their own interests or the Mafia's but do not serve us at all. The prices are notoriously high, and the practices are often racist, sexist and anti-working class. This materially oppresses female, black and poor homosexuals and also reinforces the false consciousness (racism, sexism, class-chauvinism) which divides us as a group and, in the end, oppresses us all.

c. Education: We have no stake in education which is racist, male-chauvinist, anti-working class and anti-homosexual. The schools are not people's schools and therefore do not serve the people. They certainly do not serve us as homosexuals, but teach ideology that is destructive to us and helps to keep us social outcasts. What child would have disdain for homosexuals? They have to be taught that. There are no positive educational programs on homosexuality which would alleviate anti-homosexual prejudice and our own self-hate, which comes when we discover what we are. The subject is avoided in the schools, and is usually assumed to be taboo and dirty by the students. It is wrong to mislead the people this way and perpetuate attitudes which harm us. The only models for love and sexuality according to our "educators" are heterosexual ones in the context of state-sanctioned monogamous white relationships which oppress women. Homosexual authors are usually ignored, especially if they write about their homosexuality, like James Baldwin. Others, like Walt Whitman or Gertrude Stein, are taught but never as homosexual writers. Like blacks and women, we are taught, by omission, that we have no heroes and heroines and certainly no role-models.

d. Medical care: The branch of medicine we are most concerned with is psychiatry. The American medical profession is oblivious to the needs of oppressed people, and psychiatrists are clearly hostile to homosexuality. They (not Freud) have created and spread the ideology that we are sick, neurotic, paranoid and other bullshit. Yet they never hesitate in taking money from brothers and sisters who are fed up with having to live in such a sick society, and who could use some *honest* advice. Because psychiatrists emphasize "adjustment" and conformity rather than liberation, because they tell us to become good citizens rather than good revolutionaries, because they favor individual solutions rather than social change, we recognize that they are not the helpers of homosexuals or any oppressed people, but serve our oppressors.

4. Culture.

Although we have certainly contributed to this country's cultural life as a group we have been robbed of our culture. The culture of any period is defined by a ruling elite; and the rulers of Amerika have defined homosexuals as outcasts. The culture available to us is clearly heterosexual and alienating to us. Athletics are based upon men competing with each other, one winning at the other's expense; while homosexual men relate by loving each other, not by competition. In movies or on TV, women are always shown as objects of the love (?) of men, but homosexual women love each other; and the standards of female beauty, defined by society as what *men* want, is irrelevant to lesbians. Art, books, plays don't relate to homosexuality except in trying to say how bad it is. As individuals we are prevented from cultural expression, for sexuality cannot be suppressed without suppression of personality at the same time. And our sexuality must be suppressed because of the legal, economic and social penalties for it. We see culture not as the output of a few great men and women, but as a possession of all people and as activities (whether sports, hobbies or arts) which all people can participate in. In spite of the restrictions homosexuals have, in fact, become artists, athletes, writers, but the masses of homosexuals have had no benefit from this fact. We have had to depend on the ruling elites who have taken over our talents and used them for their own profit, like the Kennedys who decorated their court with Gore Vidal. This is an expropriation of our cultural resources. We refuse to entertain them any longer with "camp" for their profit.

5. Class status and homosexuality.

Homosexuals from the proletariat (whether working-class or lumpen) lead a particularly prison-like, straight-jacketed existence. Because of their particular relationship (actual or potential) to production, the custom is to marry at a young age. It is not surprising that white working-class communities are among the most up-tight about homosexuals due to the role of the family structure in the capitalist mode of production. Homosexuals from these communities often marry and have children before discovering their homosexuality. All the doors that can be opened by middle-class privilege are closed. The women cannot afford to follow their homosexual preferences; they are tied economically to men due to the low salaries and restricted job opportunities open to women in general. The men cannot afford divorce, support of their family and the expense of setting up a new life as a homosexual. Nor can they afford the notoriously high legal fees used to pay off the pigs, which keep middle-class and wealthy homosexuals out of jail.

6. Sexual capitalism.

a. Social attitudes: The most frequently described grievance is the prejudice most homosexuals find in heterosexuals. Anti-homosexual feeling among the masses of Americans cannot be our ultimate problem; in fact straight people too are harmed by rigid, stereotyped ideas about sex and sex-roles. These ideas can only persist because of the institutions which support them: news media, entertainment media, schools, medical establishment, etc. These institutions are not owned by the people, and only a small minority profit from them. Certainly the masses of American people receive no long-range benefits from their contempt for homosexuals.

b. Psychological attitudes: Possibly the most devastating aspect of these attitudes is that we learn them ourselves during our "formative years" and are therefore filled with self-contempt when we become homosexual. In American society, we are taught that people are supposed to get what they *deserve* rather than what they *need*. It is a "meritocracy," not a democracy. Translated into sexual life, we see how this defeats us. Through advertising and the entertainment media, artificial standards of beauty are learned and internalized. Youth, white Aryan aggressive "masculinity" and submissive "femininity" are constantly stressed. We begin to act as though only certain "types" who approach these phony standards *deserve* our love and sexual attention, and we become more and more unresponsive to people's *needs* for love and sex. We respond to what "turns us on," and we have learned to be "turned on" by merit and not by other's needs. Taking on, as individuals, the ethic of the capitalist system which despises the needs of the people, especially the poor and oppressed, we act against our own long-run interests. Those who do not approach the stereotypes because they may be older, homely, physically deformed, etc., may be among the most miserable and lonely people in society. And we do not even have the family structure which helps most people to help these lonely persons forget how unhappy they are.

I.D., LEADERSHIP AND VIOLENCE

Charles P. Thorp

This is the text of the Keynote Speech for The National Gay Liberation Front Student Conference, August 21, 1970, San Francisco, California.

Sisters and Brothers,
   This around you concretely is San Francisco where the last *Pink Floyd* concert started by the group coming on stage and saying, "I've been Gay all my life and you'd better be ready for this set," and no one was. I'd like that as my opening comment.

I.D.
Gay Vs. Homosexual
   As we begin to see who we are, we've got to see that little seemingly unimportant details such as words and labels tell a story, a fairytale of sorts. So let me say a little about "Gay" as *opposed* to "Homosexual." They are opposites, and not just two words expressing similar objects, because only one talks about objects. In order to understand these words we must understand that this society is a multi-cultured one, but in reality it recognizes only one culture, the others are under genocidal attack. Webster's Abridged Dictionary, which sets standards for this one "official culture," the silent majority culture, accepts for the Black

American the scientific term Negro and the derogatory term Nigger. A study of Gay produces similar results in word usage: the scientific term Homosexual and the derogatory term Queer. Those who say they like the word Homosexual better than Gay say in essence they accept our sick-psychiatrist friends' definition of us. They also miss out on the difference between the words. Homosexual is a straight concept of us as sexual. Therefore, we are in a *sexual* category and become a sexual minority and are dealt with in this way legally, socially, economically, and culturally...rather than as an ethnic group, a people! But the word Gay has come to mean (by street usage) a life style in which we are not just sex machines; when something goes wrong it is not blamed on our sexuality alone. We are whole entities, and breakdowns economically may not always be the cause of our sexuality and if our sexuality does enter into it, it is only the oppression, not the sexuality which is of importance. Also important is that the word Black was once held in contempt by the Black community and society, but is now looked on as a proud distinction. It was found by the Blacks that what was a "hate weapon" in the hands of others could become in their own hands, a weapon of pride, of even greater strength, when behind the trigger is a dedication stronger than hate. So now for us it is a beautiful thing to be blatent where as at one time it was looked down upon. We have come to see that it is the fairies, faggots, queens, etc. that were, through their blatentness, the first to challenge the system. In essence, saying they had a right to be Super-Gay because Blatent is Beautiful. We also know that it will not be until what straights call "blatent behavior" is accepted with respect that we are in any sense, any of us, free. For it is Blatent Faggotry that they really hate. We are all blatent, unless we're ashamed of being Gay, and this is why we are all hated. We are all hated as part of the blatent myth of our mysterious corruption of manhood and childhood. Also deep back in their minds is the fact that we must completely change the social structure to have any kind of reasonable justice. So where does Gay come from. We hear so much about the Geisha girls. Well, the word Gei (pronounced Gay) means a person of the arts. Isn't it true we've had most of our known history in the arts and also most of our acceptance in the arts? In fact, isn't it more honest to say Gay is Creativity, rather the Gay is Good? Gay is a life-style. It is how we live. It is our oppression. It is our Tiffany lamps and our guns. Gay is our history and the history we are just beginning to become.[1]

1. Article / "Gay: Semantic History" (a critique of Reed Severin's "Advocate" article). Authored by Charles P. Thorp.

Establishment Thinking

Now that we see the depth of control and oppression, let's explore the establishment's thinking a little more. It is the straight establishment that has tried to quench its thirst with our blood, and now we find "good Queers" eating up the crap that straights drop on us and then thanking master for token-life. What we must keep in mind is that the enemy is straight society, not Gay. Straights have been our masters for 4000 years; and it has been only a few years that Gays have organized to play the role of pacifying agents. The straight establishment has taken any notion of identity from us by trick-or-treating us into believing that we are a sexual entity, therefore, we'll suck cock and be quiet. (You will see it is hard to speak with a cock in the mouth.) Also, this helps in their minds to put them in the right no matter how they treat us. For in our Judeo-Christian society the only way one may kill and treat his neighbor like dirt is to reduce his official standing to less-than-human or to that of animal. If the "other society" can believe that we are a sexual entity (which they do believe: notice it is only *illegal* to perform a homosexual act and not to be homosexual), then they may think of us as animals and treat us as they wish. I'm sure you've heard the phrase time and again: "You're just animals; all you think about is sex." It is important to notice that animal is equated with sex. Also it is important to notice how many people think of us as "its." This is their way of linking us to the animal world, for an animal can be eaten in a civilized world, but not humans. So our people are killed and their bodies and souls eaten until there is no existence for us. Through the confessional, straights have called us sinners, and through sterile medical doors, called us sick. But through sick and through sin, they really mean *sex*. And if their attitudes are changing now, it is only because they believe they must treat animals "humanely." Gays too have adopted the belief that we are purely physical, and this is why so many envision a brotherhood as nonsense. You hear so many gays tell the young revolutionaries, "I can't agree with your views, but how about coming up to my place for a cup of coffee?" This too is part of the reason that appearance is so important, in fact looks are drawn in importance till they are a caricature-significance. The reason for so many married homosexuals is not only because they feel pressured into looking straight for the sake of capturing a few moments of neurotic security, but also because they don't realize that they are copping-out on the brothers and sisters. They believe that homosexuality is exactly that: Homo—sex—uality. And they refuse to see that they are turning their backs on a whole life-style that it is their obligation to develop. We are Homosexual-Sapiens (how's that for a scientific bag?) not just physical entities. One of the most effective tactics that straights use on us is our own belief that we are sexual entities; that way we can be easily kept in "our place." Our place being the three Big B's: the Bars, the Beaches and the Baths. These are to keep us happy, controlled and patrolled. Also the straights perform their "pervert hunts" (equal to Salem easily), shame us and kill a few to keep the "flock" down. Then back at the homestead the "men" pump the women full of little perverts to be thrashed for another generation: except that this is where it all ends!

THIS PUNISHING OF OUR PEOPLE EITHER *ENDS* OR (AS IT WAS IN NEW YORK AND SO IT SHALL BE . . .) *THE FIRE NEXT TIME!!* . . . to quote James Baldwin.

One of the other tactics used by straights is that of suicide; in this way straights have proof of their sick-sin theory and also eliminate some of us. This is accomplished by educating us to believe that we are unnatural, worthless, and then they lead us to the cliffs where they will do everything in their power to make us jump except push!

Gay Liberation has been made up mostly of young Gays, because, as in the rest of society, it is *young* Gays, as it is young Blacks or young white radicals, it is the young that are *aware* and aware is synonymous with *desperate*. That means a new culture, a new society and a new education. This has scared the don't-rock-the-boat older Gays. They believe, and possibly very rightly so, that the establishment will come down on our backs. So the Gay Estab-in-the-back-lishment will try to prevent us from doing our freedom in the ass, but we can't stop because it feels too good. We could care less about the consequences because we have more to do than spend seven days in bed trying to get a piece. To quote Sister Morrison . . . "We want the world, AND WE WANT IT *NOW!*" [2]

Talkin' at Work: Oppression can be very subtle; for instance a conversation I had at work with some straight workers. The dig went:

Boy 1: I could use a chick.

Black girl: Everyone needs a chick.

Boy 2: Not Charles.

Me: I heard that. It isn't just Charles that doesn't need a chick. There are 13 million others and there are 9 million women that

2. Manifesto / "*A Gay Liberation Manifesto*": Establishment thinking. Authored by Charles P. Thorp.

don't need men and that makes 22 million of us that don't need any of you.

SO WHO ARE WE: First we're all Closet Queens—or babies.

Closet Queens: Closet Queens are our people hiding in Plato's legendary cave afraid to step into the light. We cannot expect them to "come out" unless those who are strongest make the way safer for those who are too sensitive. But also they must remember this is not the age of "Tea and Sympathy" anymore. As Sister Jagger says, you can have "Coke and Sympathy" and she doesn't mean Raquel Welch. Closet Queens need someone to bleed on, and Honey tell them they can bleed on us. But I'm tired of hearing money always used as an out. It makes me sick to hear "Gay Marriage" (the bastard child of Straight Respectability) justified in terms of economics. Something is wrong when dollars come up . From a poem:

I'm tired Amerika of your
castration of yourself
and my people/turned
us all into TV's
trans(invest)ites . . . [3]

Gay Liberation Front: And when We become Gay Liberation we must demand that we are accepted as such and not let it ride along with our families and friends for the sake of "family-peace" and untroubled existence (there is no such thing). That is liberalism and death to your movement in life and ours also. In a poem my mother is asked of me or more specifically the Virgin Mary is asked of Christ;

. . . but if he died on a cross
4-Gay Liberation
wood-she love him
separate from his actions
or would she love
his hole [4]

We must recognize the dead things such as our family and not let them pass easily, because they are out of our ethnocentric scope. We are not they any more. It was obvious to me when, after not

---

3. Poem / "i'm tired . . . i want to fuck Amerika (not be fucked over)." Authored by Charles P. Thorp.

4. Poem / "His christian Mother / er" 3/8/70. Authored by Charles P. Thorp.

seeing my little brother for quite some time, he came to visit and we had nothing to say. I wanted to say, "lay with boys, don't carry a basketball to school carry a gun," I said *nothing* and he said *nothing*;

> . . . *i don't recognize my family-brother*
> *(playing-football-feeling-up-the-chicks)*
> *for the society that is committing*
> *genocide*
> *on my people*
> *has made heroin out of his thoughts . . .*[5]

and made me;

> . . . *want to lock my brother in a room*
>   *with a twelve-year-old gay*
>   *rapist*
> *i want his ass sore*
> *i want his mouth sore*
> *i want his breath free again*
>   *the SAD STRAIGHT SOCIETY has dulled*
>   *sense*
>   *in my brother . . .*[6]

Get away from the desensitized straightworld. Do not stand among the falling ruins. CREATE. MOVE. Do not be killed as its institutions are falling to the ground; save your souls. Get away from marriage. Get away from family-tightness. When it all goes under you either better have been helping build upon Atlantis or be close enough to jump to this new life and new continent.

A Myth Without Heroes

We are much myth. Mostly destructive myth. We are part of the myth that I call "the great magneticwash" *i.e.* that opposites attract and negatives repel. This is instilled as scientific fact from the time you are very young so that when you are older you look at a trick/lover and say "that repels me" (scientifically speaking of course). But that does not stop one from the drive toward a love-sex drive deep within. But the contradictions go deeper and are more complex, but this little scientific law is important because

---

5. Poem / "Brother-meat." Authored by Charles P. Thorp.
6. Poem / "Brother-meat." Authored by Charles P. Thorp.

science in its pseudo-forms has tried in this enlightened age to use science as proof of or in place of sin. The new form is called sickness. So science in all its Mesozoic miracle work invents electric-shock therapy—castration to cure its patients, whose sickness is love and life with the same sex. Those who claim cure are without a doubt destroyers who melt away the brain or reduce us to a Pavlovian dog. Robert Fox, talking on the new machine methods of teaching foreign language, gives us a good insight into these cure-psychologists' main error. He says:

. . . Learning is treated by these pedagogues as nothing more than controlled responses to external stimuli, an organism "interacting" with its environment.

All areas of academic speculation having been permeated by this erroneous concept of nature, it is not surprising that the pedagogy of foreign-language learning also has surrendered to the "controlled response" domination. Still, the theory has some curious results in the field of language. The new methods of foreign-language instruction seems, superficially viewed, to "work"; their advocates profess to have enjoyed impressive successes. And a certain success is possible, given the unfortunate ability of a human person to reduce himself, for a time, to the condition of a mere animal organism. Quite as certain animals and certain machines can be made to talk even though they cannot think, so a human being can be persuaded to talk without thinking, occasionally with a high degree of fluency.[7]

So they cure our animal and kill our soul. These curers must be destroyed once and for all. Another important part of myth is the "child-destroyer-myth" which I think is adequately answered:

. . . Amerika i'm tired of your
    whole "i'm frightened
    for my children" jive
    (we are your children)[8]

As for straights that belong in the rape-myth category, i.e. those that say, "Oh I don't mind if that's your trip just as long as you don't touch me," I'd like to quote from a poem:

7. Article / from *The University Bookman* Quarterly Review Vol. VII No. 3 copyright Spring 1967. "Thought Control and The Teaching of Language." Authored by Robert W. Fox.
8. Poem / "i'm tired . . . i want to fuck Amerika (not be fucked over)." Authored by Charles P. Thorp.

Your:
. . . guilt:
you think we're going to
  rape you-
you know straight boy
  i want to rape your
  ass
  i want to rape your
  soul
i want to hang your balls-
  (in my mouth-rope)
i want to Knife your heart-
  (fill it with come-fill it
  with love . . .[9]

So the straight world doesn't believe we exist in reality because they have covered their naked-homosexual-feelings with myth and procreate each upcoming Gay generation with the same old stomach-to-stomach myths. Like 1001 nights until death, their fairytail, drags-(T.V.'s) across ours-and-their lives slowly onward . . . And as we grow up in myth we find it has no heroes or does it? Well, none that they (the other) will let us claim without struggle or at least without totally degrading until they no longer are heroes. It is hoped that G.L.F. will find our heroes and educate the masses about their contributions. But, I have one I dug out of my soul. I'd like to tell you our story in the form of poetry. The title is, "HeShe surface/survive we," it reads:

We did not seek
  the underground
  like rabbits
  timid from birth
we were called passive pansies
  now we come to the surface
  to redefine ourselves
we are violent fairies
  each of us has that hate
  for those that in Poe-like
  fashion buried our souls alive
we were driven
  from the sun that

9. Poem / "(we shall) overcome." Authored by Charles P. Thorp.

we should never
  see it as the light
  of ourselves
  that we should see
  only in whispers
  and that
we should never know of
  heroes for
we were to be enemies of the State
  and but half-lovers of our Community
we need not have sympathy for our devil
  HeShe rises to be light upon
  all mountains
  where never again will
we be hidden undersight
  for through and with HeShe our devil-god
we are all of us together to be reborn

Leadership and Violence

Once we realize ourselves we realize our oppression. And once we realize our oppression we must deal with it. There is the possibility of ignoring it . . . for ten cents folks you can step right in the street tent and watch your sisters and brothers die . . . or you can call for non-violent reformism or finally call for revolution. Frantz Fanon says this of the choice, our politics should be:

. . . national, revolutionary, and social and those new facts which the native will now come to know exist only in action. They are the essence of the fight which explodes the old colonial truths and reveals unexpected facets, which brings out new meanings and pinpoints the contradictions camouflaged by these facts. The people engaged in the struggle who because of it command and know these facts, go forward, freed from colonialism and forewarned of all attempts at mystification, inoculated against all national anthems. Violence alone, violence committed by the people, violence organized and educated by its leaders, makes it possible for the masses to understand social truths and gives the Key to them. Without that struggle, without that knowledge of the practice of action, there's nothing but a fancy-dress parade and the blare of the trumpets. There's nothing save a minimum of readaptation, a few reforms at the top, a flag waving: and down there at the bottom an undivided mass, still living in the middle ages, endlessly marking time.[10]

So I see little choice, but revolution. I never saw any choice, but to fight for freedom, for people, for *our* people.
Mao says:

As far as our own desire is concerned, we don't want to fight a single day. But if circumstances force us to fight, we can fight to the finish.[11]

I said similarly in poetry,

Revolution means community
if we must have these by blood
then let me carry a Knife
if not let me walk naked
if so let me have rifle and Knife
if not let me walk in the sun . . .[12]

What is a revolution? I have heard so many people call themselves revolutionaries and yet could watch the soul and body of a sister or brother stomped and react with statements of calmness and non-violence.
   I'd like to quote Mao once again. He says:

A revolution is not a dinner party, or writing an essay, or painting a picture, or doing embroidery; it cannot be so refined, so leisurely and gentle, so temperate, kind, courteous, restrained and magnanimous. A revolution is an insurrection, an act of violence . . .[13]

So I assert once again, I want not to fight but I will until I am placed back into my river form—until I am water. But does violence only commit destruction? Is it but one side of the birth-death cycle? Jean-Paul Sartre says:

The rebel's weapon is proof of his humanity. For in the first days of the revolt you must kill: to shoot down a European is to kill two birds with one stone, to destroy an oppressor and the man he

   10. Book / *The Wretched of the Earth*, page 147. Chapter on "Spontaneity: Its Strength and Weakness." Grove Press Inc. Authored by Frantz Fanon.
   11. Book / *Quotations of Chairman Mao*. Chapter on "Dare to Struggle Dare to Win." Authored by Mao Tse-Tung.
   12. Poem / "Revolution means Community." Authored by Charles P. Thorp.
   13. Book / *Quotations of Chairman Mao*. Chapter on "Classes and Class Struggle." Authored by Mao Tse-Tung.

oppresses at the same time: there remain a dead man, and a free man . . .[14]

So Sartre tells us there are two natures to violence, whereas our leaders are telling us the same jive that the enemy is telling us; "don't hate nothin' at all except hatred" (Bob Dylan). Our leadership would do well to remember what Mao says; "Leaders must march ahead of the movement, not lag behind it." So far the leaders have consistently been behind in action of where the people are at. The leaders must lead—if the spontaneity of the people is toward violent acts then the leaders should lead the people successfully to the victory in these acts. Leaders should not try to determine the people against violence or try to confuse the violence of their souls, but instead be light for their path (for it is a long heavy path that must be followed).

Frantz Fanon says, "At the level of individuals, violence is a cleansing force." So it is that I wrote my first poem affirming that Gays would struggle for life and not let "passive-genocide" as was committed upon Jews, be their fate. A part of that poem talks to straights warning:

> . . . we are bursting
>   we are dreams
>   we are bursting dreams
>   you will not escape in sleep
>   for violent fairies will
>   visit you even in your dreams and
>   castrate you at night
>   as you have castrated so
>   many of my people . . .[15]

So to the leaders of the movement who still can't tell the people from the pigs; I speak to you in rhythmed-tongue:
> . . . we are
> all aware (within the Community)
> who the pigs are
>
> Their death is our survival
> if you know no differences then
> do not take up a gun, but please

14. Essay / "Introduction" to *Wretched of the Earth* by Frantz Fanon. Authored by J. P. Sartre.

15. Poem / "(we shall) over come." Authored by Charles P. Thorp.

do take up our souls and lead us either
in the Snake Pit: we were born
        crawl out
the world awaits Your bite[16]

I will not stand by and watch our people die. There needs to be struggle. There needs to be revenge committed against the enemy for both the dead and the living. Frank Bartley and Larry Turner were not Martyr, they were Murder, and senselessly at that. Will we stop these murders in our community or are we to sit and wait for them to be stopped out of the love of straights for dead Gays. Are we to fast Reverend Perry when much of our community, especially our children, is selling its ass on the street to keep from starvation. Violent Fairies rise in defense of your community. Those of us who are revolutionaries and are not reformists ". . . also believe in (our) community and want no more blood and tears shed. In this count we will not sit as passive pansies (we are "violent fairies"). We will not watch the government slaughter our people and kill their pride. We will struggle. Violence as a means of oppression is being used and we are told we must accept that. Bullshit. If violence shall oppress us so shall it liberate. Our Community is a Community of Lovers and because of oppression we've become an Army of Lovers.

And dig it—we'll win . . ."[17]

ALL POWER TO THE PEOPLE—RIGHT ON!!!

WHAT WE WANT, WHAT WE BELIEVE

Third World Gay Revolution (New York City)

Our straight sisters and brothers must recognize and support that we, gay women and men, are equal in every way within the revolutionary ranks.

We each organize our people about different issues, but our struggles are the same against oppression, and we will defeat it together. Once we understand these struggles, and gain a love for our sisters and brothers involved in these struggles, we must learn how best to become involved in them.

16. Poem / "Snake Pit Shit" 7/24/70. Authored by Charles P. Thorp.
17. Letter / *To The Editor "Advocate"* July 8-21, 1970. Authored by Charles P. Thorp.

The struggles of the peoples of the world are our fight as well; their victories are our victories and our victories are theirs. Our freedom will come only with their freedom.

Together, not alone, we must explore how we view ourselves, and analyze the assumptions behind our self-identity. We can then begin to crack the barriers of our varying illnesses, our passivity, sexual chauvinism—in essence, our inability to unabashedly love each other, to live, fight, and if necessary, die for the people of the earth.

As we begin to understand our place in this international revolution, and join with others in this understanding, we must develop the skills necessary to destroy the forces of repression and exploitation, so as to make it possible for a new woman and man to evolve in a society based on communal love.

While we understand that in the United States our main enemy is the socio-economic-political system of capitalism and the people who make profits off our sufferings, fights and divisions, we also recognize that we must struggle against any totalitarian, authoritarian, sex-controlled, repressive, irrational, reactionary, fascist government or government machine.

What We Want:
What We Believe:

1. We want the right of self-determination for all Third World and gay people, as well as control of the destinies of our communities.

We believe that Third World and gay people cannot be free until we are able to determine our own destinies.

2. We want the right of self-determination over the use of our bodies: the right to be gay, anytime, anyplace; the right to free physiological change and modification of sex on demand; the right to free dress and adornment.

We believe that these are human rights which must be defended with our bodies being put on the line. The system as it now exists denies these basic human rights by implementing forced heterosexuality.

3. We want liberation for all women: We want free and safe birth control information and devices on demand. We want free 24-hour child care centers controlled by those who need and use them. We want a redefinition of education and motivation (especially for Third World women) towards broader educational opportunities without limitations because of sex. We want truthful teaching of women's history. We want an end to hiring practices

which make women and national minorities 1) a readily available source of cheap labor; and 2) confined to mind-rotting jobs under the worst conditions.

We believe that the struggles of all oppressed groups under any form of government which does not meet the true needs of its people will eventually result in the overthrow of that government. The struggle for liberation of women is a struggle to be waged by all peoples. We must also struggle within ourselves and within our various movements to end this oldest form of oppression and its foundation—male chauvinism. We cannot develop a truly liberating form of socialism unless we fight these tendencies.

4. We want full protection of the law and social sanction for all human sexual self-expression and pleasure between consenting persons, including youth. We believe that present laws are oppressive to Third World people, gay people, and the masses. Such laws expose the inequalities of capitalism, which can only exist in a state where there are oppressed people or groups. This must end.

5. We want the abolition of the institution of the bourgeois nuclear family.

We believe that the bourgeois nuclear family perpetuates the false categories of homosexuality and heterosexuality by creating sex roles, sex definitions and sexual exploitation. The bourgeois nuclear family as the basic unit of capitalism creates oppressive roles of homosexuality and heterosexuality. All oppressions originate within the nuclear family structure. Homosexuality is a threat to this family structure and therefore to capitalism. The mother is an instrument of reproduction and teaches the necessary values of capitalist society, i.e., racism, sexism, etc., from infancy on. The father physically enforces (upon the mother and children) the behavior necessary in a capitalist system: intelligence and competitiveness in young boys and passivity in young girls. Further, it is every child's right to develop in a non-sexist, non-racist, non-possessive atmosphere which is the responsibility of all people, including gays, to create.

6. We want a free non-compulsory education system that teaches us our true identity and history, and presents the entire range of human sexuality without advocating any one form or style; that sex roles and determination of skills according to sex be eliminated from the school system; that language be modified so that no gender takes priority; and that gay people must share in the responsibilities of education.

We believe that we have been taught to compete with our sisters and brothers for power, and from that competitive attitude grows sexism, racism, male and national chauvinism and distrust of our sisters and brothers. As we begin to understand these things within ourselves, we attempt to free ourselves of them and are moved toward a revolutionary consciousness.

7. We want guaranteed full equal employment for Third World and gay people at all levels of production.

We believe that any system of government is responsible for giving every woman and man a guaranteed income or employment, regardless of sex or sexual preference. Being interested only in profits, capitalism cannot meet the needs of the people.

8. We want decent and free housing, fit shelter for human beings.

We believe that free shelter is a basic need and right which must not be denied on any grounds. Landlords are capitalists, and, like all capitalists, are motivated only by the accumulation of profits, as opposed to the welfare of the people.

9. We want to abolish the existing judicial system. We want all Third World and gay people when brought to trial, to be tried by people's court with a jury of their peers. A peer is a person from similar social, economic, geographical, racial, historical, environmental, and sexual background.

We believe that the function of the judicial system under capitalism is to uphold the ruling class and keep the masses under control.

10. We want the reparation for and release of all Third World, gay and all political prisoners from jails and mental institutions.

We believe that these people should be released because they have not received fair and impartial trials.

11. We want the abolition of capital punishment, all forms of institutional punishment, and the penal system.

We want the establishment of psychiatric institutions for the humane treatment and rehabilitation of criminal persons as decided by the people's court. We want the establishment of a sufficient number of free and non-compulsory clinics for the treatment of sexual disturbances, as defined by the individual.

12. We want an immediate end to the fascist police force.

We believe that the only way this can be accomplished is by putting the defense of the people in the hands of the people.

13. We want all Third World and gay men to be exempt from compulsory military service in the imperialist army. We want an end to military oppression both at home and abroad.

We believe that the only true army for oppressed people is the people's army, and Third World, gay people, and women should have full participation in the People's Revolutionary Army.

14. We want an end to all institutional religions because they aid in genocide by teaching superstition and hatred of Third World people, homosexuals and women. We want a guarantee of freedom to express natural spirituality.

We believe that institutionalized religions are an instrument of capitalism, therefore an enemy of the People.

15. We demand immediate non-discriminatory open admission/membership for radical homosexuals into all left-wing revolutionary groups and organizations and the right to caucus.

We believe that so-called comrades who call themselves "revolutionaries" have failed to deal with their sexist attitudes. Instead they cling to male supremacy and therefore to the conditioned role of oppressors. Men still fight for the privileged position of man-on-the-top. Women quickly fall in line behind-their-men. By their counterrevolutionary struggle to maintain and to force heterosexuality and the nuclear family, they perpetuate decadent remnants of capitalism. To gain their anti-homosexual stance, they have used the weapons of the oppressor, thereby becoming the agent of the oppressor.

It is up to men to realistically define masculinity, because it is they, who, throughout their lives, have struggled to gain the unrealistic roles of "men." Men have always tried to reach this precarious position by climbing on the backs of women and homosexuals. "Masculinity" has been defined by capitalist society as the amount of possessions (including women) a man collects, and the amount of physical power gained over other men. Third World men have been denied even these false standards of "masculinity." Anti-homosexuality fosters sexual repressions, male-supremacy, weakness in revolutionary drive, and results in an inaccurate non-objective political perspective. Therefore, we believe that all left-wing revolutionary groups and organizations must immediately establish non-discriminatory, open admission/membership policies.

16. We want a new society—a revolutionary socialist society. We want liberation of humanity, free food, free shelter, free clothing, free transportation, free health care, free utilities, free education, free art for all. We want a society where the needs of the people come first.

We believe that all people should share the labor and products of society, according to each one's needs and abilities, regardless of race, sex, age, or sexual preferences. We believe the land, technology, and the means of production belong to the people, and must be shared by the people collectively for the liberation of all.

PHOTOGRAPH BY DIANNA DAVIES

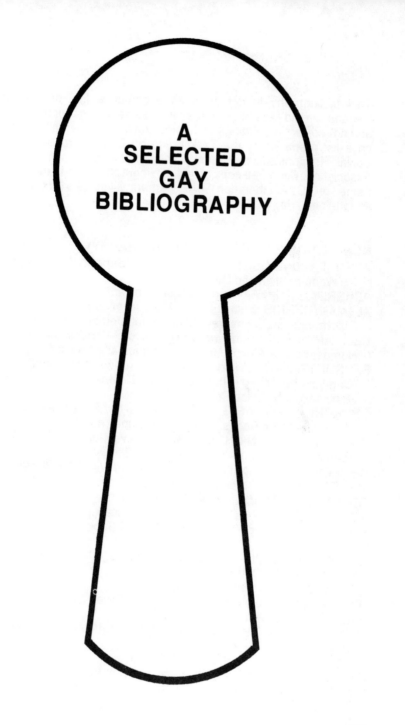

A
SELECTED
GAY
BIBLIOGRAPHY

This bibliography is not seen as a complete list, or even a "recommended" list, but rather as a cross-section of some recent and not-so-recent readings on homosexuality. It is partially based on a list prepared by the Task Force on Gay Liberation of the Social Responsibilities Round Table of the American Library Association. For a free copy of their bibliography, write to the Task Force on Gay Liberation, c/o Barbara Gittings, Box 2383, Philadelphia, Pa. 19103.

NON-FICTION (INCLUDING AUTOBIOGRAPHY)

ABBOTT, SIDNEY, and LOVE, BARBARA. *Sappho Was A Right On Woman*. Stein and Day, 1972.

ACKERLY, J.R. *My Father and Myself.* Coward, McCann, 1969.

ALTMAN, DENNIS. *Homosexual: Oppression and Liberation.* Outerbridge and Dienstfrey, 1971. Distributed by E.P. Dutton.

BELL, ARTHUR. *Dancing the Gay Lib Blues: A Year in the Homosexual Liberation Movement.* Simon and Shuster, 1971.

BENSON, R.O. *What Every Homosexual Knows.* Ace, paper. (Originally published in hardcover as *In Defense of Homosexuality*, Julian Press, 1965.)

CHURCHILL, WAINWRIGHT. *Homosexual Behavior Among Males.* Hawthorn Books, 1967. Prism, paper, 1971.

CLARK, LIGE, and NICHOLS, JACK. *I Have More Fun With You Than Anybody.* St. Martin's Press, 1972.

DE BECKER, RAYMOND. *The Other Face of Love.* Grove, 1969.

FISHER, PETER. *The Gay Mystique.* Stein and Day, 1972.

GENET, JEAN. *Thief's Journal.* Grove, 1964.

GERASSI, JOHN. *The Boys of Boise.* Macmillan, paper, 1968.

HOFFMAN, MARTIN. *The Gay World.* Basic Books, 1968. Bantam, paper.

HUMPHREYS, LAUD. *Tearoom Trade.* Aldine-Atherton, 1970.

HYDE, H. MONTGOMERY. *Famous Trials No. 9: The Trial of Roger Casement,* Penguin Books.

HYDE, H. MONTGOMERY. *The Love That Dared Not Speak Its Name.* Little, Brown, 1970.

HYDE, H. MONTGOMERY. *Oscar Wilde: The Aftermath.* Farrar, Straus, 1963.

LEDUC, VIOLETTE. *La Batarde.* Dell, 1967.

MILLER, MERLE. *On Being Different.* Random House, 1971.

MURPHY, JOHN. *Homosexual Liberation: A Personal View.* Praeger, 1971.

OBERHOLTZER, W. DWIGHT, ed. *Is Gay Good?* Westminster Press, 1971.

ONGE, JACK. *The Gay Liberation Movement.* Alliance Press, 1971. (order for $1.50 from Alliance Press, 741 Briar Pl., Chicago, Ill. 60657.)

PITTENGER, W. NORMAN. *Making Sexuality Human.* Pilgrim Press, 1970.

PITTENGER, W. NORMAN. *A Time for Consent.* SCM Press, Ltd., 1970. (order for $1.15 from Morehouse-Barlow Co., 14 E. 41 St., New York, N.Y. 10017.)

RICHMOND, LEN, and NOGUERA, GARY. *The Gay Liberation Book: Writings by Gay Men.* Ramparts Press, 1972.

TEAL, DONN. *The Gay Militants.* Stein and Day, 1971.

TOBIN, KAY, and WICKER, RANDY. *The Gay Crusaders.* Paperback Library, 1972.

WESTWOOD, GORDON. *Society and the Homosexual.* Dutton, 1953.

WILLIAMS, COLIN J., WEINBERG, MORTON S. *Homosexuality and the Military: A Study of Less than Honorable Discharge.* Harper and Row, 1971.

WINANT, FRAN. *Looking at Women.* Violet Press, 1971. (Order for fifty cents and ten cents postage from Violet Press, Box 398, New York, N.Y. 10009.)

FICTION

BALDWIN, JAMES. *Giovanni's Room.* Dial, 1962. Dell, paper, 1970.

FORSTER, E.M. *Maurice.* Norton, 1971.

GENET, JEAN. *The Miracle of the Rose.* Grove, 1968.

GENET, JEAN. *Our Lady of the Flowers.* Grove, 1963. Bantam, paper, 1970.

HALL, RADCLYFFE. *The Well of Loneliness.* Pocket Books, 1959. (originally published, 1928)

KING, LOUISE. *The Day We Were Mostly Butterflies.* Doubleday, 1964.

KING, LOUISE. *The Velocipede Handicap.* Doubleday, 1966.

MILLER, ISABEL. *Patience and Sarah.* McGraw Hill, 1972.

MORGAN, CLAIRE. *The Price of Salt.* McFadden-Bartel, 1968.

RECHY, JOHN. *City of Night.* Grove, 1964.

RULE, JANE. *Against the Season.* McCall, 1971.

RULE, JANE. *The Desert of the Heart.* McCall, 1969.

RULE, JANE. *This Is Not for You.* McCall, 1970.
   Gay readers should become familiar with the Oscar Wilde
   Memorial Bookshop, 291 Mercer St., New York, N.Y. 10003,
   phone 212-673-3539. Write for their current catalogue. Also
   write for the price list of the Gay Liberation Book Service, Box
   40397, San Francisco, Calif. 94140.

RELATED READINGS IN FEMINISM

GORNICK, VIVIAN, and MORAN, BARBARA K., eds. *Women in
   Sexist Society: Studies in Power and Powerlessness.* Basic
   Books, 1971.
MILLETT, KATE. *Sexual Politics.* Doubleday, 1970. Avon, paper,
   1971.
MORGAN, ROBIN, ed. *Sisterhood Is Powerful.* Random House,
   1971.

GAY PERIODICALS (NOT INCLUDING NEWSLETTERS OF THE VARIOUS GAY ORGANIZATIONS)

The Advocate / P.O. Box 74695
   Los Angeles, Calif. 90004 / Biweekly.
The Body Politic / Kensington Ave., Toronto,
   Ontario, Canada / Sample copy available for 35 cents.
Come Out / Box 233 Times Sq. Station
   New York, New York 10036 / Quarterly. Sample copy
   and back issues, 50 cents each.
Faggotry / c/o Templar Press, Box 98,
   F.D.R. Station, New York, New York 10022
   Sample copy available for 50 cents.
Fag Rag / c/o Red Book / 91 River Street
   Cambridge, Mass. 02139/ Sample copy available for 35 cents.
Focus: A Journal for Gay Women / c/o D.O.B.
   /419 Boylston Street / Boston, Mass. 02116 / Monthly
The Furies / Box 8843, South East Station
   Washington, D.C. 20003
Gay / P.O. Box 431, Old Chelsea Sta.
   New York, New York 10011 / Biweekly.
The Gay Blade / 232 North Fillmore Street
   Arlington, Va. 22201
Gay Liberator / Box 631-A
   Detroit, Mich. 48232
Gay Sunshine / Box 40397
   San Francisco, Calif. 94140 / Monthly. Sample copy
   and back issues available for 50 cents.

The Ladder / P.O. Box 5025, Washington Sta.
   Reno, Nev. 89503 / Bi-monthly. Back issues and sample
   copy available for $1.25 each.
The Lesbian Tide / 1124 1/2 North Ogden Drive
   Los Angeles, Calif. 90046
Manroot / Box 982 /
   South San Francisco, Calif. 94080
Nuntius / 4615 Mt. Vernon
   Houston, Tex. 77006 / Monthly
Southern Gay Liberator / P.O. Box 1054
   Delray Beach, Fla. 33444
Proud Woman / Box 8507
   Stanford, Calif. 94305

PHOTOGRAPH BY ELLEN SHUMSKY

Christmas Gift Rates

**First 1 year subscription
(your own or a gift)**

$10

**Each additional 1 year
gift subscription**

$9

PERFORATION

n the United States

First Class
Permit No. 17501
New York, N.Y.

AN
INTERNATIONAL
DIRECTORY
OF GAY
ORGANIZATIONS

Editors' Note: If you cannot contact any group listed here, you can obtain current information about local groups from the following: Gay Sunshine, Box 40397, San Francisco, Calif. 94140, or National Gay Movement Committee, c/o Gay Activists Alliance Box 2 Village Sta., New York, N.Y. 10014.

ALABAMA

Gay People
c/o Left Face
Box 1595
Anniston, Ala. 36201

ARIZONA

Gay Liberation Front
c/o Chuck Ashmore
820 N. 6
Tucson, Ariz. 85705

Gay Liberation Front
c/o Alan Butcher, GSA
1842 N. 12 St.
Phoenix, Ariz. 85006
602-252-8335

Gay Liberation Arizona
Desert (GLAD)
Box 117
Tempe, Ariz. 85281
602-968-2475

Gay Liberation Arizona
Desert (GLAD II)
838 N. 4th Ave.
Tucson, Ariz. 85705

Gay Liberation
c/o People's Center
412 N. 4th Ave.
Tucson, Ariz. 87505

CALIFORNIA

Nova
Box 6184
Albany, Calif. 94706

Gay Liberation Front
Box 3488
Anaheim, Calif. 95351
209-537-7442

Gay People's Project Office
2200 Parker
Berkeley, Calif.
415-845-9630

Gay Women's Liberation
2828 Benvenue
Berkeley, Calif. 94705
415-849-4465

Gay Seminarians (Berkeley)
415-524-0399

The Effeminist
Box 4089
Berkeley, Calif. 94704
415-843-6982

Free Particle
2516 Regent
Berkeley, Calif. 94704
415-845-9017

Gay Students Union
Eshleman Hall, 3rd floor
University of California
Berkeley, Calif. 94720
415-848-4349

Gay Liberation Front of Contra Costa
c/o Gary Allen
1894 Farm Bureau Rd.
Concord, Calif. 94520
415-687-5698

Daughters of Bilitis
Box 193
El Cajon, Calif. 92022

Gay Liberation Front
c/o Art Lopez
2240 N. Van Ness Ave.
Fresno, Calif. 93407

Gay Freedom Alliance / Gay Students Union
P.O. Box 3935
Hayward, Calif. 94544

Gay Students Union
Hayward State College
Hayward, Calif. 94542

Gay Switchboard
c/o Daniel Histo
440 Medford
Hayward, Calif. 94541
415-549-0649

Metropolitan Community Church News
1149 1/2 N. Virgil St.
Hollywood, Calif. 90029

In Unity Magazine (Metropolitan Community Church)
Box 38098
Hollywood, Calif. 90039

UNIDOS (Latin Gays)
c/o Steve Jordan
Box 1154
Huntington Park, Calif. 90255
213-660-0050

Daughters of Bilitis
Box 3237 Hollywood Station
Los Angeles, Calif. 90027

One
2256 Venice Blvd.
Los Angeles, Calif. 90006
213-735-5252

Gay Liberation Front
Box 29280
Los Angeles, Calif. 90029
213-660-2990

Gay Liberation Front
Box 17715
Los Angeles, Calif. 90004
213-665-1881

Gay Community Service Center
1614 Wilshire Blvd.
Los Angeles, Calif.
213-482-3062

Gay Liberation House
1322 Van Ness
Los Angeles, Calif.
213-464-9050

Gay Liberation House
1168 N. Edgemont
Los Angeles, Calif.

Dignity (Gay Catholics)
P.O. Box 6161
Los Angeles, Calif. 90048
213-463-2058

Gay Community Alliance
525 N. Laurel Ave.
Los Angeles, Calif. 90048
213-463-2058

Gay Fellowship
c/o Dick Nash
3338 Andrita St.
Los Angeles, Calif. 90065

Gay Women's Service Center
1542 Glendale Blvd.
Los Angeles, Calif.
213-483-9223

Gay Liberation Front
Occidental College
Box 41035
Los Angeles, Calif. 90041
213-254-9781

Help (Homophile Effort for Legal Protection)
P.O. Box 3007
Los Angeles, Calif. 90028
213-463-3146

Lesbian Feminists
1027 S. Crenshaw Blvd.
Los Angeles, Calif. 90019
213-937-3965

Metropolitan Community Church
2201 S. Union
Los Angeles, Calif. 90007
213-748-0123

Southern California Council on Religion and the Homosexual
3330 W. Adams Blvd.
Los Angeles, Calif. 90018

Society of David
Gay Fellowship in the Arts
701 S. Gramercy
Apt. 120
Los Angeles, Calif. 90005

SPREE
1545 N. Detroit St.
Los Angeles, Calif. 90046

Gay Liberation Front
University of California at Los Angeles
c/o Randy Shrader
2128 Bently Ave.
Los Angeles, Calif. 90025

National League for Social Understanding
7080 Hollywood Blvd.
Los Angeles, Calif. 90006

Prosperos
8840 Evanview Dr.
Los Angeles, Calif. 90068

Tangents
Homosexual Information Center
3473 1/2 N. Cahuenga Blvd.
Los Angeles, Calif. 90028

Gay Liberation Front
1263 Pine Ave.
Long Beach, Calif. 90813
213-463-7710

Gay Liberation Front
c/o Vanich Shatley
1711 Dallas
Modesto, Calif. 95351
209-537-7442

Daughters of Bilitis
Box 727
Manhattan Beach, Calif. 90266

Peninsula Gay Switchboard
383 Miravelle Ave.
Mountain View, Calif. 94040
415-964-7268

San Gabriel Valley Liberation Front
Altadena Community Church
943 E. Altadena
Pasadena, Calif. 91107

Gay Liberation Front
c/o Rob Boblett
3631A Comer Ave.
Riverside, Calif. 92507

Gay Liberation Front
c/o Edgar Carpenter
2215 P St.
Sacramento, Calif. 95816

Association for Responsible Citizenship
Box 895
Sacramento, Calif. 95814

Gay Encounter
Box 15765
Sacramento, Calif. 95813

Gay Liberation Front
Box 2882
San Diego, Calif. 92112

Daughters of Bilitis
3591 Madison Ave.
San Diego, Calif. 92116

Metropolitan Community Church
906 North 47th St.
San Diego, Calif. 92101

Gay Liberation Front
Box 40397
San Francisco, Calif. 94140

Emmaus Group Switchboard
Box 6361
San Francisco, Calif. 94101
415-626-2019

Bay Area Gay Alliance
P.O. Box 40263
San Francisco, Calif. 94140

San Francisco Bay Area Gay Teenagers
c/o Seth 415-548-4190
Gay Sunshine
P.O. Box 40397
San Francisco, Calif. 94140
415-824-3184
San Francisco State Gay Liberation Front
Student Activities Building
San Francisco, Calif. 94132
Institute for the Study of Gay Power
3343 22nd St.
San Francisco, Calif. 94110
415-647-9772
Gay Activists Alliance
Box 1528
San Francisco, Calif. 94101
415-239-9001 or 415-864-8205
Free Gay Student Association
c/o Student Activities
San Francisco City College
San Francisco, Calif.
Lesbian Mothers Union
651 Duncan St.
San Francisco, Calif. 94131
Metropolitan Community Church
Community Center and Switchboard
150 6th St.
San Francisco, Calif. 94103
415-864-3576 or 415-864-3063
Daughters of Bilitis
1005 Market St. Rm. 208
San Francisco, Calif. 94103
415-861-8689
Society for Individual Rights (SIR)
340 9th St.
San Francisco, Calif.
Mattachine Society
348 Ellis St.
San Francisco, Calif. 94102
Council on Religion and the Homosexual
330 Ellis St.
San Francisco, Calif. 94102
Gay Social Organization
Box 298
San Francisco, Calif. 94102
San Francisco Homophile League
1683 Page St.
San Francisco, Calif. 94117

Gay Liberation Front
Box 4087
San Jose, Calif. 95126
408-292-3028

Santa Barbara Gay Liberation Front
U.C.S.B.
900 Embarcadero del Mar Suite B
Isla Vista, Calif. 93017
805-968-0912

Gay Students Union
Sonoma State College
Sonoma, Calif 95476
707-795-9950

Manroot
Box 982
South San Francisco, Calif. 94080

Gay Students Union
Stanford Union Box 9376
Stanford, Calif. 94305

Lavender People
Box 994
Venice, Calif. 90291

COLORADO

Gay Liberation Front
Box 1402
Boulder, Colo. 80302

Daughters of Bilitis
2239 King
Denver, Co. 80211
(mailing address: Box 9057
South Denver Sta.
Denver, Co. 90209)

Gay Youth
c/o Tony Cartwright
1041 Ogden 204
Denver, Co. 80218

Alliance for Homosexual Equality
c/o DeWar
5635 S. Bannock
Littleton, Colo. 80120

CONNECTICUT

Kalos Society—Gay Liberation
796 Grand St.
Bridgeport, Ct. 06604
203-333-5884

Institute of Social Ethics
Box 3417 Central Sta.
Hartford, Ct. 06103

Project "H" Committee
Christ Church Cathedral
45 Church St.
Hartford, Ct. 06103
Kalos Society
Box 572
Hartford, Ct. 06101
203-547-0940
Gay Liberation Front
c/o Hank Major
622 Howard Ave.
New Haven, Ct. 06519
Gay Women's Liberation of New Haven
phone only 203-432-2913

DELAWARE

Human Enlightenment
Box 92 Federal Sta.
Newark, Del. 19711

DISTRICT OF COLUMBIA

National Gay Student Center
2115 S St. N.W.
Washington, D.C. 20008
202-387-5100
Gay Liberation Front
1620 S St. N.W.
Washington, D.C. 20009
Mattachine Society
Box 1032
Washington, D.C. 20013
Washington Area Council on Religion and the Homosexual
Box 5618
Washington, D.C. 20016
Gay People's Alliance
427 Marvin Center
800 21st St. N.W.
Washington, D.C. 30013
Guild Press
507 8th St. S.E.
Washington, D.C. 20003

FLORIDA

Transvestite/Transsexual Action Organization (TAO)
Box 261
Coconut Grove, Fla. 33133
Gay Liberation Front
1628D N.W. 3rd St.
Gainesville, Fla. 32601
or
Box 13883 University Sta.
Gainesville, Fla. 32601

Gay Liberation Front
2175 N.W. 26th St.
Miami, Fla. 33142
Young Peoples Group
2175 N.W. 26th St.
Miami, Fla. 33142
Metropolitan Coummunity Church
Box 5077
Miami, Fla. 33131
Slavonic Orthodox Church
c/o The Rev. Richard E. Drews
Box 4893
Miami, Fla. 33101
Florida League for Good Government
Box 301
Miami, Fla. 33101
305-374-4591
Gay Liberation Front
c/o Koulianos
New College No. 255
P.O. Box 1958
Sarasota, Fla. 33578
Gay Liberation Front
607 E. Park No. 1
Tallahassee, Fla. 32301
Gay Task Force
c/o Student Mobilization Committee
University of South Florida
Ctr. Box 378
Tampa, Fla. 33620

GEORGIA

Gay Liberation Front
c/o Great Speckled Bird
Box 7847
Atlanta, Ga. 30309
404-874-1658
Daughters of Bilitis
1620 Hollywood Rd. N.W. No. 3A
Atlanta, Ga. 30318

HAWAII

Gay Students Union
University of Hawaii
c/0 Jon Moore
1545 Piikoi 302
Honolulu, Ha. 96822

Gay Liberation Front
Southern Illinois University
c/o Dr. W. Gray
RFD No. 3
Carbondale, Ill. 62901

Red Butterfly
c/o Bill Stanley
1112 S. 2nd St.
Champaign, Ill. 61820
317-344-3770

Gay Liberation Front
University of Illinois
289 Illinois Union
Champaign, Ill. 61801
217-367-2781

One
P.O. Box 62
Chicago, Ill. 60690

Third World Gay Revolution
c/o Joe Hall
1952 N. Orchard
Chicago, Ill. 60613
312-472-2967

Loyola University Gay Liberation
Campus Center
6525 N. Sheridan Rd.
Chicago, Ill. 60626

Gay Liberation Front
c/o Step May
2618 N. Orchard
Chicago, Ill. 60614
312-248-1996 or 312-525-5268

Gay Alliance and Community Center
171 W. Elm St.
Chicago, Ill. 60610
312-664-4708 or 312-944-8393

University of Illinois GLF
c/o Chicago Circle Center
750 S. Halsted
Rm. 312C
Chicago, Ill. 60607
312-663-4843

Gay Women's Caucus
7621 Saginaw
Chicago, Ill. 60649

Gay Spirit Collective
2034 N. Halsted
Chicago, Ill. 60614

Fiery Flames Collective
628 Buckingham Pl. No. 201
Chicago, Ill. 60657

Gay Liberation Front
University of Chicago
Ida Noyes Hall
1212 E. 59th St.
Chicago, Ill. 60637
312-753-3274

Gay People's Legal Committee
Chicago, Ill.
phone only 312-947-9346

Gay Liberation Front
Northern Illinios University
Student Activities Office
Box 74
University Center
DeKalb, Ill. 60115
815-758-5570 or 815-758-2221

Gay Liberation Front
Northwestern University
Evanston, Ill. 60201

Mandrake
1312 Iowa
Madison, Ill. 62060

Gay Liberation Front
Illinois State University
Normal, Ill. 61761

Society Advocating Mutual Equality (SAME)
Box 775
Rock Island, Ill. 61202

INDIANA

Gay Liberation Front
c/o Jim Doherty
415 E. Smith St. 2
Bloomington, Ind. 47401

IOWA

Gay Liberation Front
University of Iowa
Student Activities Center
University of Iowa
Iowa City, Iowa 52240
515-338-3307·

Sebastian Quill
c/o Hibbard
725 E. College St.
Iowa City, Iowa 52240

KANSAS

Gay Liberation Front
Box 234
Lawrence, Kan. 66044

The Liberties
Box 3012
Shawnee Mission, Kan. 66203

KENTUCKY

Gay Liberation Front
Box 175
Louisville, Ky. 40201
502-637-6030

LOUISIANA

Gay Liberation Front
Box 19001
New Orleans, La. 70119

Daughters of Bilitis
Box 24033
Lakeview Sta.
New Orleans, La. 70124

MARYLAND

Gay Liberation Front
1811 Park Ave.
Baltimore, Md.
or
c/o Free Medical Clinic
3028 Greenmount Ave.
Baltimore, Md. 21218
301-685-2770

Student Homophile Association
Student Union
University of Maryland
College Park, Md. 20740

Homophile Social League
5601 Longfellow St., 301
Riverdale, Md. 20840

MASSACHUSETTS

Gay Liberation Front
Box 761
Amherst, Mass. 01002

Student Homophile League
Student Activities Office
RSO 368
Lincoln Campus Center
University of Massachusetts
Amherst, Mass. 01002

Boston Council on Religion and the Homosexual
131 Cambridge St.
Boston, Mass. 02114

Daughters of Bilitis
Box 221
Prudential Center Sta.
Boston, Mass. 02199
617-262-1592

Homophile Community Health Service
419 Boylston St.
Rm. 405
Boston, Mass. 02116
617-266-5477

Student Homophile League
c/o Mission Church
33 Bowdoin St.
Boston, Mass.
617-776-7454

Gay Male Liberation
c/o Red Book
91 River St.
Cambridge, Mass. 02139
617-354-1555

Graduate Student Homophile Association of Harvard
Biological Labs
16 Divinity Ave.
Cambridge, Mass. 02138
617-498-4237
or c/o John Boswell
31 Conant Hall
Harvard University
Cambridge, Mass. 02138

Homophile Union of Boston (HUB)
Box 217
Dorchester, Mass. 02124
617-282-9181

Homophile League
484 Chestnut St.
Holyoke, Mass. 01040

Daughters of Bilitis
Box 243 Mattapan Sta.
Mattapan, Mass. 02126

Kalos Society
c/o J. Dube
179 Pine St.
Springfield, Mass.

Out of the Closets
c/o Young
1045 High St.
Westwood, Mass. 02090

MICHIGAN

Gay Liberation Front
c/o Jim Toy
722 Arbor St.
Ann Arbor, Mich. 48110
313-665-6959

Gay Liberation Front and Gay Help Line
Elizabeth Street Collective
533 Elizabeth St.
Ann Arbor, Mich. 48104
313-663-7277

Radical Lesbians
Box 305
Ann Arbor, Mich. 48107

Revolutionary Lesbians of Ann Arbor
phone only 313-663-7635 or 313-761-2296

Daughters of Bilitis
Box 244 Greenfield Sta.
Dearborn, Mich. 48126

Daughters of Bilitis
Box 4490
Detroit, Mich. 48448

Gay Activists
Box 631-A
Detroit, Mich. 48232
313-833-7527

Gay Students Union
Box 23 U.C.B.
Wayne State Union
Detroit, Mich. 48202

Gay Youth
3025 E. Grand Blvd.
Apt. 209
Detroit, Mich.
313-874-4846

The Liberator
Box 631-A
Detroit, Mich. 48232

One
Box 7926 Kerscheval Sta.
Detroit, Mich. 48215

Gay Liberation Front
309 Student Services Building
Michigan State University
East Lansing, Mich. 48823

Western Michigan Gay Alliance
c/o Georgia Kohlbeck
454 Wealthy SE
Grand Rapids, Mich. 49503

Gay Liberation
Box 291
Student Services Bldg.
Western Michigan University
Kalamazoo, Mich. 49001

Gay Liberation Front
Box 472
Port Huron, Mich. 48060
313-982-3023

Gay Liberation Front
Box 240
Warner Hall
Mount Pleasant, Mich. 48858
517-774-5332

Order of St. Gregory
2803 Tenth St.
Wyandotte, Mich. 48192

MINNESOTA

FREE-Gay Liberation
Room B-67 Coffman Memorial Union
University of Minnesota
Minneapolis, Minn. 55455

Gay House, Inc.
216 Ridgewood Ave.
Minneapolis, Minn. 55403
612-333-6088

Minnesota Council for the Church and the Homophile
Rm. 508
122 W. Franklin
Minneapolis, Minn. 55404
612-335-1281

Gay Liberation Front
c/o Kathy Kerr
Carleton College
Northfield, Minn. 55057

MISSOURI

Gay Liberation
Box 1383
Columbia, Mo. 65201

Gay Liberation Front
Washington University
Box 1128
St. Louis, Mo. 63108
314-863-0100 Ext. 4806 or 314-725-1608

Homosexual Underground Action Committee
3800 McGee
Kansas City, Mo. 64111

Gay Liberation Front
c/o Mike Yore
4530 McPherson
St. Louis, Mo. 63108
314-FO7-1356 or 313-FO1-1772

National Homophile Center
Graduate Institute for Behavior
420 E. 37th St.
Kansas City, Mo. 64109

Phoenix Society for Individual Freedom
Box 1191
Kansas City, Mo. 64141

MONTANA

Gay Liberation Front
Box 97 Rocky Mountain College
Billings, Mont. 91802

NEBRASKA

Gay Action Group
333 No. 13th St.
Lincoln, Neb. 68508
402-475-5710 or 402-432-6561

NEW JERSEY

Gay Activists Alliance of New Jersey
32 Bridge St.
Hackensack, N.J. 07601

Daughters of Bilitis of New Jersey
Box 62
Fanwood, N.J.

Gay Rights of People Everywhere
Jersey City State College
Jersey City, N.J. 07305

Student Homophile League
RPO 2901
Rutgers University
New Brunswick, N.J. 08903

Student Homophile League
c/o Student Center
Fairleigh Dickinson University
Teaneck, N.J. 07666

NEW MEXICO

Gay Liberation Front
c/o Dan Butler
1524 Lead SE Apt. 3
Albuquerque, N.M. 87106

Gay Liberation Front
University of New Mexico
c/o 310A Edith S.E.
Albuquerque, N.M. 87106

Circle of Love Companions
Box 8
San Juan Pueblo, N.M. 87566

NEW YORK

Gay Liberation Front of the Tri-Cities
Box 131
Albany, N.Y. 12201
518-462-6138 or 518-434-1202

Gay Liberation Front
Box 87
Bard College
Annandale-on-Hudson, N.Y. 12504
914-758-8522

Gay Liberation
Box 2000
Harpur College
State University of New York
Binghamton, N.Y. 13901

Gay Alliance
P.O. Box 662
Brooklyn, N.Y. 11202
212-596-0235

Mattachine Society of the Niagara Frontier
Box 975 Ellicot Square Sta.
Buffalo, N.Y. 14205

Women's RL
344 Linwood
Buffalo, N.Y. 14209

Gay Liberation Front
180 Pearl St.
Buffalo, N.Y. 14202

Gay Liberation Front
Norton Hall
State University of New York
Buffalo, N.Y. 14214

Gay Liberation Front
24 Willard Straight Hall
Cornell University
Ithaca, N.Y. 14850
607-256-3729

Gay Activists Alliance (GAA)
Box 2 Village Sta.
New York, N.Y. 10014
212-226-8572

Faggot Effeminists
c/o Elliott
G.P.O. Box 3012
New York, N.Y. 10001

Gay Activists Alliance Firehouse
99 Wooster St.
New York, N.Y. 10012
212-226-8572

Mattachine Society
243 West End Ave.
New York, N.Y. 10023
212-799-0916

American Orthodox Church
300 Ninth Ave.
New York, N.Y. 10001
212-691-4422

Gay Counseling Service
149 E. 60 St. No. 5F
New York, N.Y. 10022
212-834-1159

Gay Women's Liberation Front
c/o Women's Center
243 W. 20th St.
New York, N.Y. 10011
212-254-8514 or 212-691-1860

Radicalesbians
c/o Women's Center
243 W. 20th St.
New York, N.Y. 10011
212-596-9764 or 212-691-1860

Daughters of Bilitis
c/o Church of the Holy Apostles
300 Ninth Ave.
New York, N.Y. 10001
212-475-9870

Gay Youth
c/o Church of the Holy Apostles
300 Ninth Ave.
New York, N.Y. 10001

Queer Blue Light Videotape Group
c/o Ecstasy
Box 410 Old Chelsea Sta.
New York, N.Y. 10011

Oscar Wilde Memorial Book Shop
291 Mercer St.
New York, N.Y. 10003

Council on Equality for Homosexuals
Box 539 Stuyvesant Sta.
New York, N.Y. 10009

Street Transvestites Action Revolutionaries (STAR)
211 Eldridge St., Apt. 3
New York, N.Y. 10002

Gay Student Liberation
Washington Square South
New York University
New York, N.Y. 10012

Gay People at Columbia
104 Earl Hall
Columbia University
New York, N.Y. 10027

Gay People at City College
Finley Student Center
City College of New York
133rd St. and Convent Ave.
New York, N.Y. 10031

East Side Gay Group
209 E. 76th St.
New York, N.Y. 10028

West Side Discussion Group
Box 502 Cathedral Sta.
New York, N.Y. 10025

Third World Gay Revolution
c/o Ecstasy
Box 410 Old Chelsea Station
New York, N.Y. 10011

Queens Liberation Front
Box 538 Stuyvesant Sta.
New York, N.Y. 10009

Gay Activists Alliance of Long Island
c/o N.D.C.
334 Eagle Ave.
West Hempstead, N.Y. 11552
or Box 493
Valley Stream, N.Y. 11580
516-825-8729

The Red Butterfly
Box 3445 Grand Central Sta.
New York, N.Y. 10017

The Erickson Foundation (for transsexuals)
1045 Park Ave.
New York, N.Y. 10028

Mattachine Society of the Cataract City
505 Third St.
Niagara Falls, N.Y. 14304

Gay Liberation Front
Todd Hall Room 202-D
University of Rochester
River Campus Sta.
Rochester, N.Y. 14627
716-275-6181

Gay Liberation Front
c/o Polity
Student Union
State University of New York
Stony Brook, N.Y. 11790
516-246-7654

Vietnam Veterans Against the War
c/o Vince Muscari
60 Carlton Rd.
Sutton, N.Y. 10910

Gay Liberation Front
Box 34
Syracuse, N.Y. 13201

Gay Liberation Front
c/o Ronald Denning
613 Nichols St.
Utica, N.Y. 13501

The Black Informer
Box 321 Main Sta.
Yonkers, N.Y. 10702

NORTH CAROLINA

Gay Liberation Front
c/o Hal Blackwelder
J-12 Kingwood Apts.
Chapel Hill, N.C. 27514

Gay Liberation Front
c/o Brad Keistler
1218 Myrtle Ave.
Charlotte, N.C. 28203

NORTH DAKOTA

Aware
Box 1283
Grand Forks, N.D. 58201

OHIO

Gay Alliance
Ohio University
c/o Ric Laufman
146 1/2 W. Union
Athens, Ohio 45701

Mattachine Society
Box 625
Cincinnati, Ohio 45201

Daughters of Bilitis
Box 20335
Cleveland, Ohio 44120

Mattachine Society
10404 Clifton Blvd.
Cleveland, Ohio 44102
216-651-3220

Gay Activists Alliance
4313 Germain Ave.
Cleveland, Ohio 44109

Gay Liberation Front
University of Ohio
P.O. Box 3062 University Sta.
Columbus, Ohio 43210

Gay Activists Alliance
Ohio Union Room 311
1739 N. High St. No. 3
Columbus, Ohio 43201
614-422-9212

Shades of Lavender
c/o Women's Liberation
1739 N. High St. No. 3
Columbus, Ohio 43201

SIR of Ohio, Inc.
Box 9761
Columbus, Ohio 43206
614-469-0154

Gay Revolution
1385 Indianola
Columbus, Ohio 43201
614-291-4055

SIR Cultural and Community Center
140 E. Spring St.
Columbus, Ohio 43215

Gay Liberation Front
Box 231 Dayton View Sta.
Dayton, Ohio 45406
513-274-0528

Gay Liberation Front
Student Activities Board
Kent State University
Kent, Ohio 44240

Gay Liberation Front
Box 30
Wilder Hall
Oberlin, Ohio 44074
216-774-6361

Personal Rights Organization
Box 4642 Old West End Sta.
Toledo, Ohio 43620

Gay Liberation Front
Antioch Union
Antioch College
Yellow Springs, Ohio 45387

Radicalesbians
c/o Women's Center
Yellow Springs, Ohio 45387

Personal Rights Organization
Box 2522
Youngstown, Ohio 45507
Cincinnati Homophile Organization
Box 1492
Cincinnati, Ohio 45201

OREGON

Gay People's Alliance
c/o Ted Edwards
Findrack Sta. Rt. 1
Box 501
High Pass Rd.
Junction City, Ore. 97448
Gay Liberation Front
3604 S.E. Belmont St.
Portland, Ore. 97214
The Second Foundation
1017 S.W. Morrison No. 506
Portland, Ore. 97205
503-227-5651

PENNSYLVANIA

LE HI HO
Box 1003 Moravian Sta.
Bethlehem, Penn. 18018
State College Homophile Movement
c/o Frederick Reed
Box 66
Kutztown, Penn. 19530
American Library Association Gay Liberation Task Force
c/o Barbara Gittings
P.O. Box 2383
Philadelphia, Penn. 19103
Urania
c/o Kiyoshi Kormiya
5046 Cedar Ave.
Philadelphia, Penn. 19143
Gay Activists Alliance
3818 Chestnut
Apt. E-401
Philadelphia, Penn.
Gay Liberation Front
Temple University
Box 98 Student Activities Center
Broad & Montgomery Streets
Philadelphia, Penn.
Homophile Action League
256 S. 45 St.
Philadelphia, Penn. 19104
215-EV7-1786

Radicalesbians
c/o Women's Center
928 Chestnut St.
Philadelphia, Penn. 19107

Gay Liberation Fellows
Box 13023
Philadelphia, Penn. 19101
215-732-8668 or 215-349-8207

Philadelphia Action Committee for Equality
c/o Jay's Place 1511 Pine St.
Philadelphia, Penn. 19103

Philadelphia Christian Homophile Church
Box 1921
Philadelphia, Penn. 19105
215-521-3264

Task Force on Religion and the Homosexual
c/o Metropolitan Christian Council of Philadelphia
1211 Chestnut St.
Philadelphia, Penn. 19107

Homophiles of Penn State (HOPS)
Box 218
State College, Penn. 16801

Gay Rights Organization of Wilkes-Barre and Scranton
(GROWS)
Box 5027 Sta. A
Wilkes-Barre, Penn. 18710

RHODE ISLAND

Gay Liberation
c/o Celt Grant
47 Farewell St.
Newport, R.I. 02840
401-847-3416

Gay Liberation Movement
c/o Student Activities
Brown University
Providence, R.I. 02912

Gay Alliance
Box 1422 Annex Station
Providence, R.I.
401-272-0465

TENNESSEE

Gay Students Union
c/o Merle DeVault
Box 8163 University Sta.
Knoxville, Tenn. 37816

TEXAS

Gay Liberation Front
Box 8107
Austin, Tex. 78712
512-478-1858

Council on Religion and the Homosexual
3133 Inwood Rd.
Dallas, Tex. 75235
Purple Star Tribe
Box 19433
Dallas, Tex. 75219
214-526-5893
Gay Liberation Front
University of Houston
6031 Cullen (U.C.)
Houston, Tex. 77004
Gay Liberation Front
Box 53221 Sam Houston Sta.
Houston, Tex. 77502
713-524-2276 or 713-667-6017
or 713-526-6257

VIRGINIA
Gay Alliance
Student Union
Virginia Tech
Blacksburg, Va. 24060
Gay Liberation Front
c/o Kenny Pederson
506 Brookside Blvd.
Richmond, Va. 23327
703-266-2691
Gay Alliance of Roanoke Valley
Box 1576
Roanoke, Va. 24007

WASHINGTON
Gay Community Center and Gay Liberation Front
102 Cherry St.
Seattle, Wash. 98104
206-MA2-9621 or 206-MA3-3862
Gay Alliance
c/o Gay Community Center
102 Cherry St.
Seattle, Wash. 98104
Gay Student Association
c/o Gay Community Center
102 Cherry St.
Seattle, Wash. 98104
Counselling Service for Homosexuals
318 Malden Ave. E.
Seattle, Wash. 98102
206-EA9-5820

Stonewall
Halfway House for Gay Parolees
4016 37th Ave.
Seattle, Wash.
206-722-1445

Dorian Society
Box 799
Seattle, Wash. 98101

The Collumns Northwest
Box 99022 Magnolia Sta.
Seattle, Wash. 98199

Gay Women's Alliance and
Gay Women's Resource Center
4224 University Ave. NE
Seattle, Wash. 98105
206-ME2-4747

Gay Liberation Front
P.O. Box 1276
Spokane, Wash. 99210

Gay Alliance of Tacoma
206-BR2-2316

Gay Liberation Front
c/o Dale Hough No. 214877
Washington State Penitentiary
P.O. Box 520
Walla Walla, Wash. 99362

WISCONSIN

Gay Sisters
c/o YWCA Women's Center
306 No. Brooks St.
Madison, Wisc. 53705

Gay Liberation Front
10 Langdon St.
Madison, Wisc. 53703
608-643-8460

Gay Liberation Front
Box 5457
Milwaukee, Wisc. 53211
414-955-7433

Gay Liberation Organization
c/o Rev. Joseph Feldhausen
1155 N. 21 St.
Milwaukee, Wisc. 53233
414-342-1722 or 414-342-1727

Radical Queens
Box 5457
Milwaukee, Wisc. 53211

Gay House
2483 N. Frederick
Milwaukee, Wisc.

Gay Peoples Union
Box 90530
Milwaukee, Wisc. 53202
414-962-8611

CAMP
Box56
E. Brisbane
Queensland 4169
Daughters of Bilitis
Box 2131T
Melbourne 3001

Homophile Association
York University
Rm. N105 Ross Bldg.
Downsview
Ontario
Homophile Association
University of Guelph
Guelph
Ontario
Gay Liberation Front
Box 15 Sta. A.
Vancouver
British Columbia
604-255-9969
Gay Activists Alliance
Box 284 Sta. A
Vancouver 1
British Columbia
604-685-4850
Gay Sisters of Vancouver
phone only: 604-738-5379
Gay Alliance Towards Equality (GATE)
105-1131 Richard St.
Vancouver
British Columbia
604-687-8048 or 604-687-6302
International Sex Equality Anonymous
CP 145 Sta. G
Montreal 18
Quebec
Front de Liberation Homosexuelle
2065 rue St. Denis
Montreal
Quebec
514-843-4425

University of Toronto Homophile Association
SAC Building
Hart House Circle
Toronto
Ontario
416-964-1918

Gay Fellowship
c/o E.F. Blair
Box 6248 Terminal A
Toronto 1
Ontario

Community Homophile Association (CHAT)
58 Cecil St.
Toronto 130
Ontario
416-964-0653

Gay Action (TGA)
58 Cecil St.
Toronto 130
Ontario
416-922-2624 or 416-920-6576

Gays of/d' Ottawa
Box 2919 Sta. D
Ottawa
Ontario

BELGIUM

CCL
281 Chansee d'Ixelles
Brussels 5

DENMARK

National League for Homosexuals
P.O. Box 1023
Copehagen K
55-29-87

FRANCE

Arcadie
61, rue du chateau d'eau
Paris 10

Front Homosexuel d'Action Revolutionnaire
c/o Tout
73 Rue Buffon
Paris 5

THE NETHERLANDS

COC
Fredriksplein 14
Amsterdam

COC Center
49A Korte Leidsedwarsstraat
Amsterdam

COC
32 Oostenstraat
Antwerp

Forbundet of 1948
Postbox 1305
Oslo

Riksforbundet for Suxuelt Likaberattigrande
Box 850
Stockholm 1

Minerva Club
C.P. 1211
Gran-pre
Geneva 16

Club 68
Postfach 417
Zurich 8022

Gay Liberation Front
5 Caledonian Rd.
London N1

GLF Media Workshop
c/o Agit-prop
160 N. Gower St.
London NW 1

Compendium Bookshop
240 Camden High St.
London NW 1
485-8944

Scottish Minorities Group
214 Clyde St.
Glasgow C1
Scotland